best of
TOMMY EMMA

Photography by Sara Corwin

Music transcriptions by Pete Billmann

ISBN-13: 978-1-4234-3175-6

7777 W. BLUEMOUND RD. P.O. BOX 13819 MILWAUKEE, WI 53213

For all works contained herein:
Unauthorized copying, arranging, adapting,
recording or public performance is an infringement of copyright.
Infringers are liable under the law.

Visit Hal Leonard Online at
www.halleonard.com

best of TOMMY EMMANUEL cgp

- 6 Blue Moon
- 12 Can't Get Enough
- 30 Classical Gas
- 45 Countrywide
- 55 Determination
- 68 Guitar Boogie Shuffle
- 82 Hearts Grow Fonder
- 93 The Hunt
- 101 Initiation
- 108 The Journey
- 119 Stevie's Blues
- 128 Up From Down Under
- 140 GUITAR NOTATION LEGEND

from *Dare to Be Different*
Blue Moon
Words by Lorenz Hart
Music by Richard Rodgers

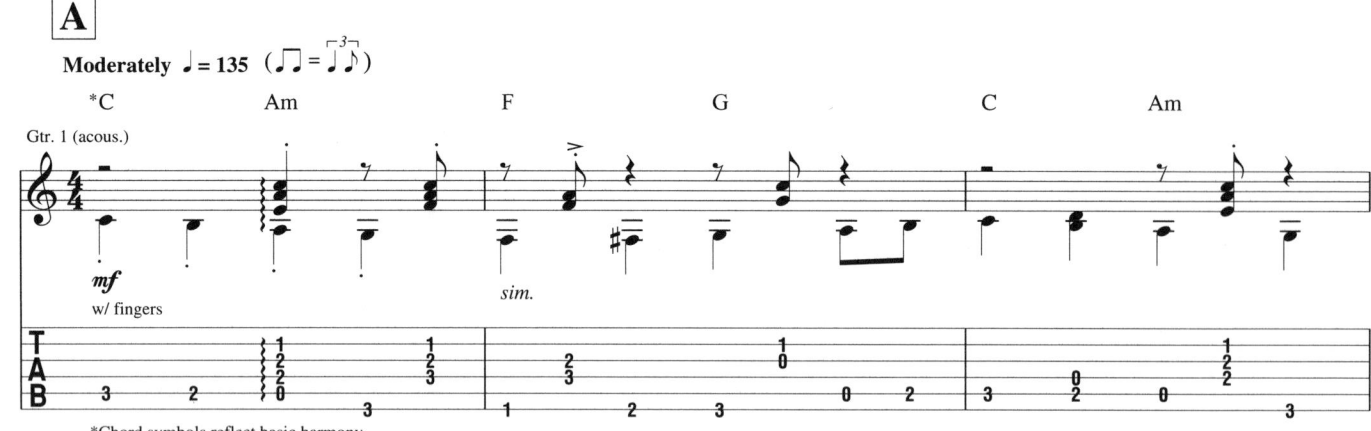

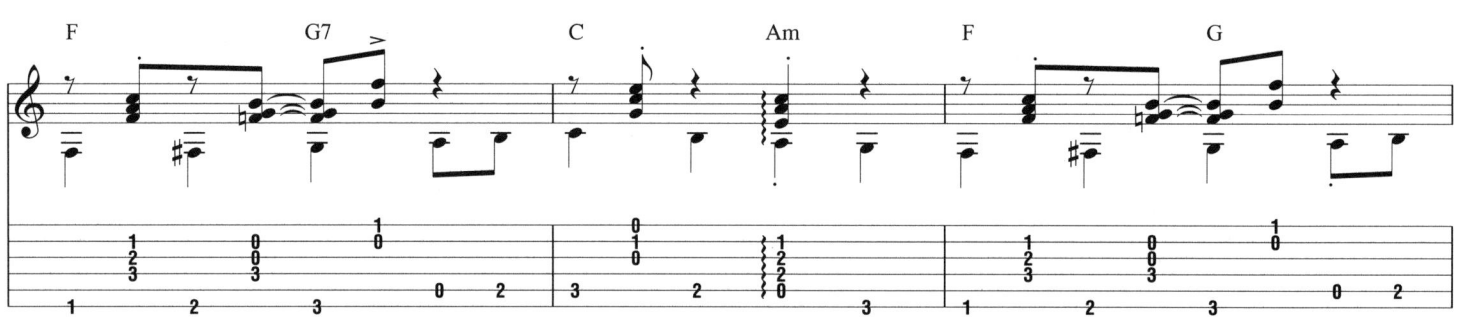

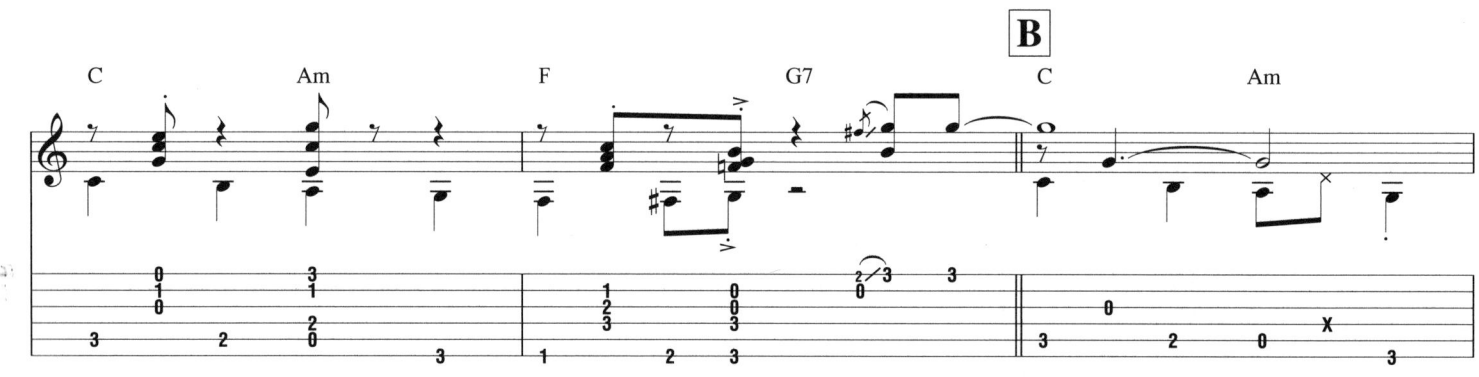

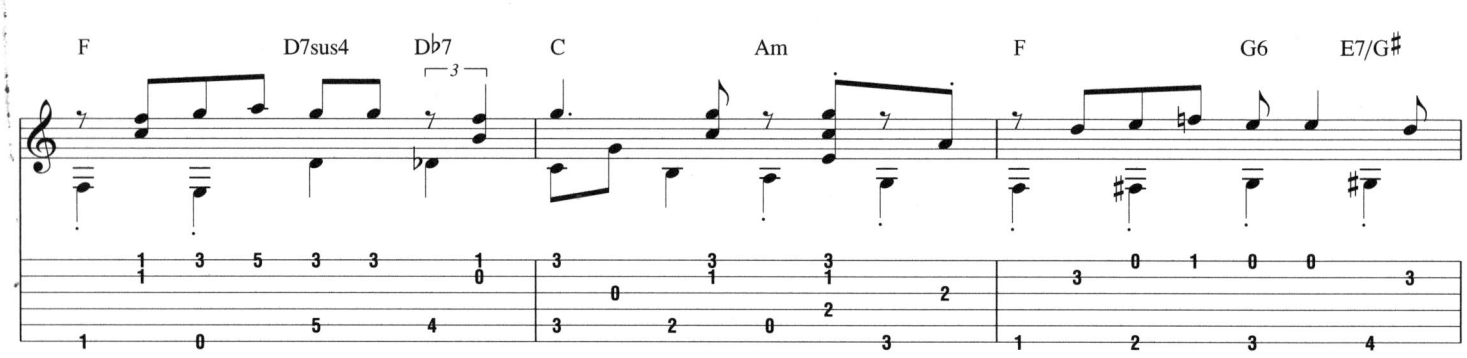

© 1934 (Renewed 1962) METRO-GOLDWYN-MAYER INC.
All Rights Controlled by EMI ROBBINS CATALOG INC. (Publishing) and WARNER BROS. PUBLICATIONS U.S. INC. (Print)
All Rights Reserved   Used by Permission

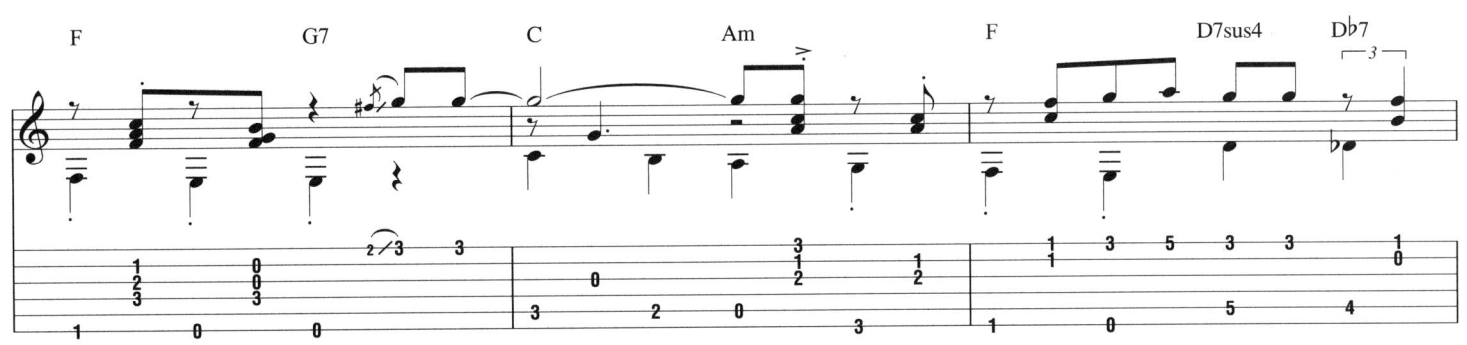
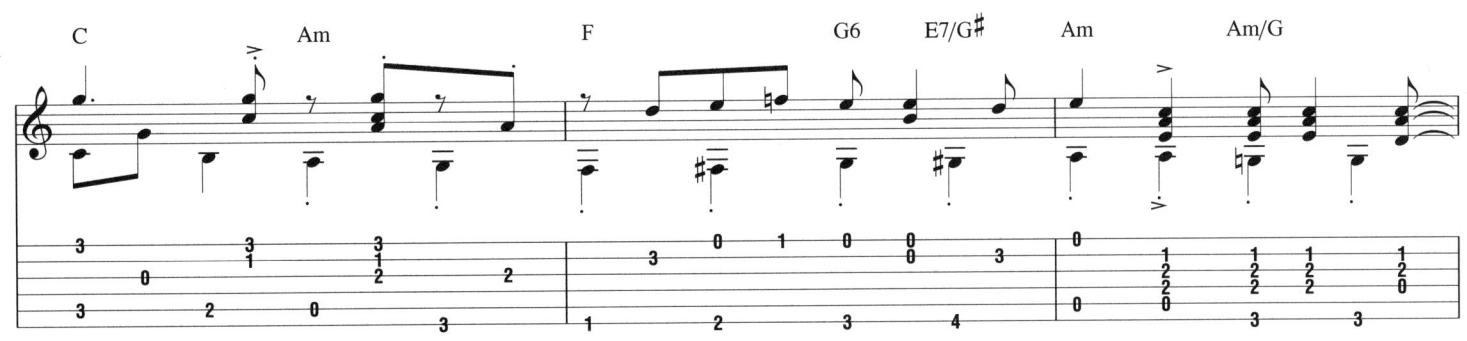
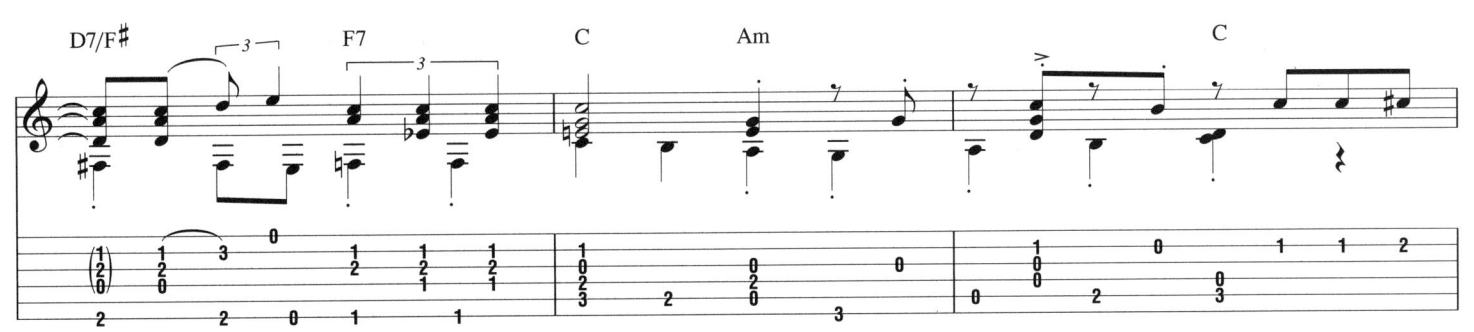

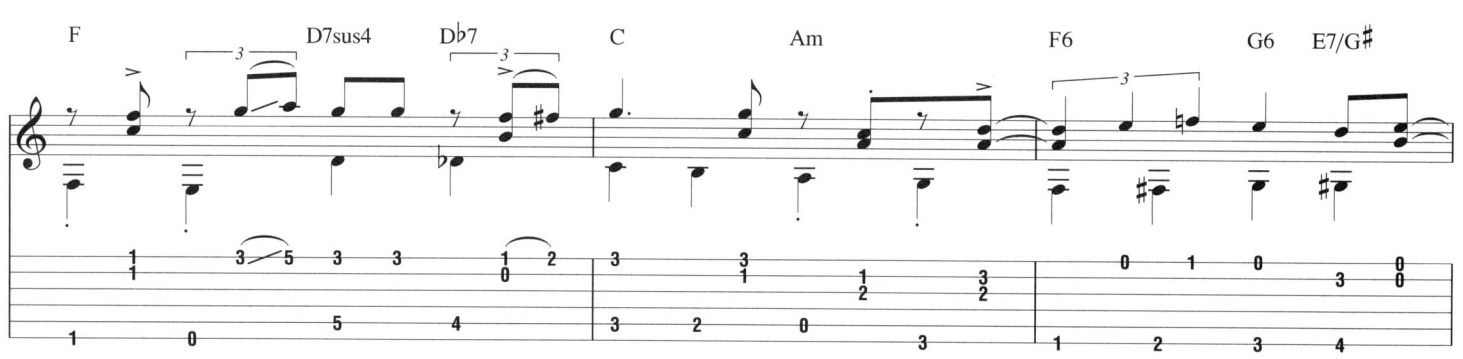

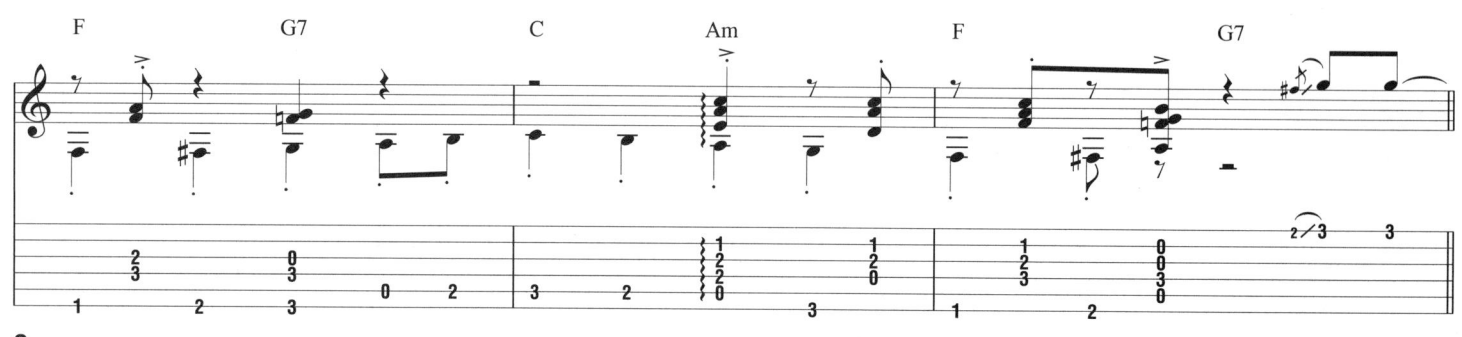

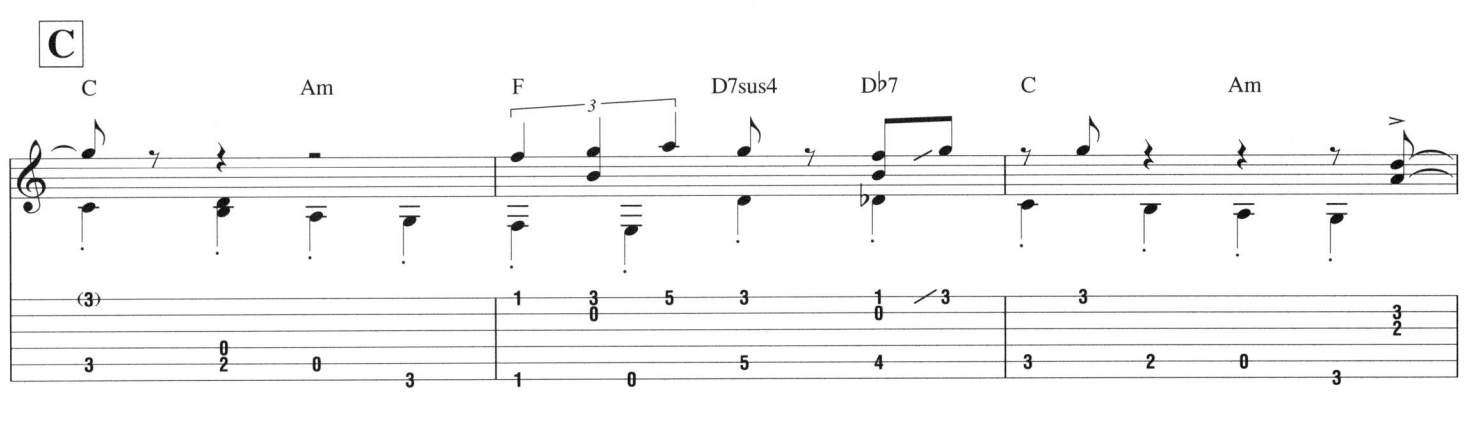
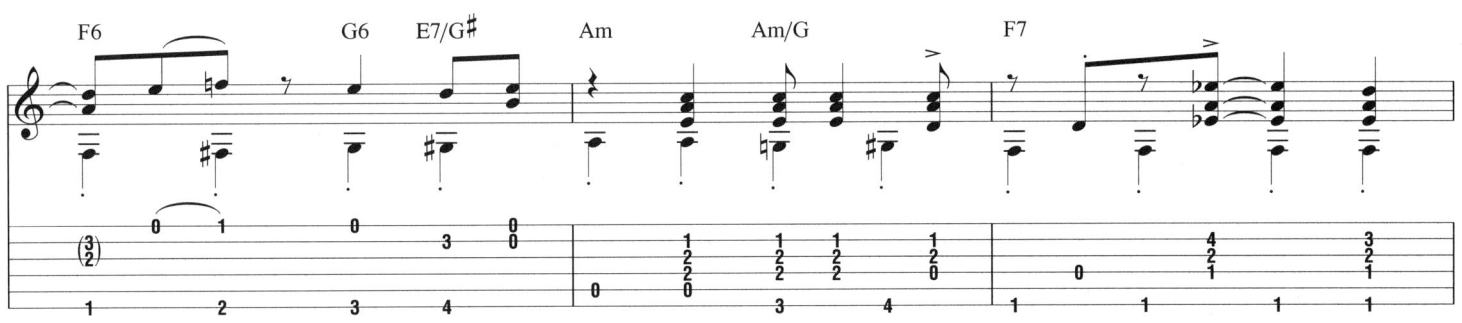
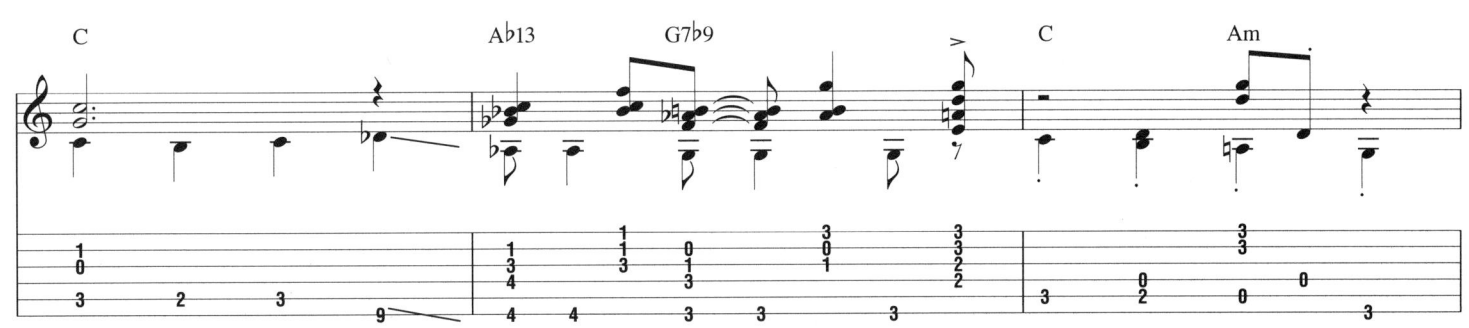
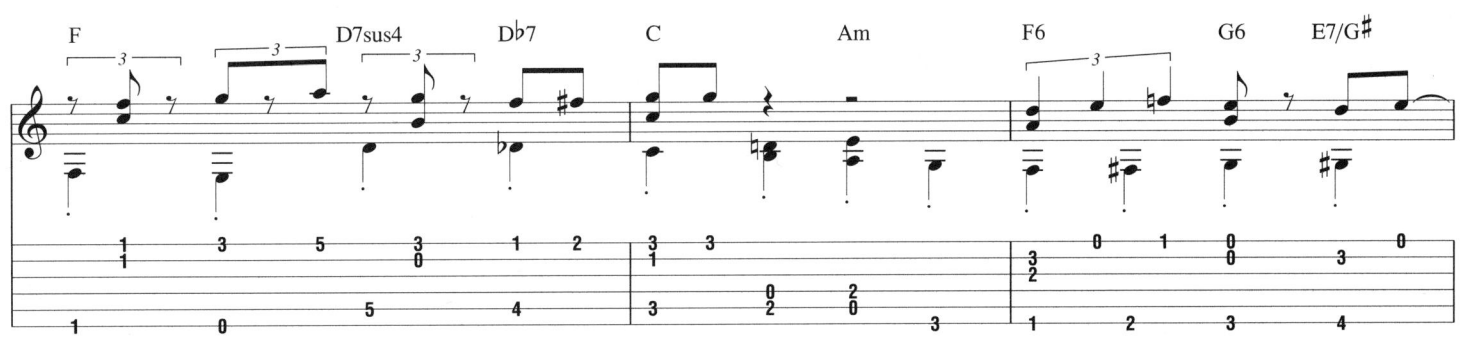
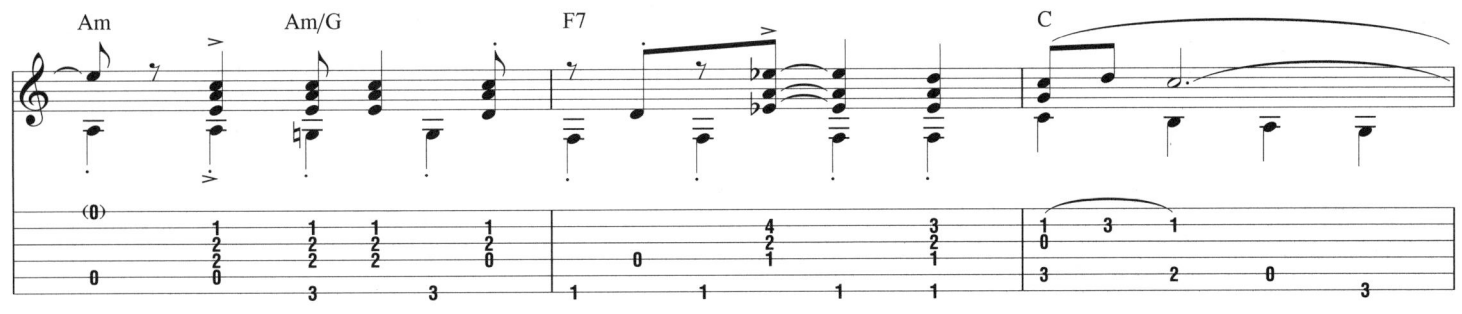

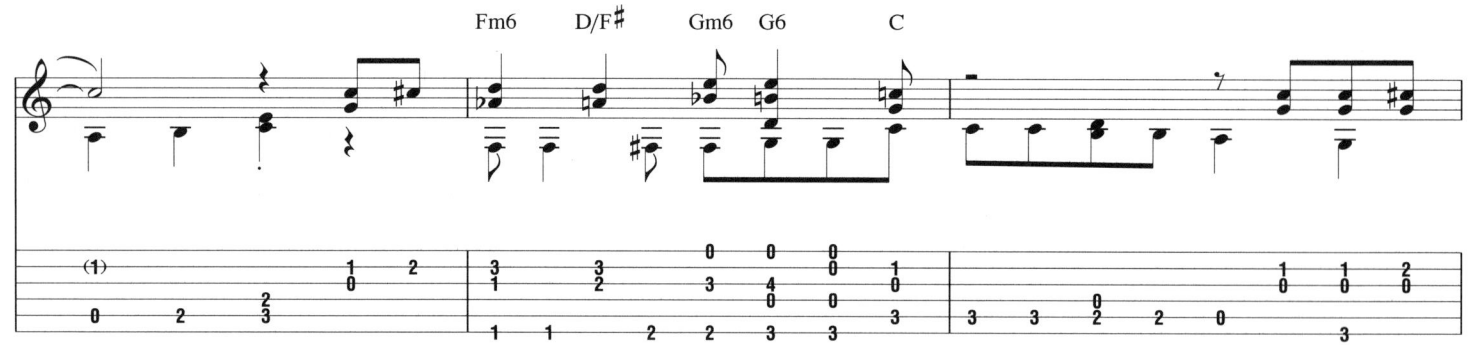
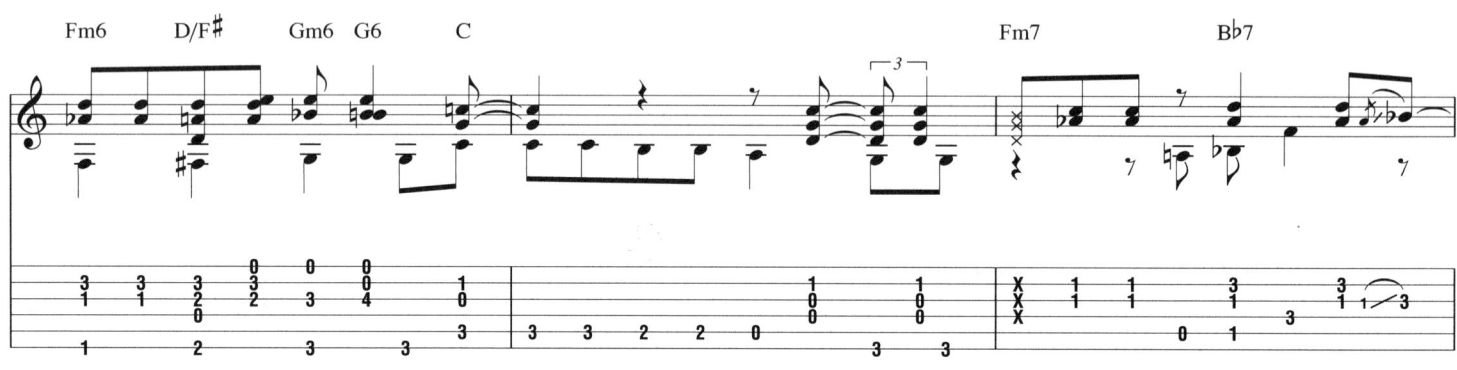
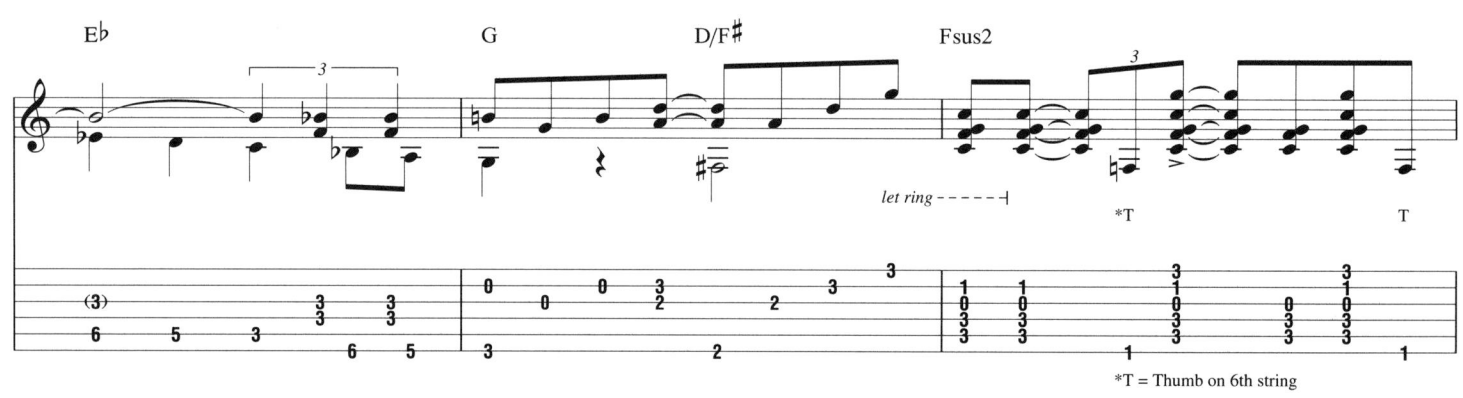

*T = Thumb on 6th string

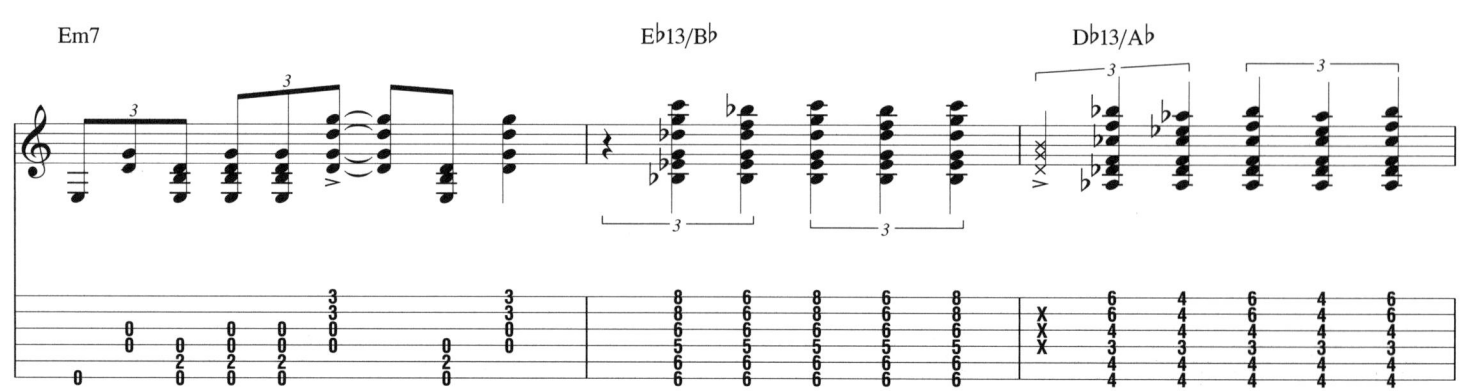

10

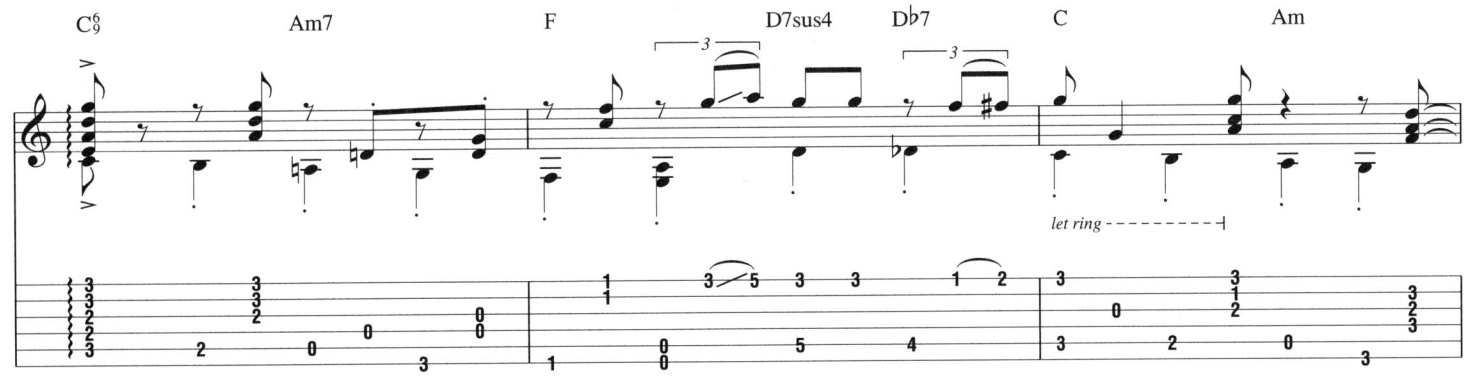
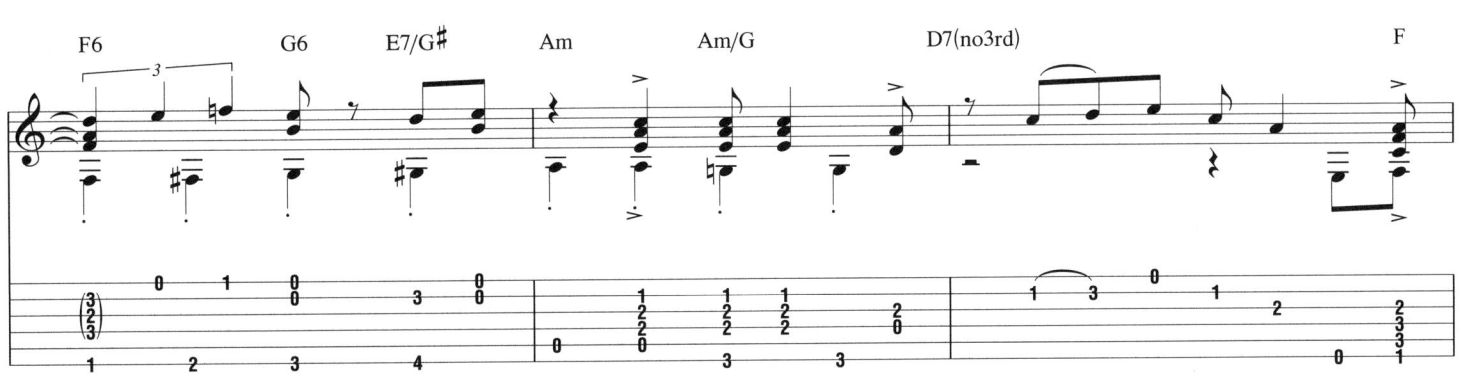
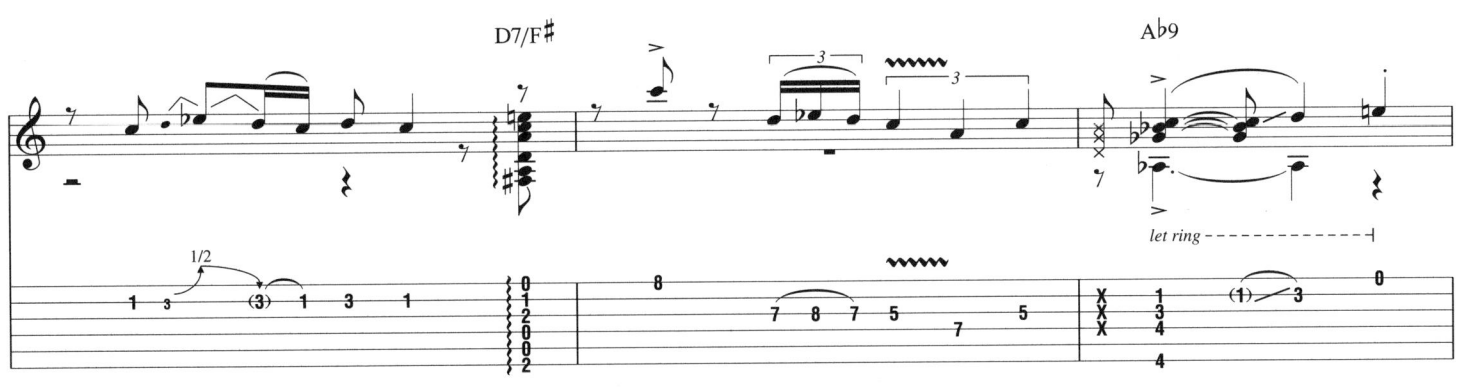
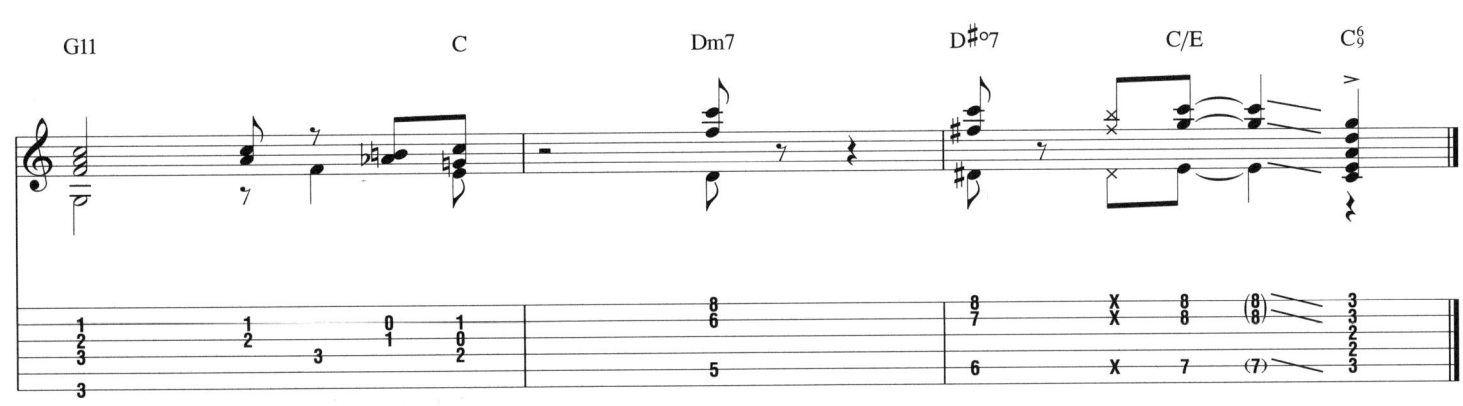

Can't Get Enough

from *Can't Get Enough*

By Tommy Emmanuel and Randy Goodrum

*Chord symbols reflect overall harmony.

Copyright © 1997 UNIVERSAL MUSIC PUBLISHING PTY. LTD., TOMMY EMMANUEL MUSIC, CHRIS GILBEY PTY. LTD. and MIGHTY GOOD MUSIC
All Rights for MIGHTY GOOD MUSIC in Central America and South America ex. Brazil Controlled and Administered by UNIVERSAL MUSICA, INC.
All Rights for TOMMY EMMANUEL MUSIC and CHRIS GILBEY PTY. LTD. in the world
ex. U.S. and Canada Controlled and Administered by UNIVERSAL MUSIC PTY. LTD.
All Rights in the United States and Canada Controlled and Administered by UNIVERSAL - POLYGRAM INTERNATIONAL PUBLISHING, INC.
All Rights Reserved   Used by Permission

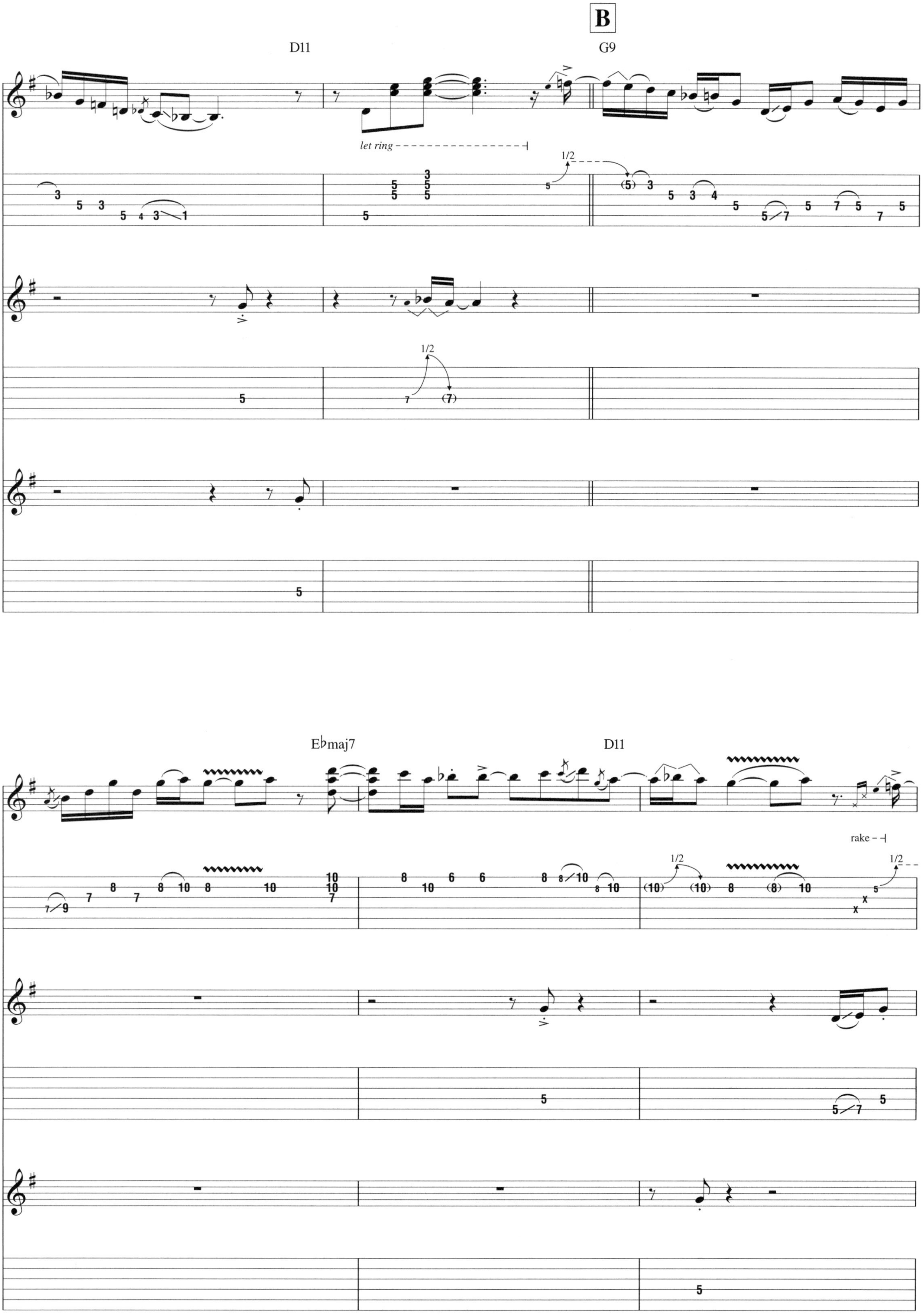
B
D11
G9
let ring
1/2
E♭maj7
D11
rake

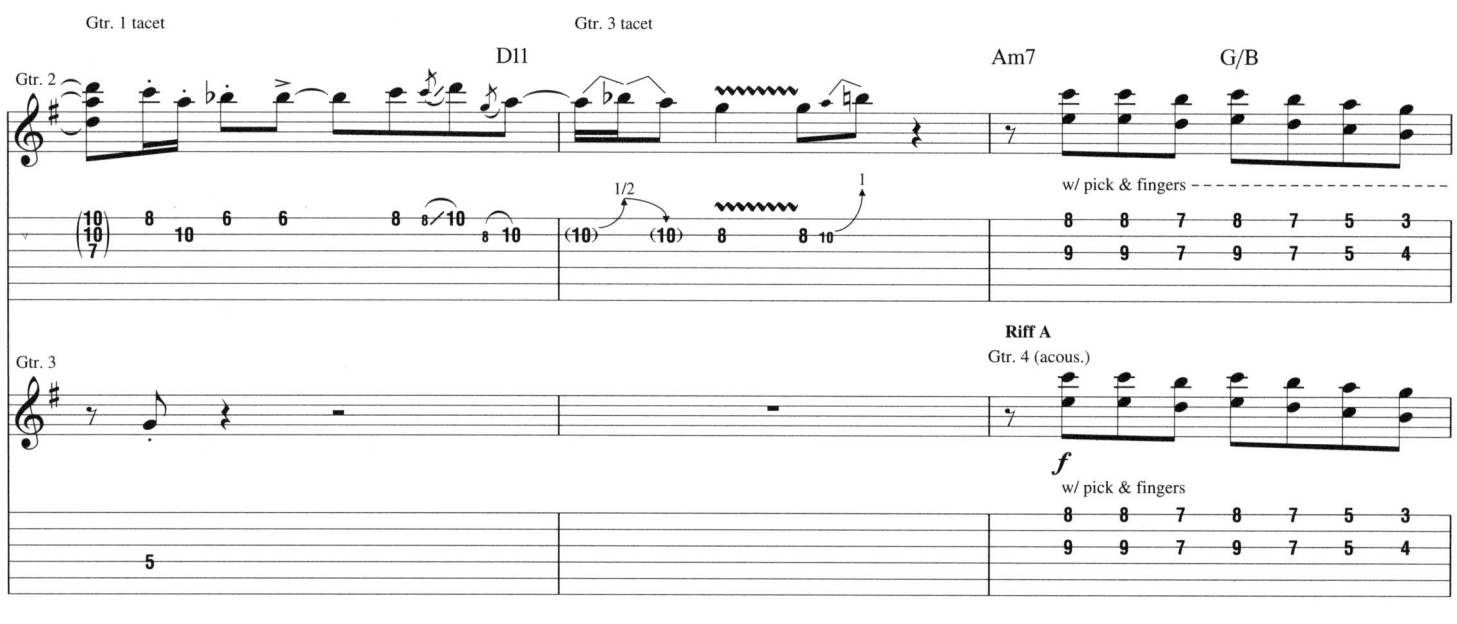
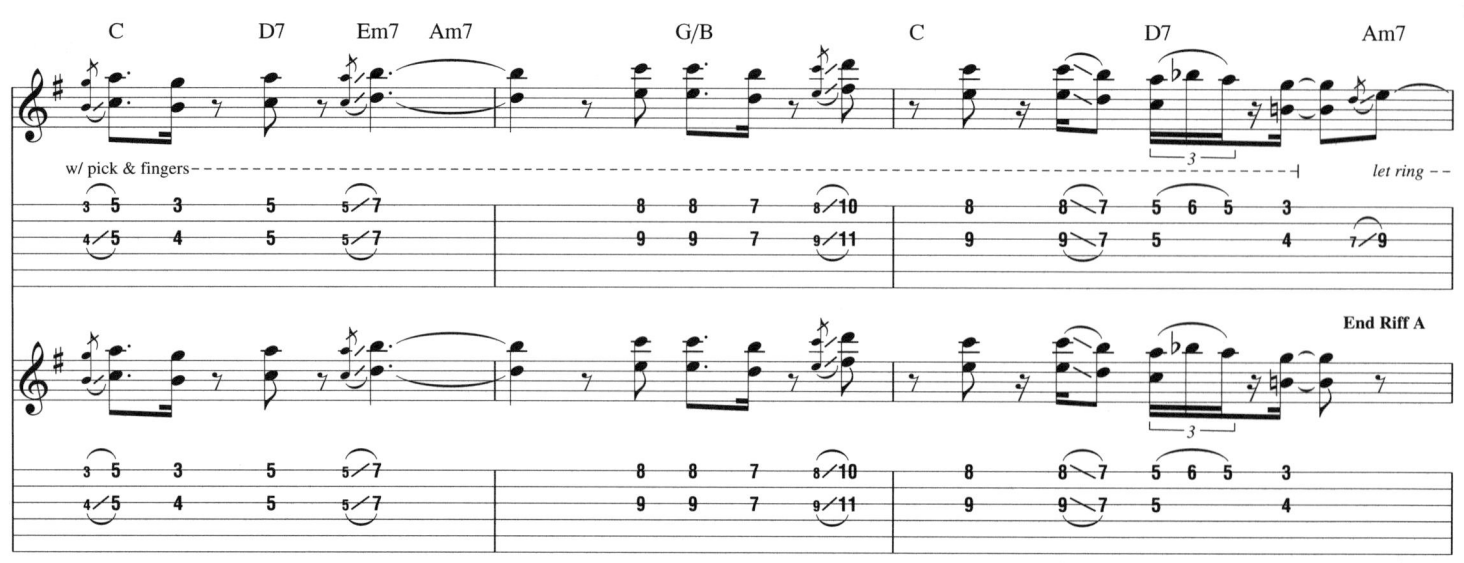

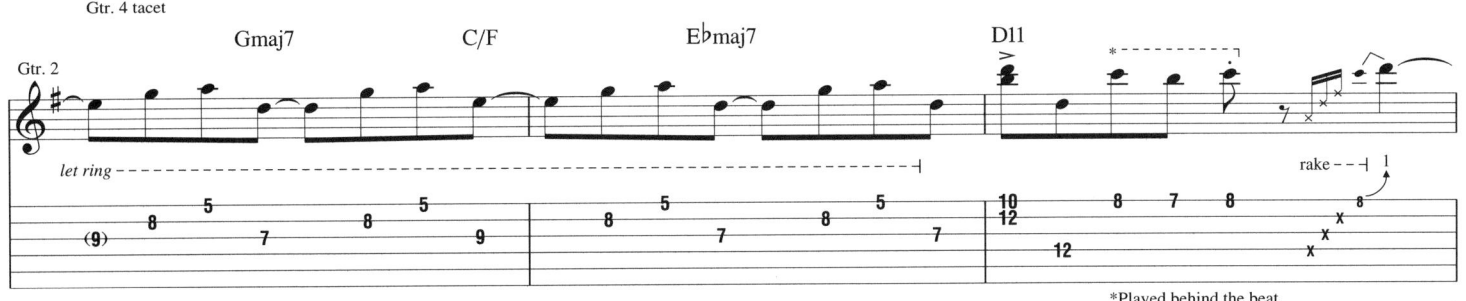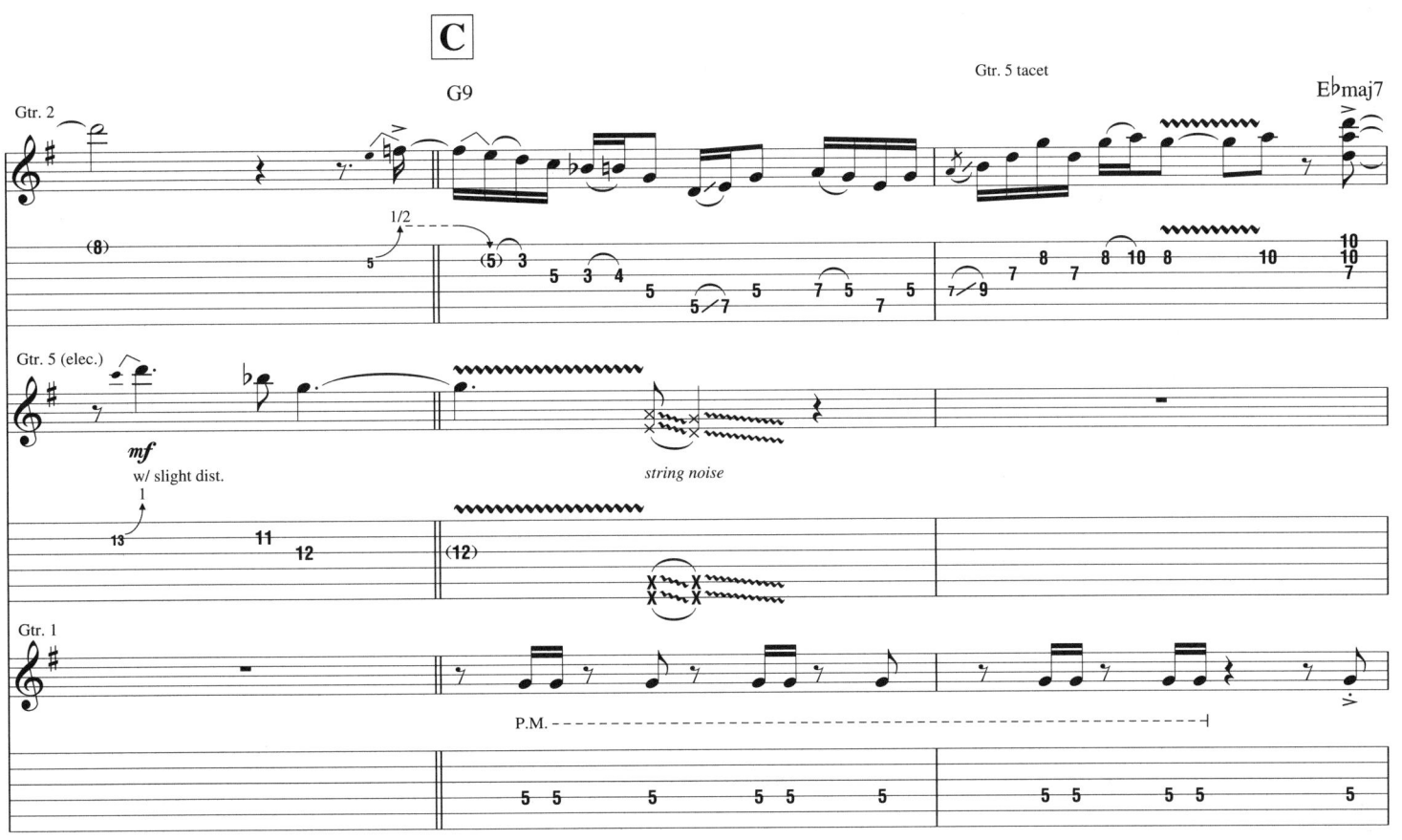

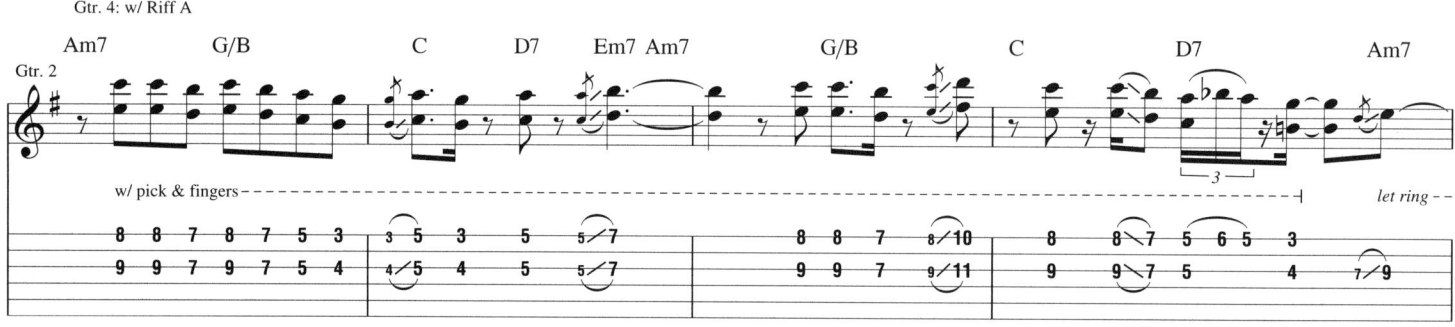
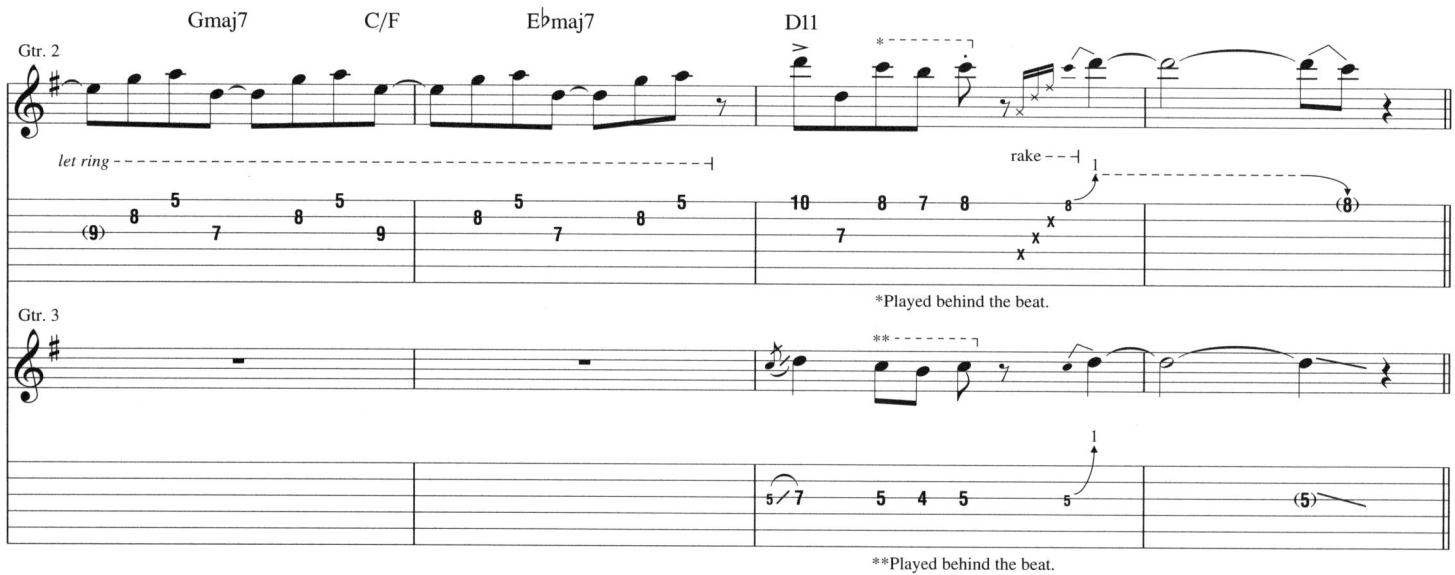

E7
Amaj7
Gmaj7
Fmaj7
Harm.
let ring
E♭maj7
D11
E
Gtr. 2 tacet
G9
E♭maj7
D11
Gtr. 3
Gtr. 2
Gtr. 1
P.M.
P.M.

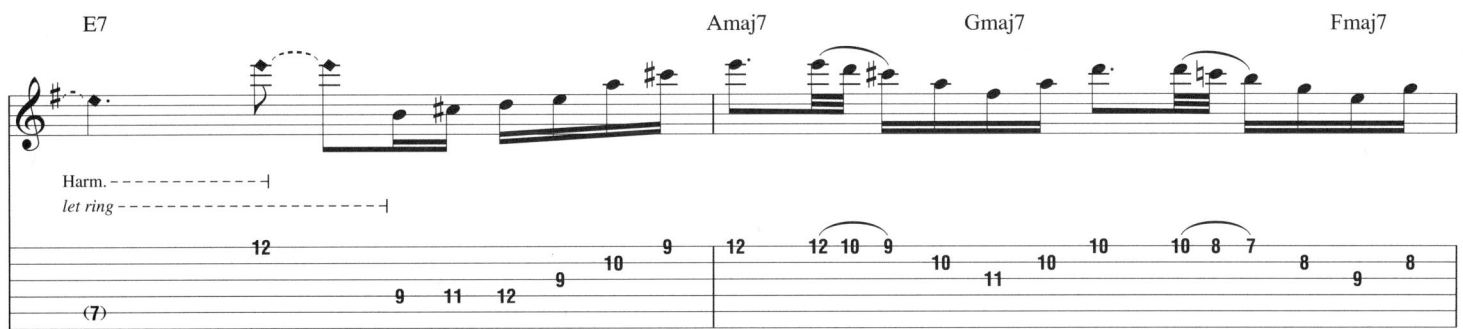

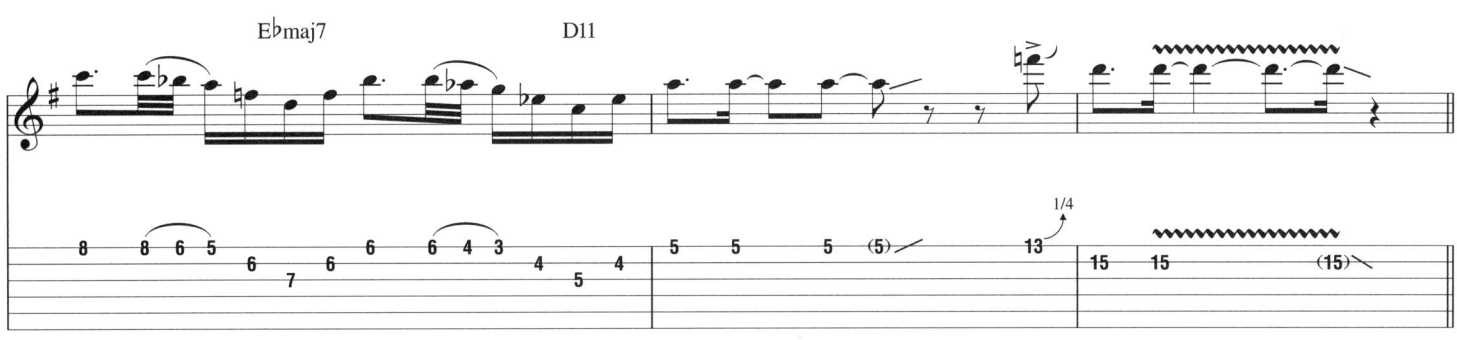

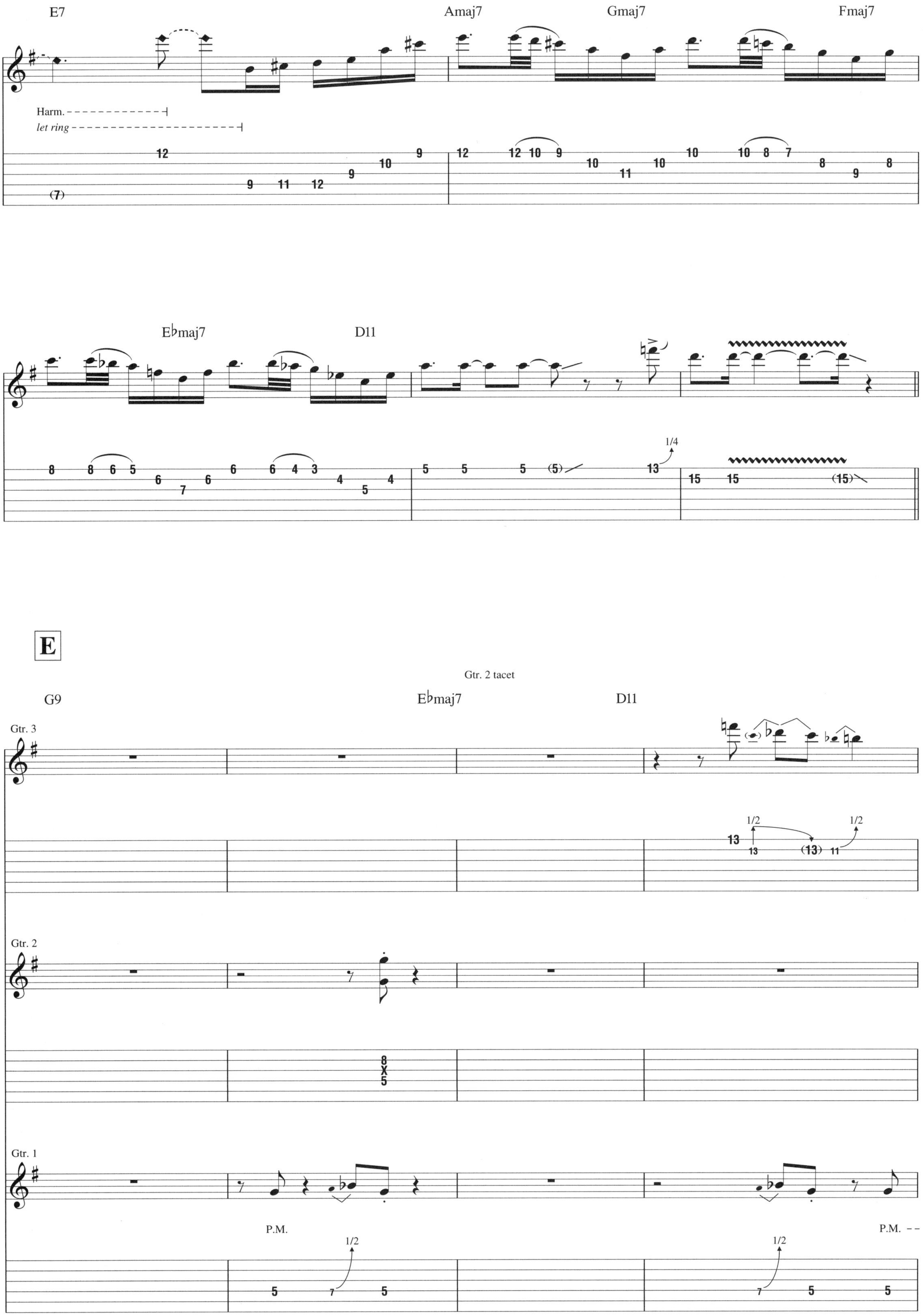

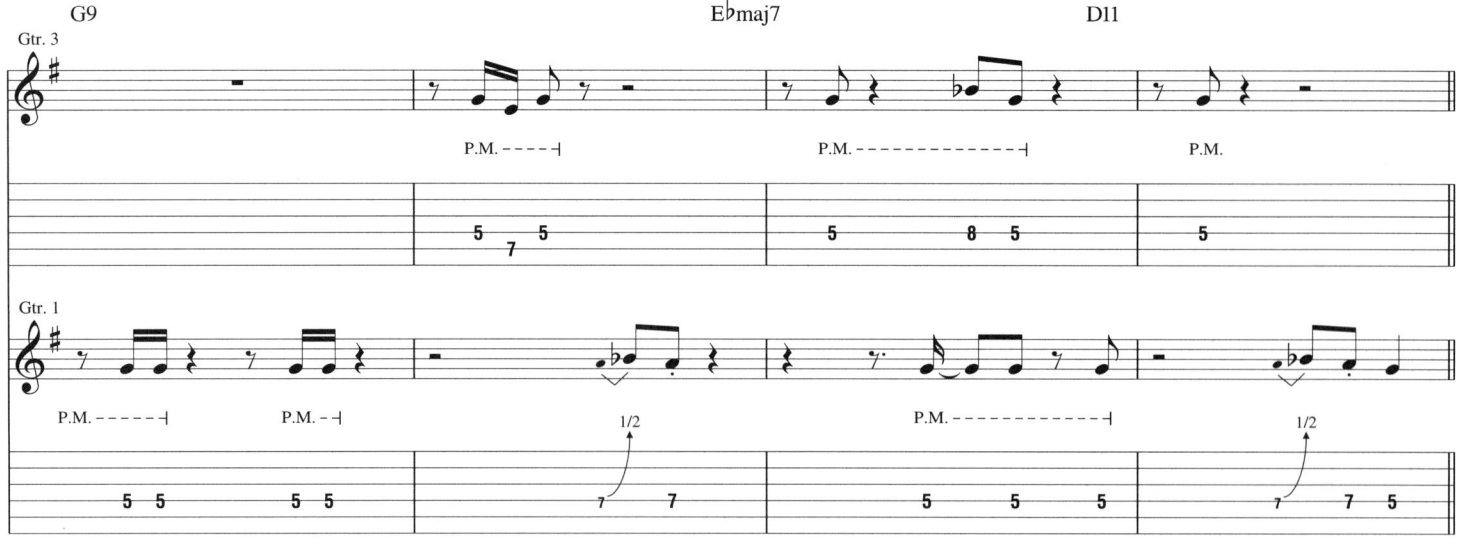
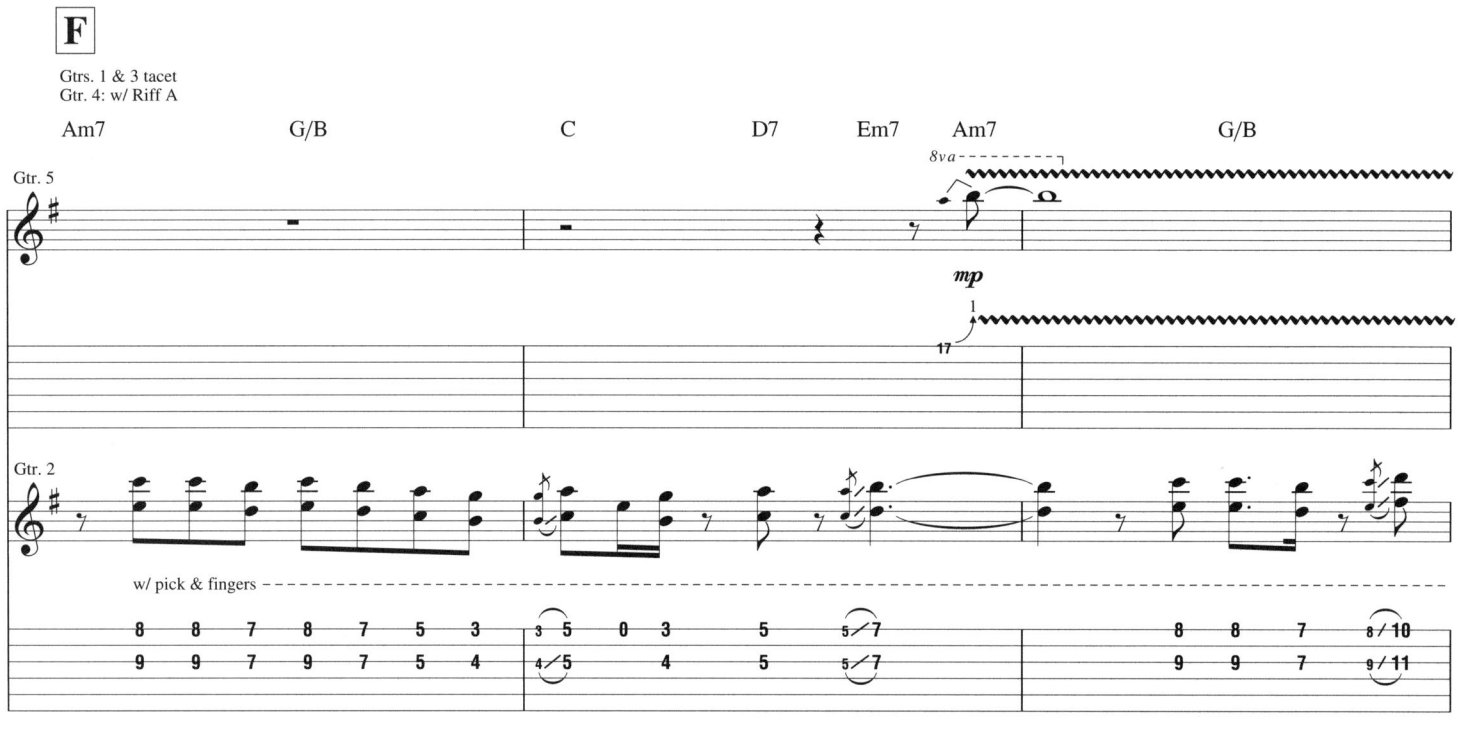
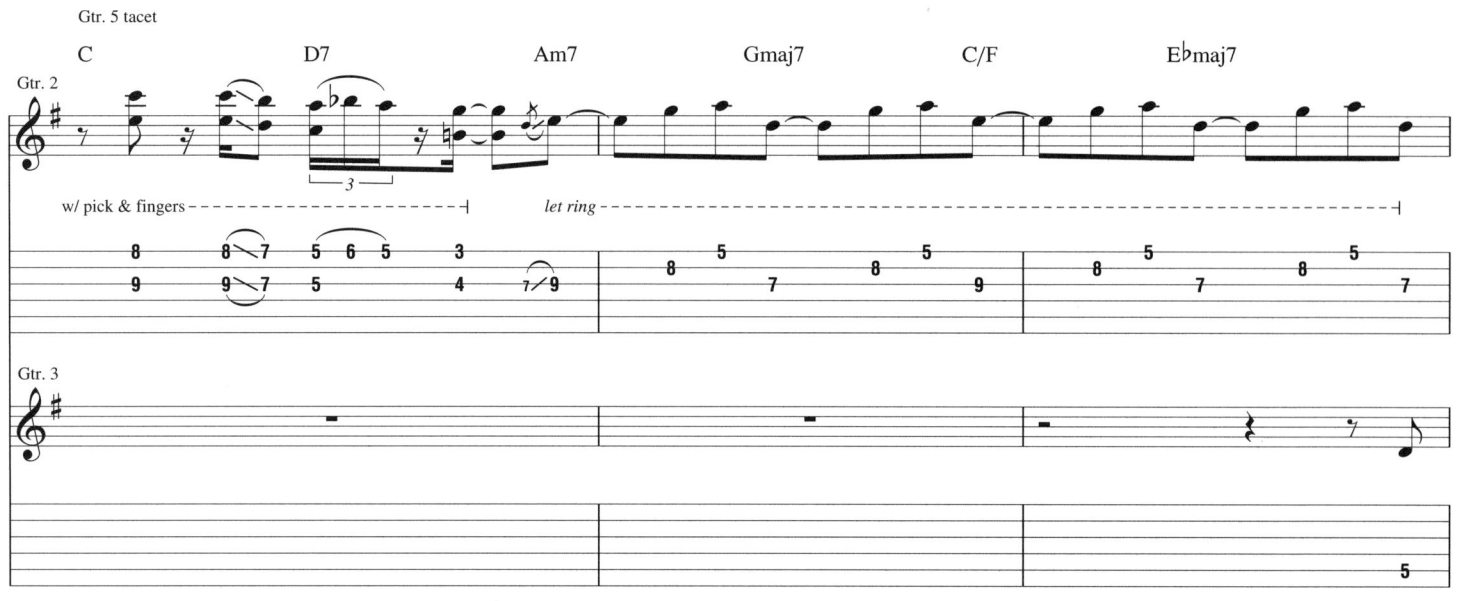

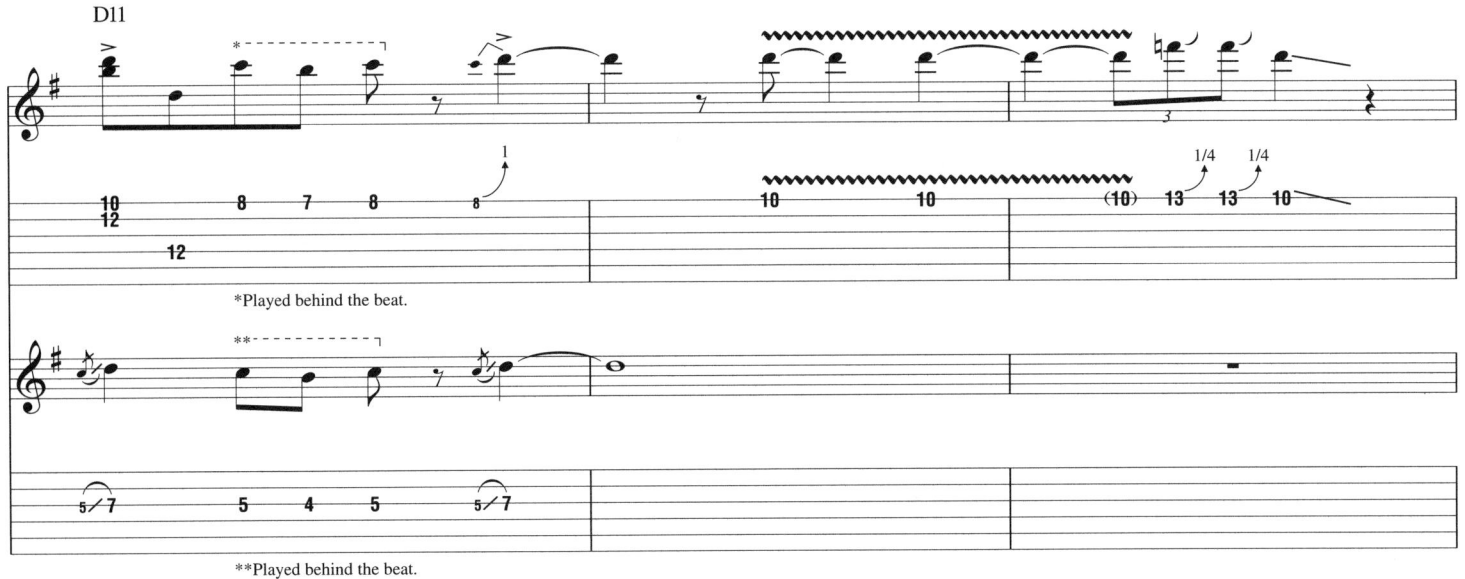
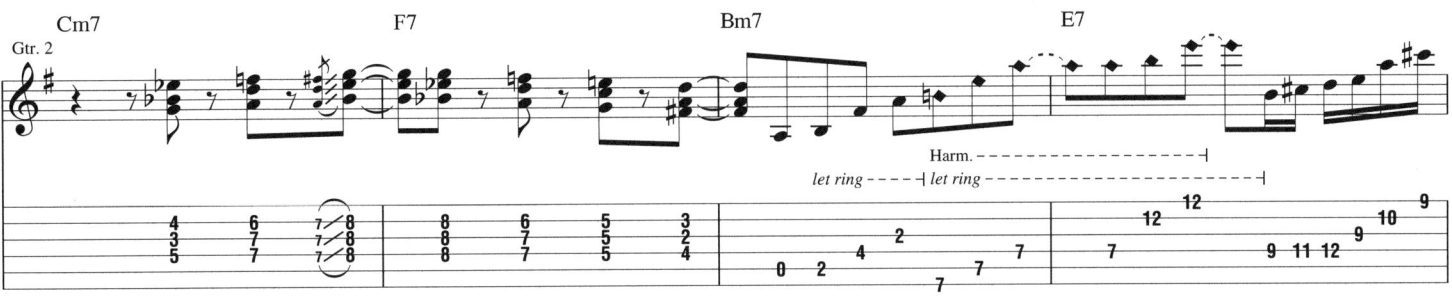
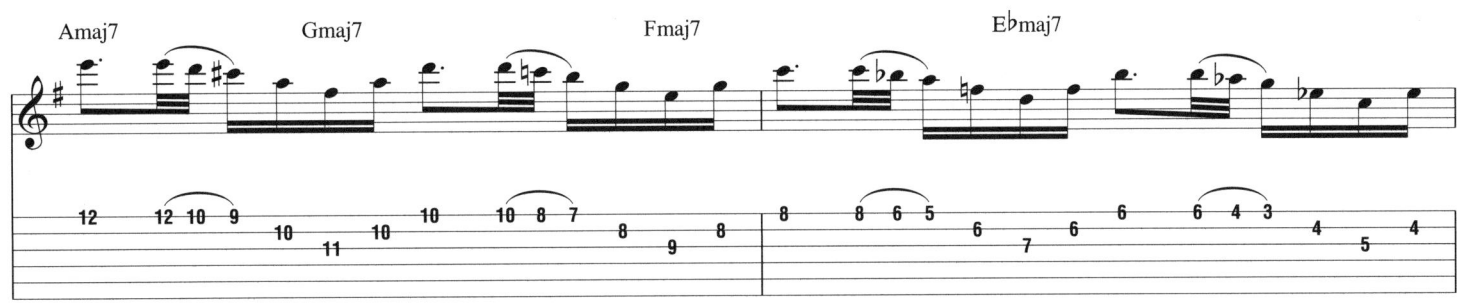
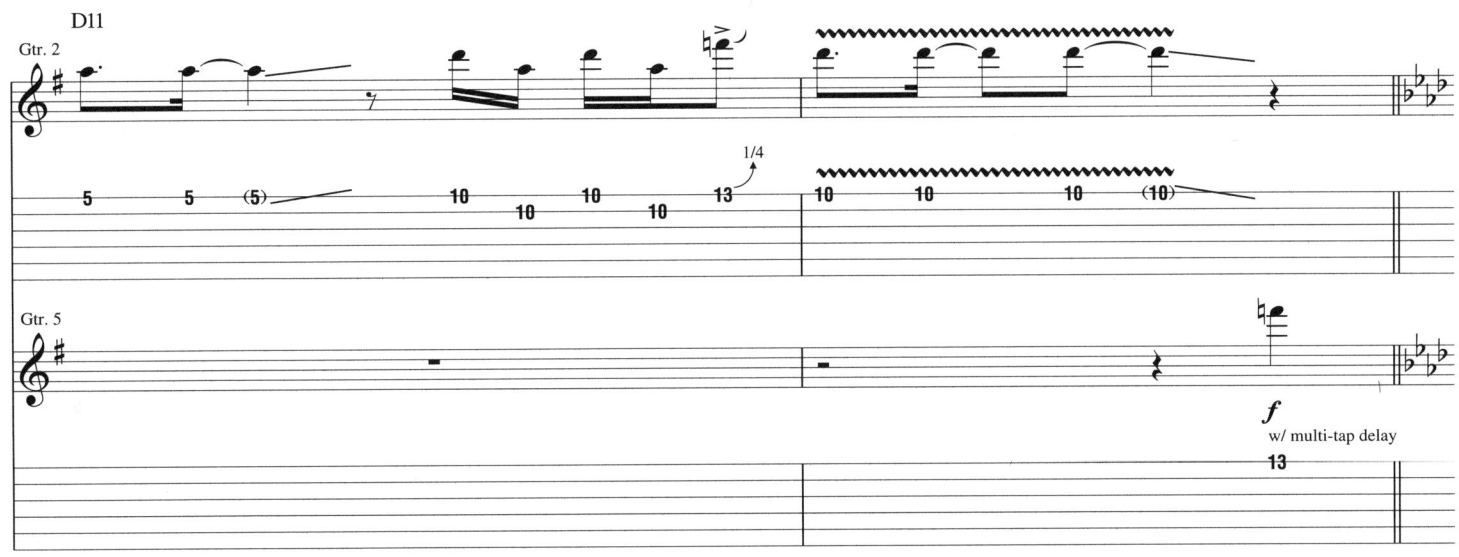

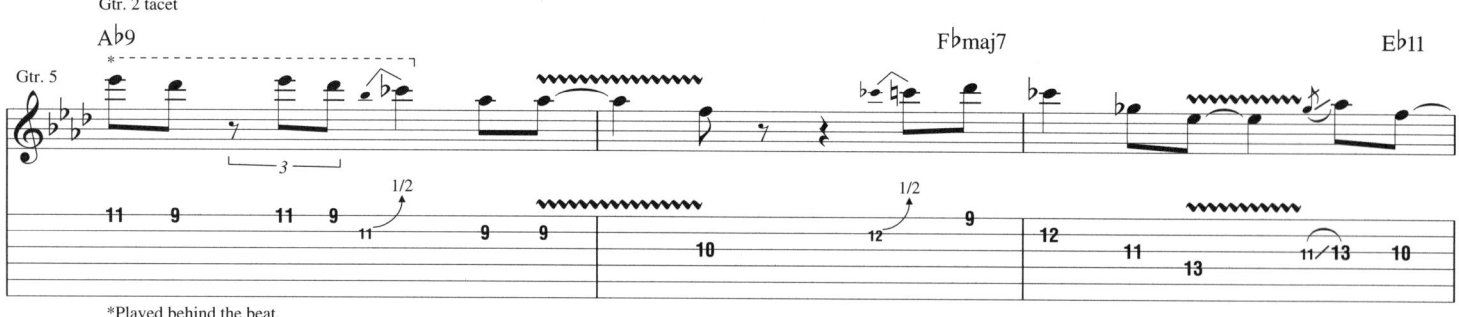
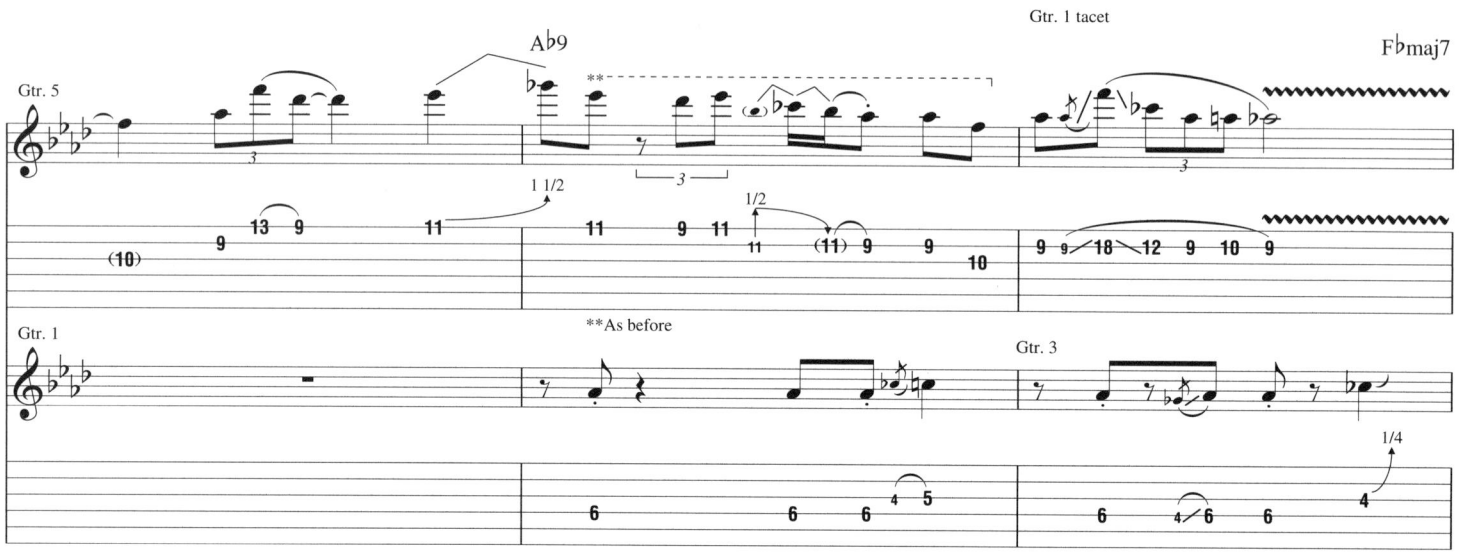

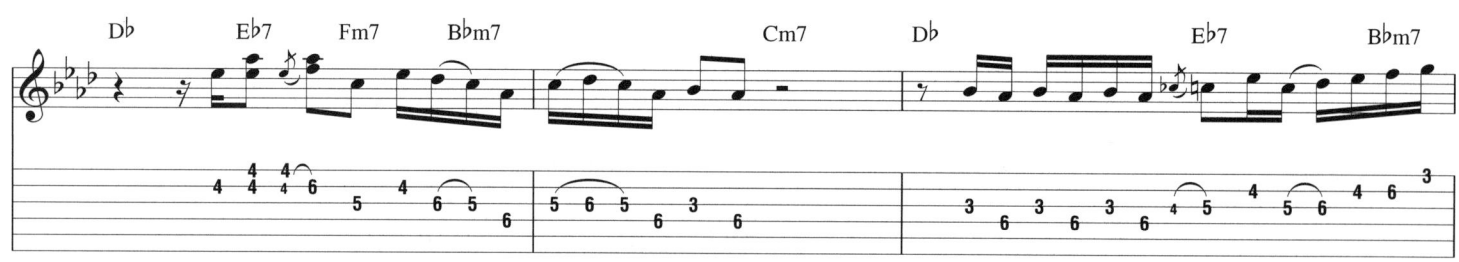
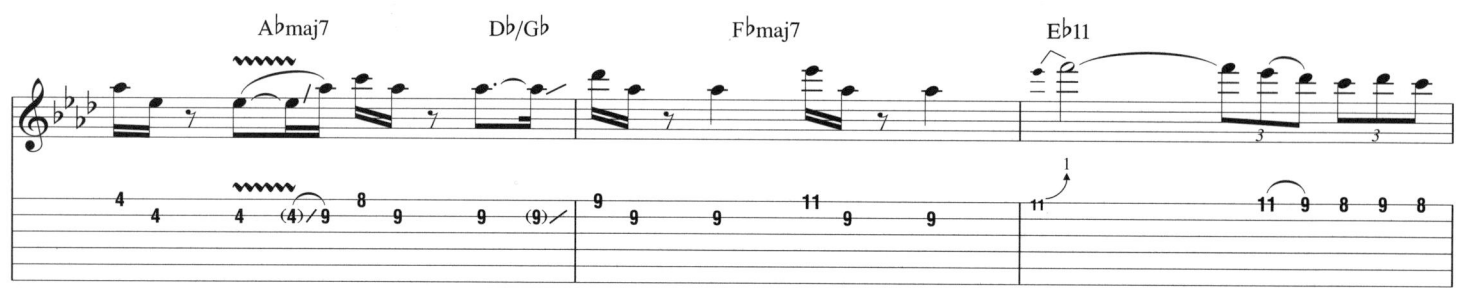

8va
H
A9
Gtr. 5
8va
loco
Gtr. 2
1/2
Gtr. 1
P.M.
Gtr. 5 tacet
Fmaj7
E11
Gtr. 2
Gtr. 1
P.M.

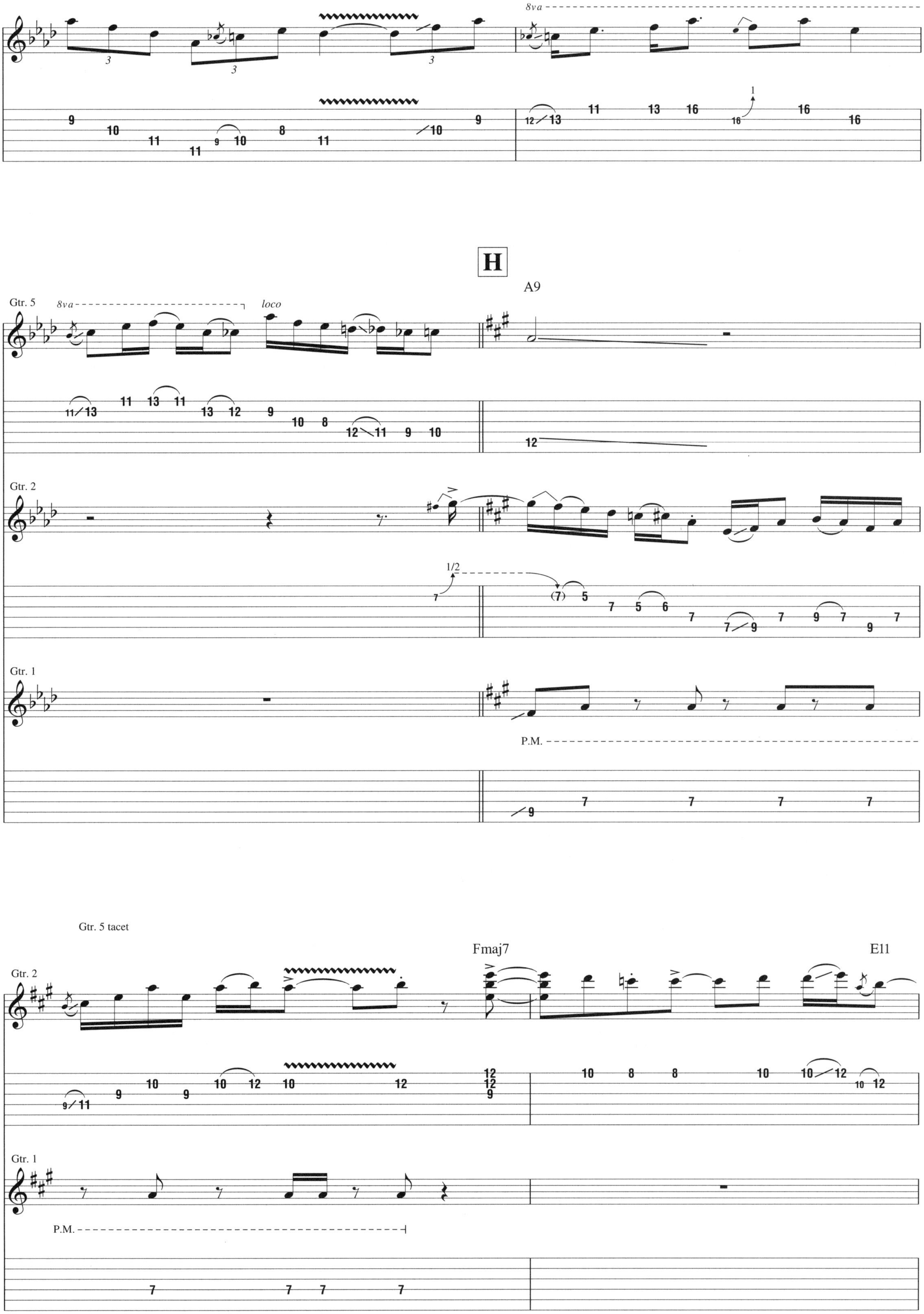

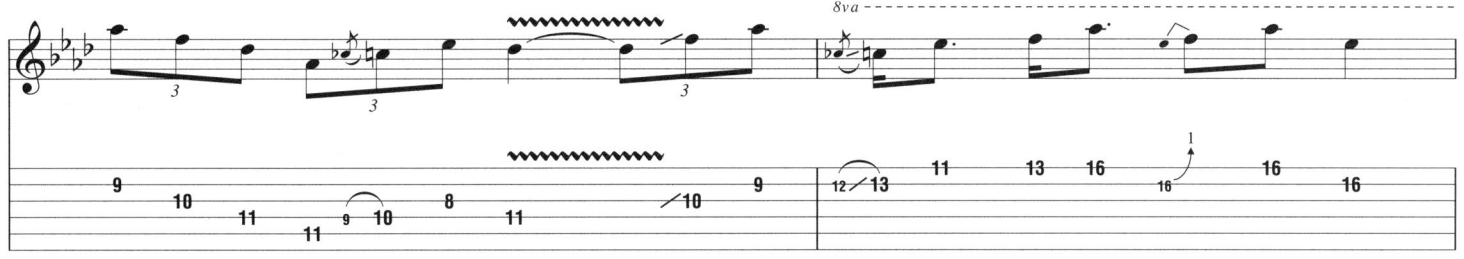

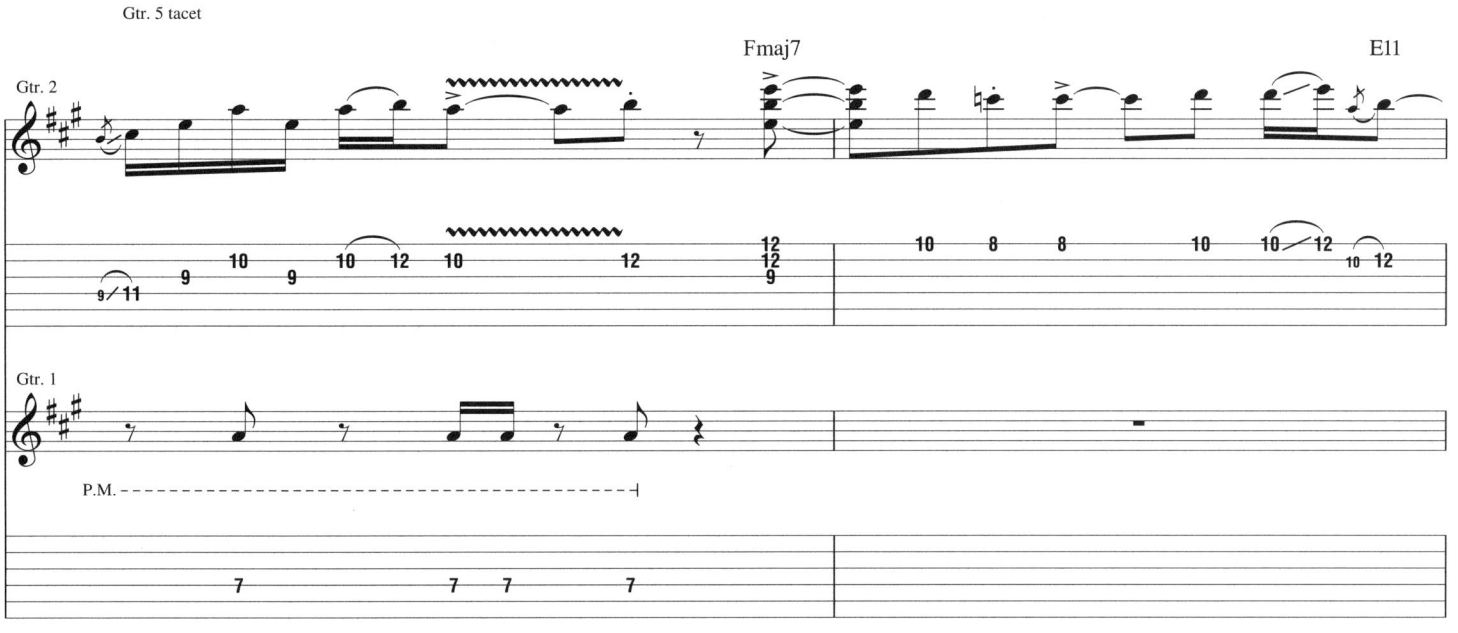

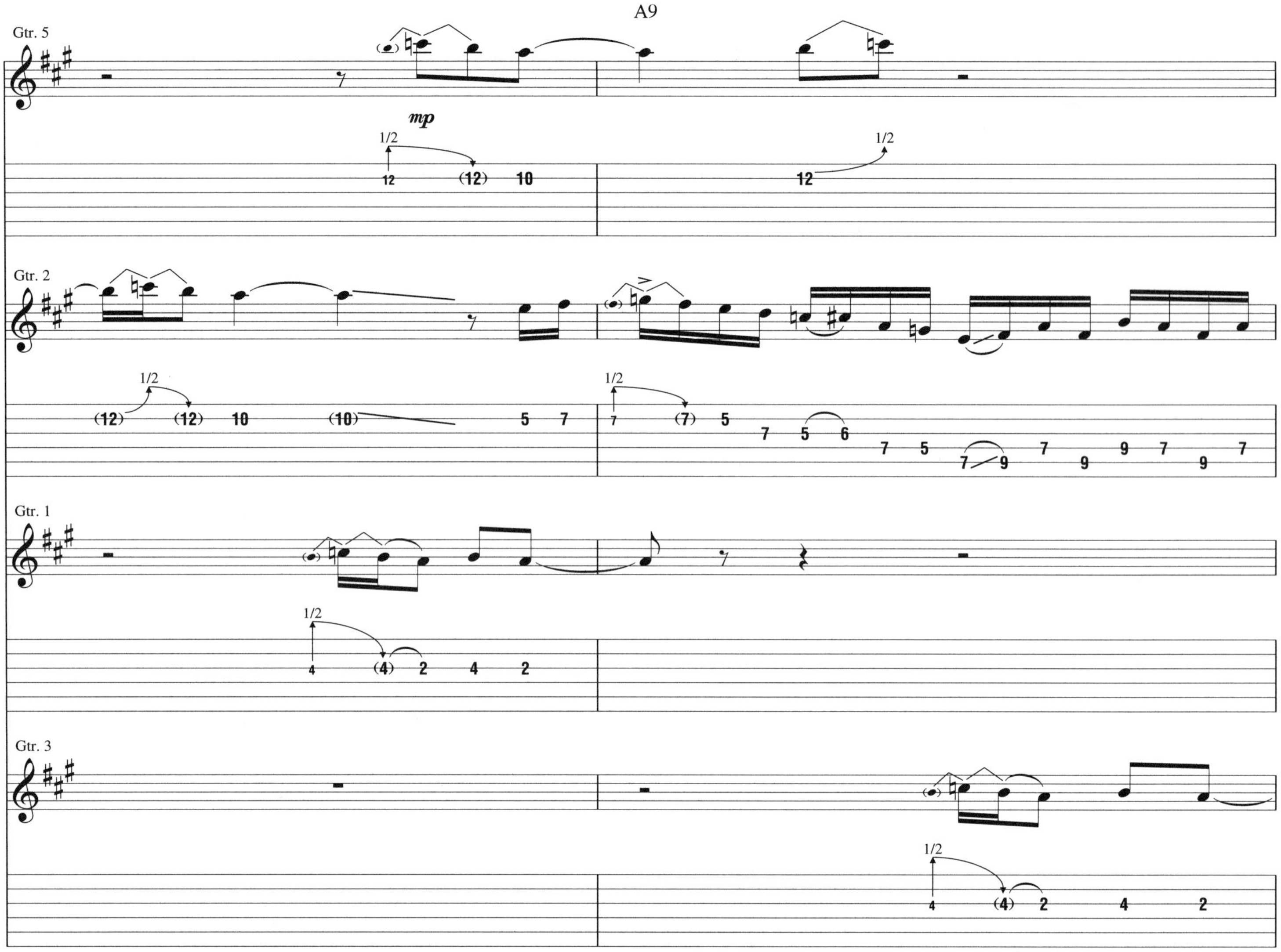
A9
Gtr. 5
mp
Gtr. 2
Gtr. 1
Gtr. 3

Gtr. 5 tacet
Gtr. 3 tacet
Fmaj7
E11
Gtr. 2
Gtr. 1
P.M.
Gtr. 3

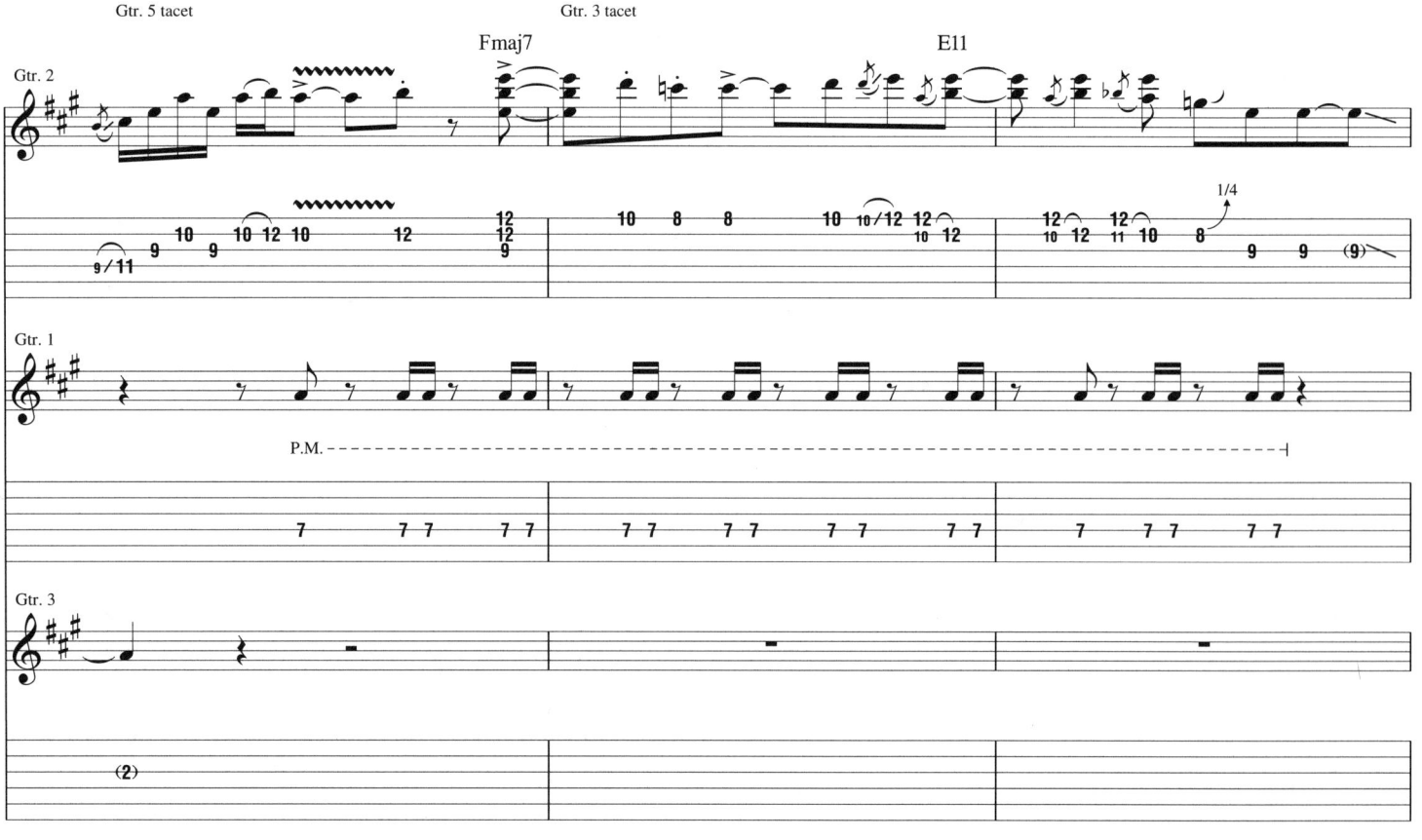

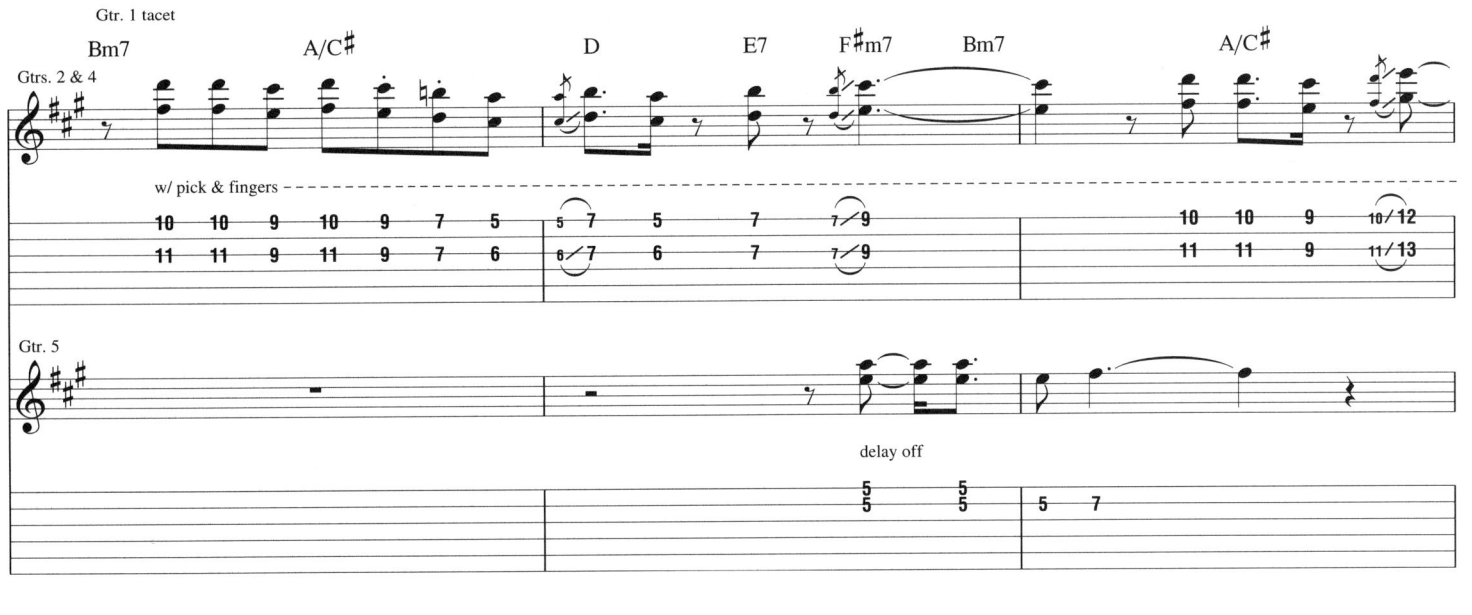
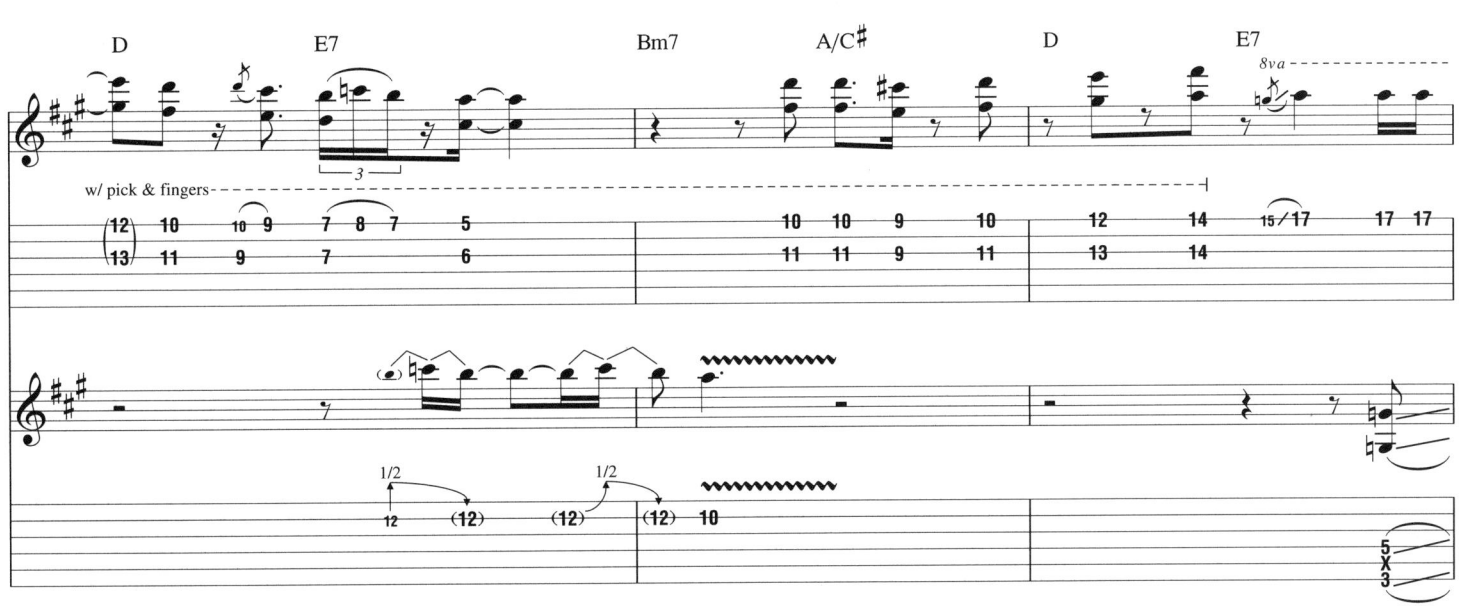
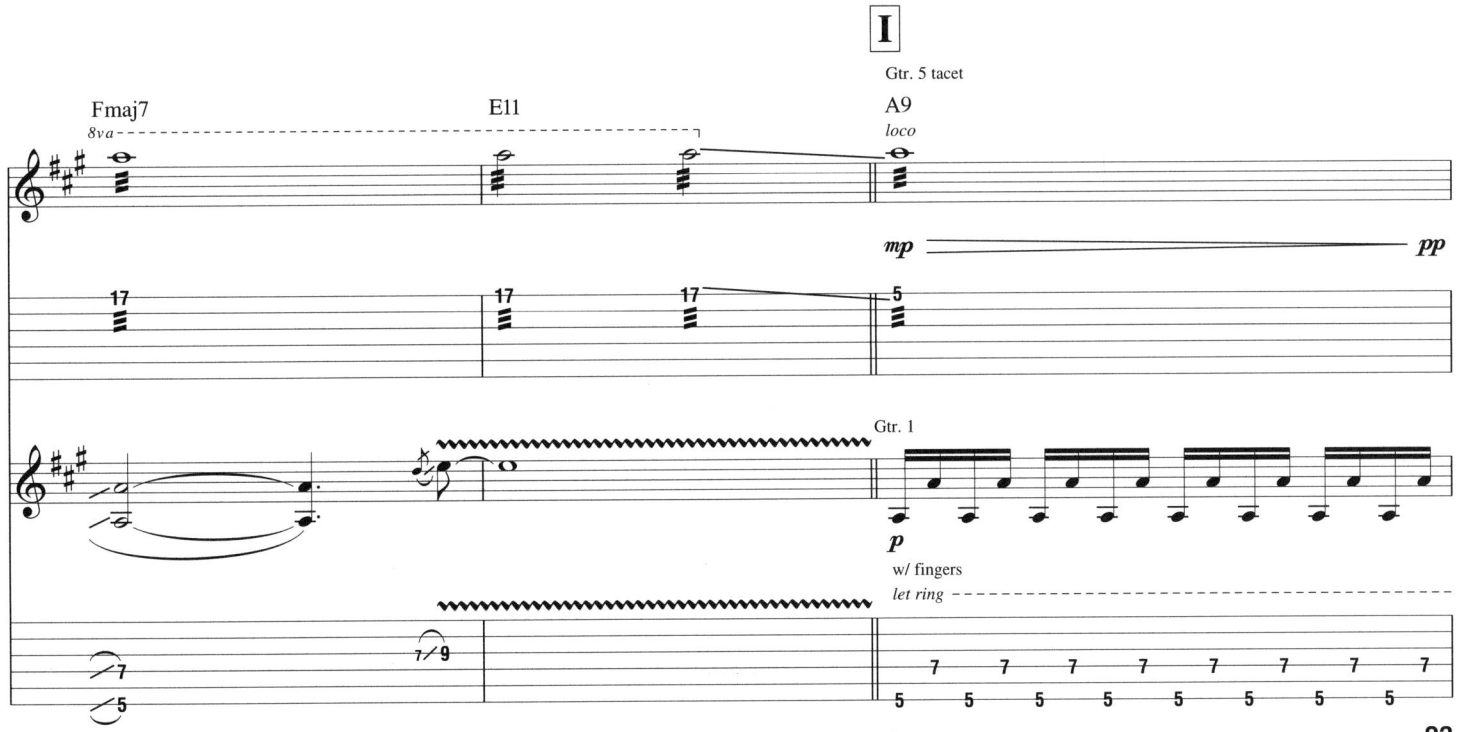

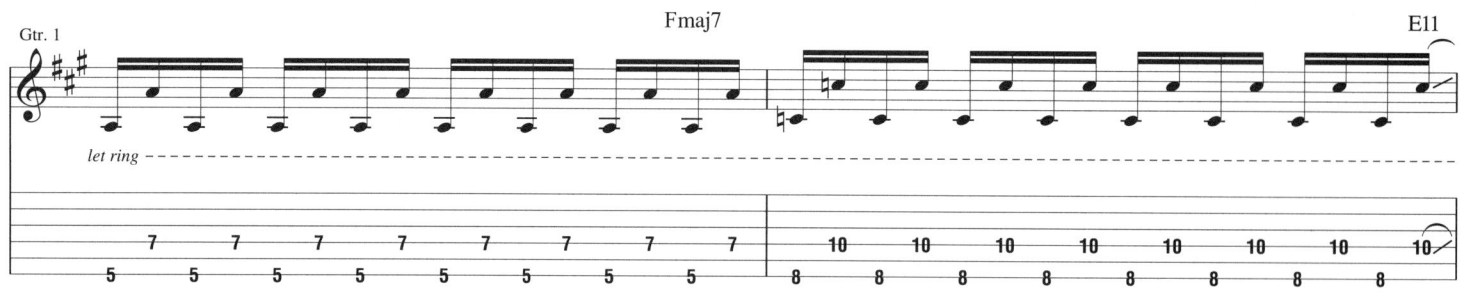
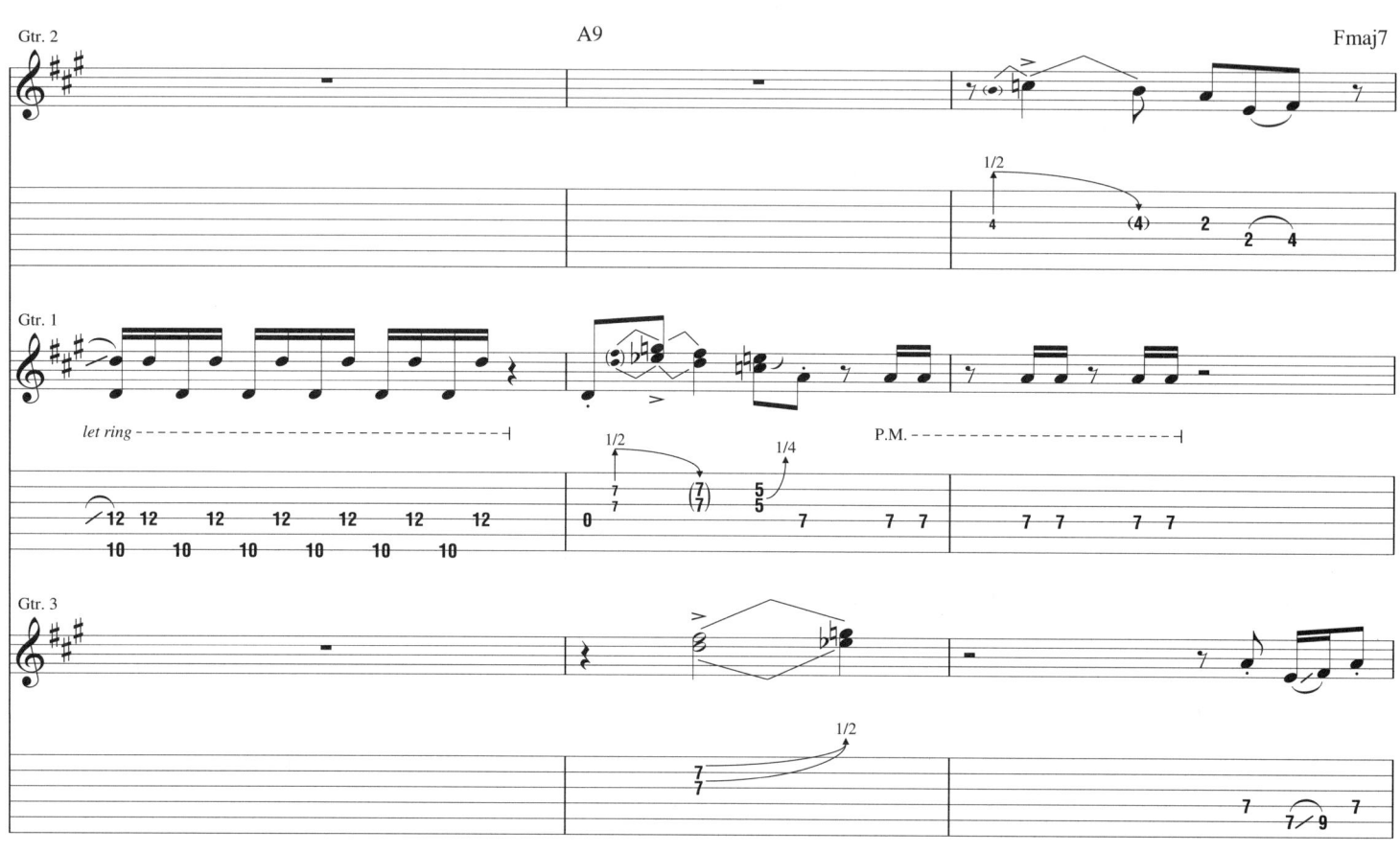
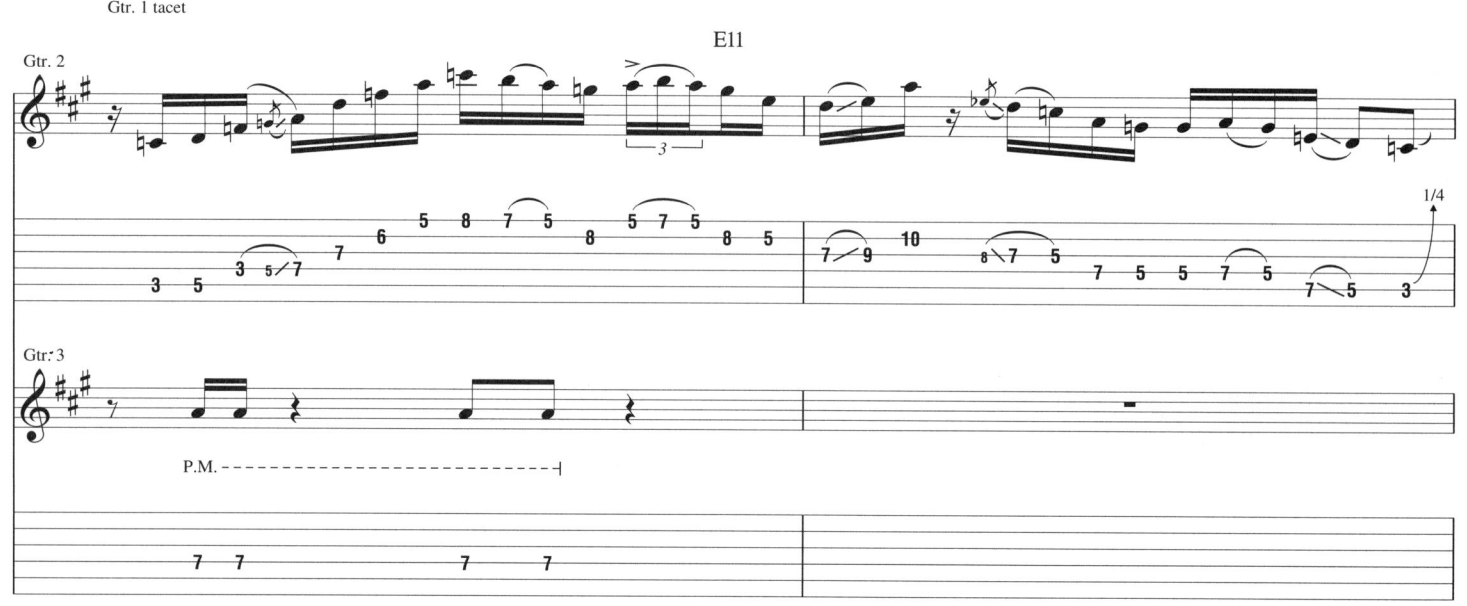

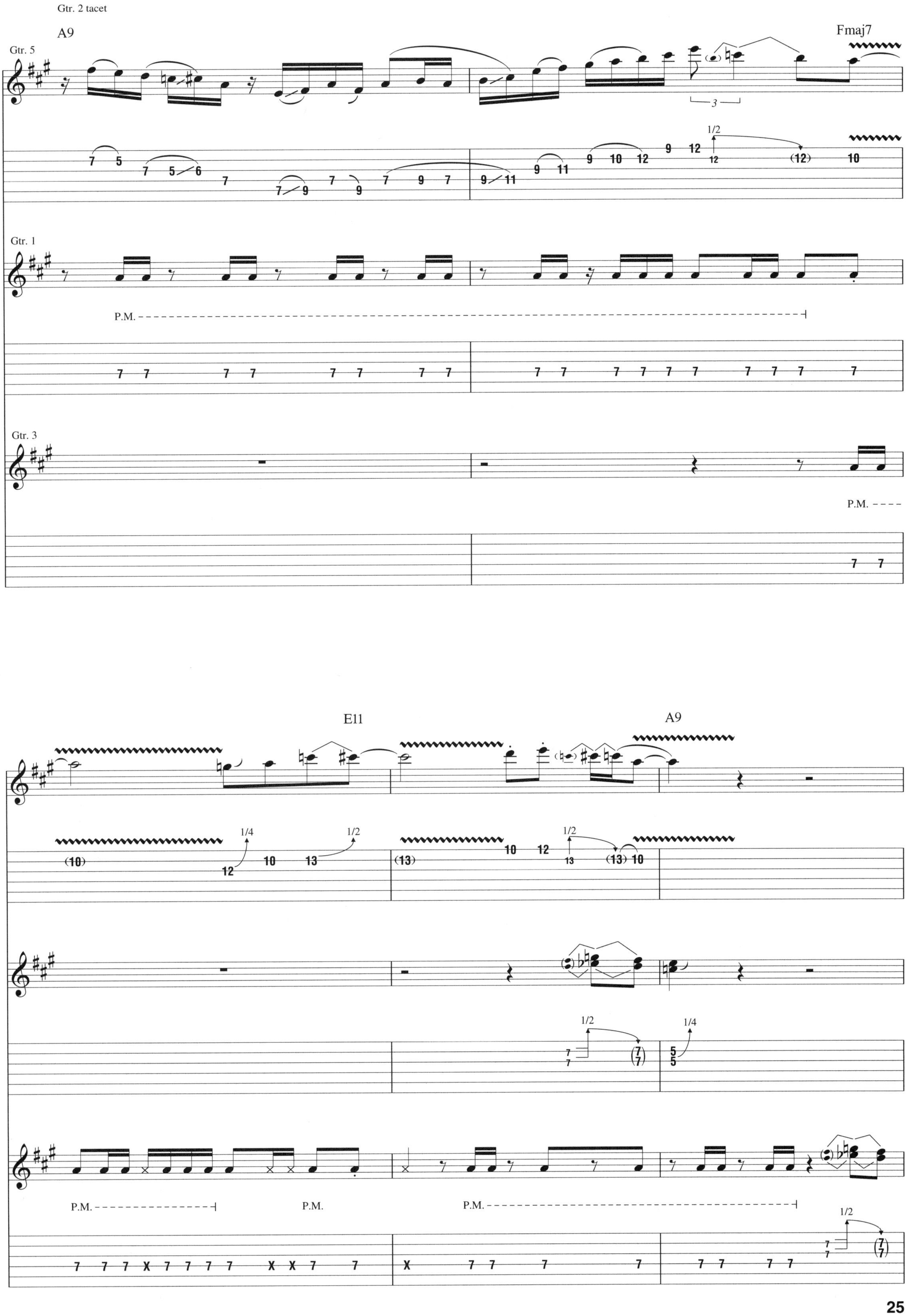
Gtr. 2 tacet
A9
Gtr. 5
Fmaj7
1/2
Gtr. 1
P.M.
Gtr. 3
P.M.
E11
A9
1/4
1/2
1/2
1/2
1/4
P.M.
P.M.
P.M.
1/2

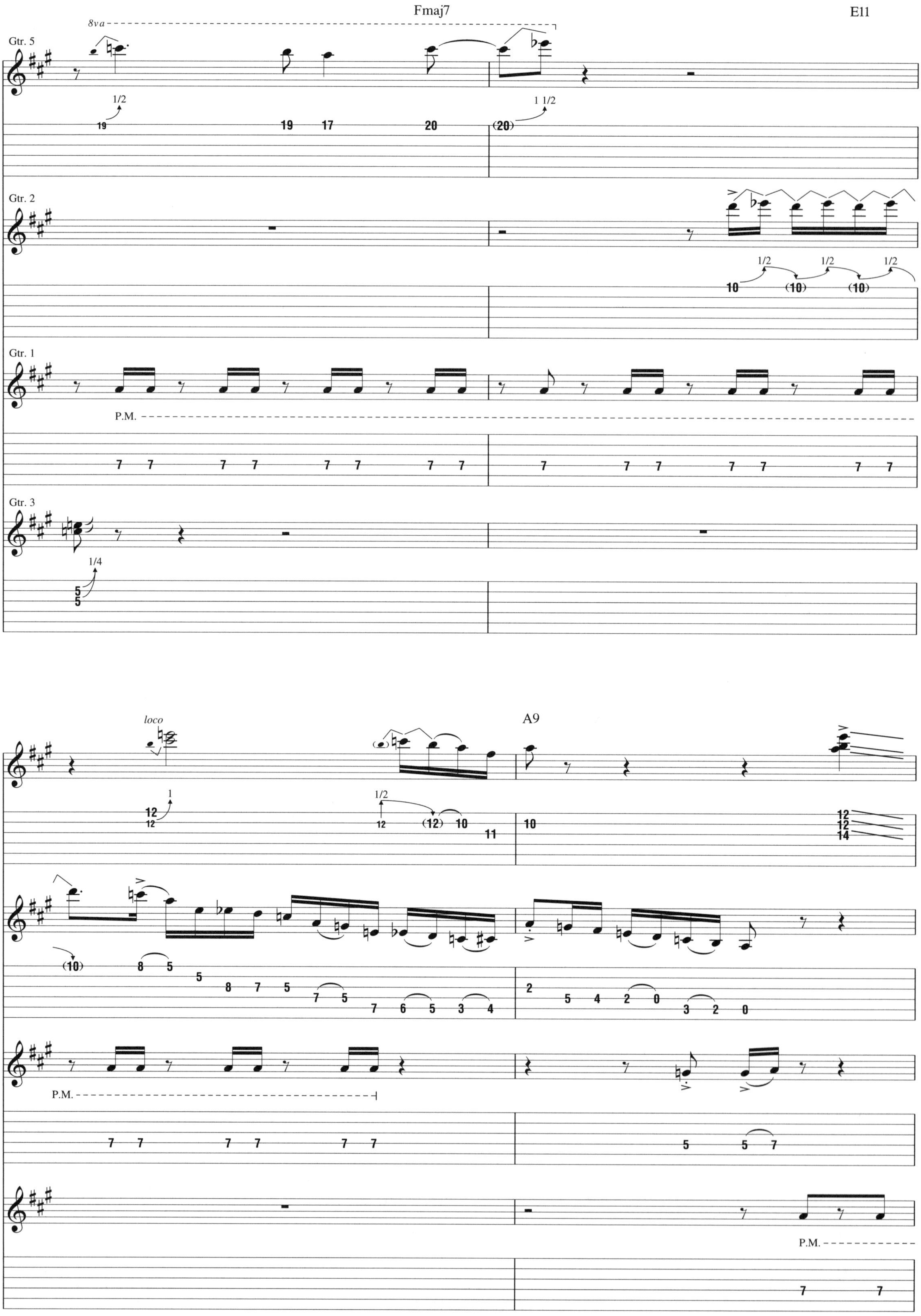
Fmaj7
E11
8va
Gtr. 5
Gtr. 2
Gtr. 1
P.M.
Gtr. 3
loco
A9
P.M.
P.M.

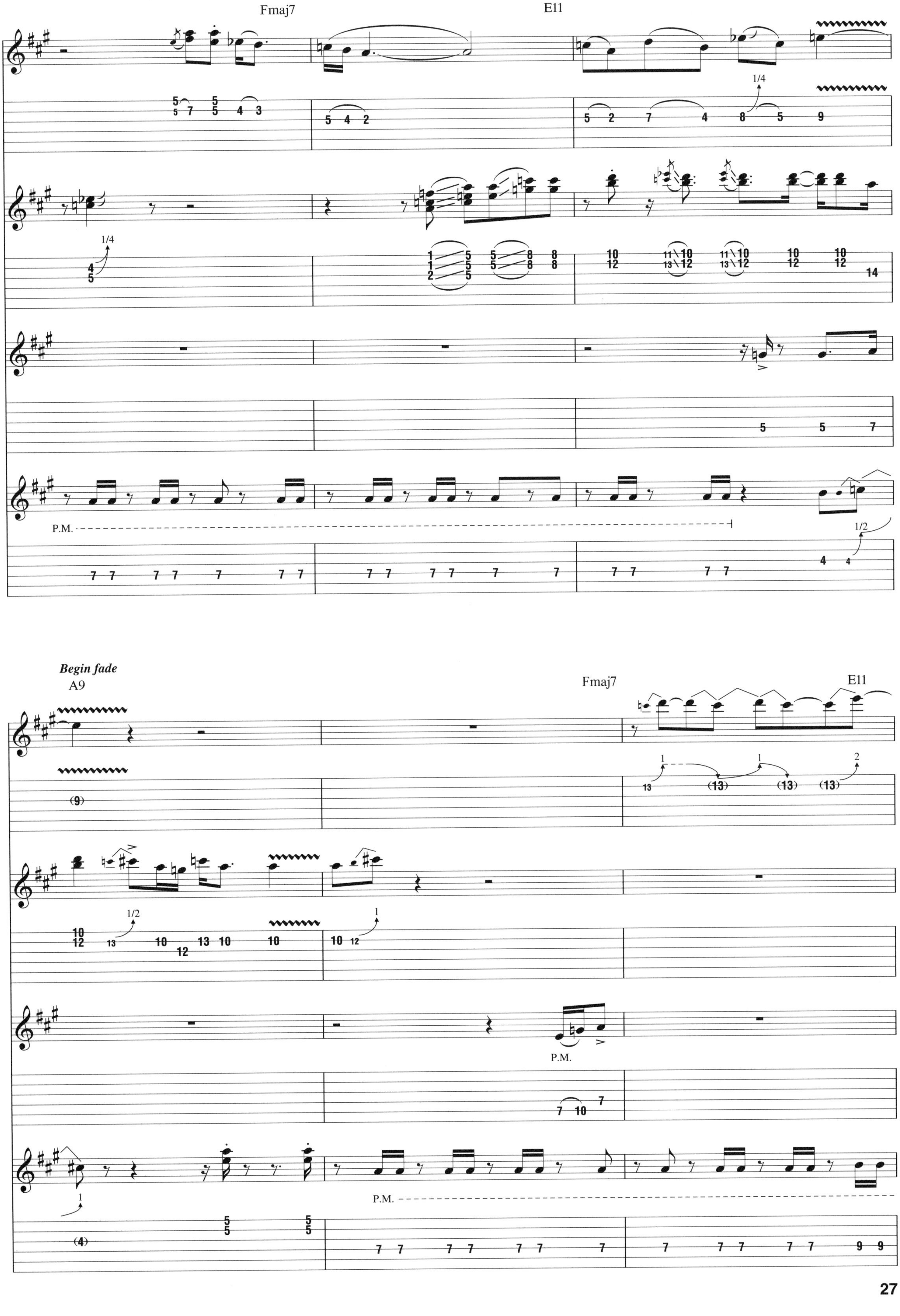
Fmaj7
E11
P.M.
Begin fade
A9
Fmaj7
E11
P.M.
P.M.

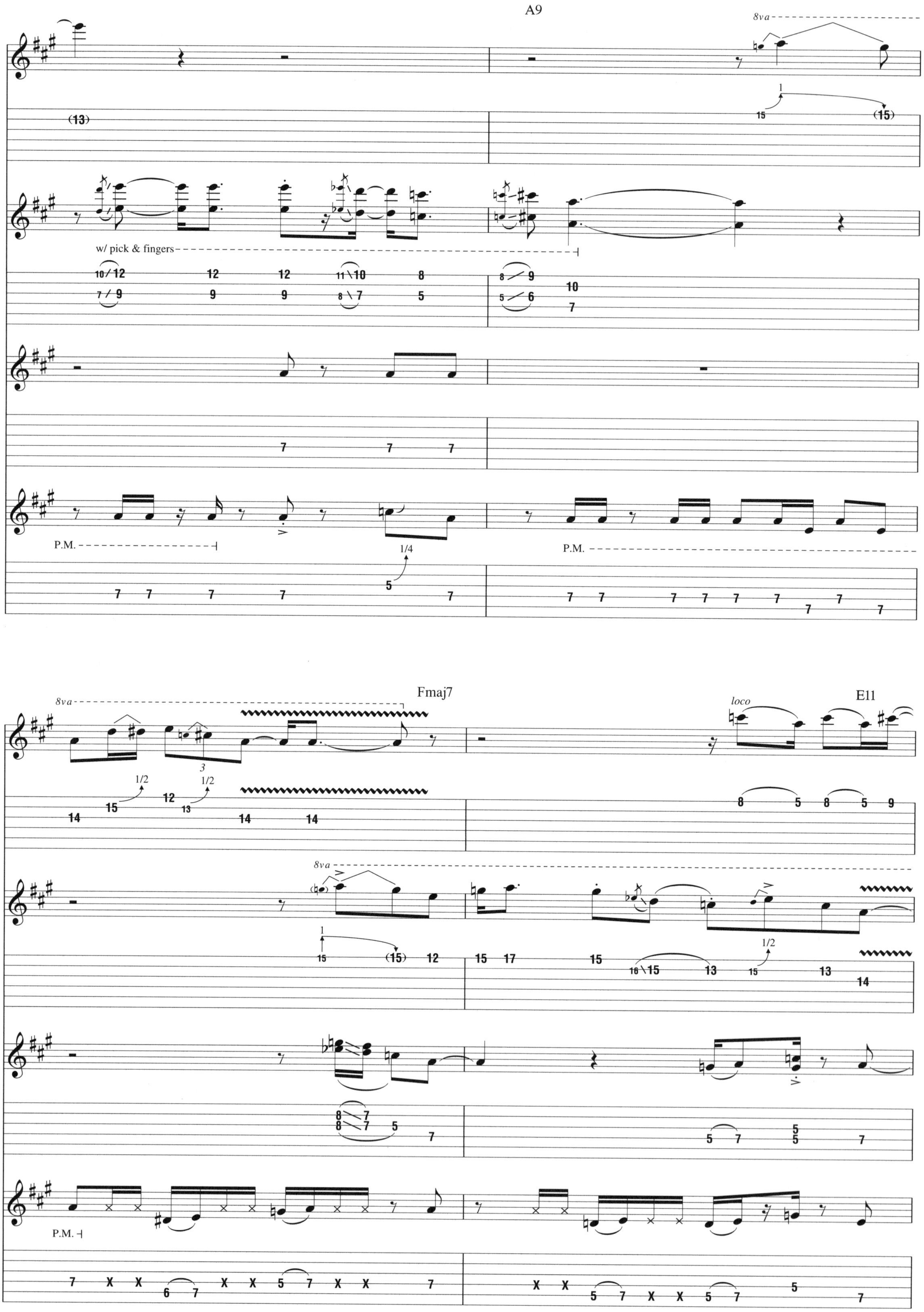
A9
8va
w/ pick & fingers
P.M.
Fmaj7
E11
loco

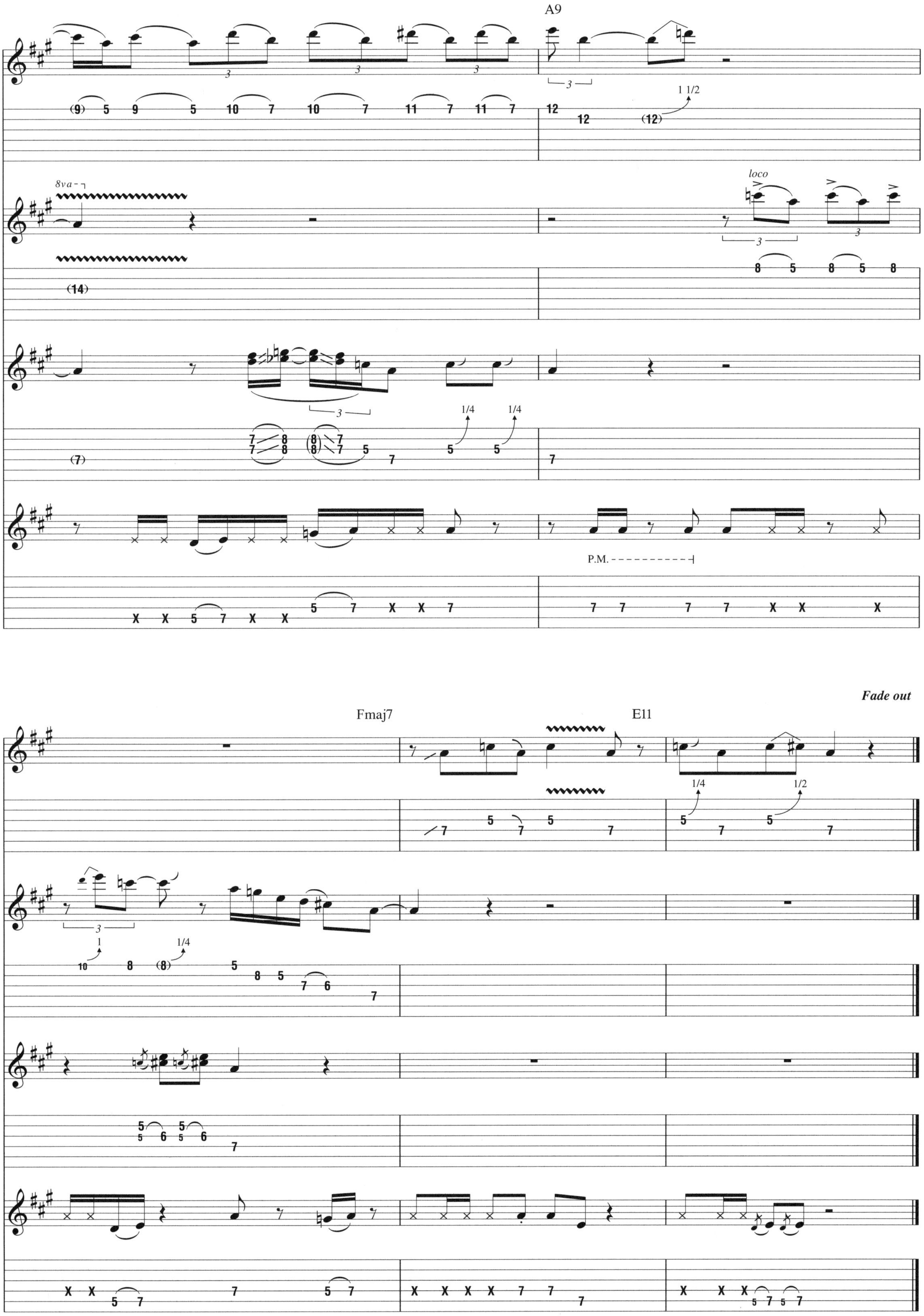
A9
8va
loco
P.M.
Fade out
Fmaj7
E11

Classical Gas

from *Classical Gas*

Music by Mason Williams

A
Free time

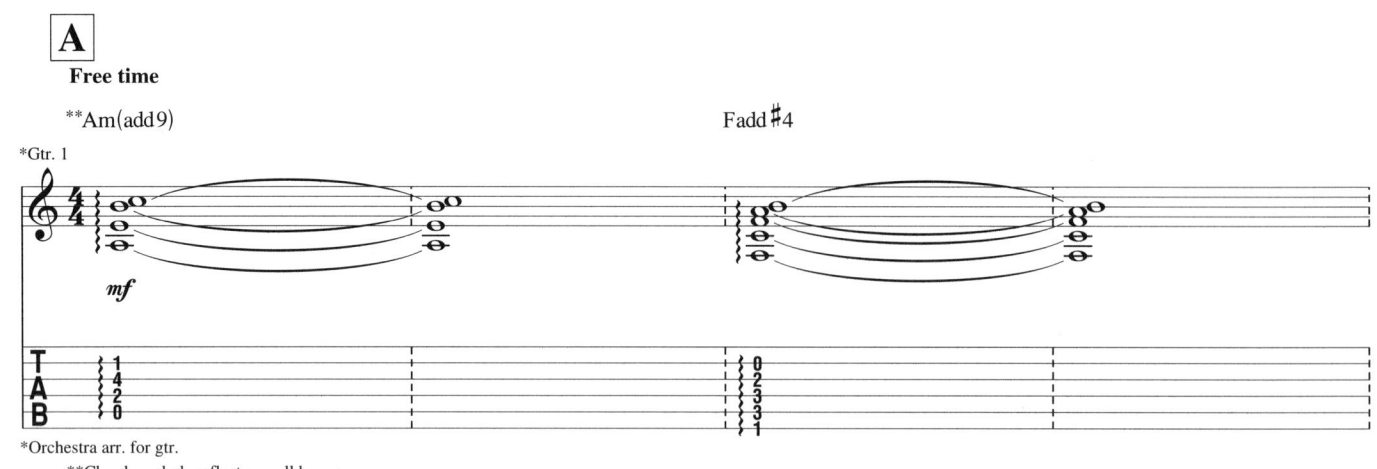

*Orchestra arr. for gtr.
**Chord symbols reflect overall harmony.

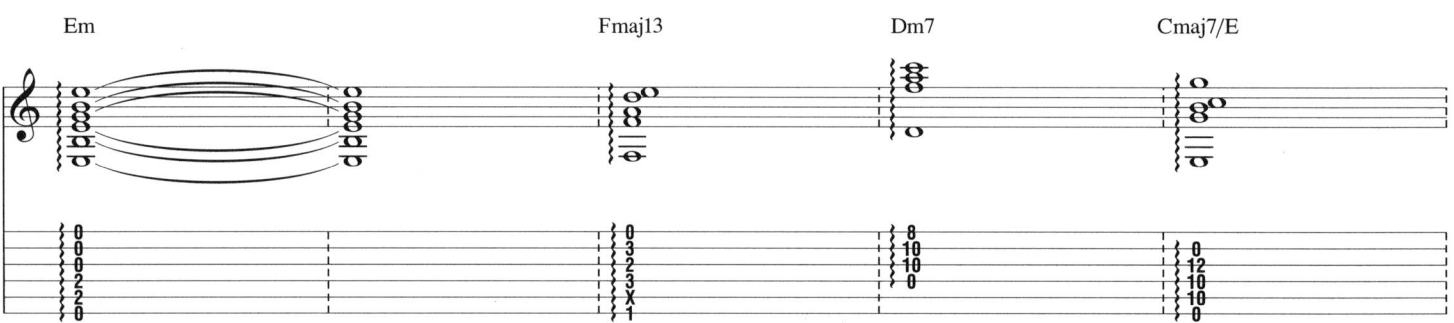

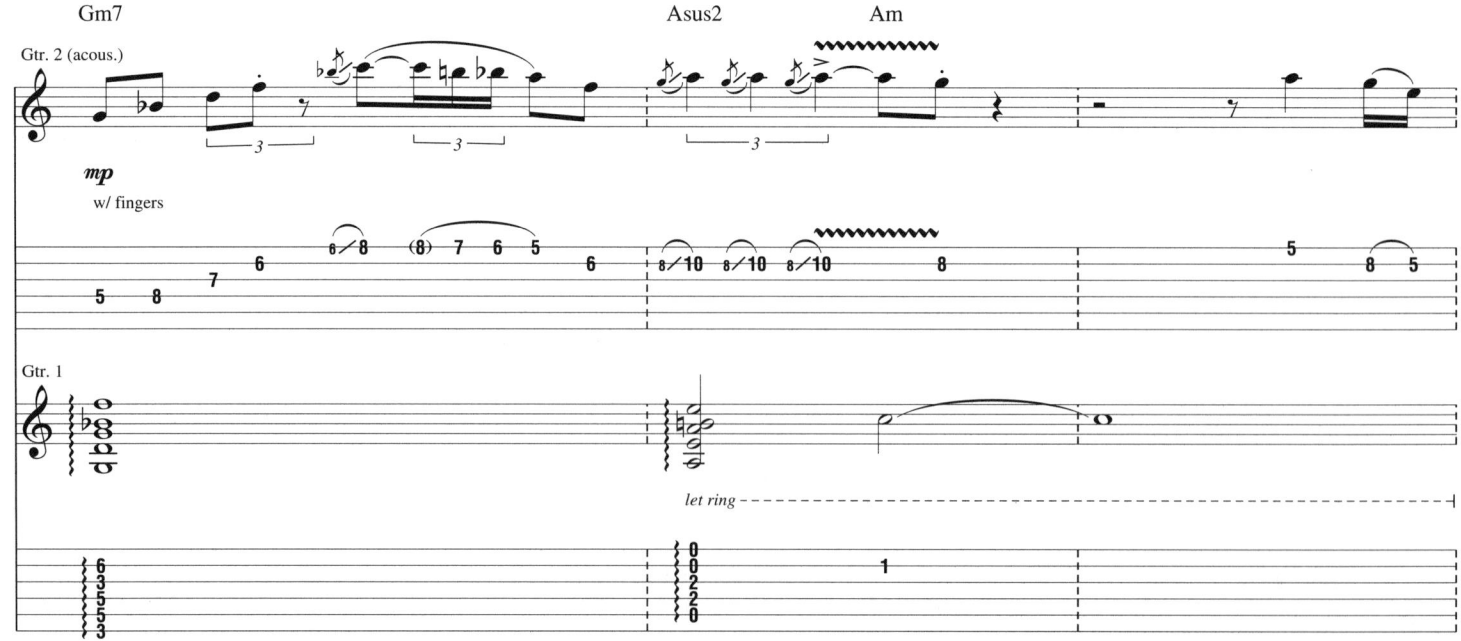

© 1967, 1968 Weems Music Co.
© Renewed 1995, 1996 Weems Music Co.
All Rights Reserved   Used by Permission

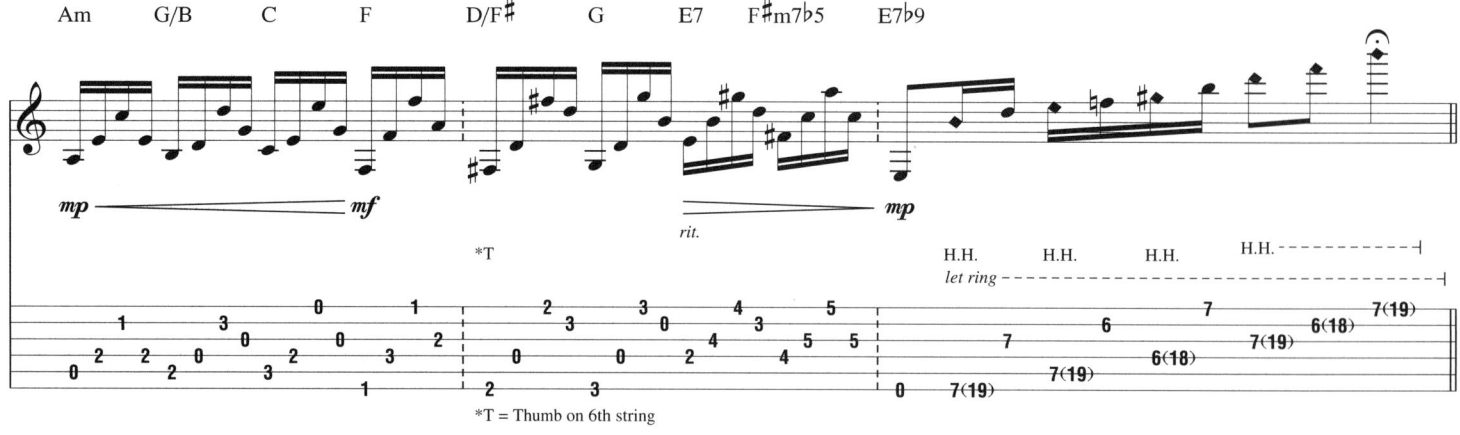
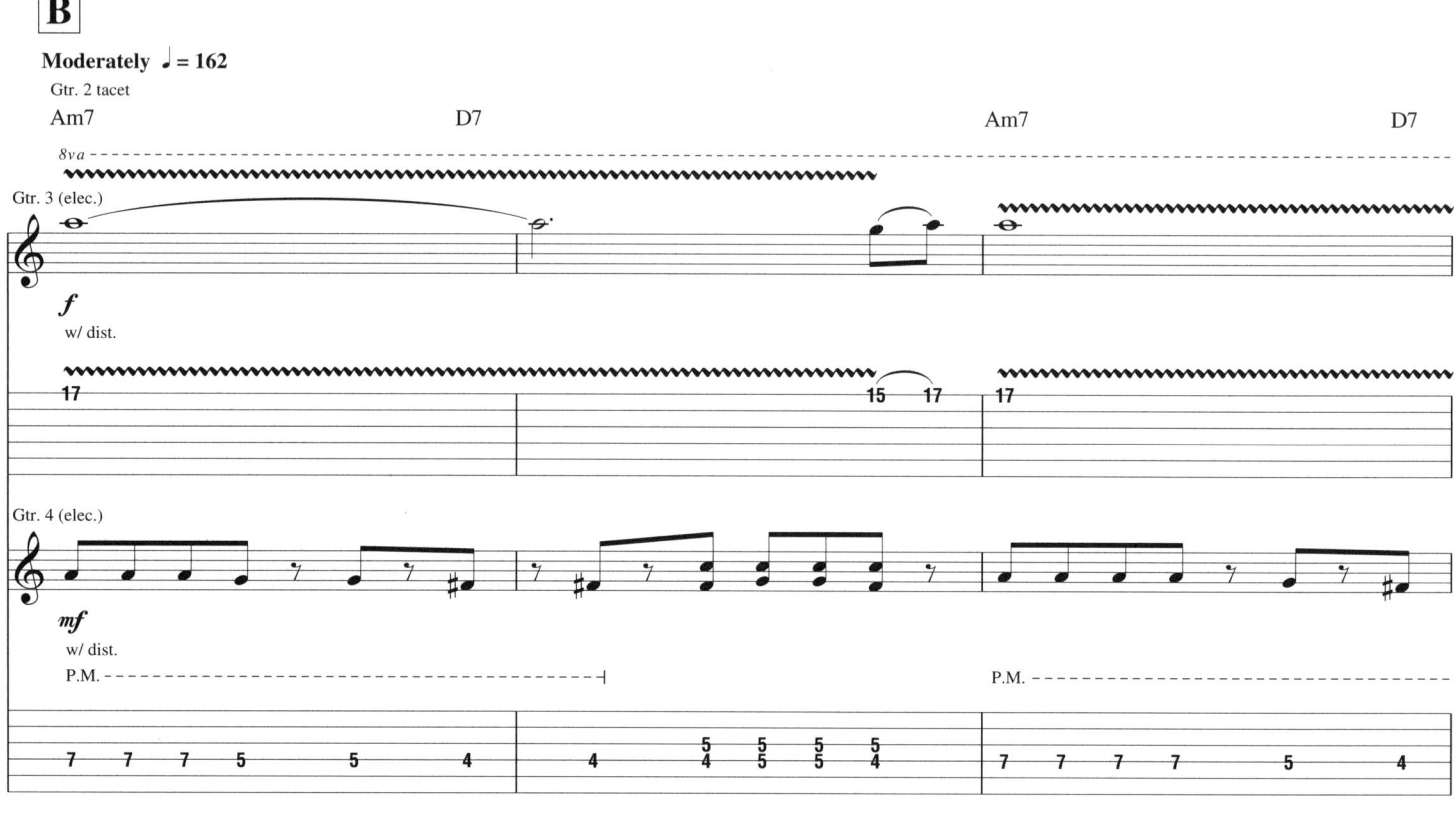
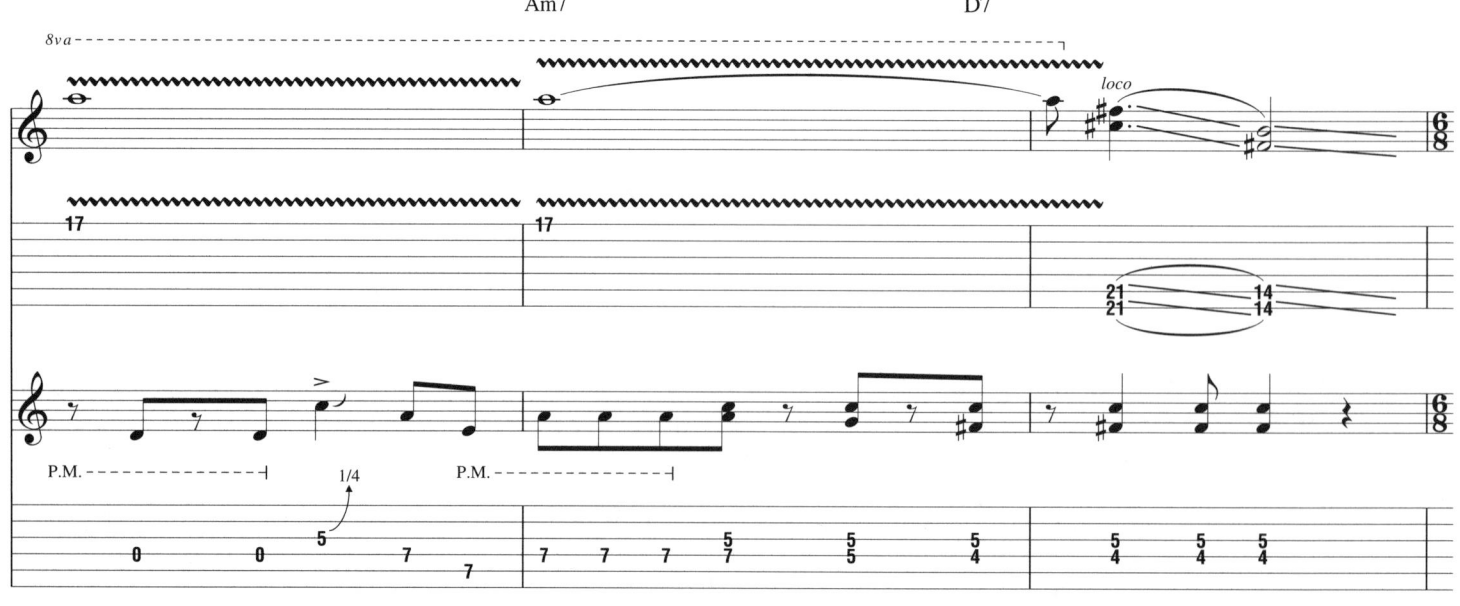

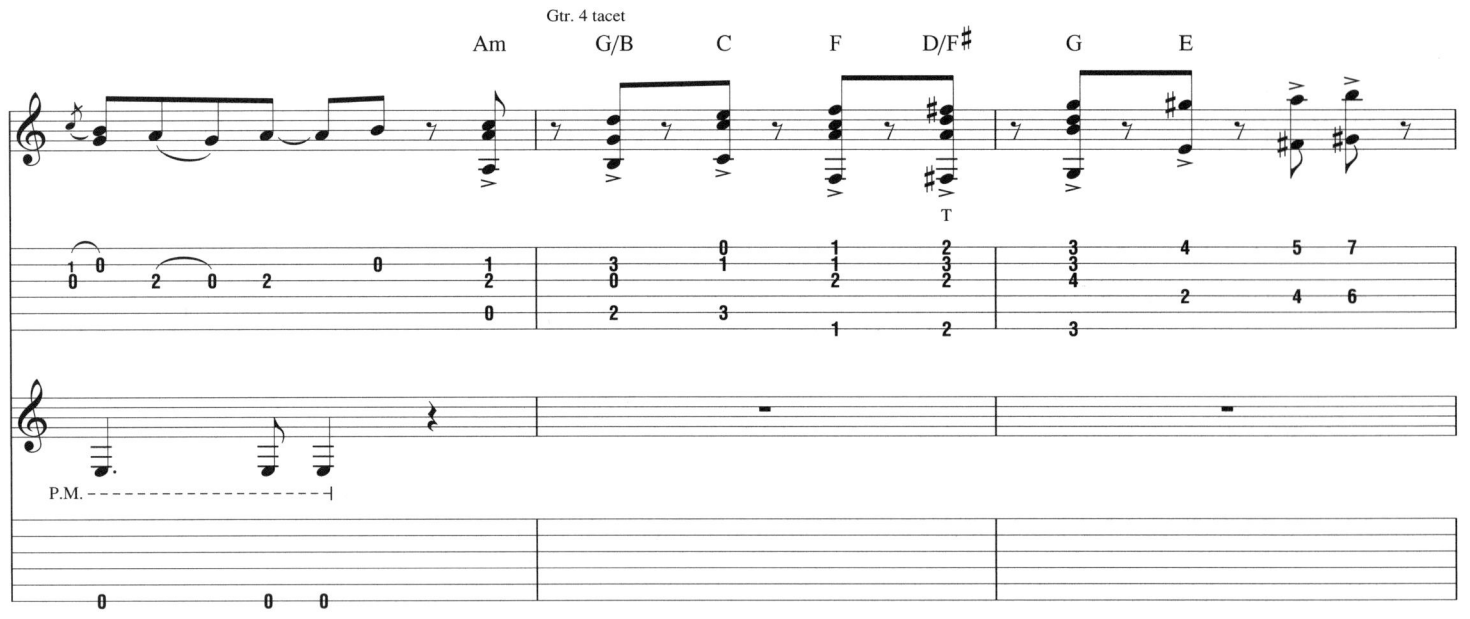
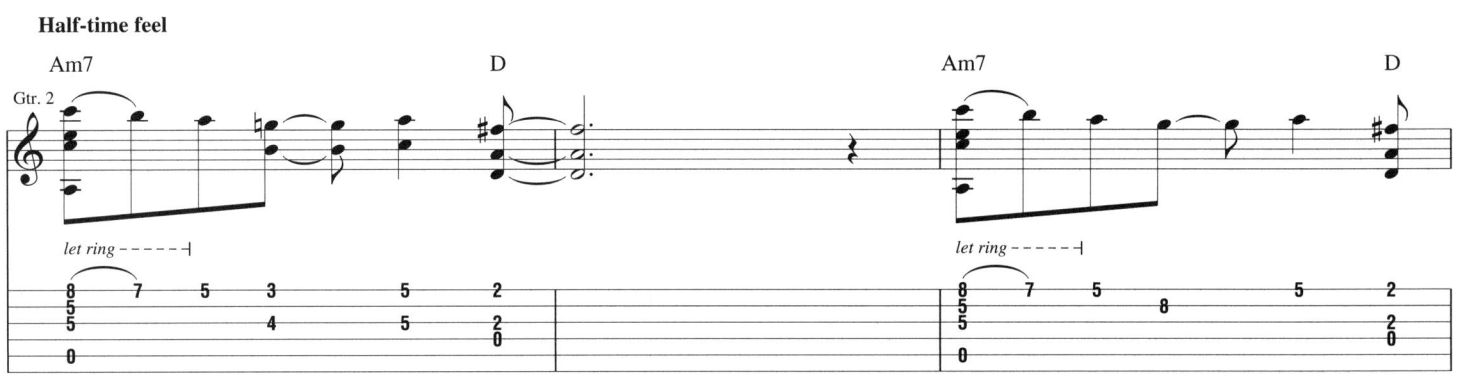
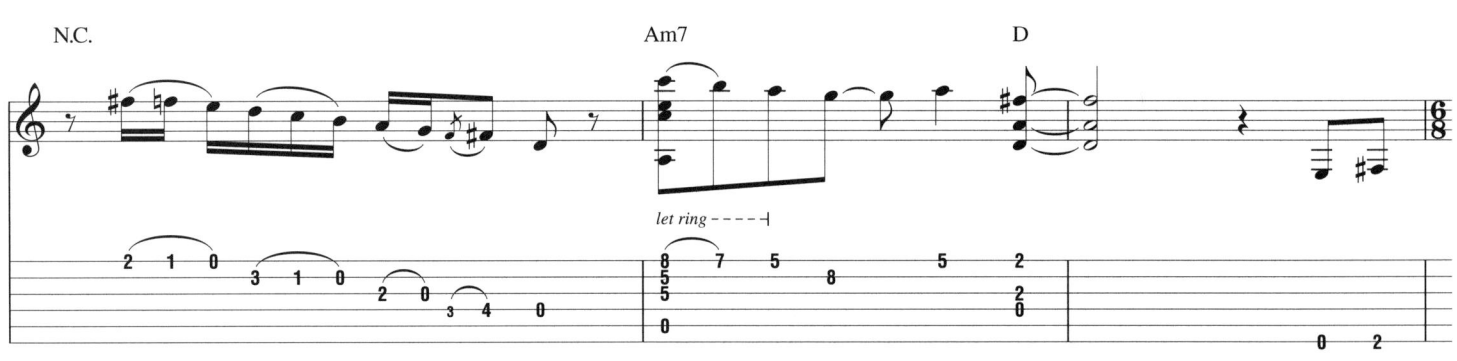
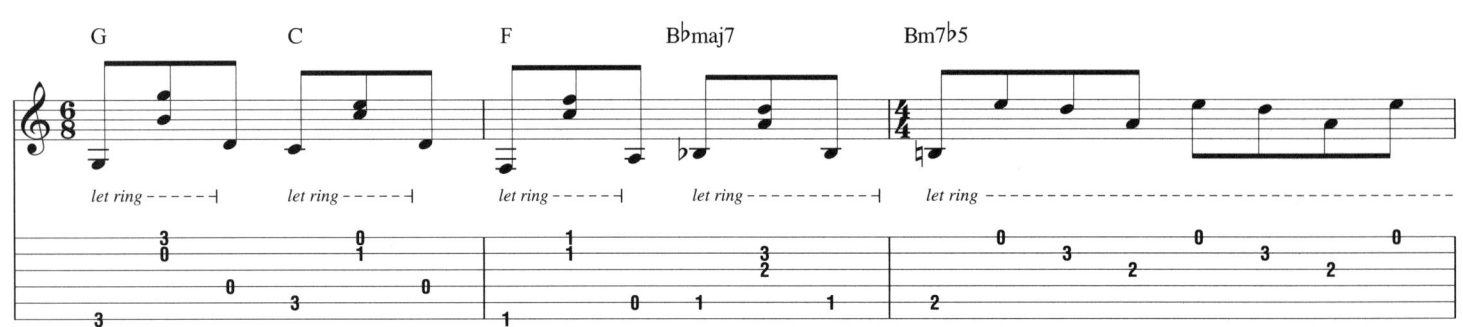

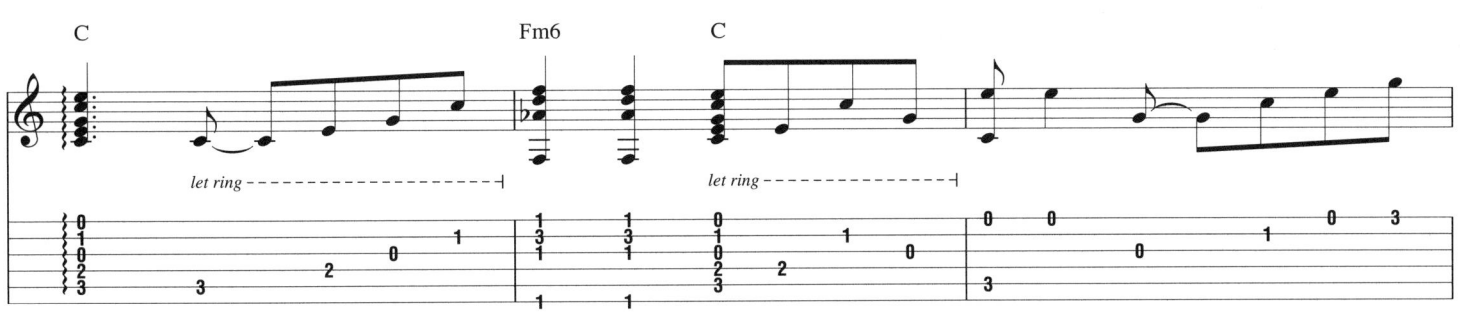
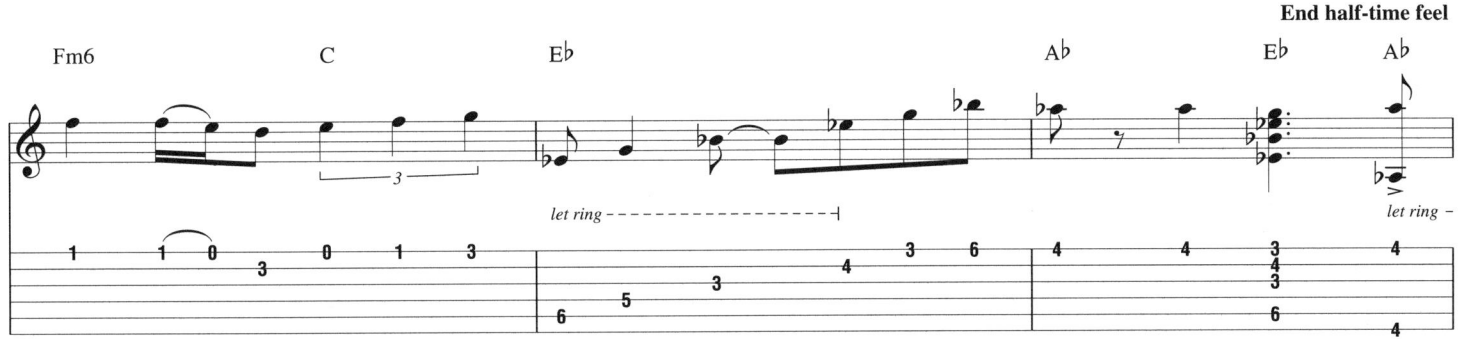
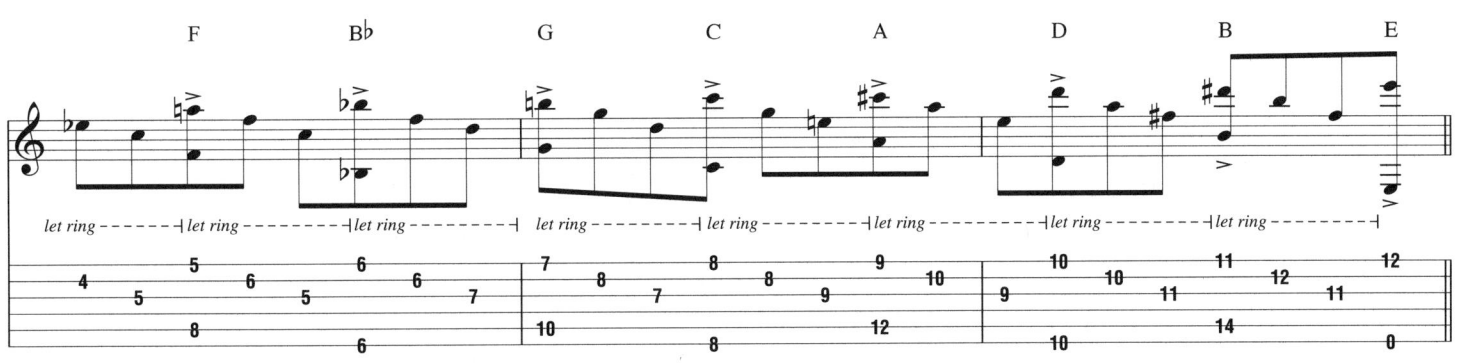
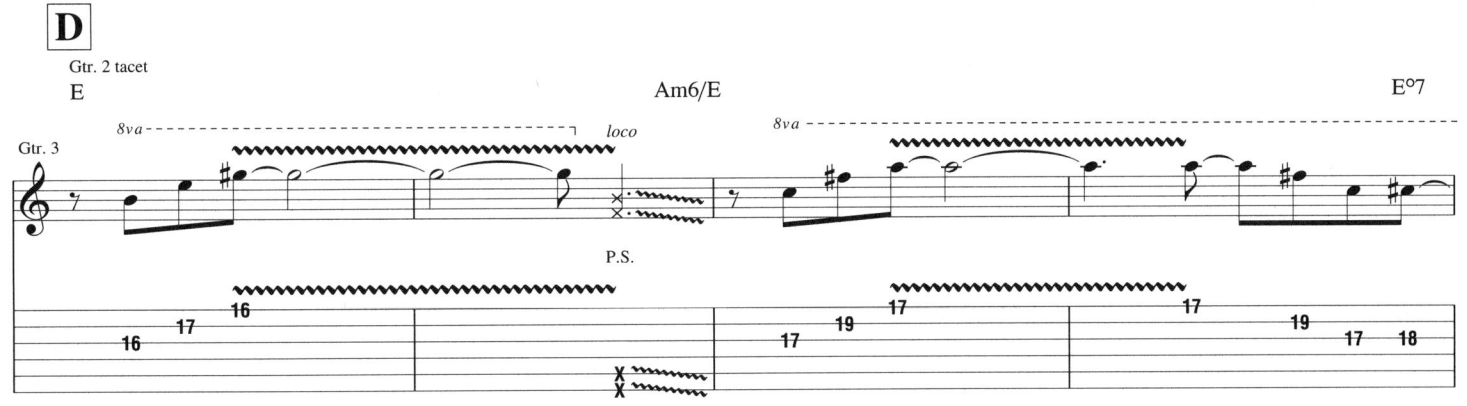

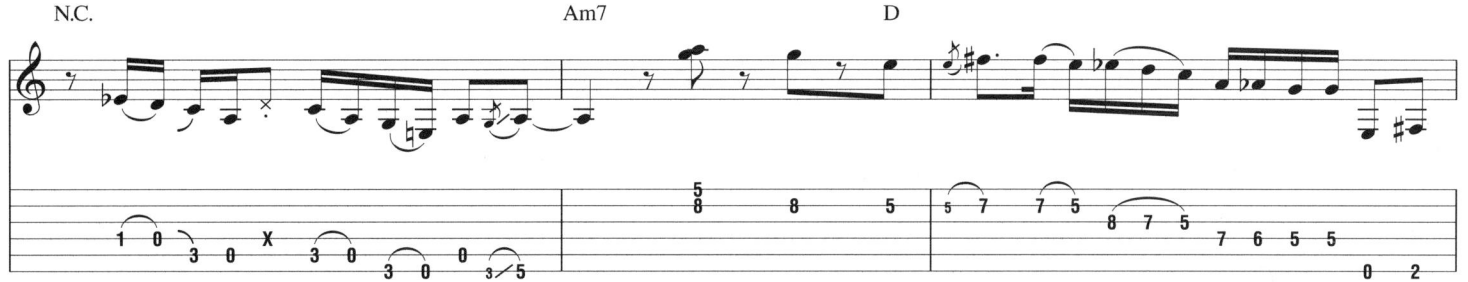
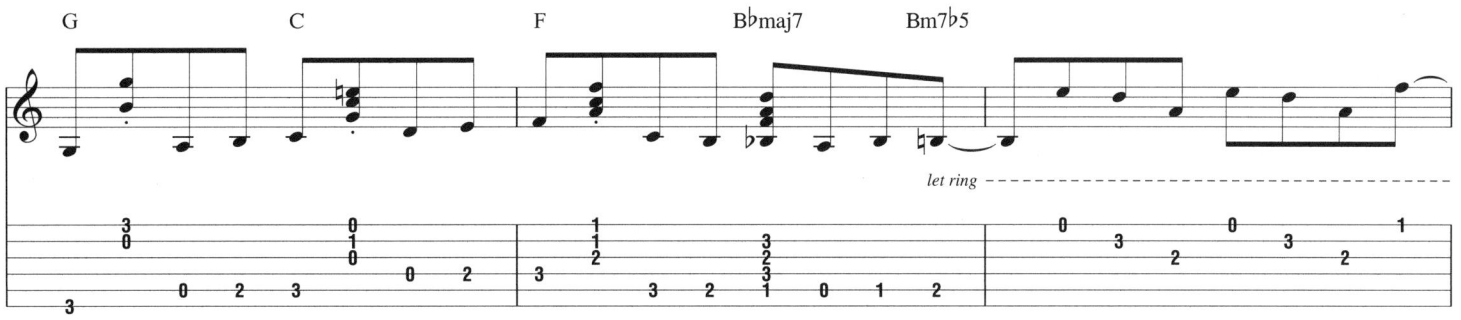
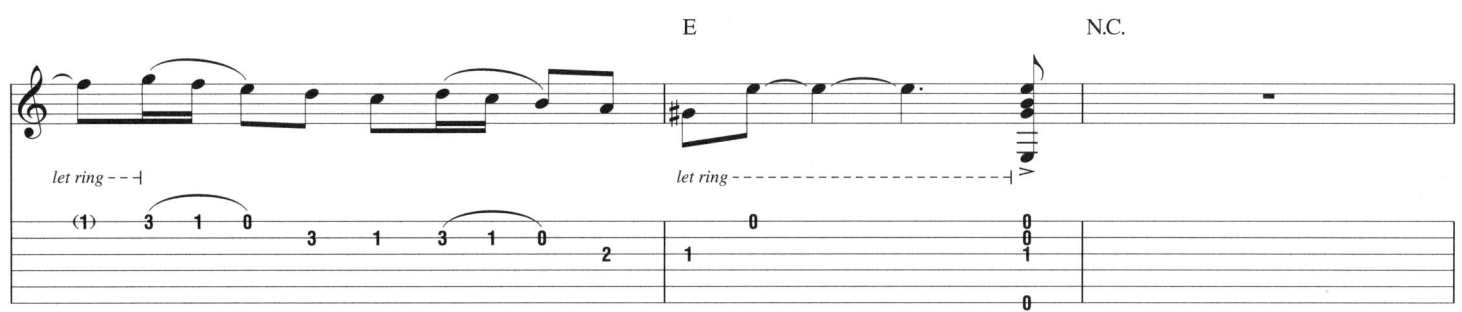
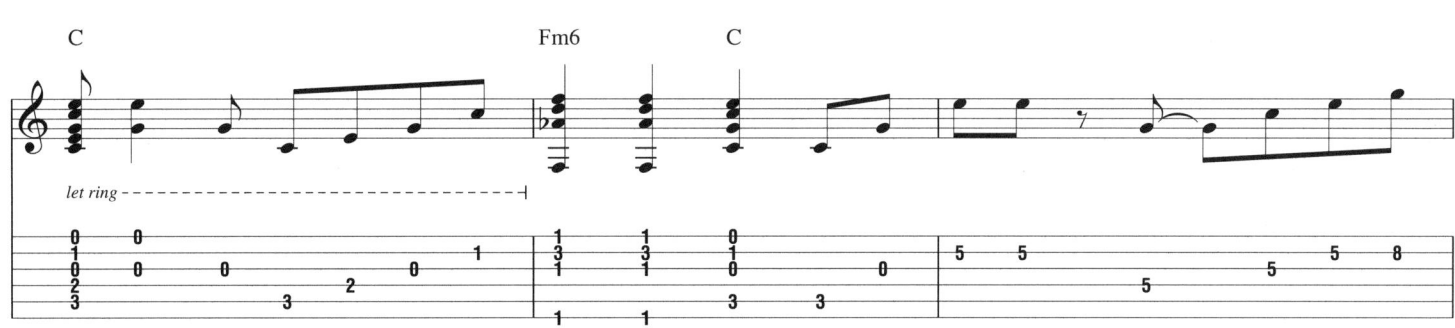
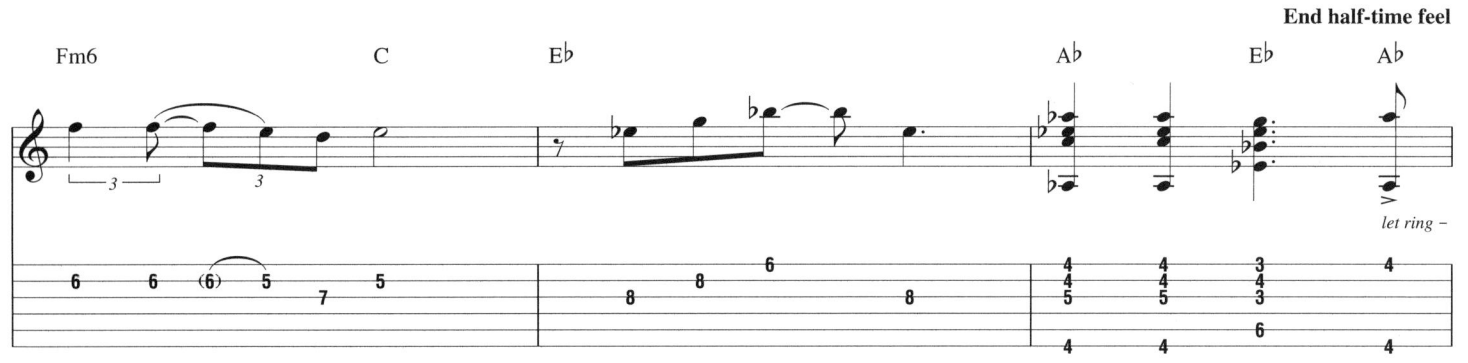

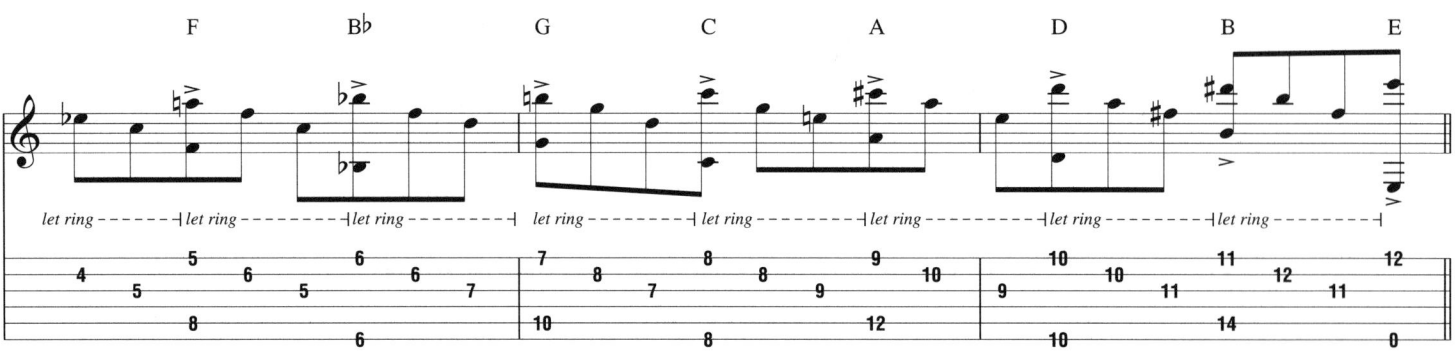
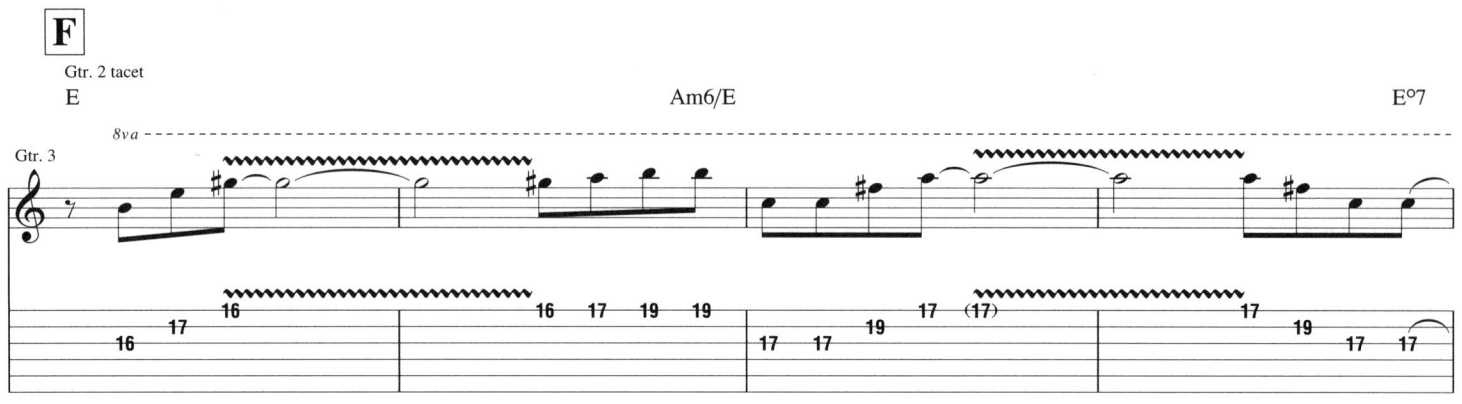
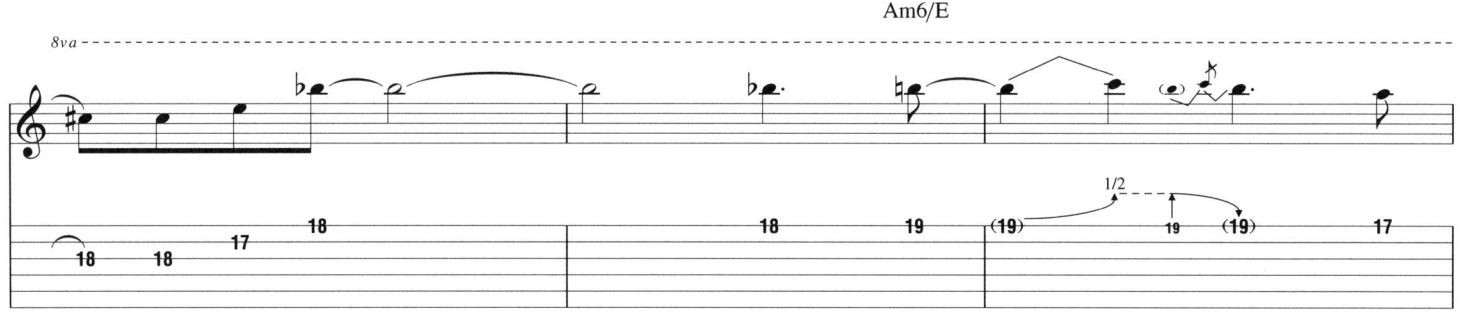

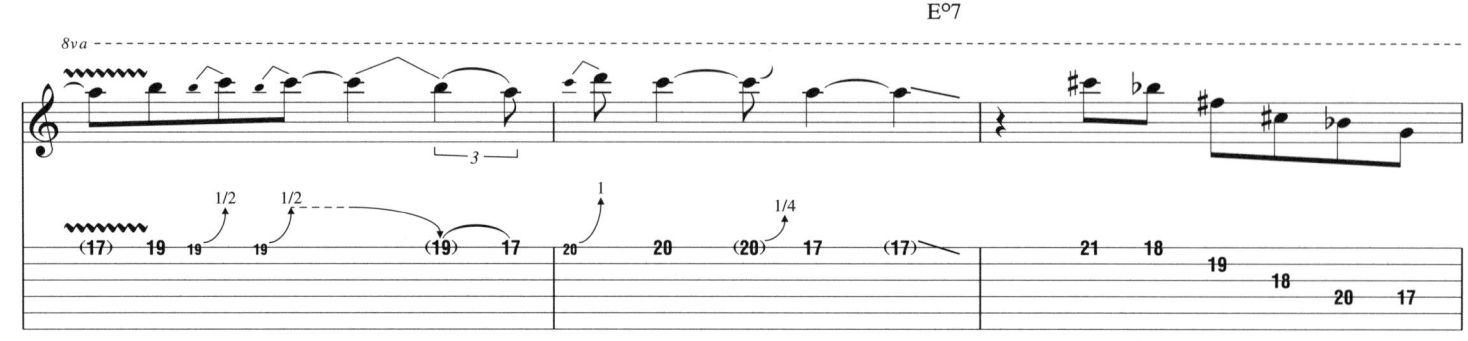

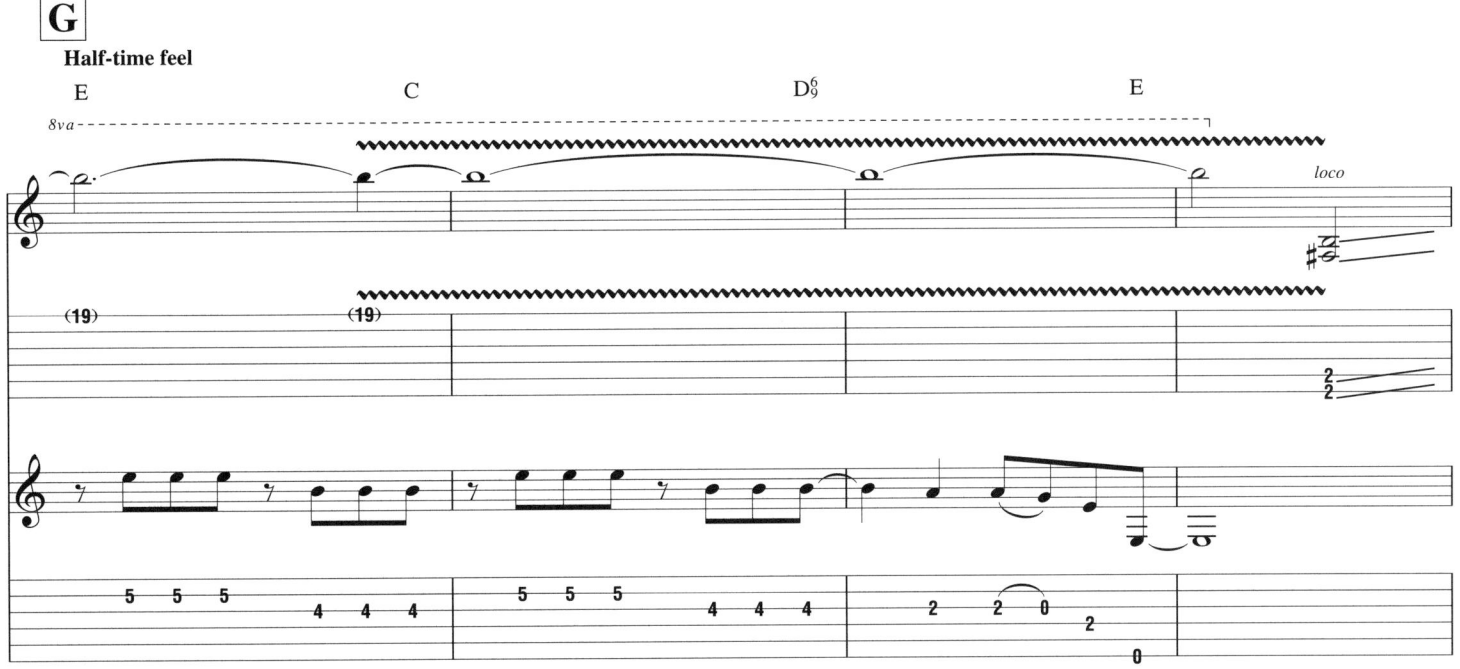
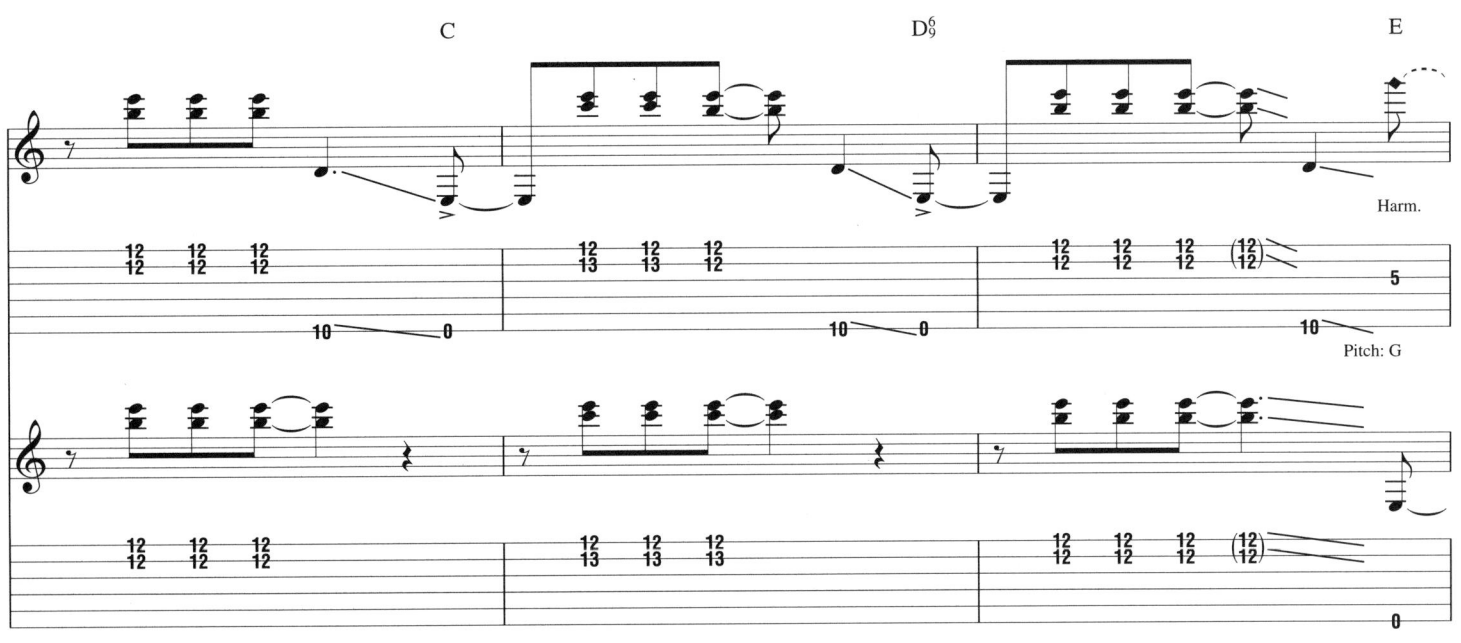

39

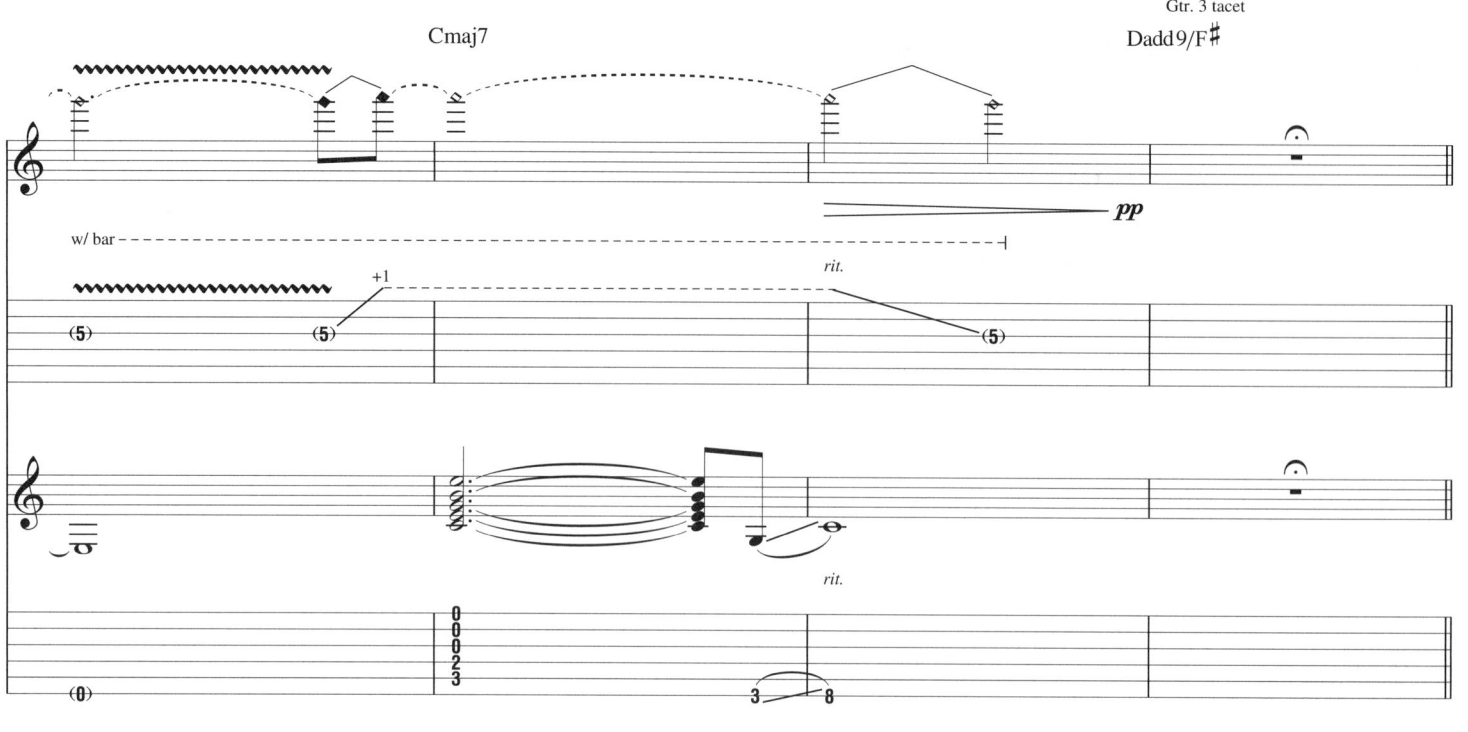
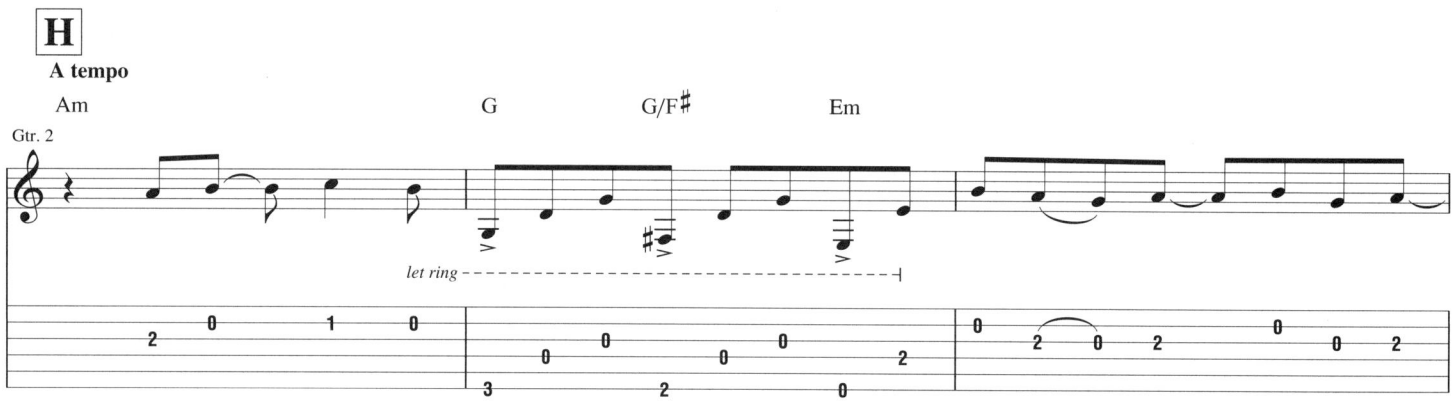

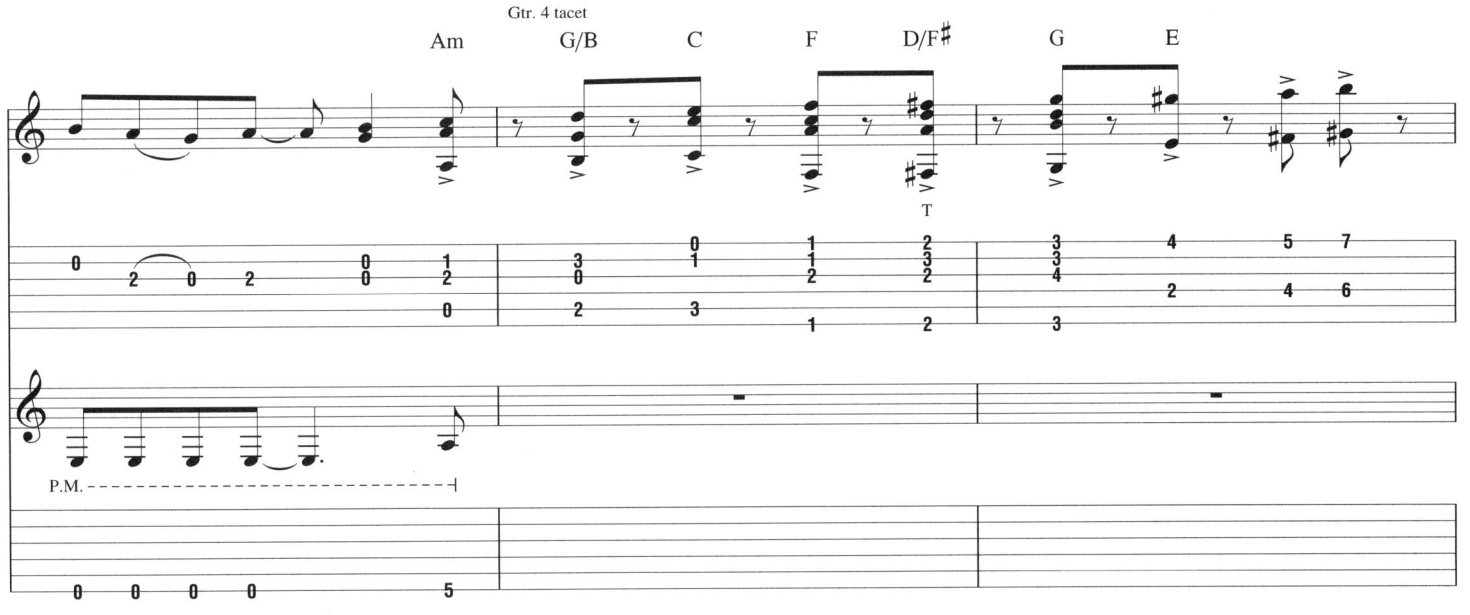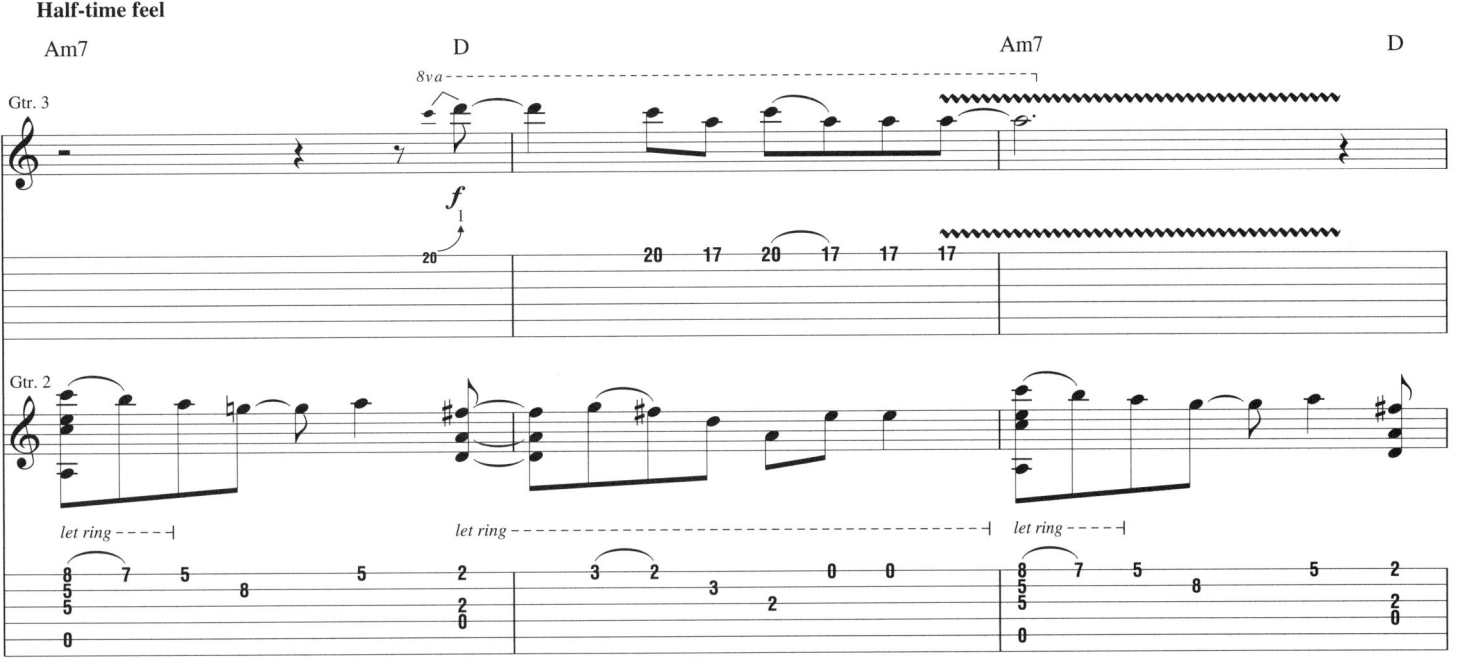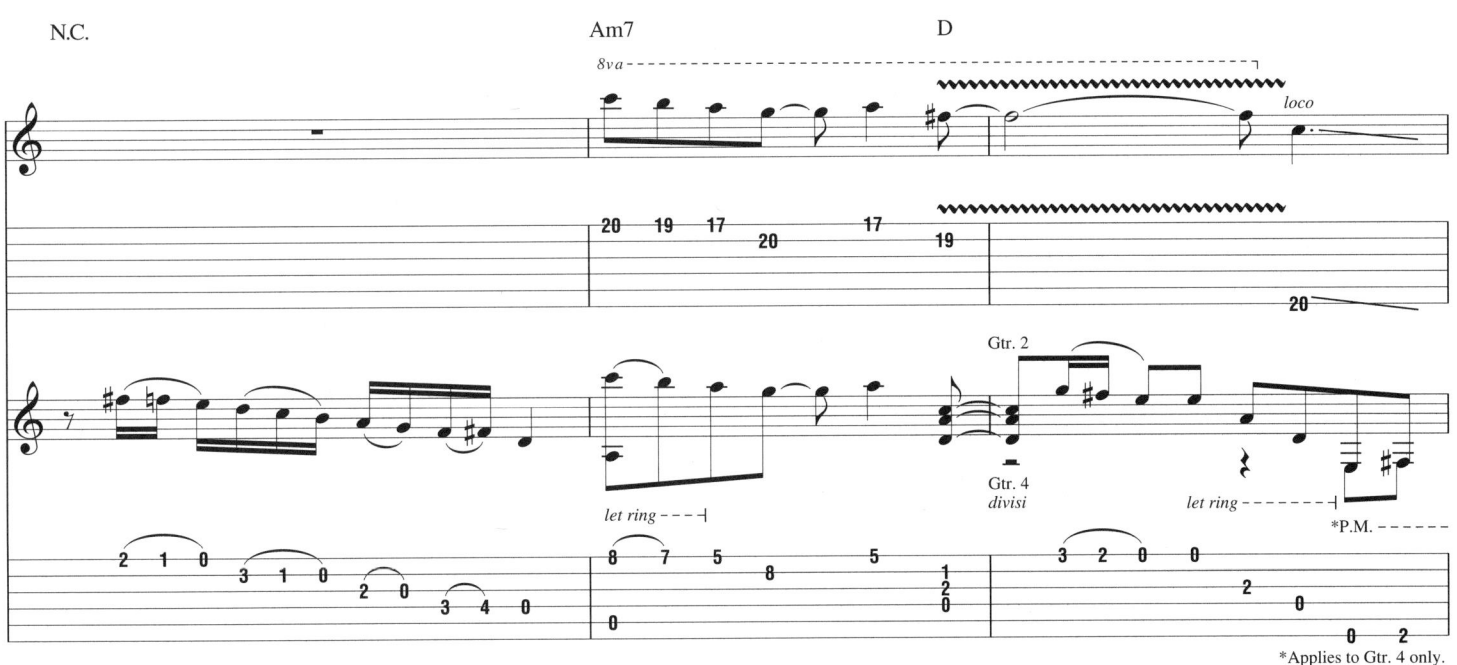

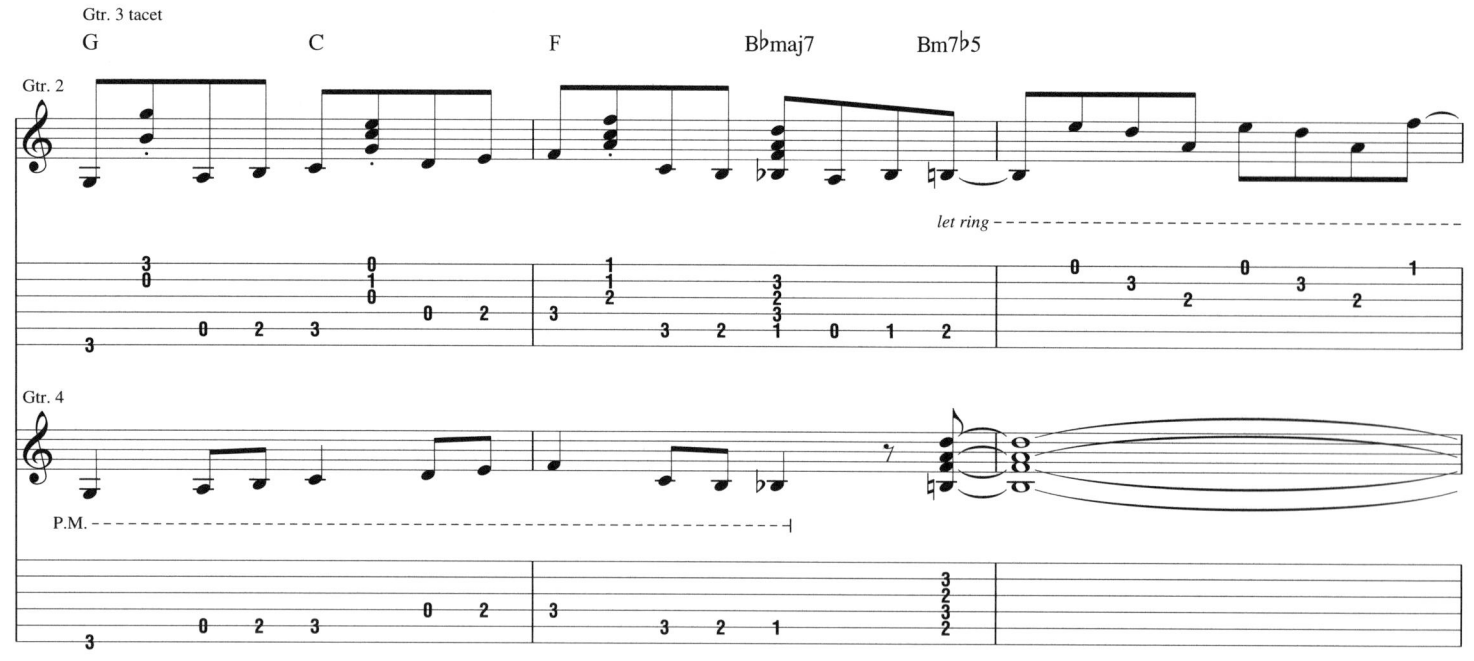
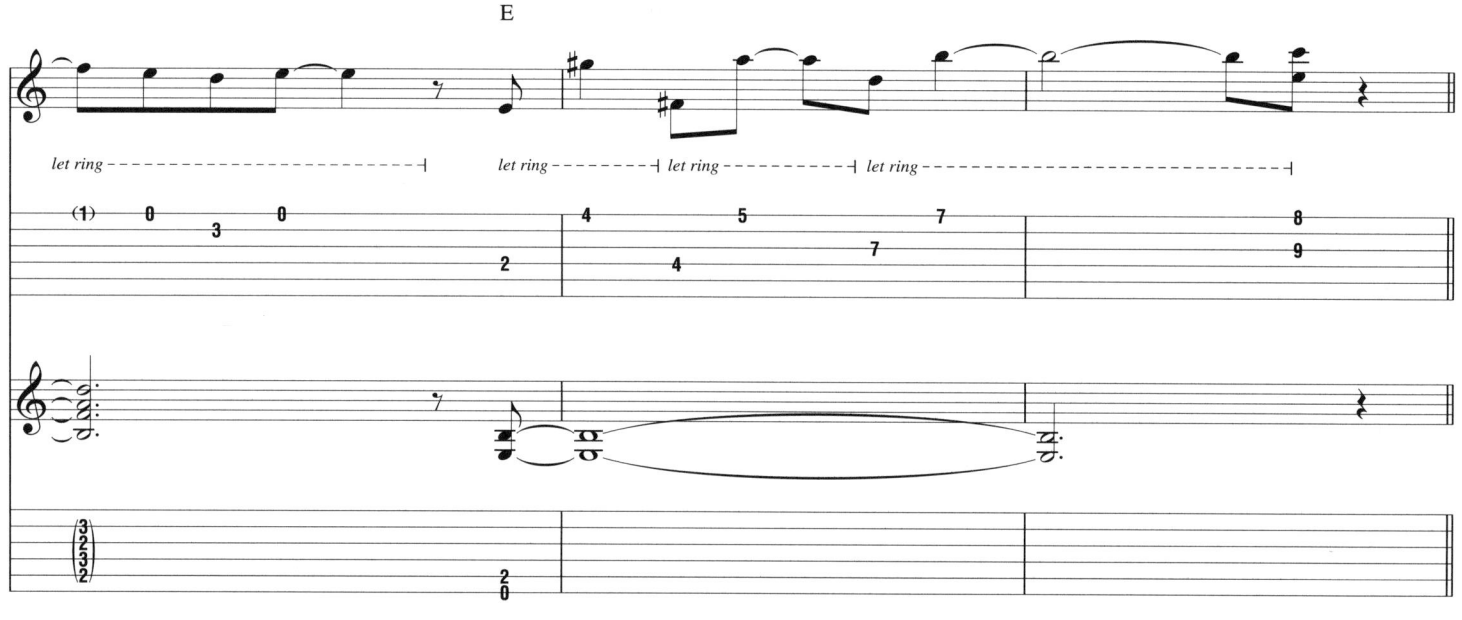
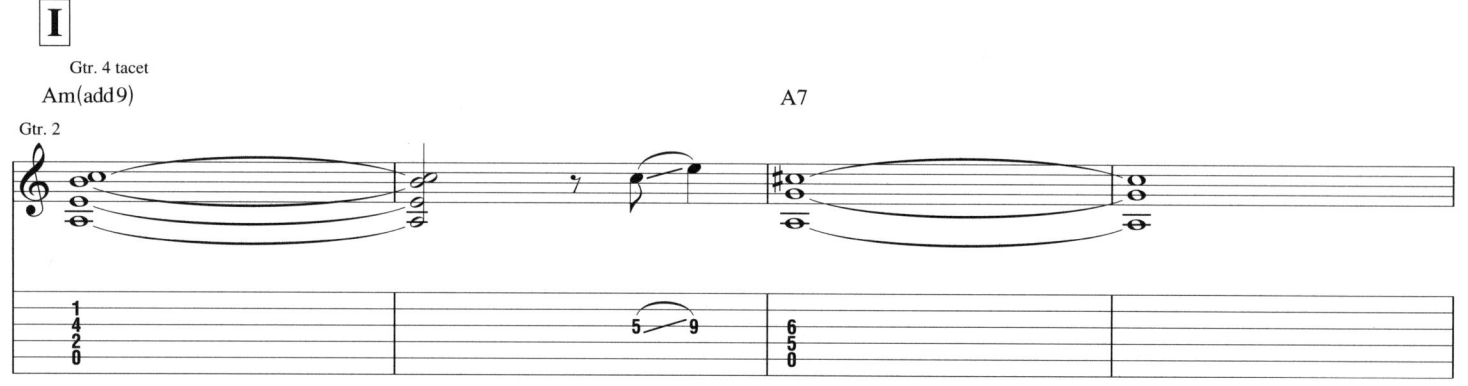

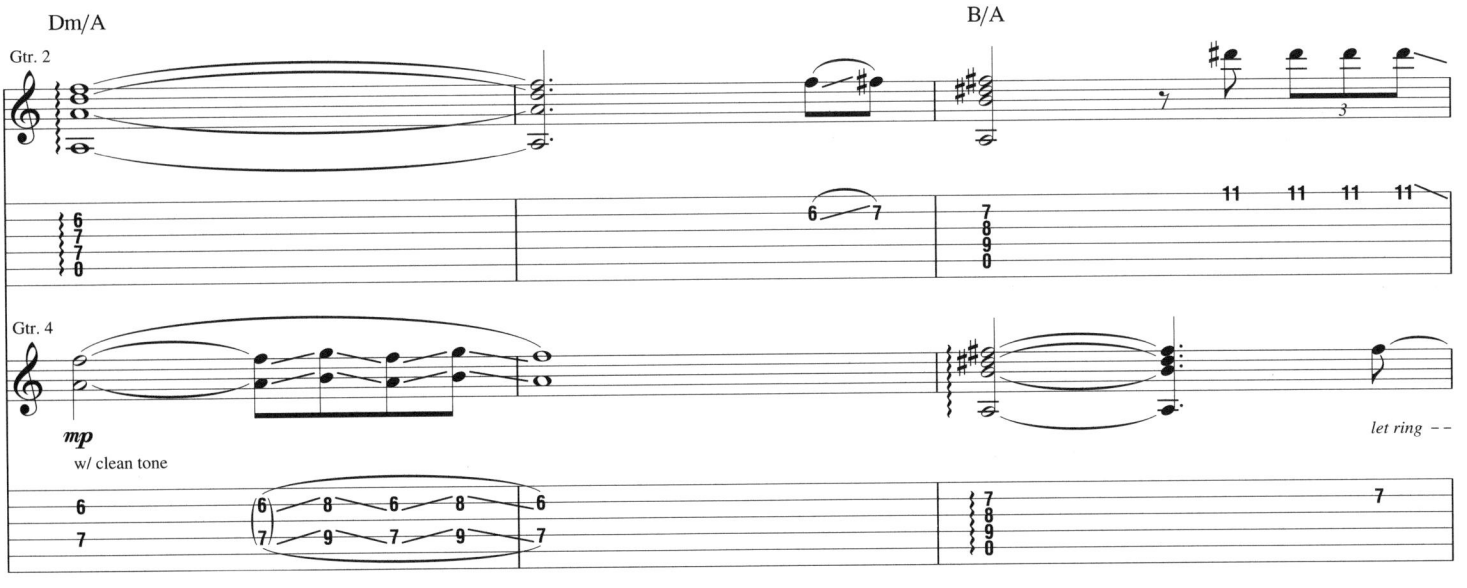
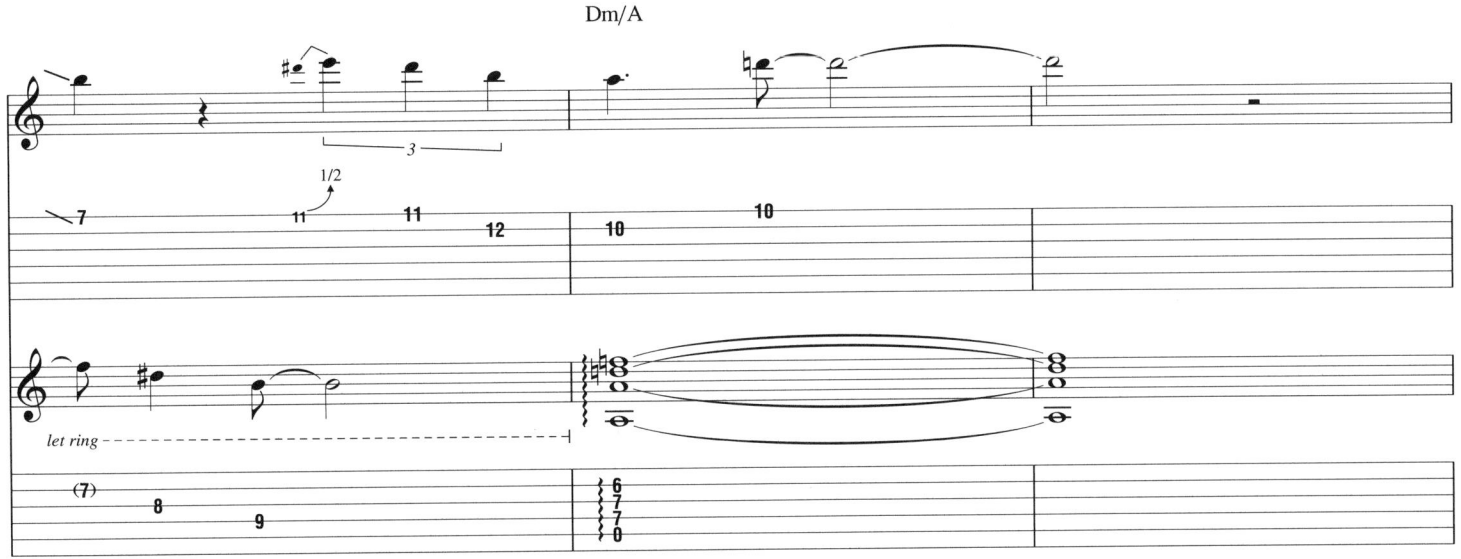
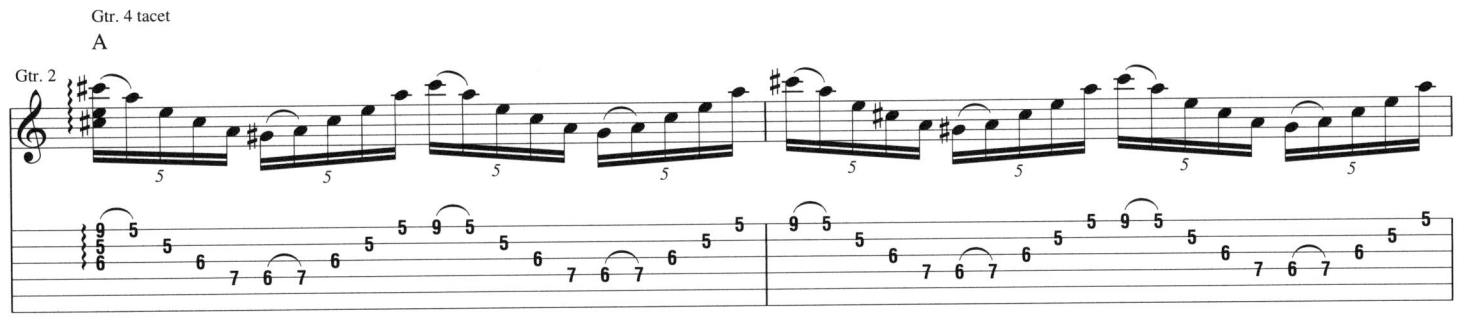
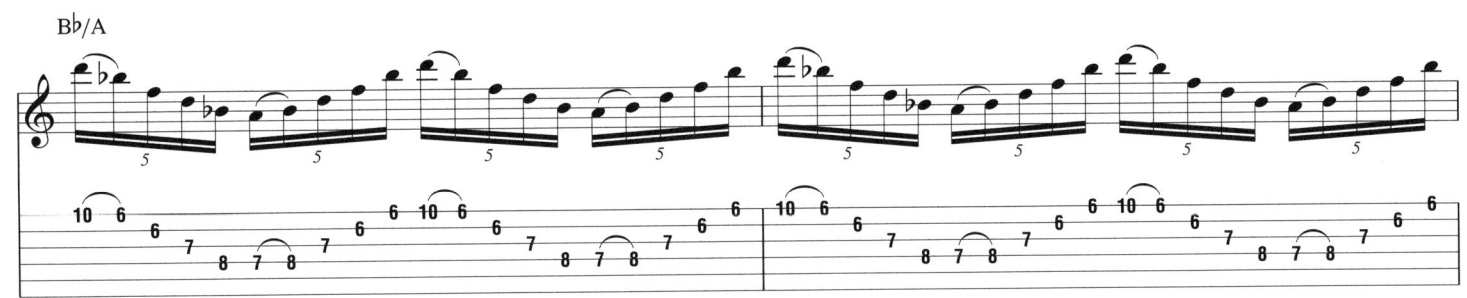

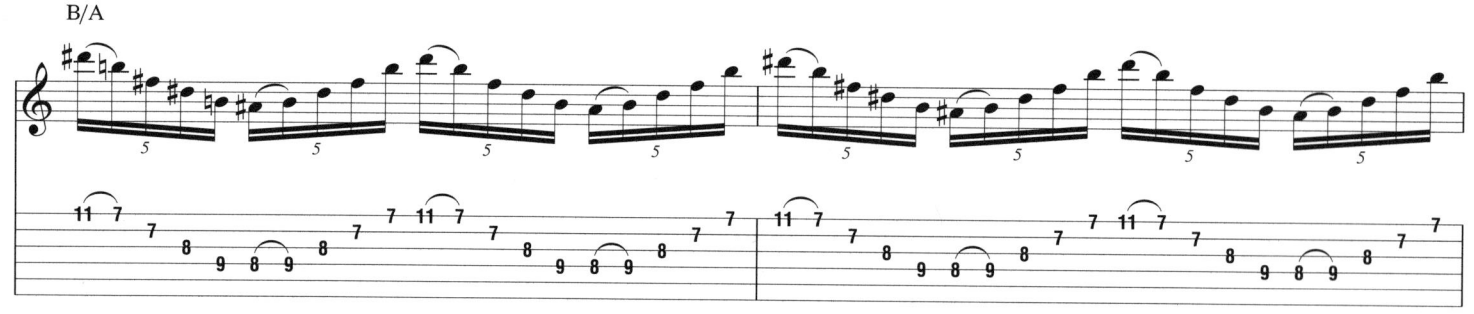

from *Dare to Be Different*
Countrywide
By Tommy Emmanuel

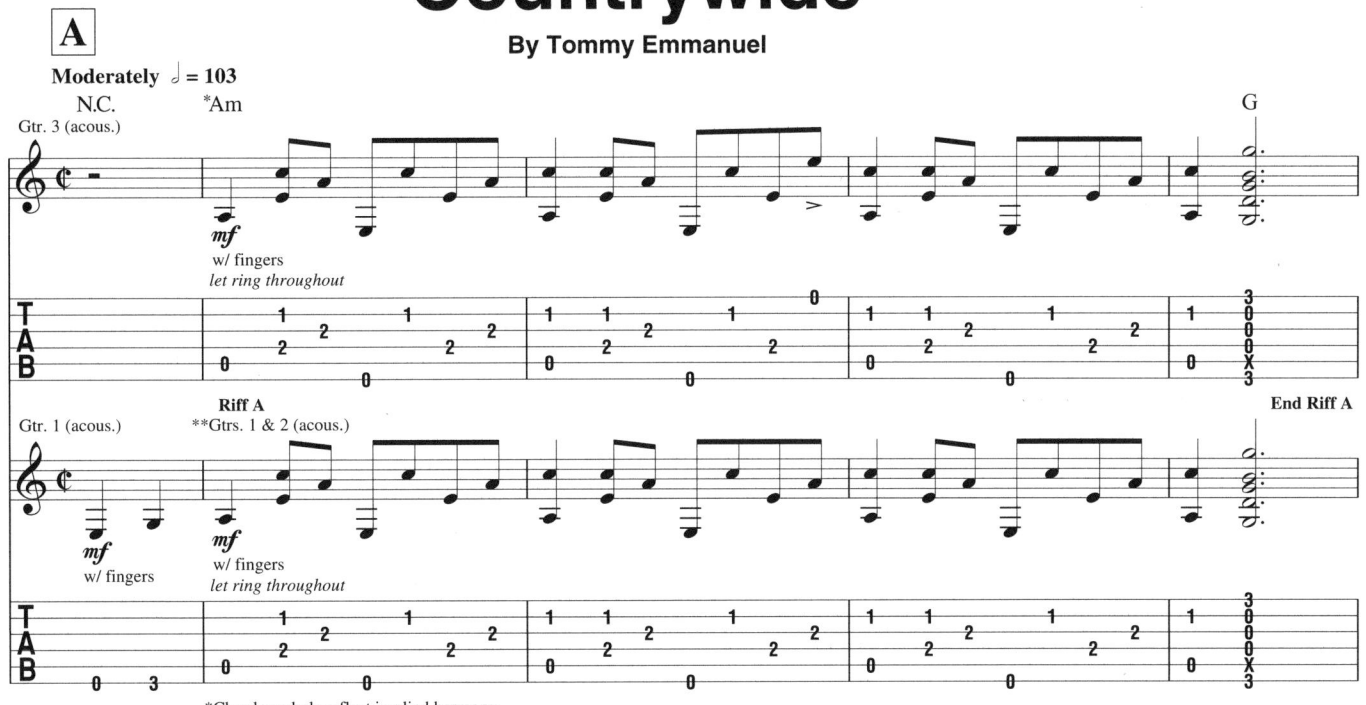

*Chord symbols reflect implied harmony.
**Gtr. 2: w/ fingers, played *mf*. Composite arrangement

Copyright © 1998 UNIVERSAL MUSIC PUBLISHING PTY. LTD.
All Rights in the United States and Canada Controlled and Administered by UNIVERSAL - POLYGRAM INTERNATIONAL PUBLISHING, INC.
All Rights Reserved Used by Permission

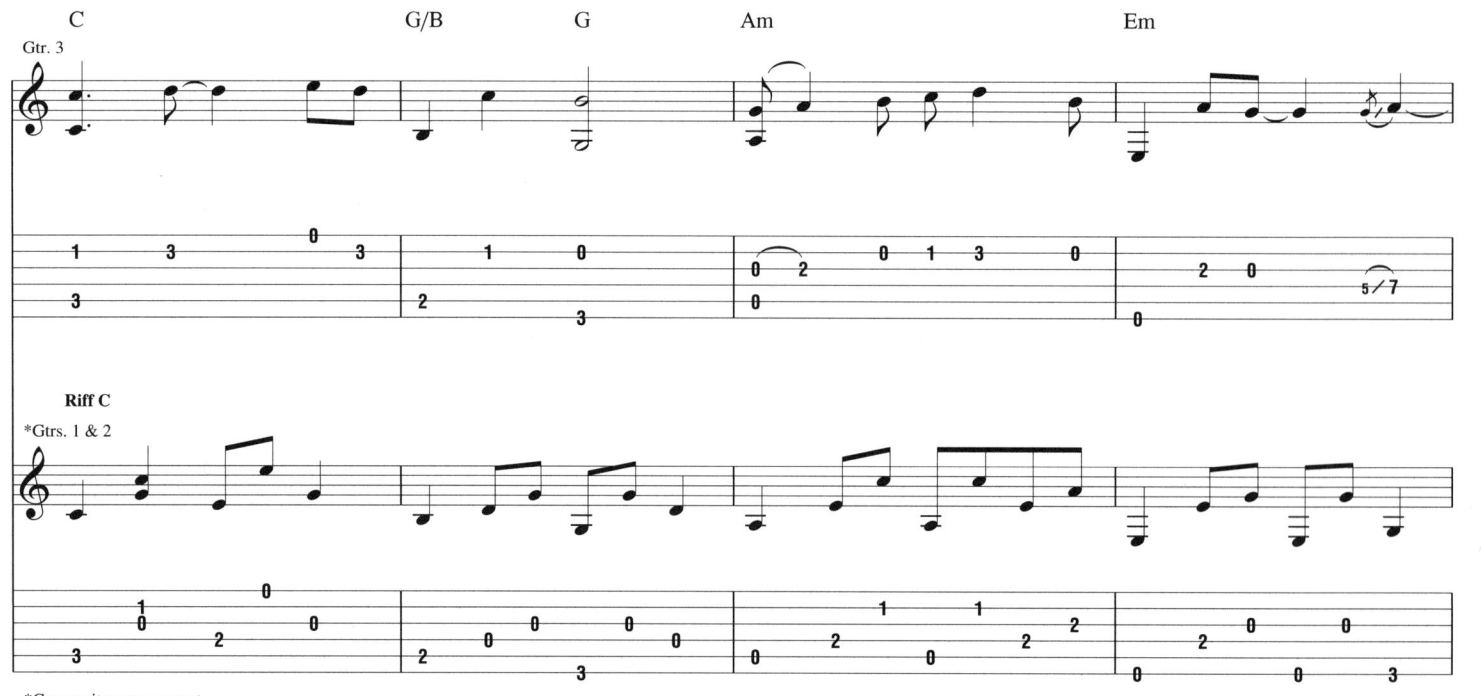

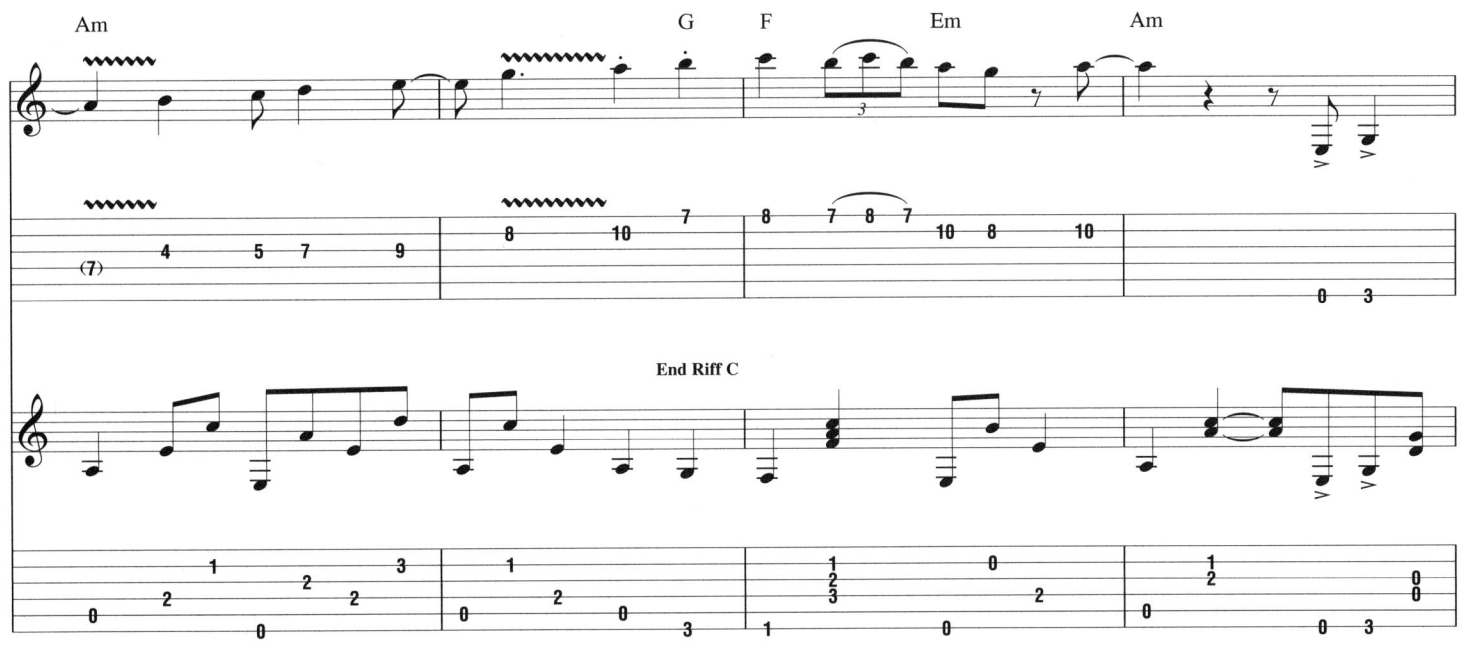
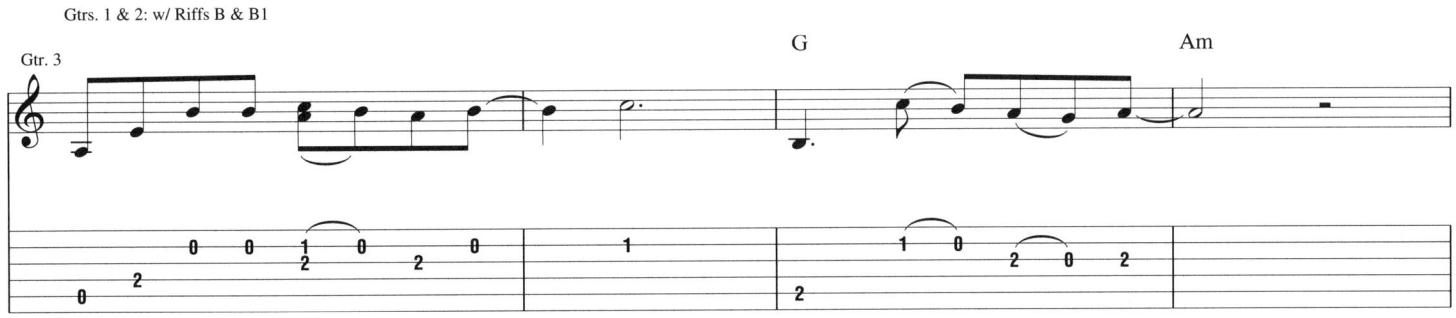

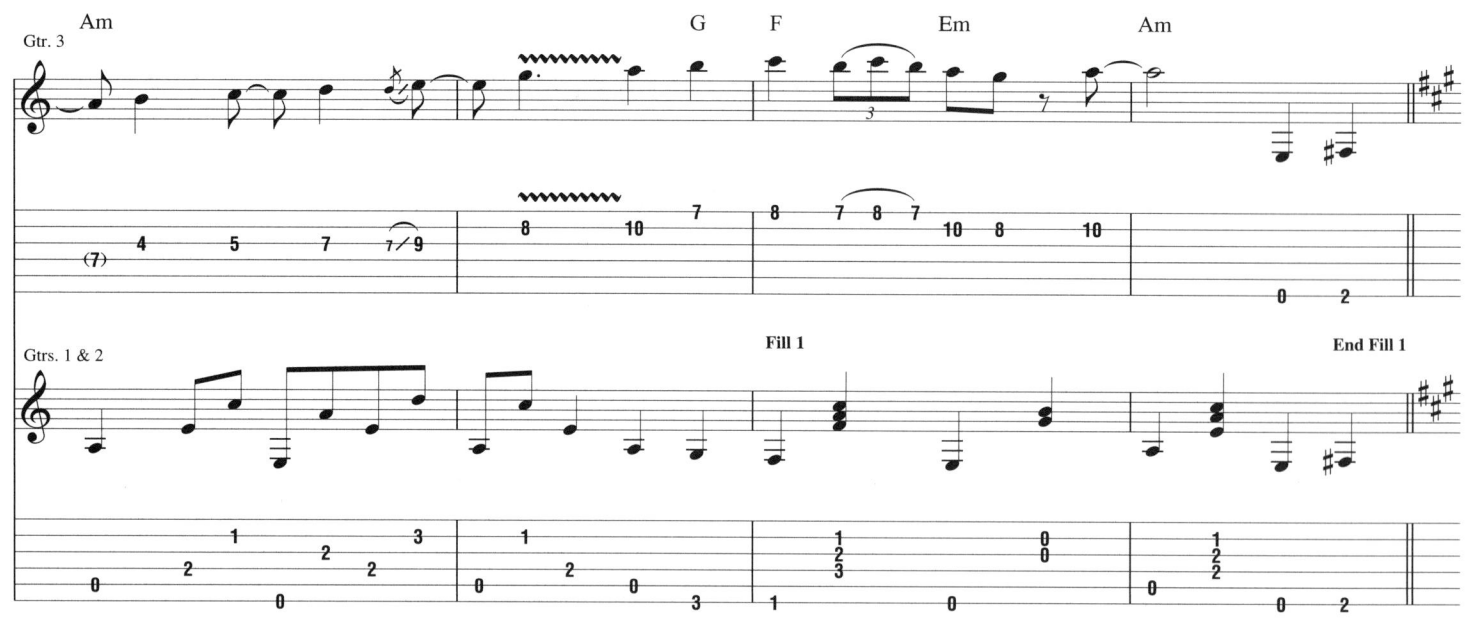

Gtrs. 1 & 2: w/ Riff D
A6
Badd11/A
Gtr. 3
F6
Bm7♭5
E7
Gtr. 3
Rhy. Fig. 1
End Rhy. Fig. 1
Gtrs. 1 & 2
D
Gtrs. 1 & 2: w/ Riffs B & B1
Bm7♭5
E7
Am
Gtr. 3
Gtr. 1
Gtr. 2
1/4

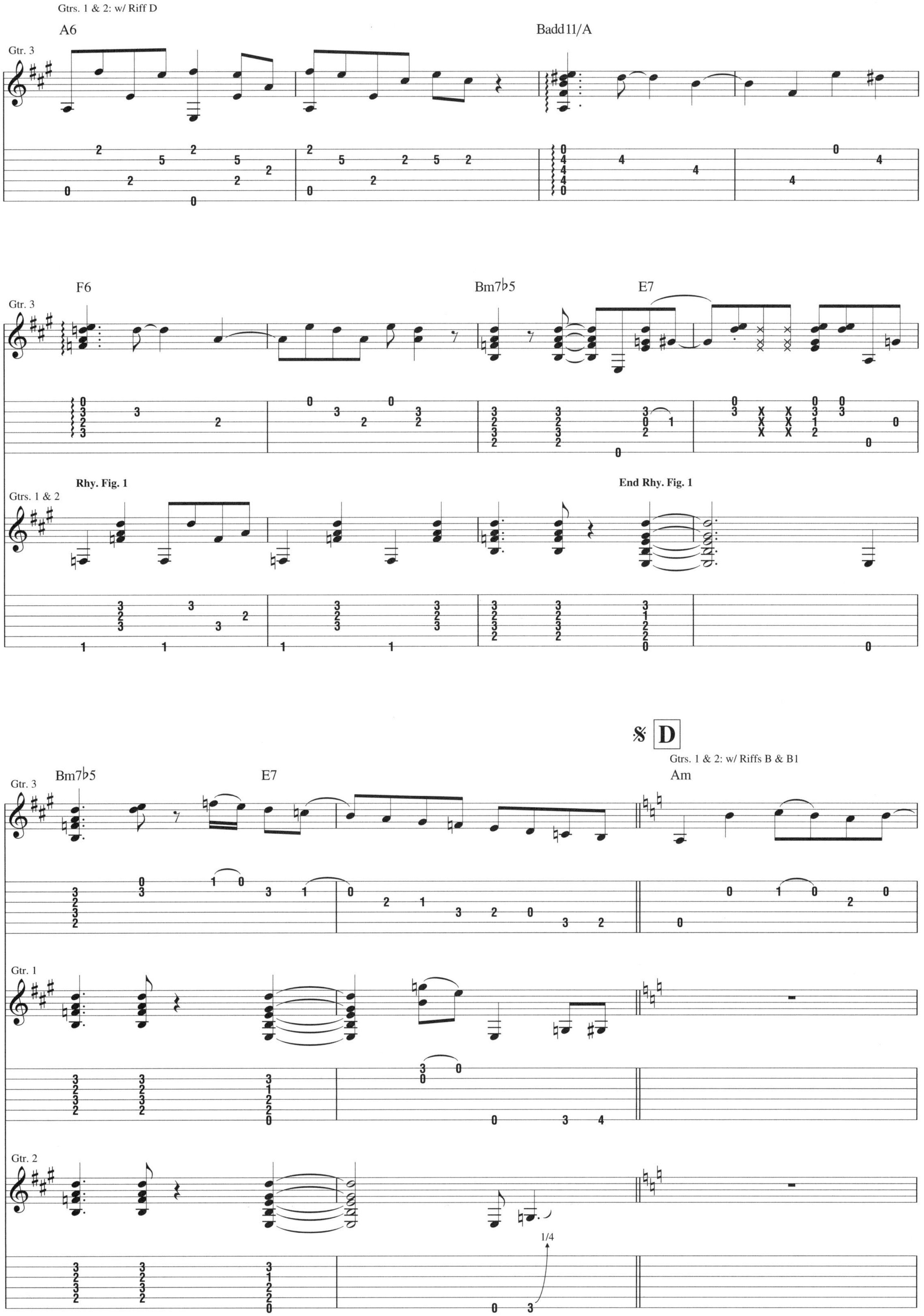

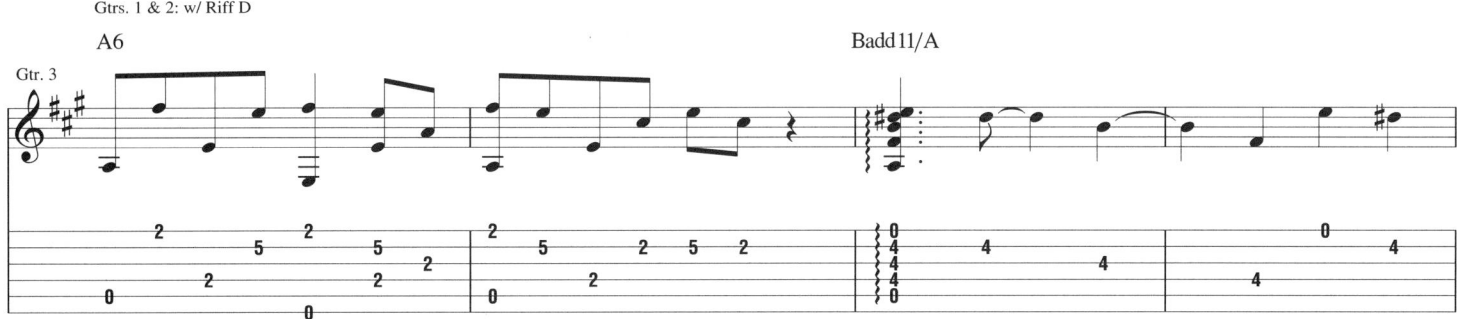

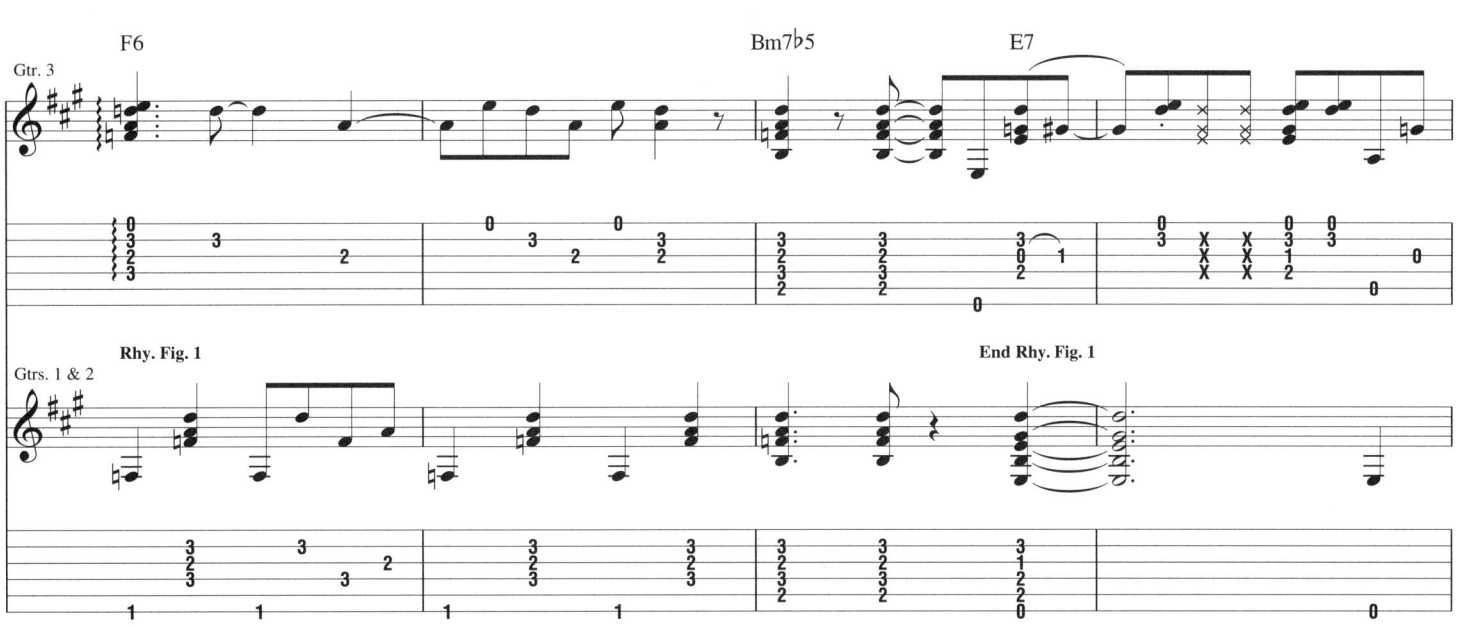

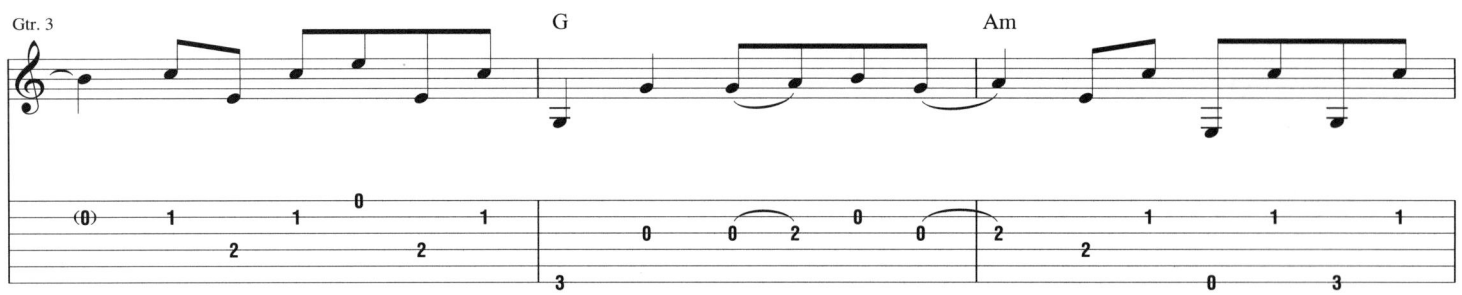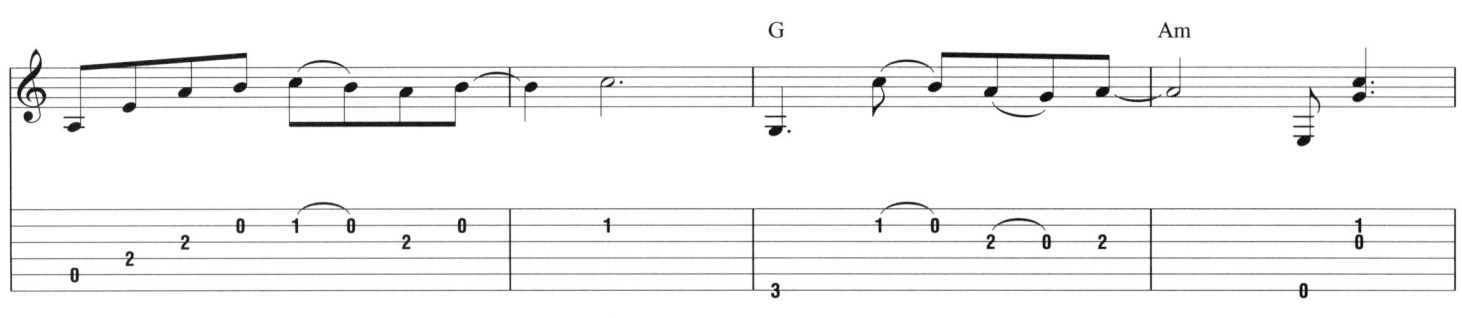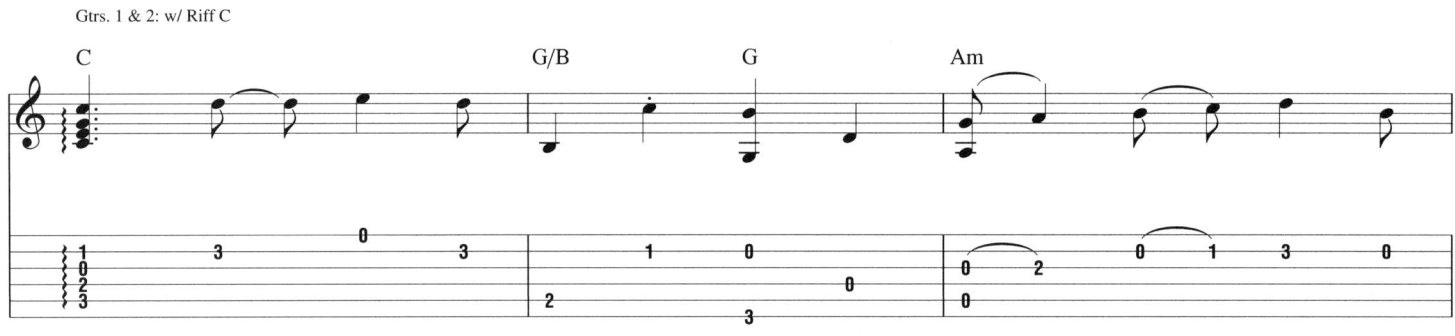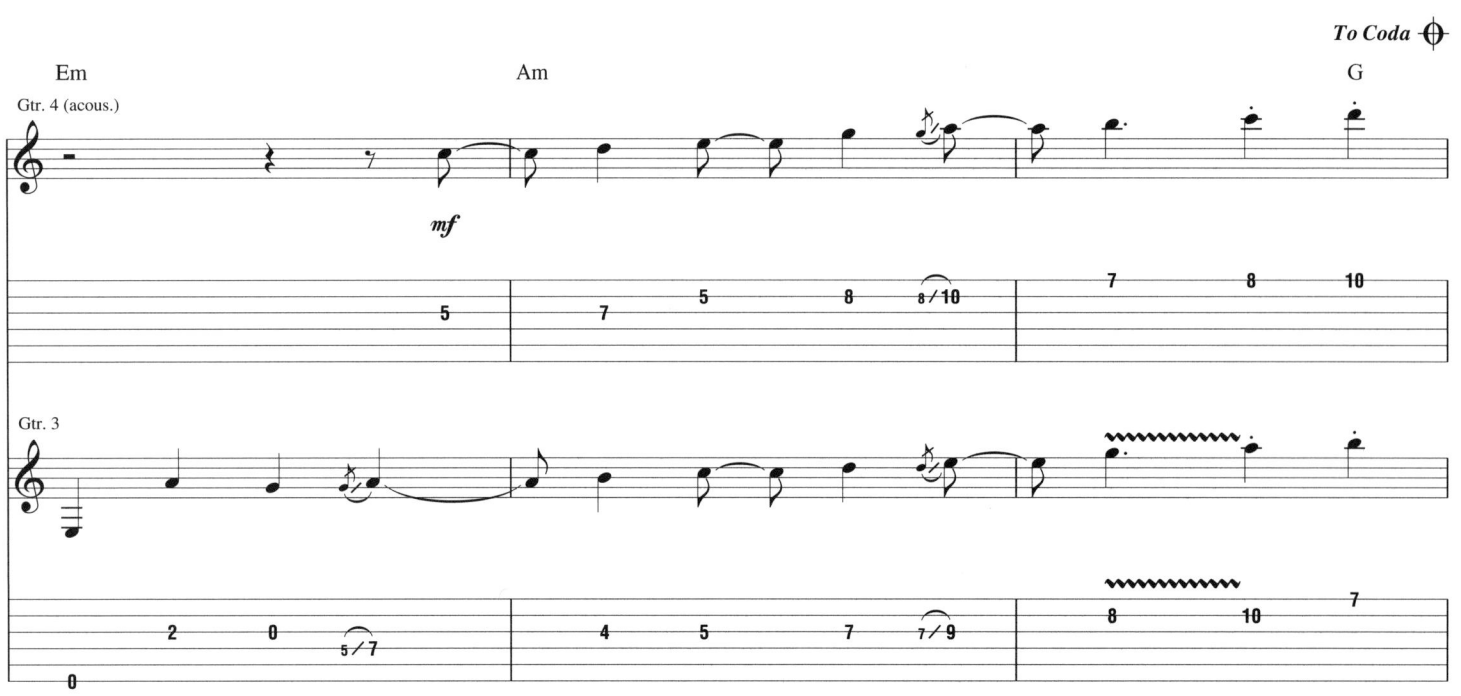

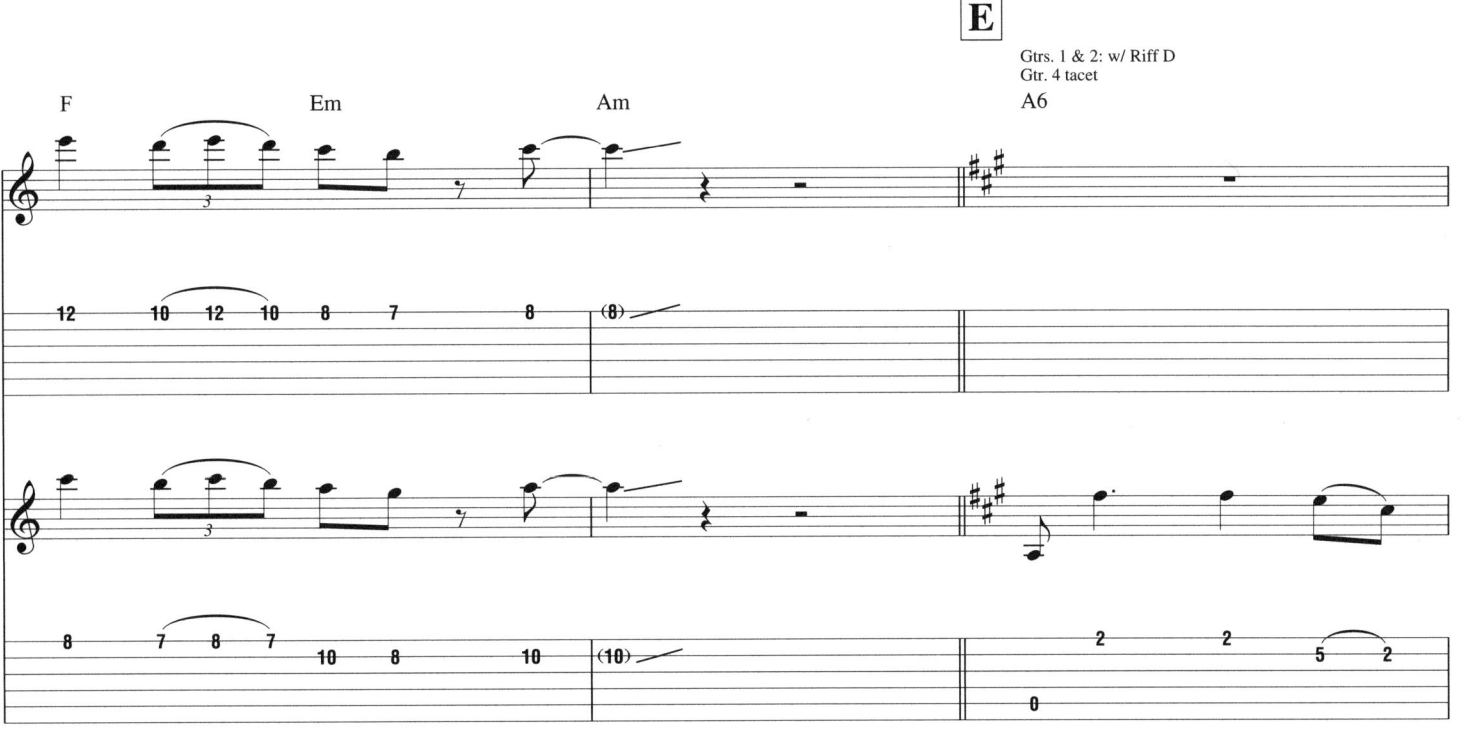

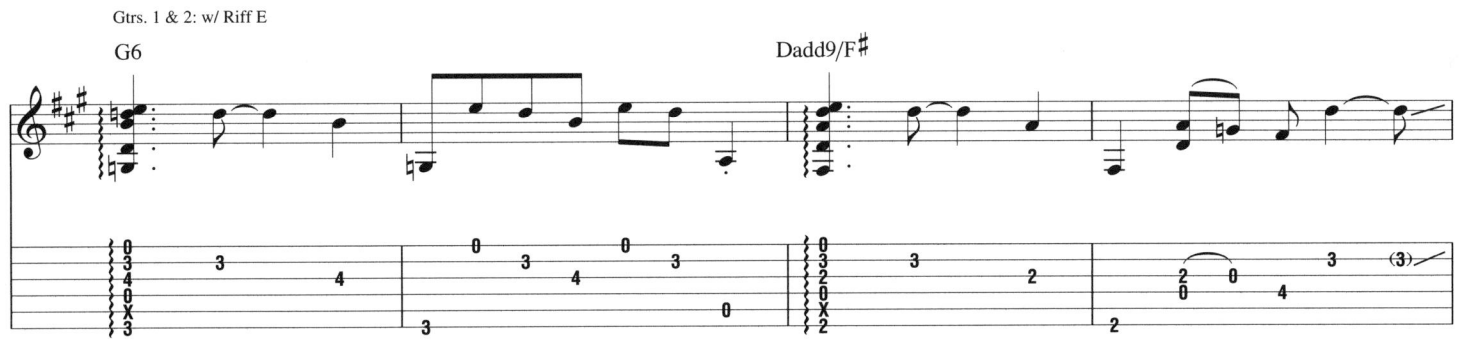
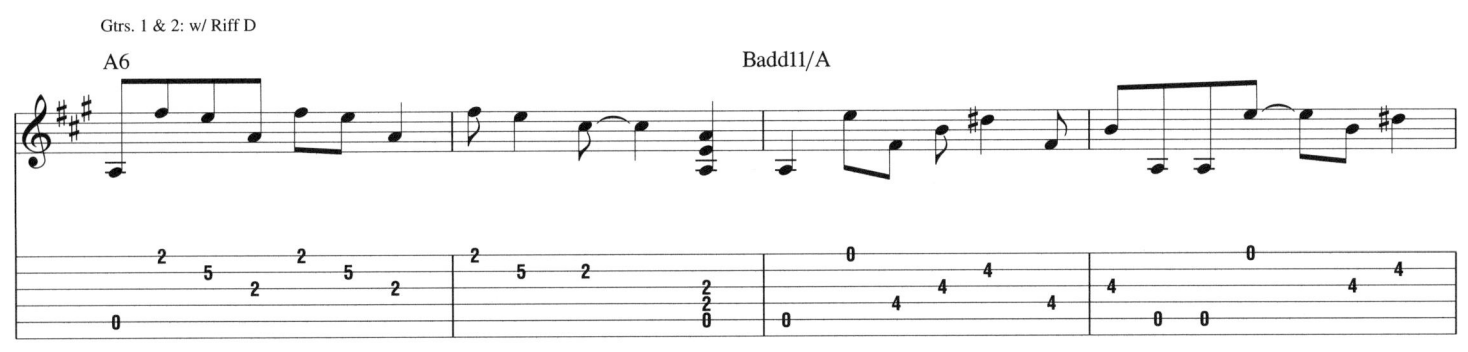

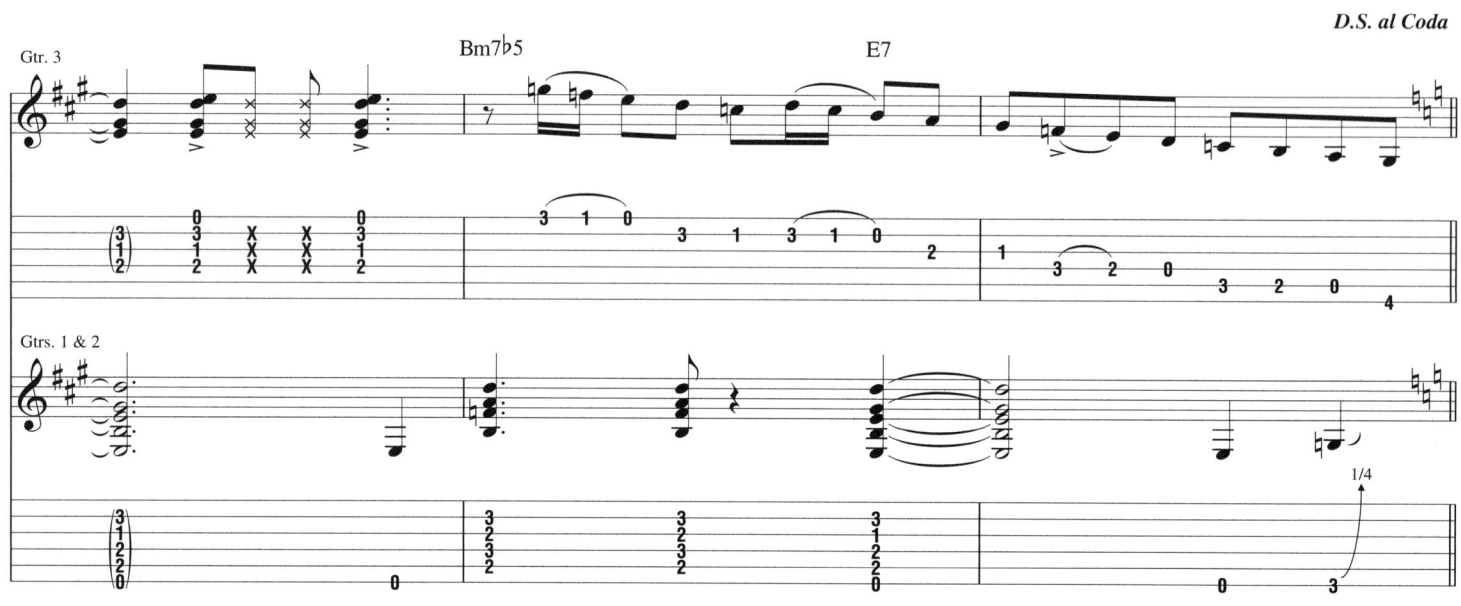

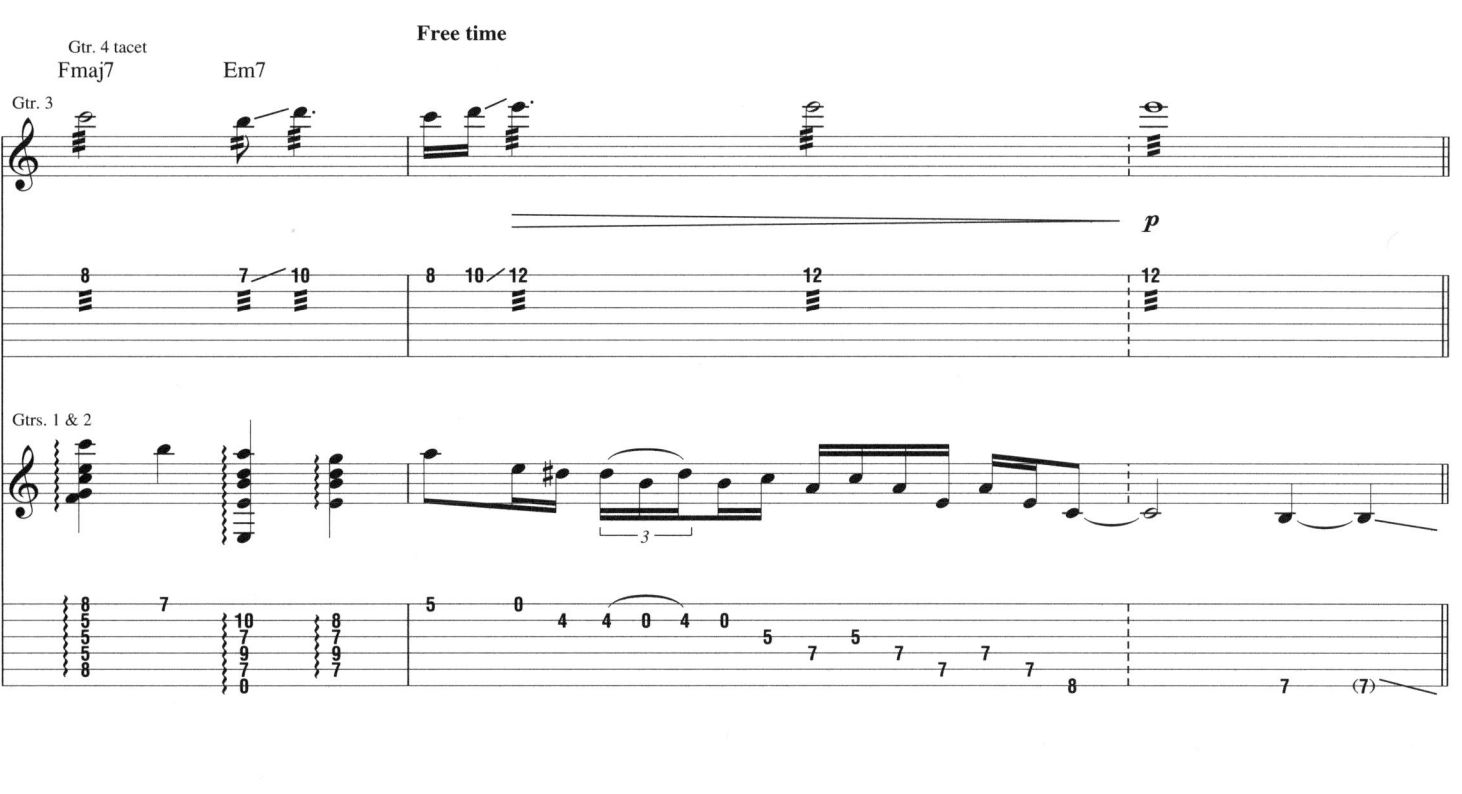
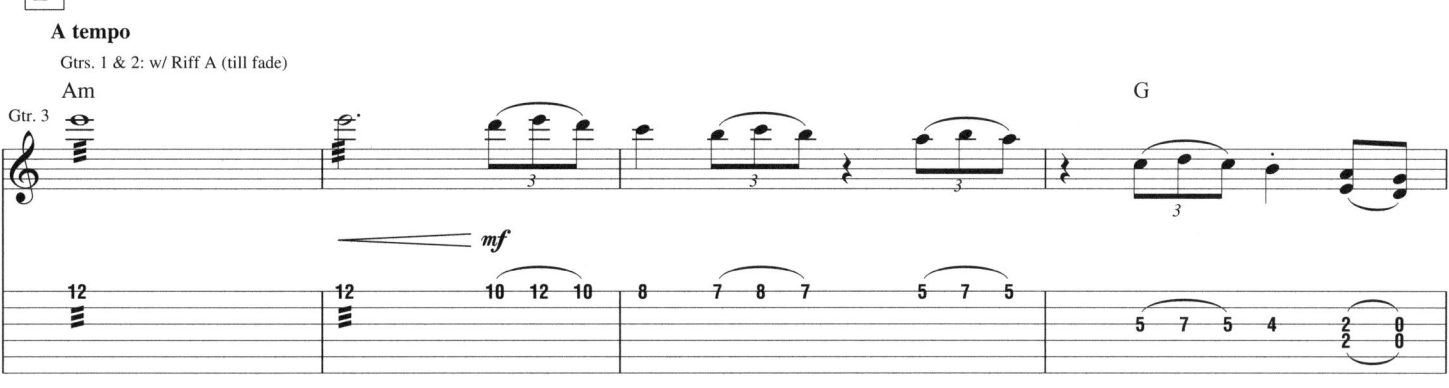
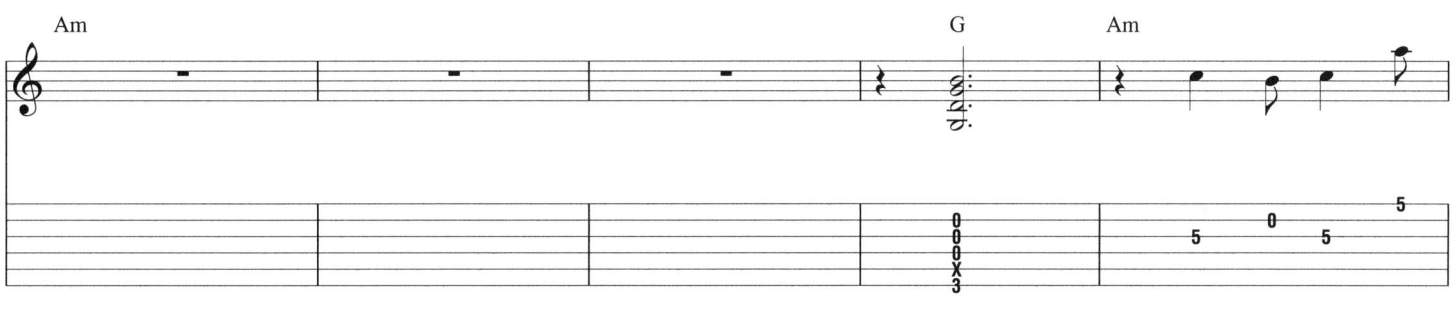
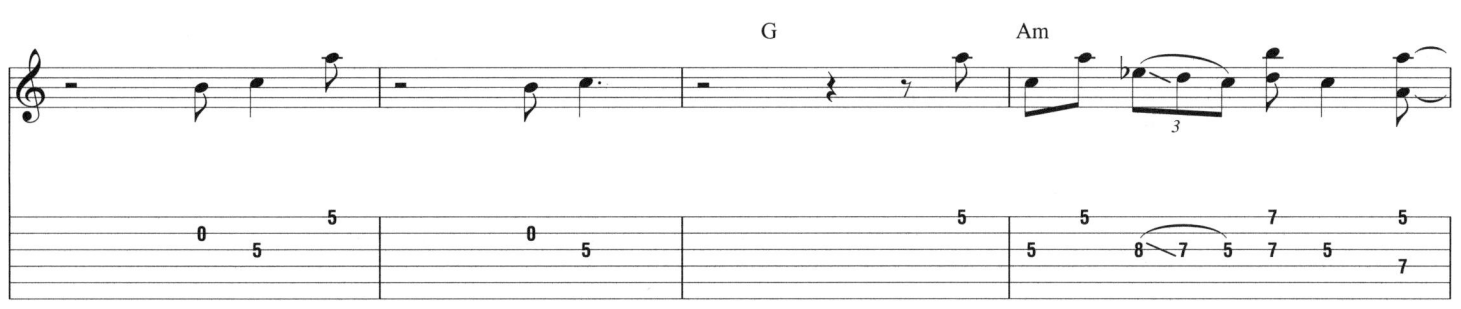

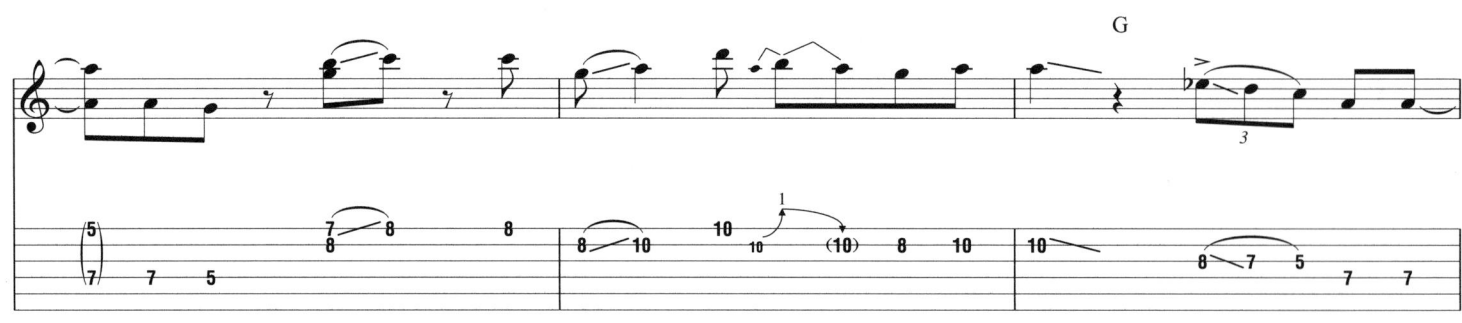
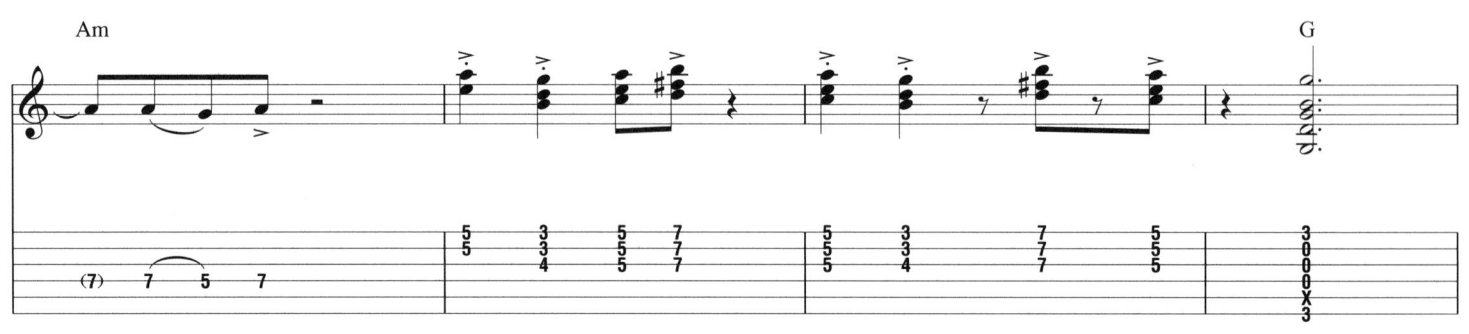
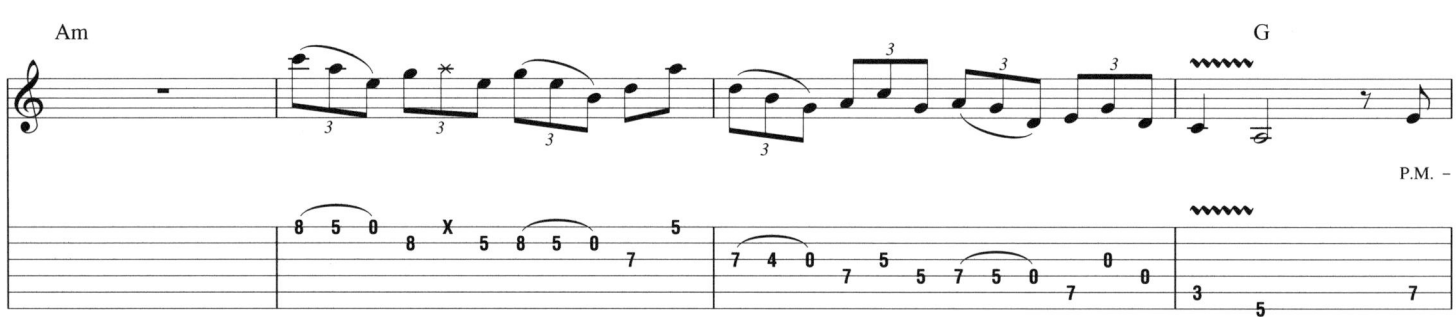

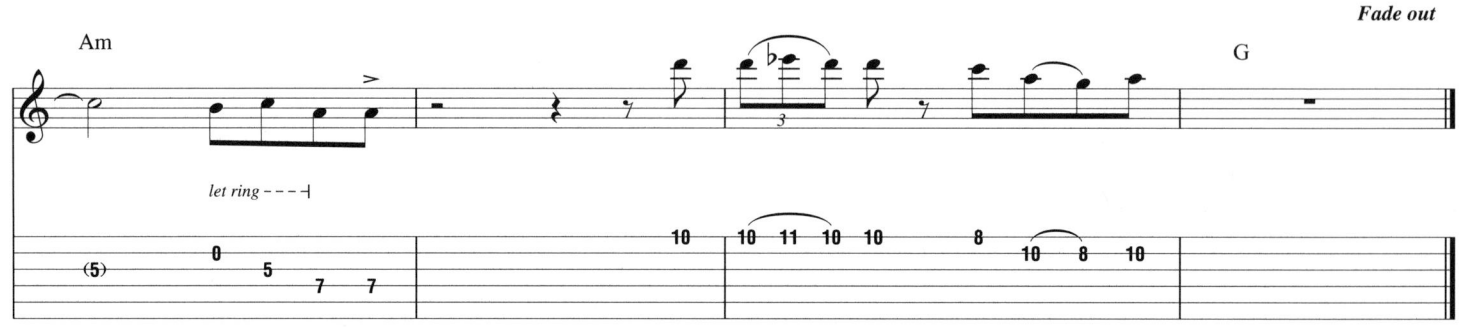

from *Determination*
Determination
By Tommy Emmanuel

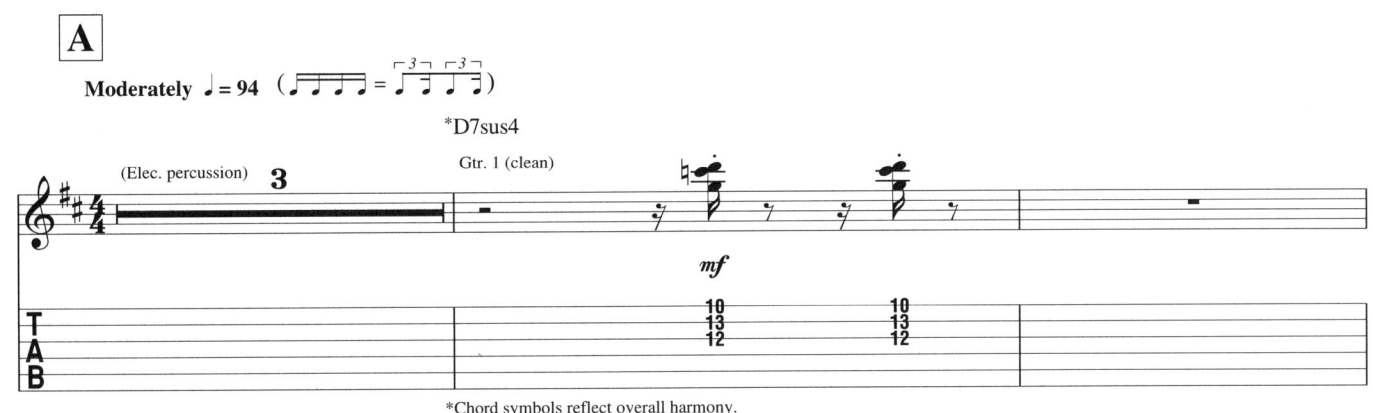

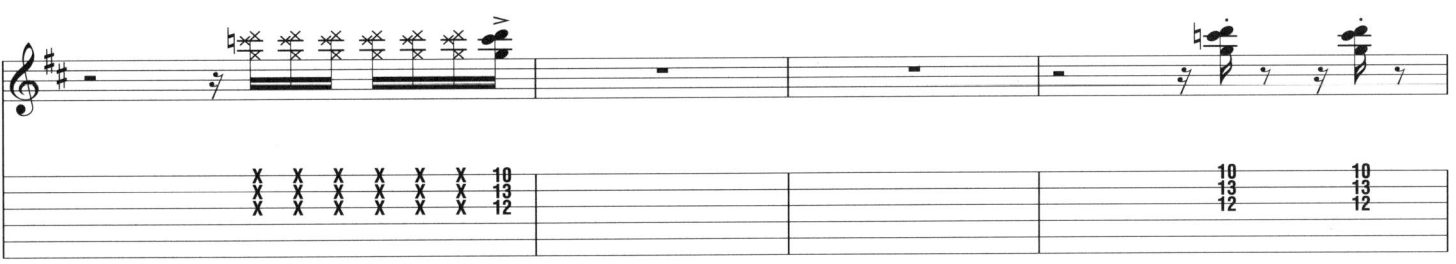

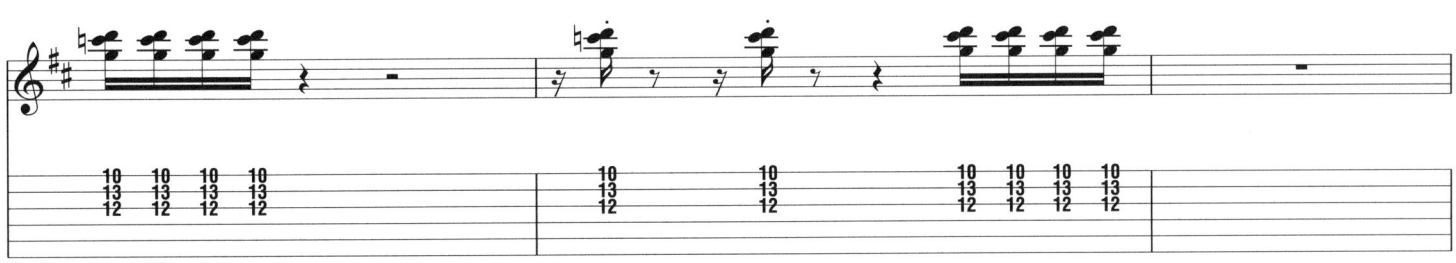

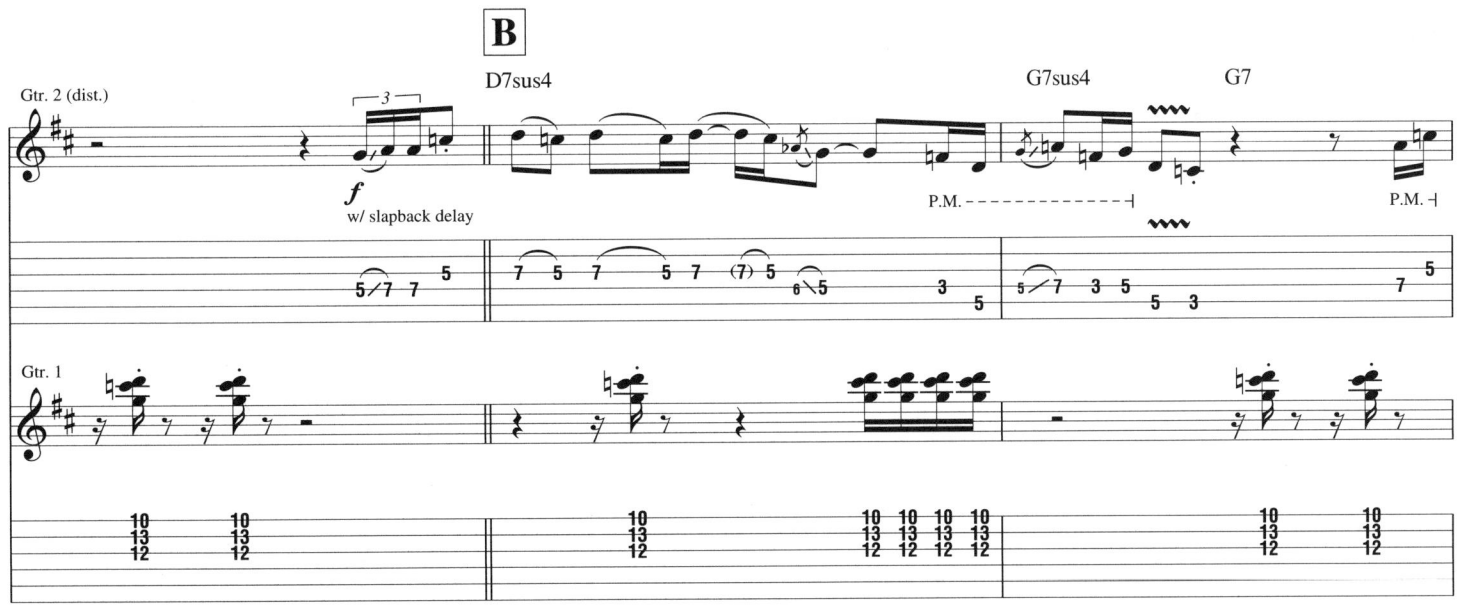

Copyright © 2000 UNIVERSAL MUSIC PUBLISHING PTY. LTD.
All Rights in the United States and Canada Controlled and Administered by UNIVERSAL - POLYGRAM INTERNATIONAL PUBLISHING, INC.
All Rights Reserved Used by Permission

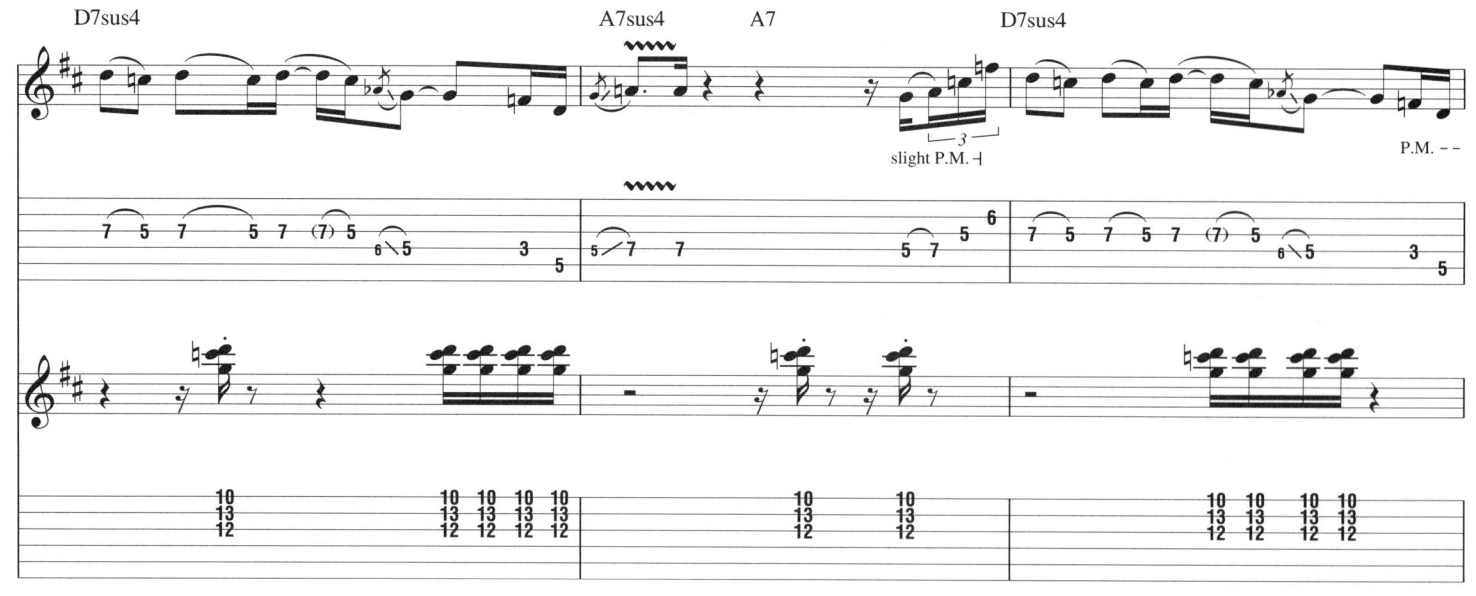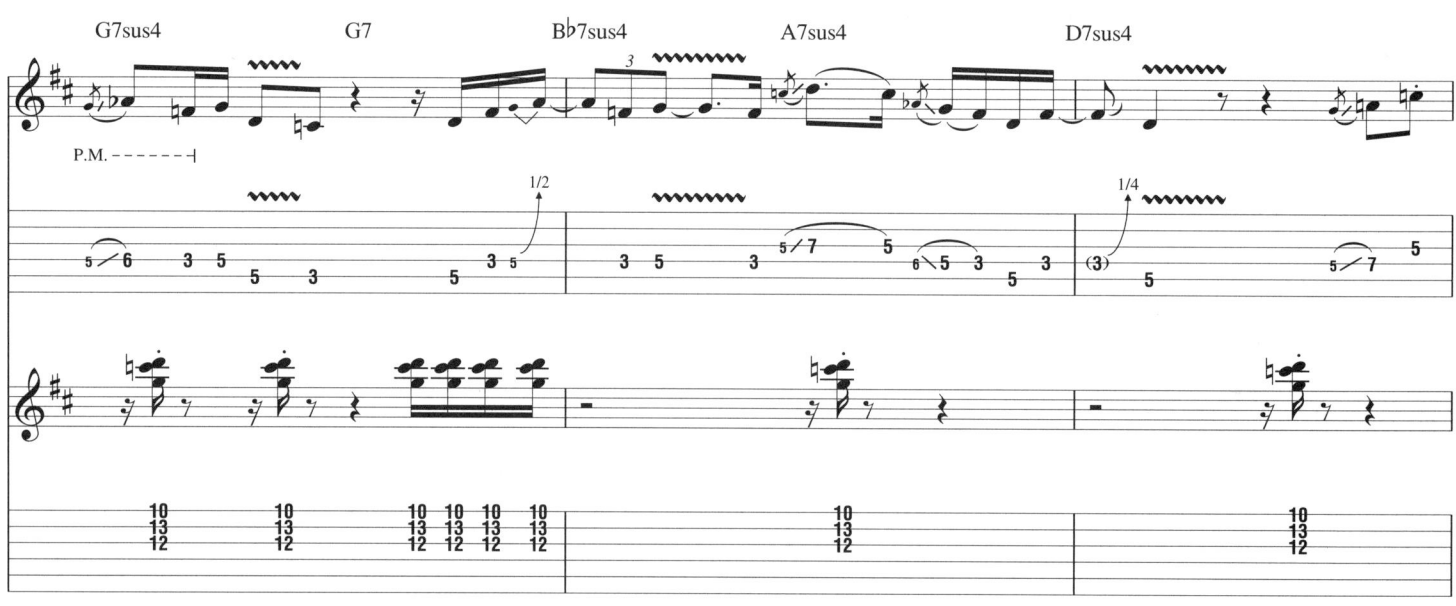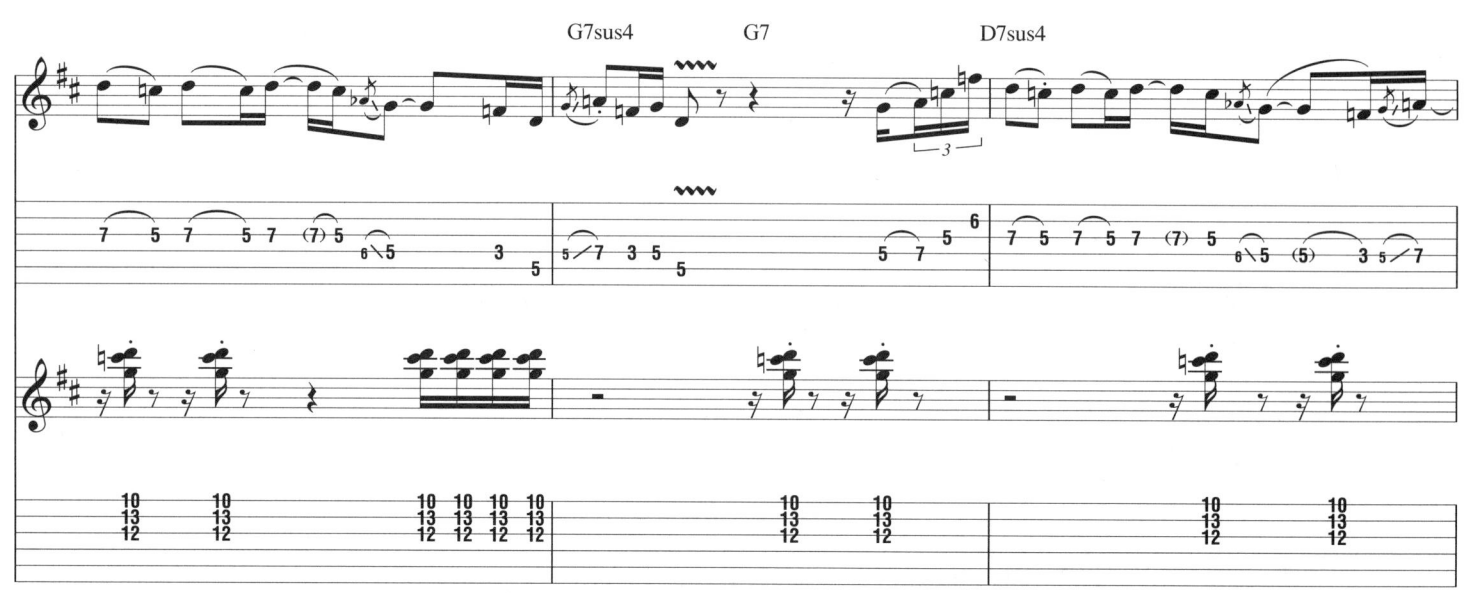

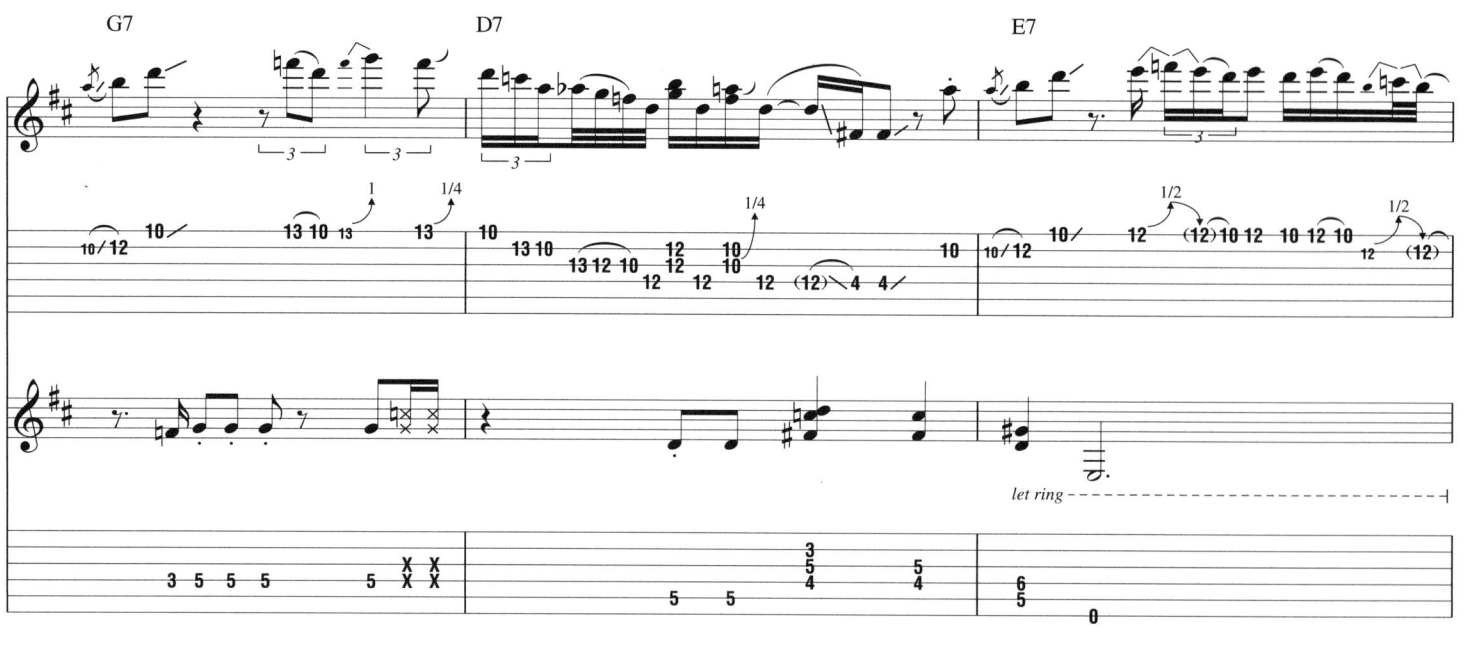
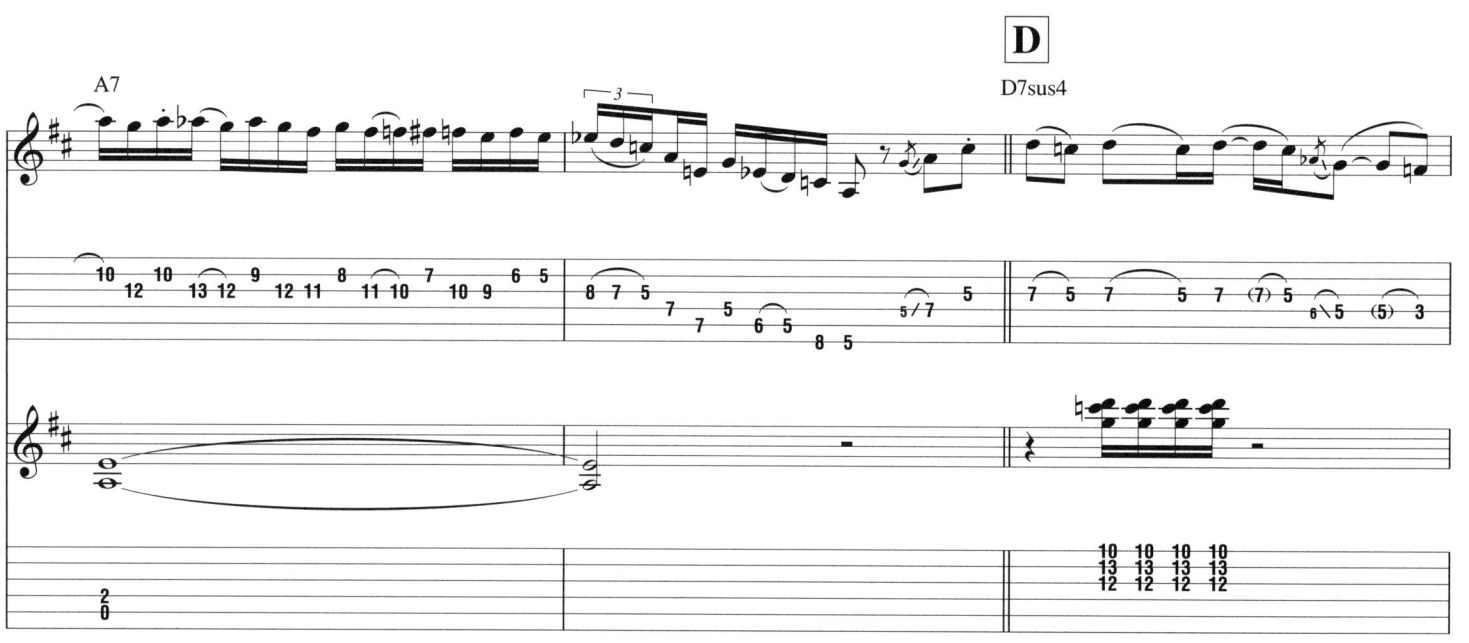
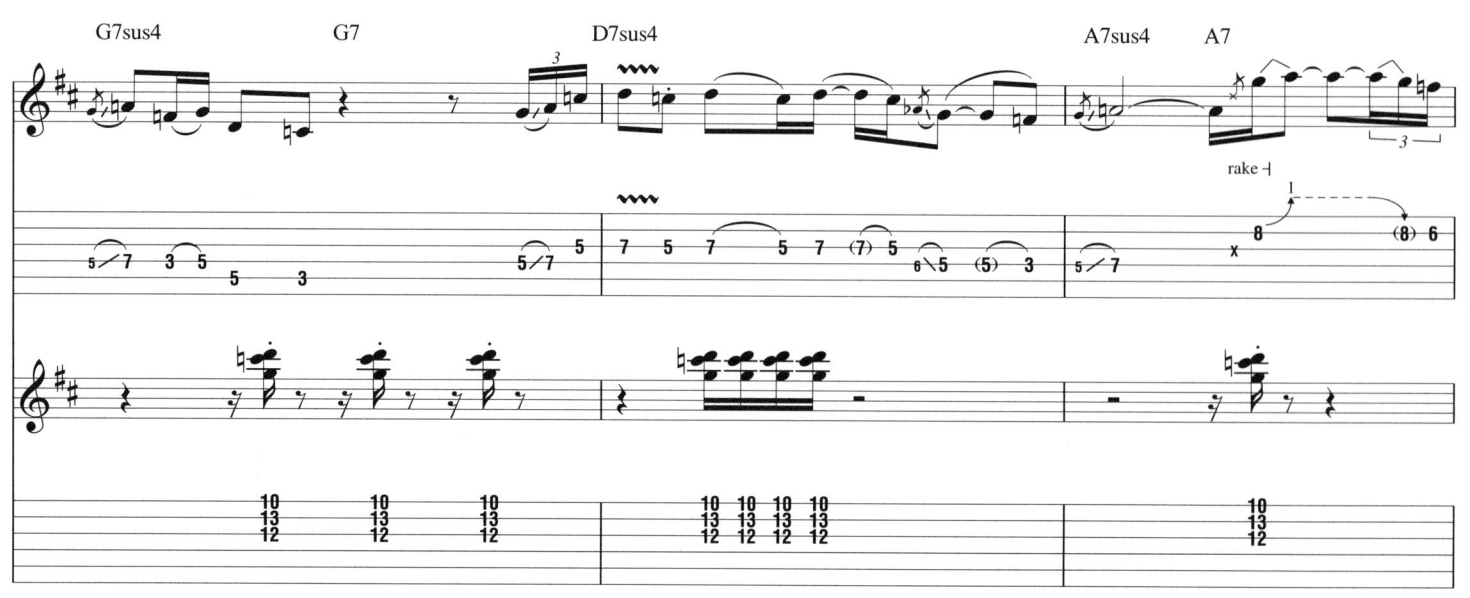

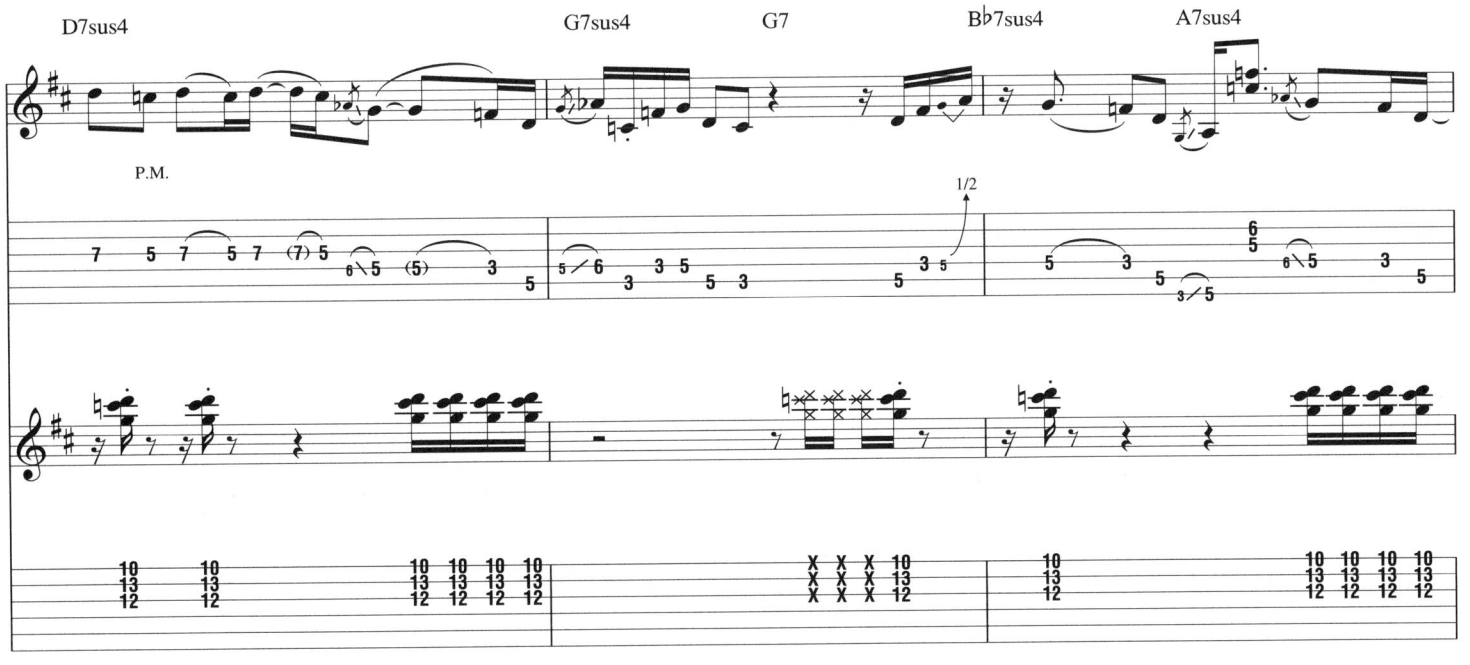

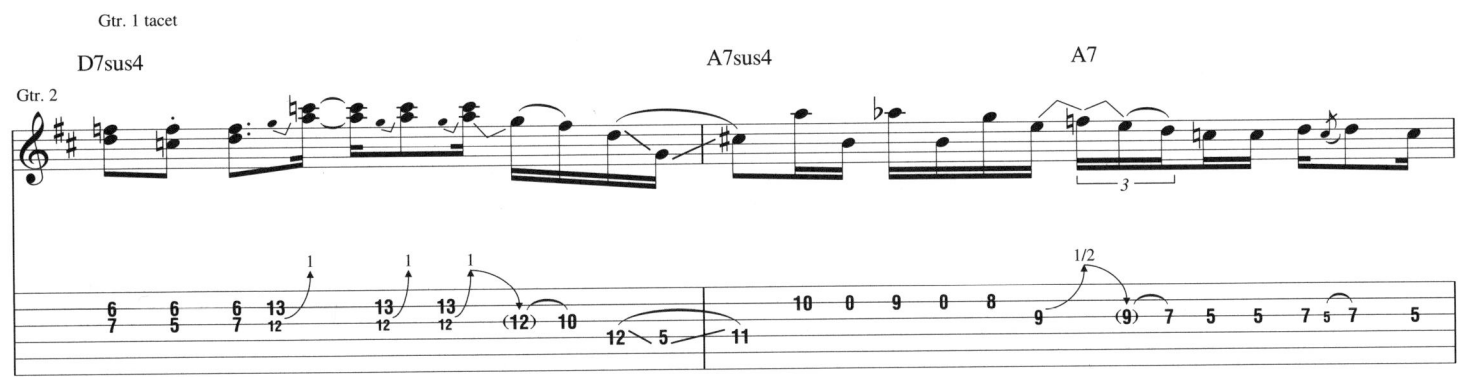

59

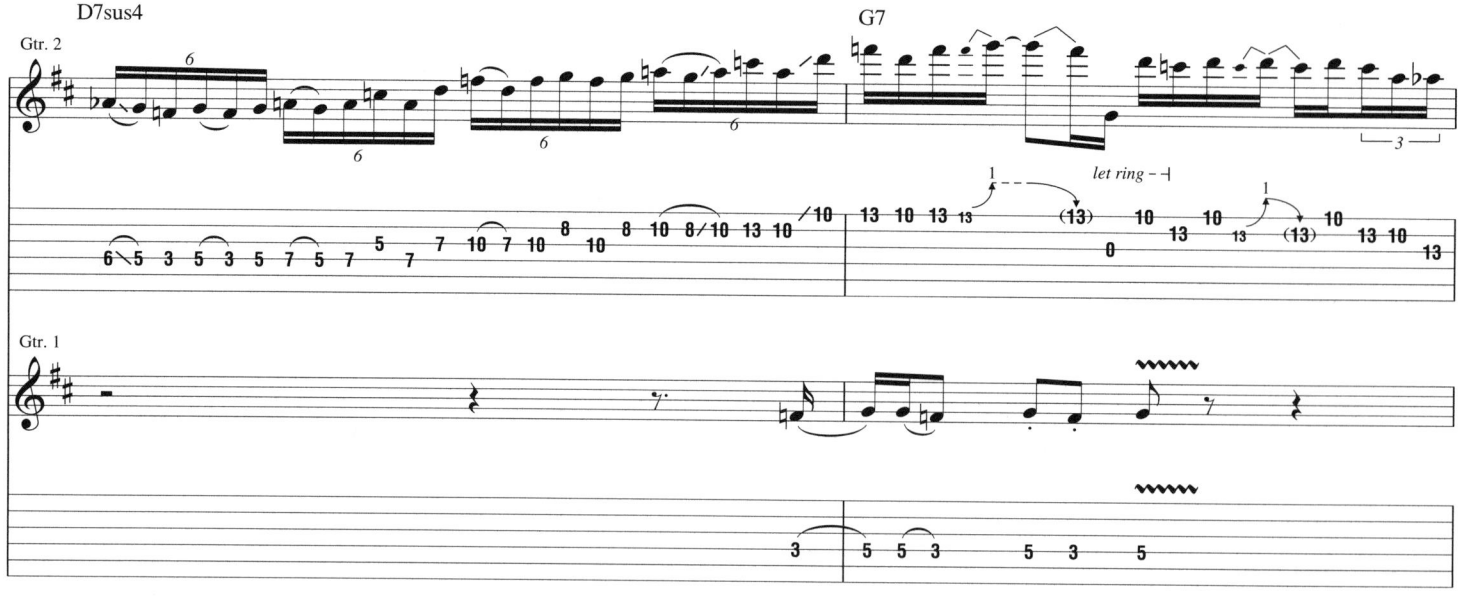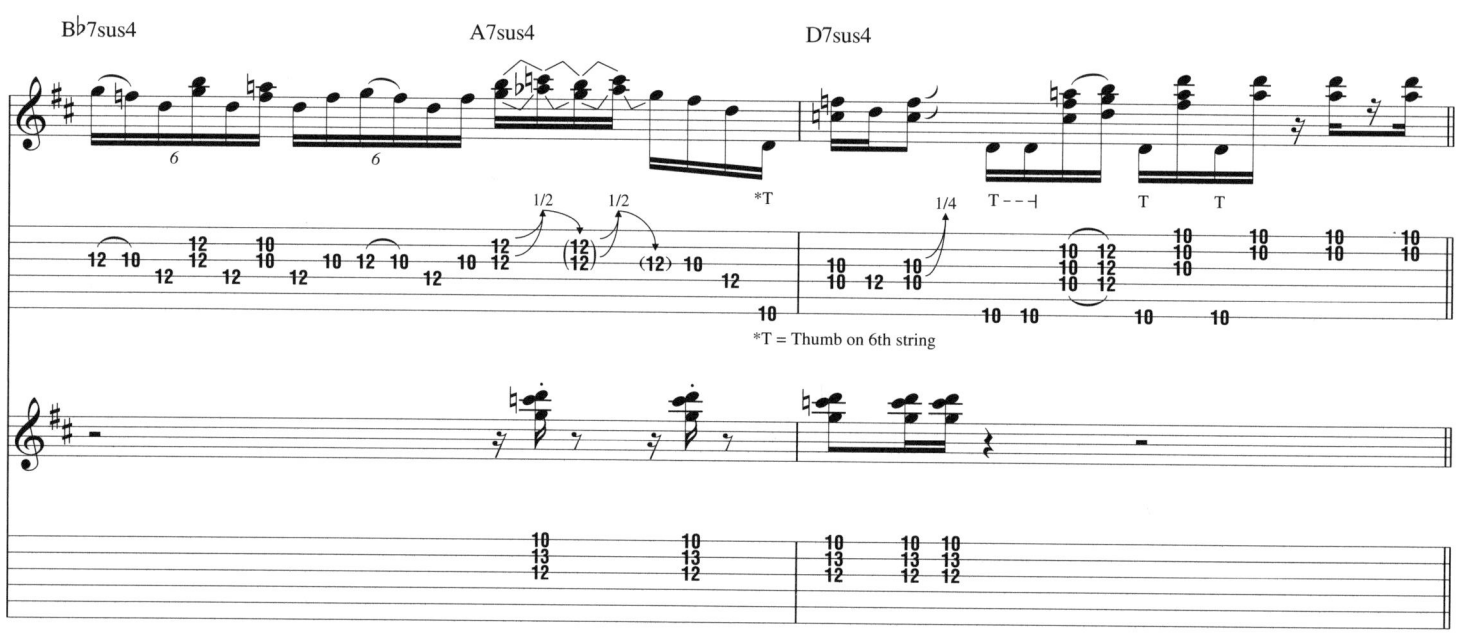

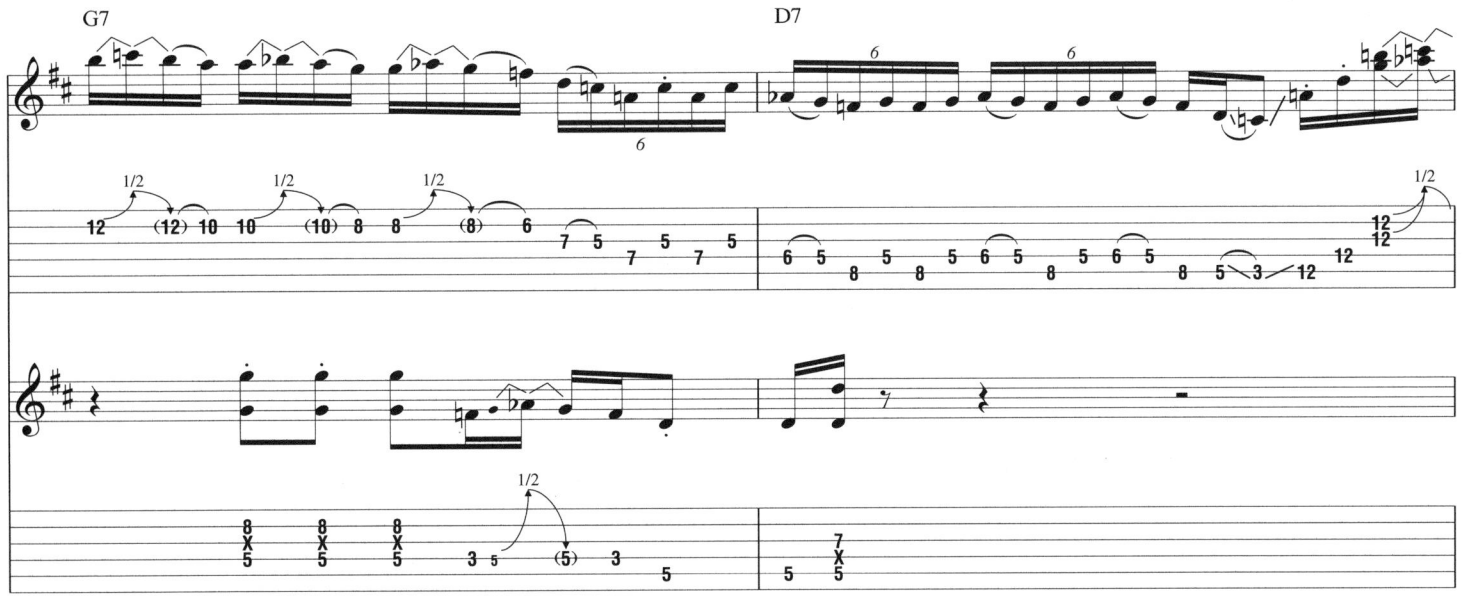

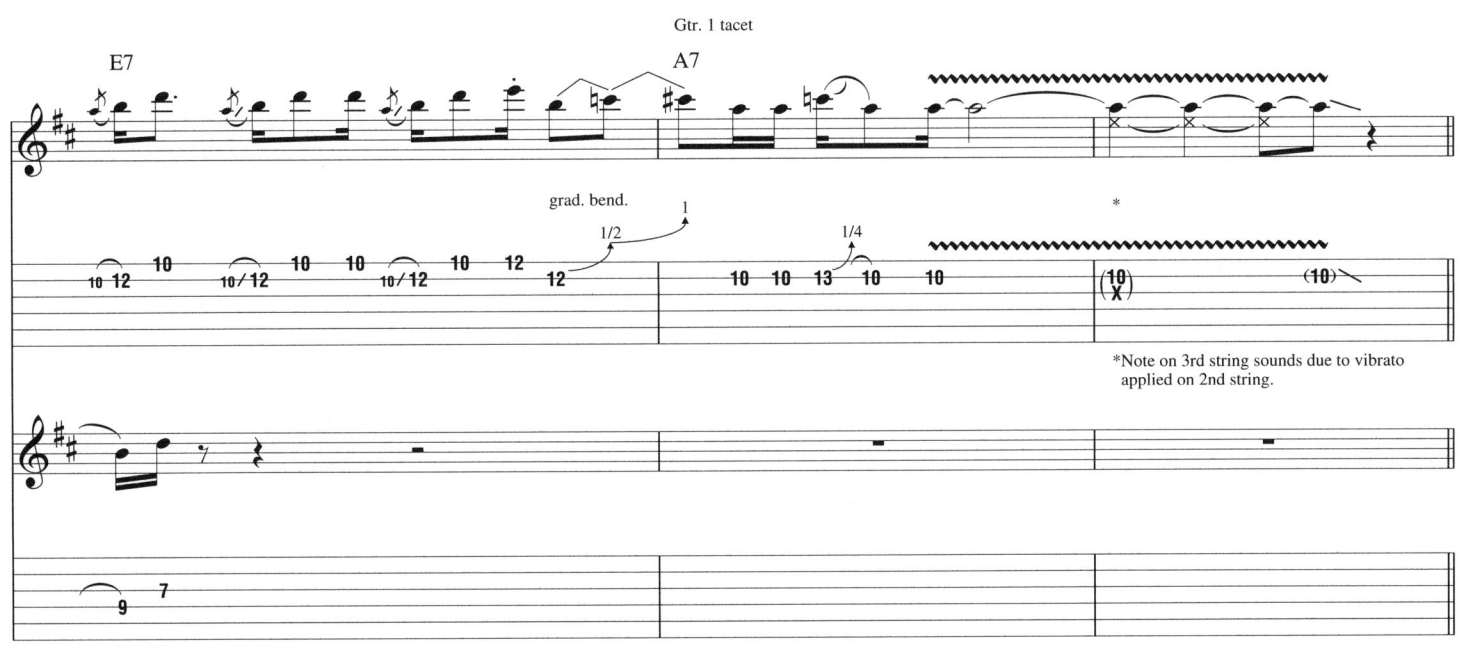

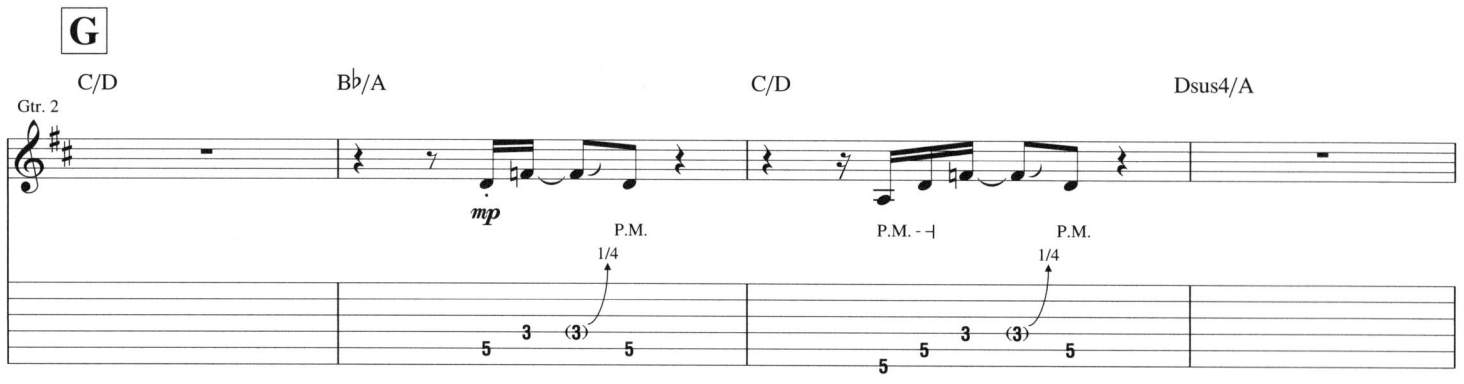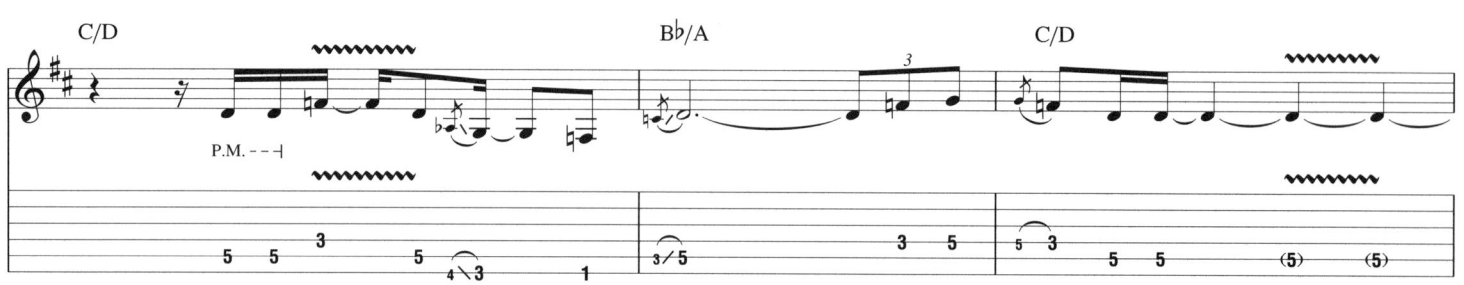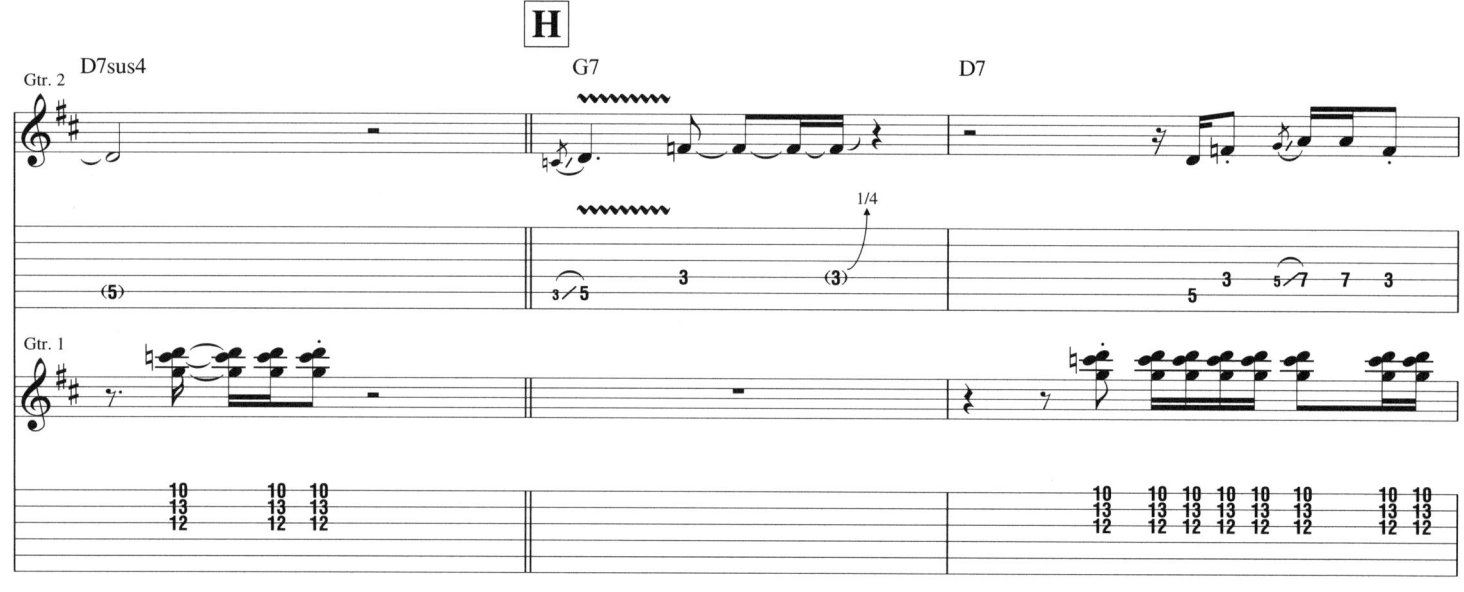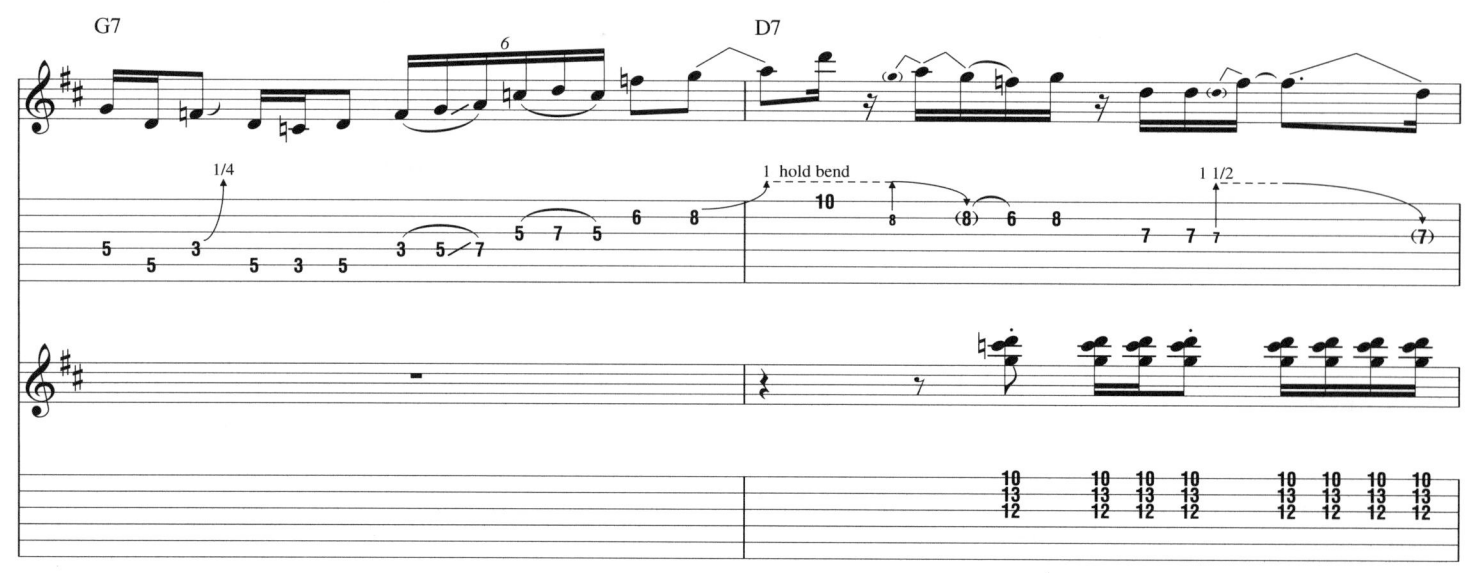

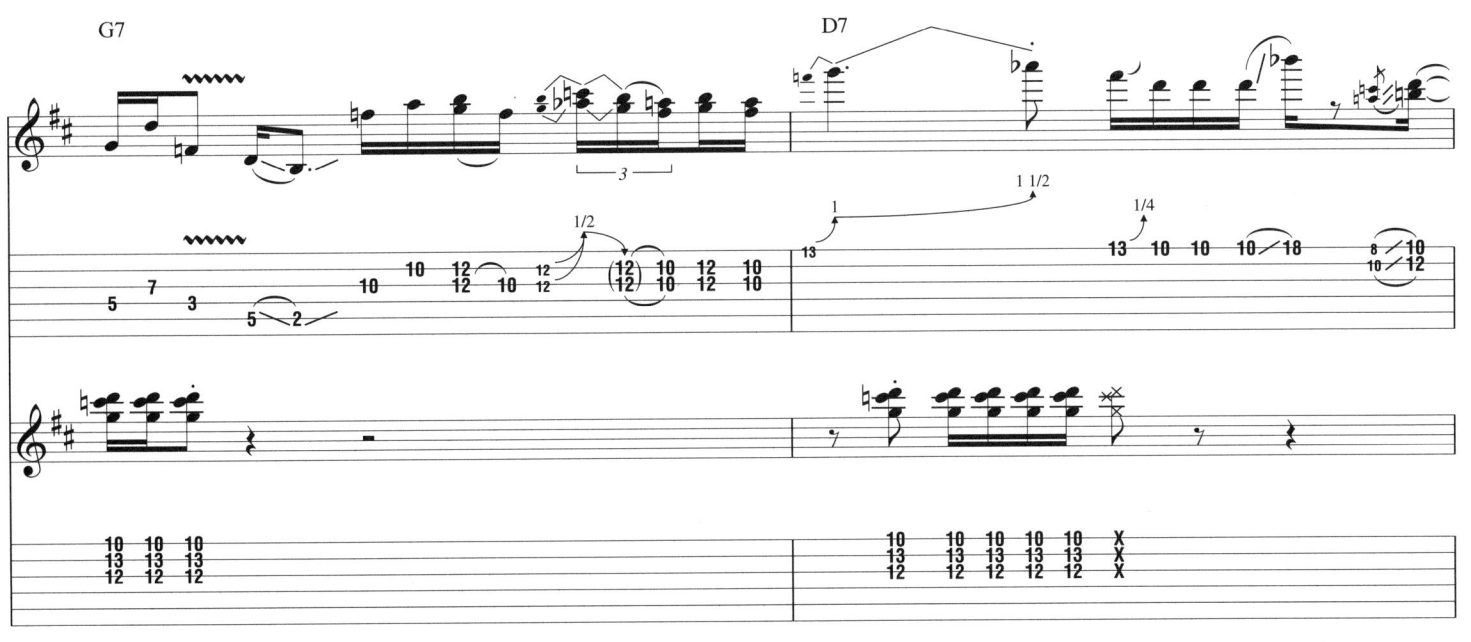
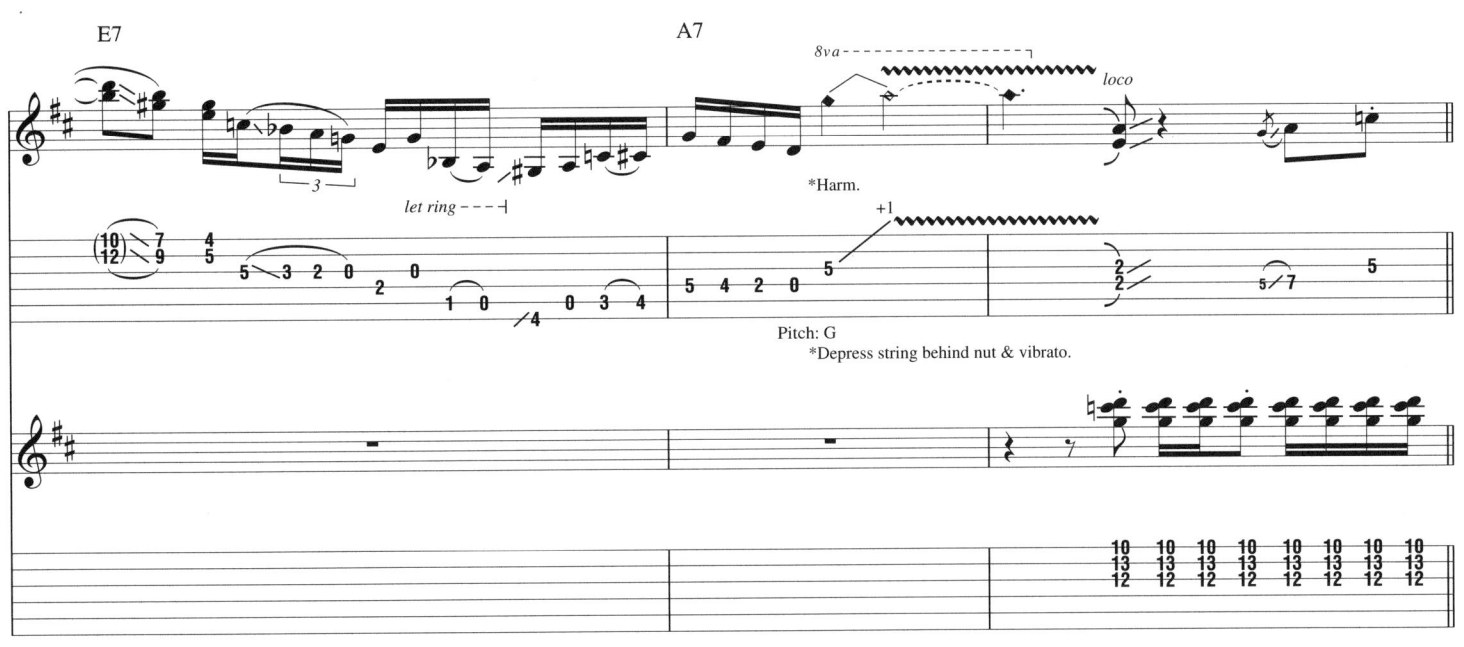
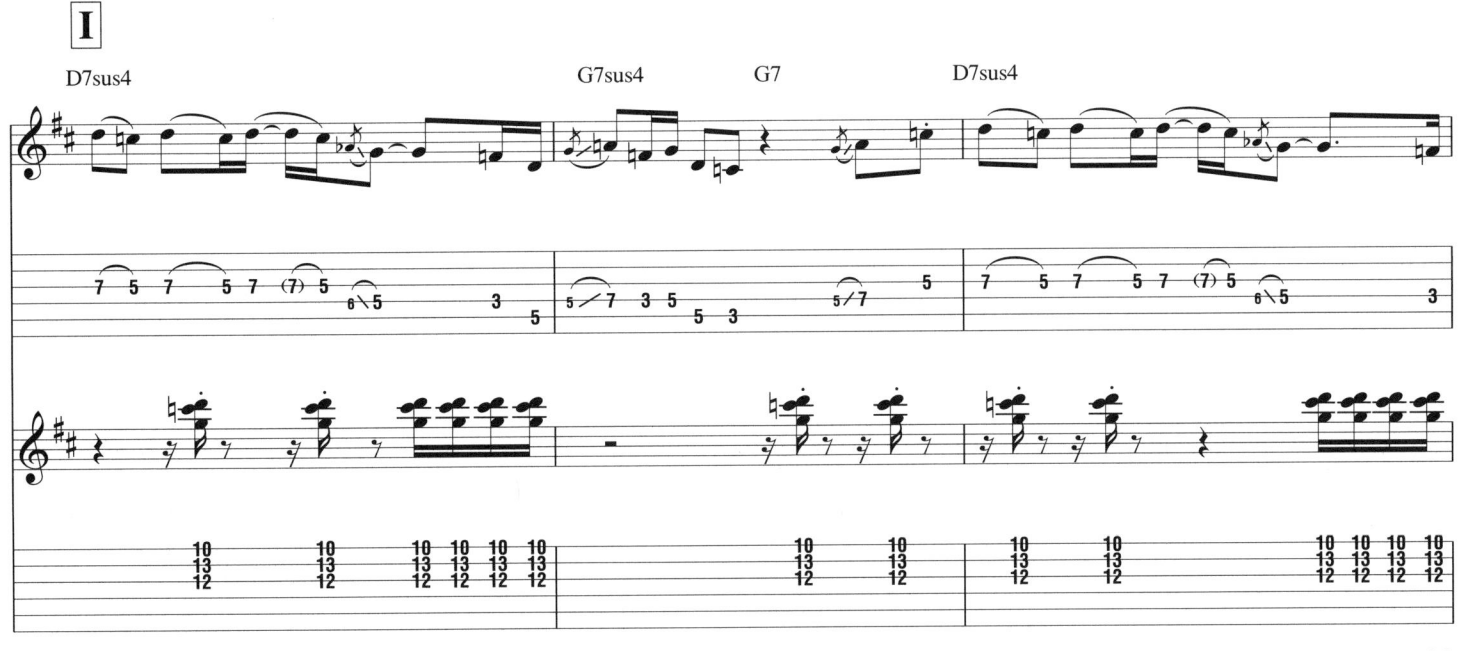

63

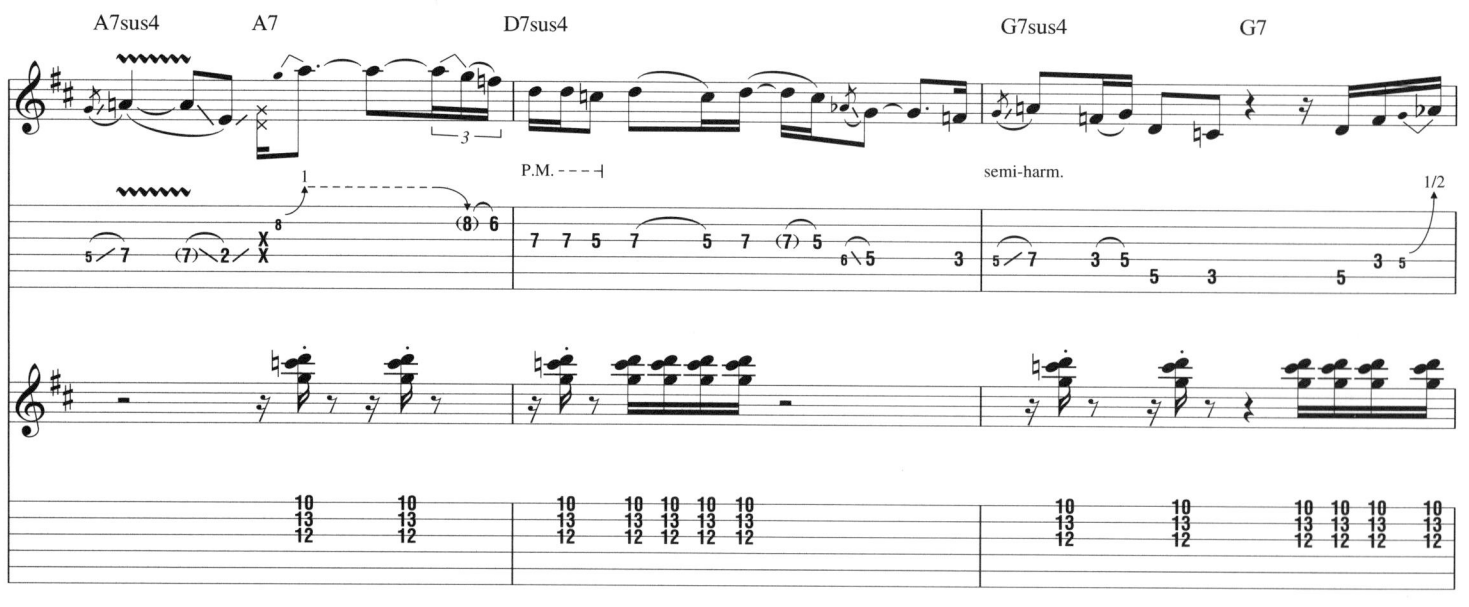
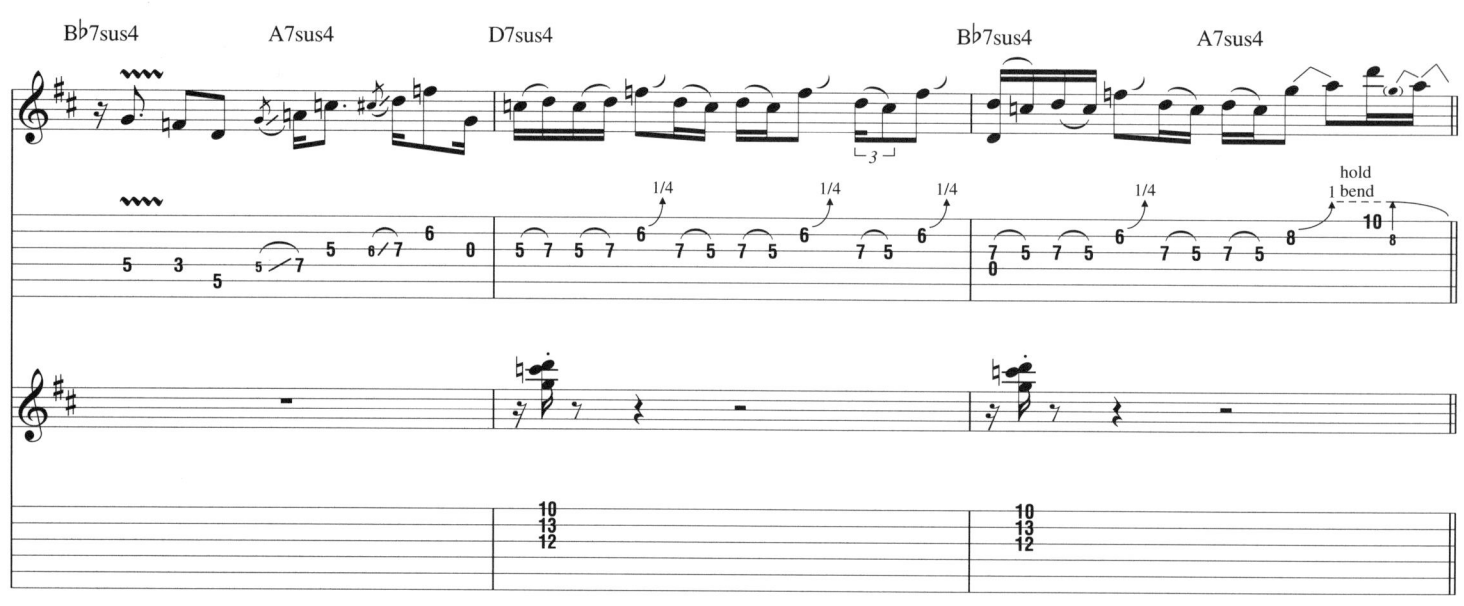
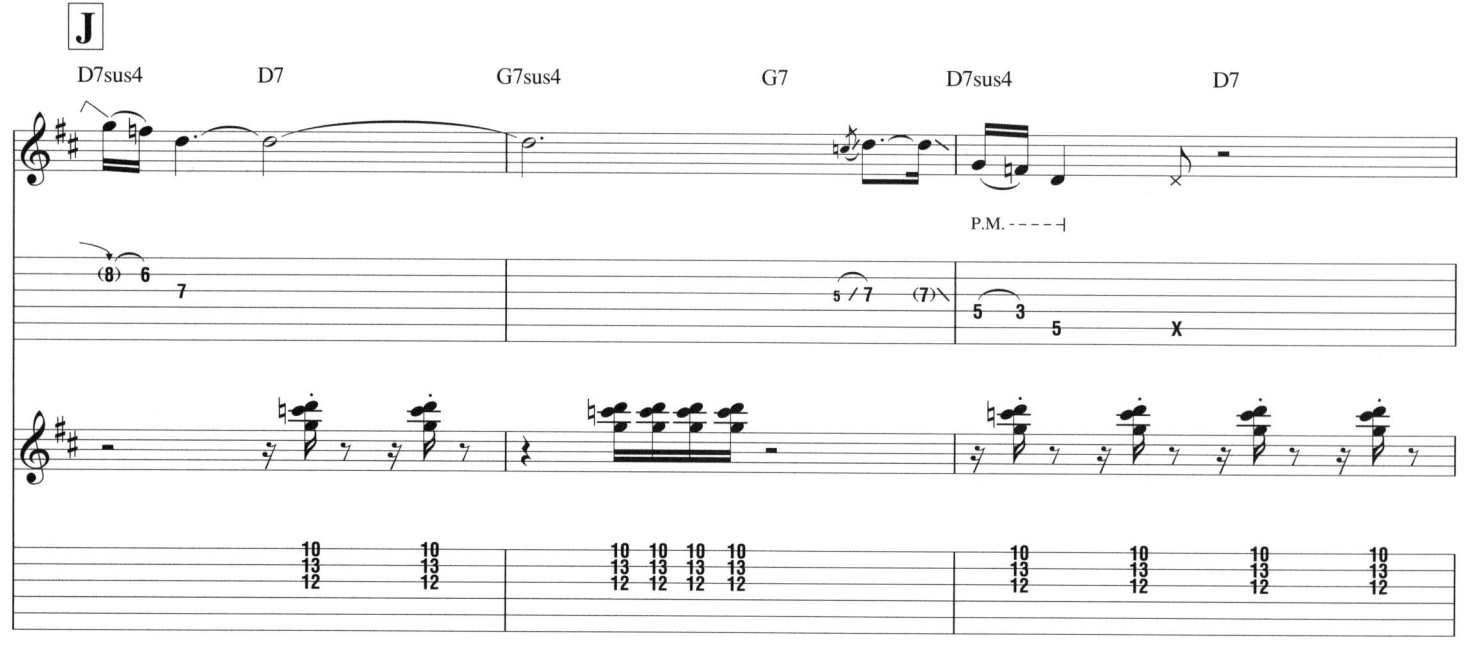

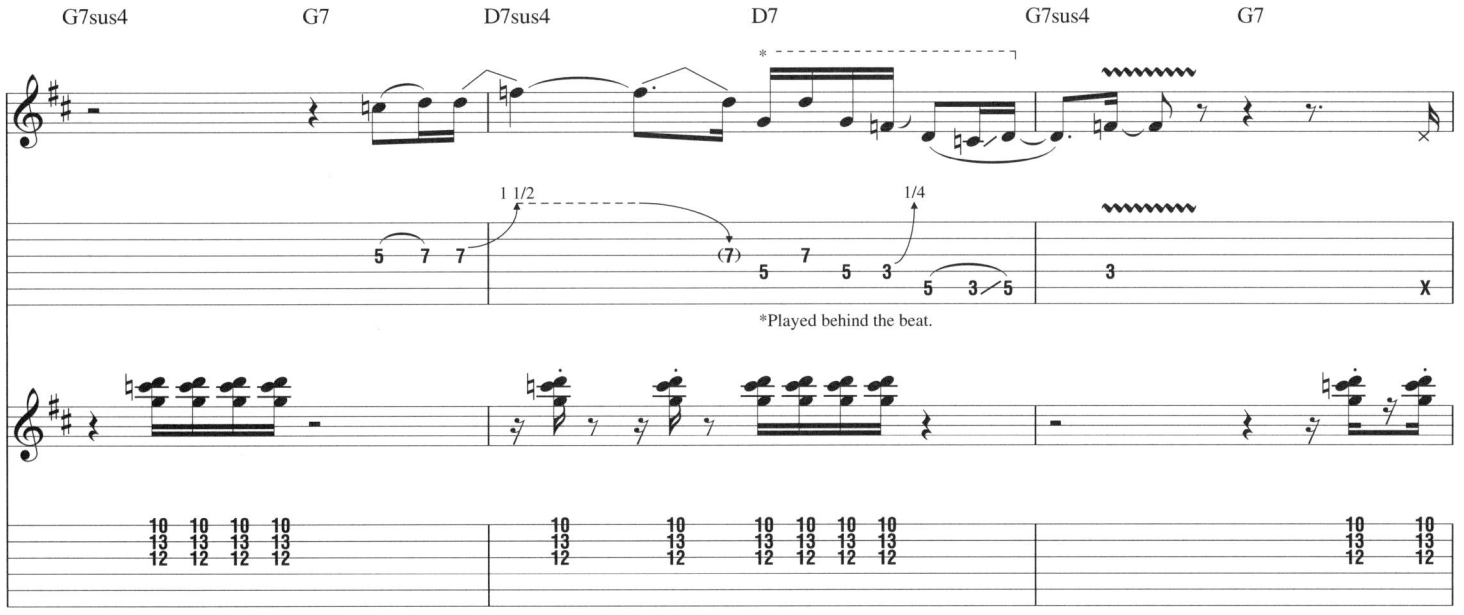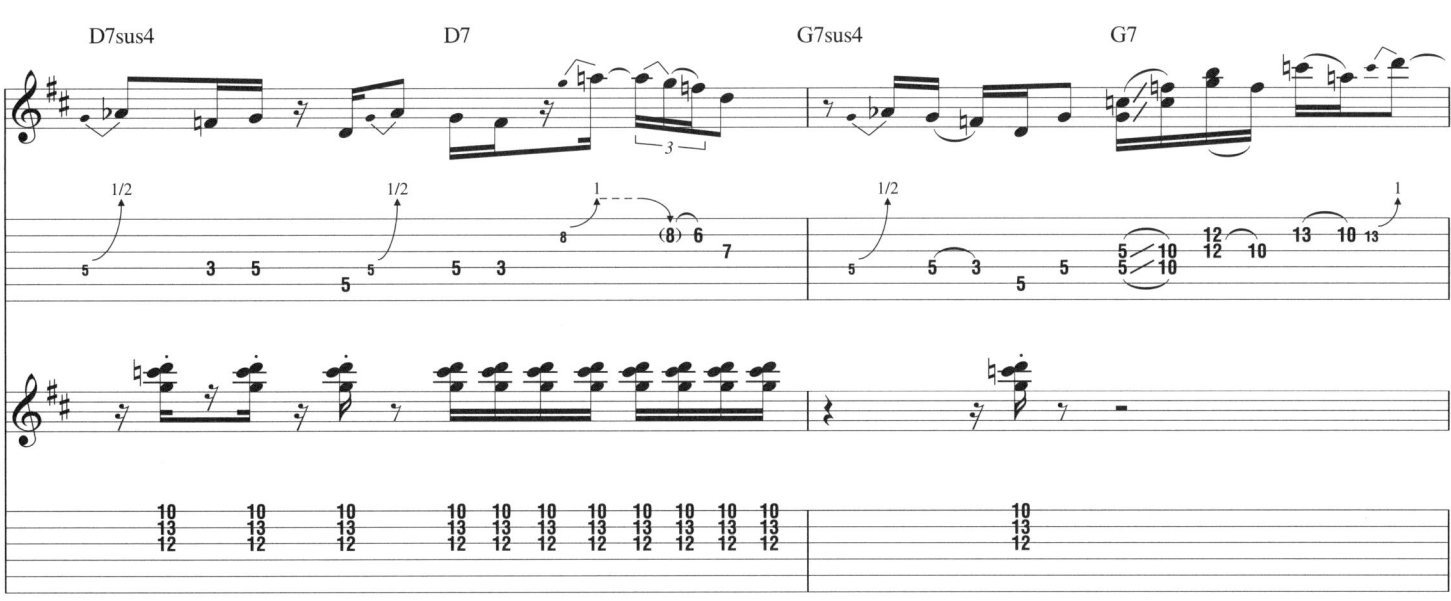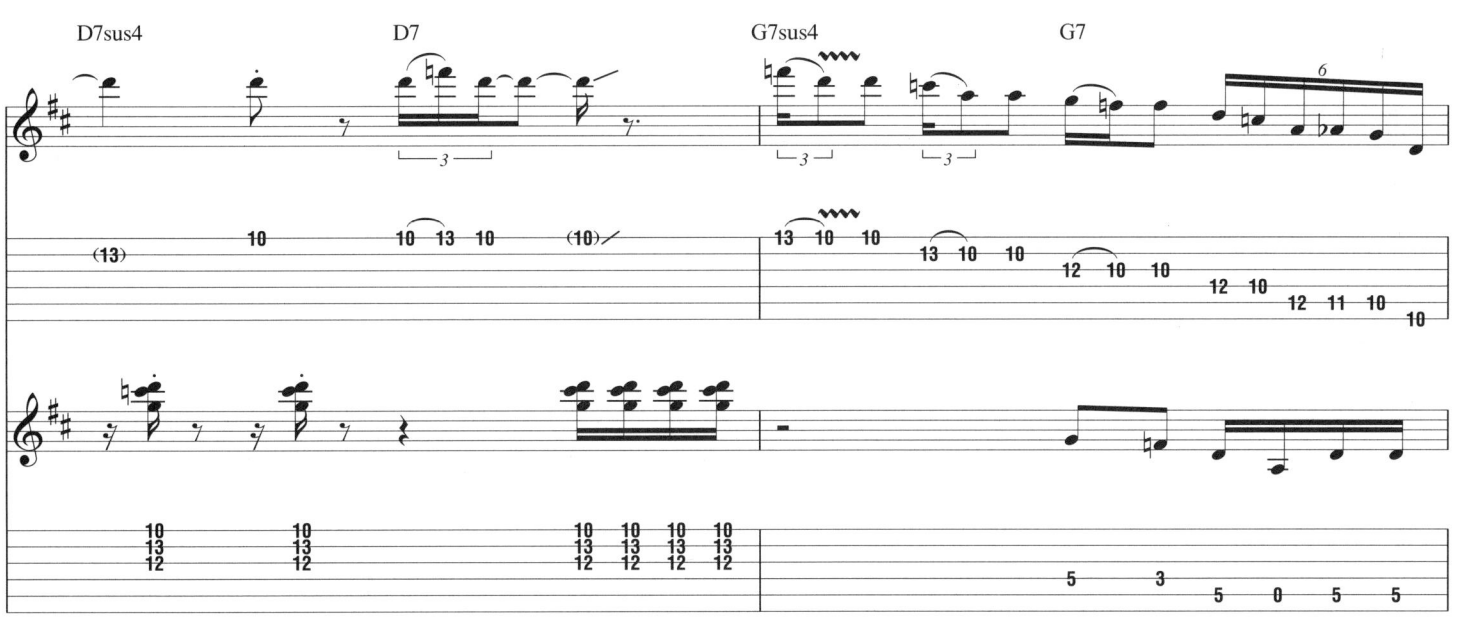

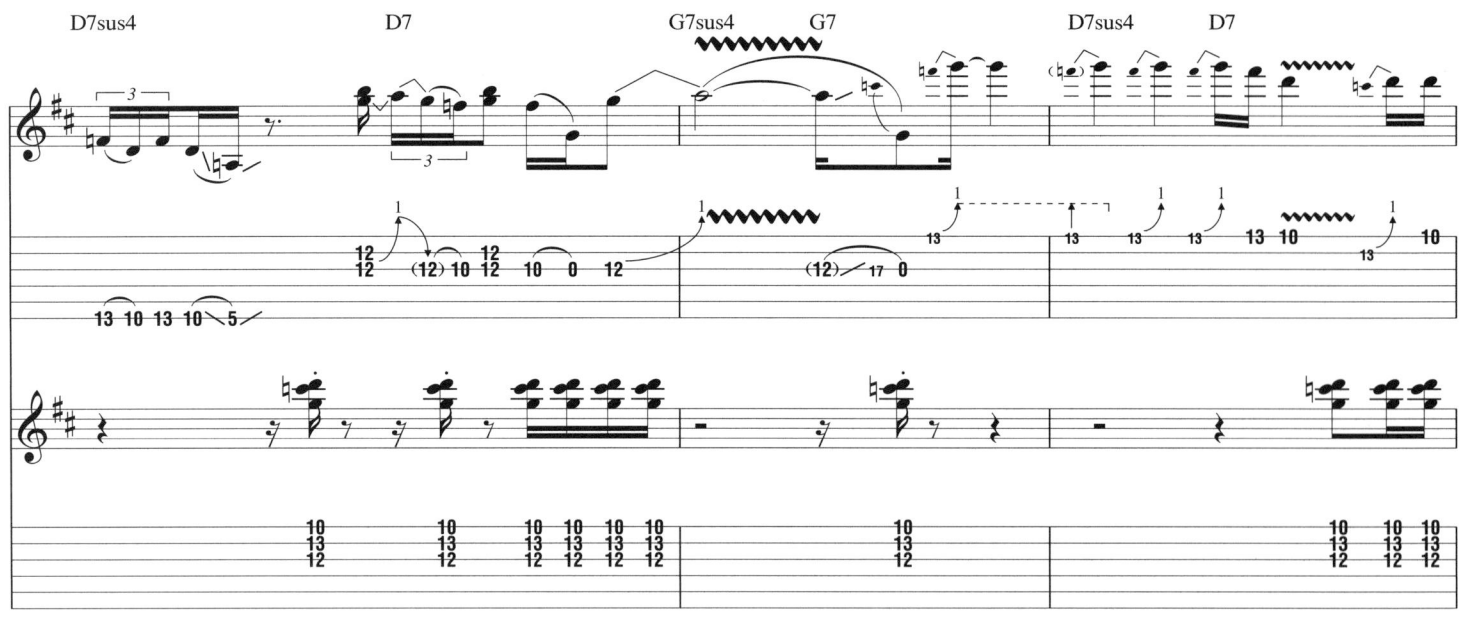
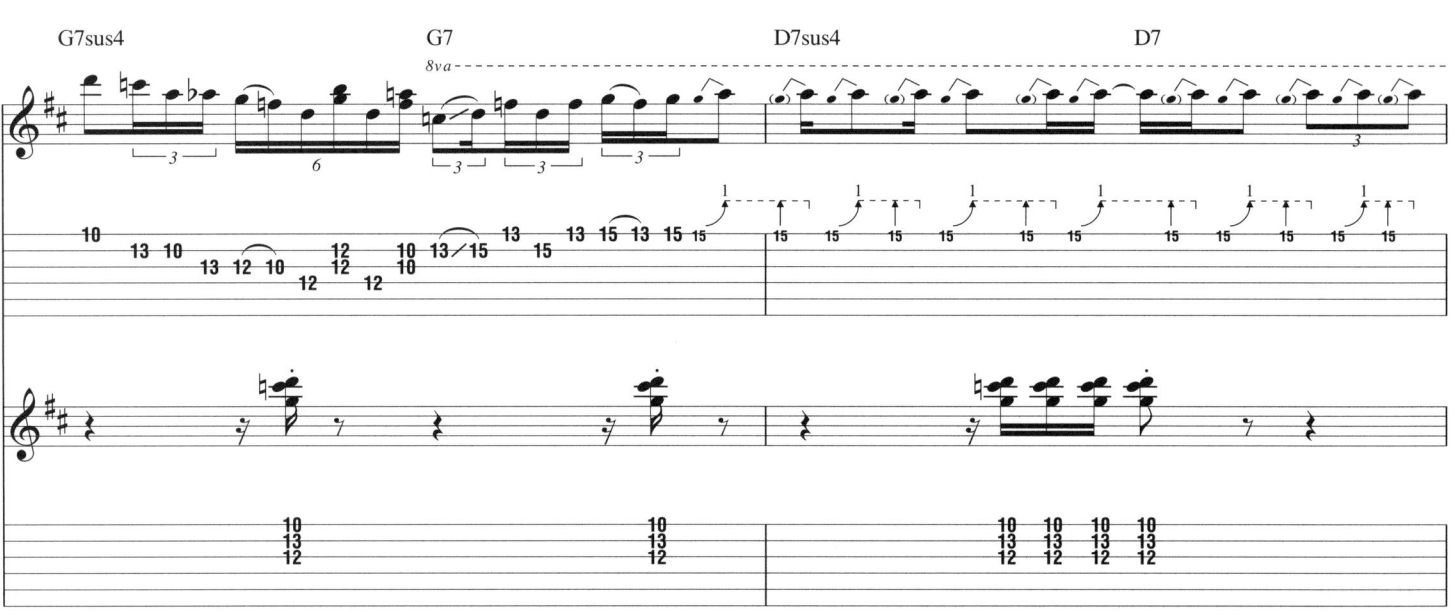
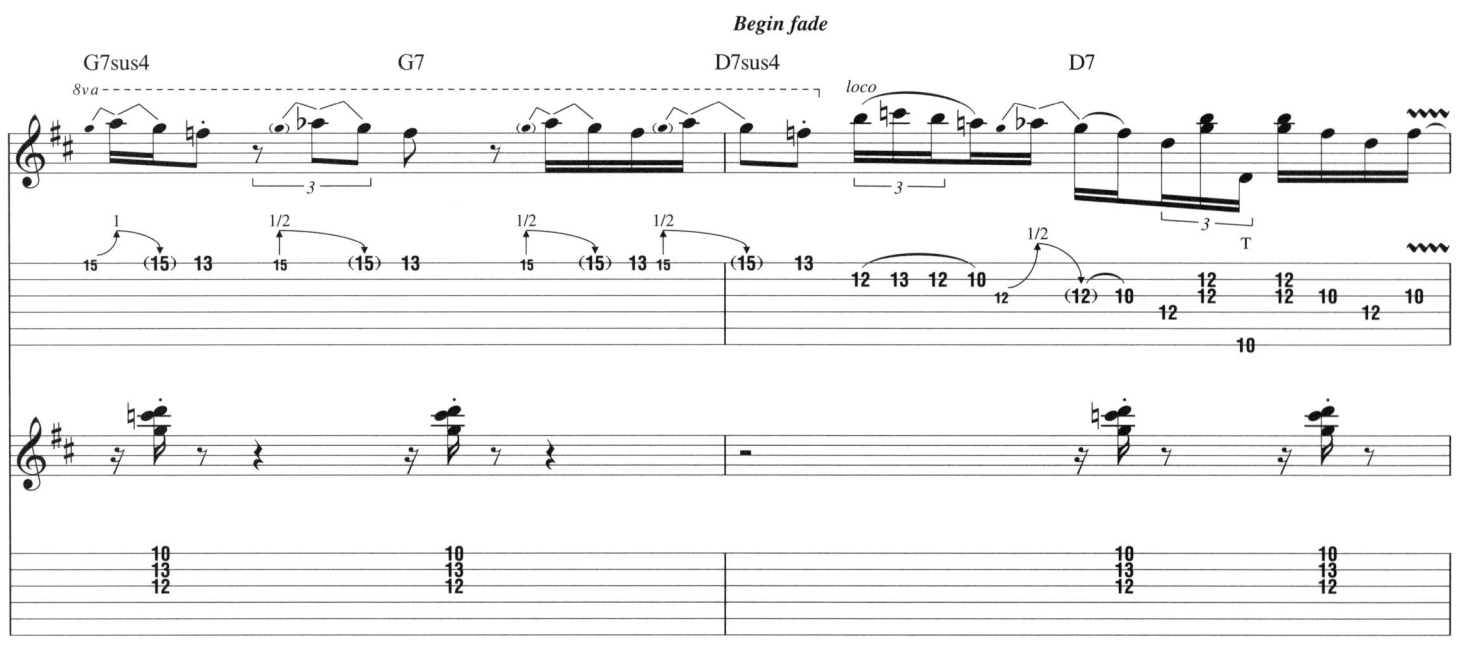

66

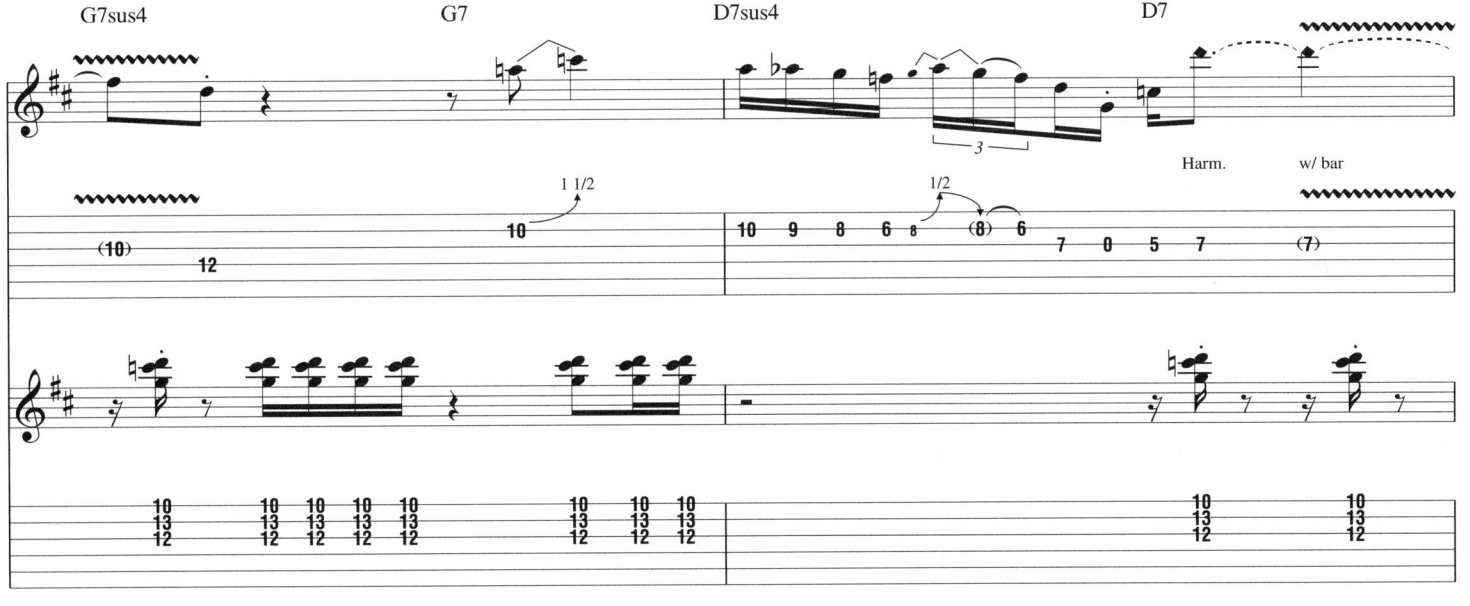
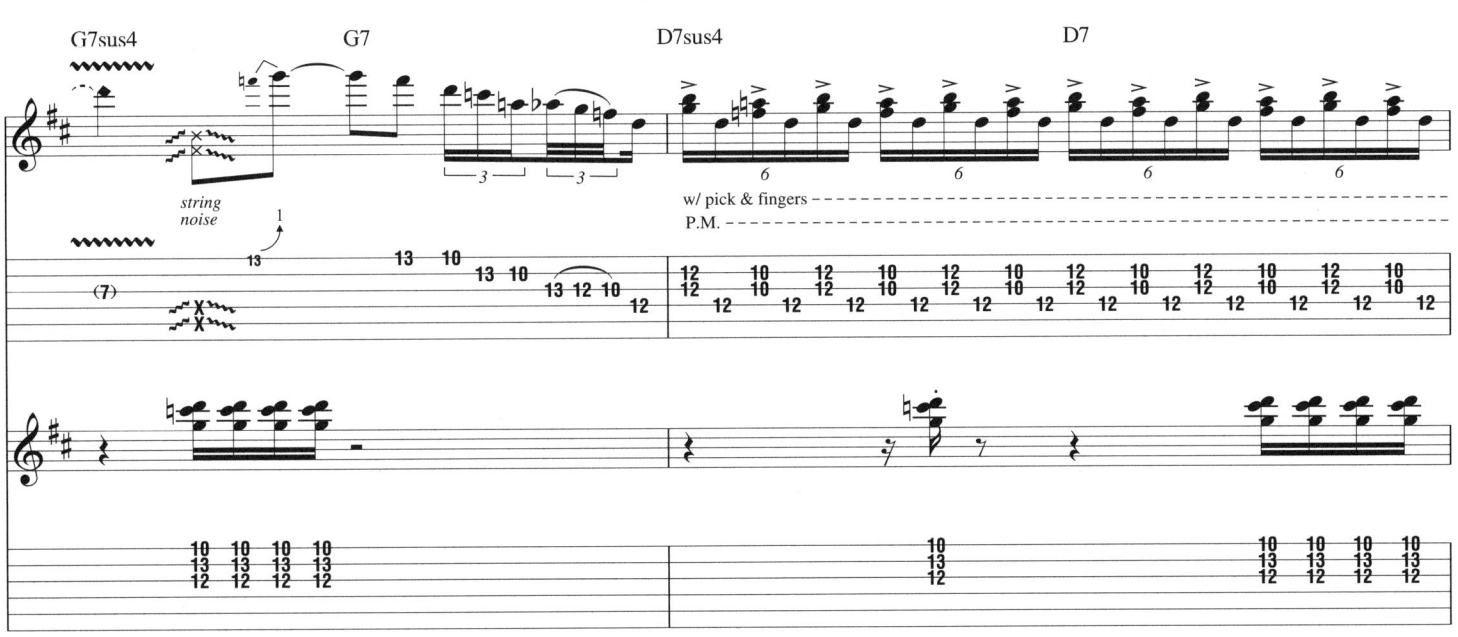
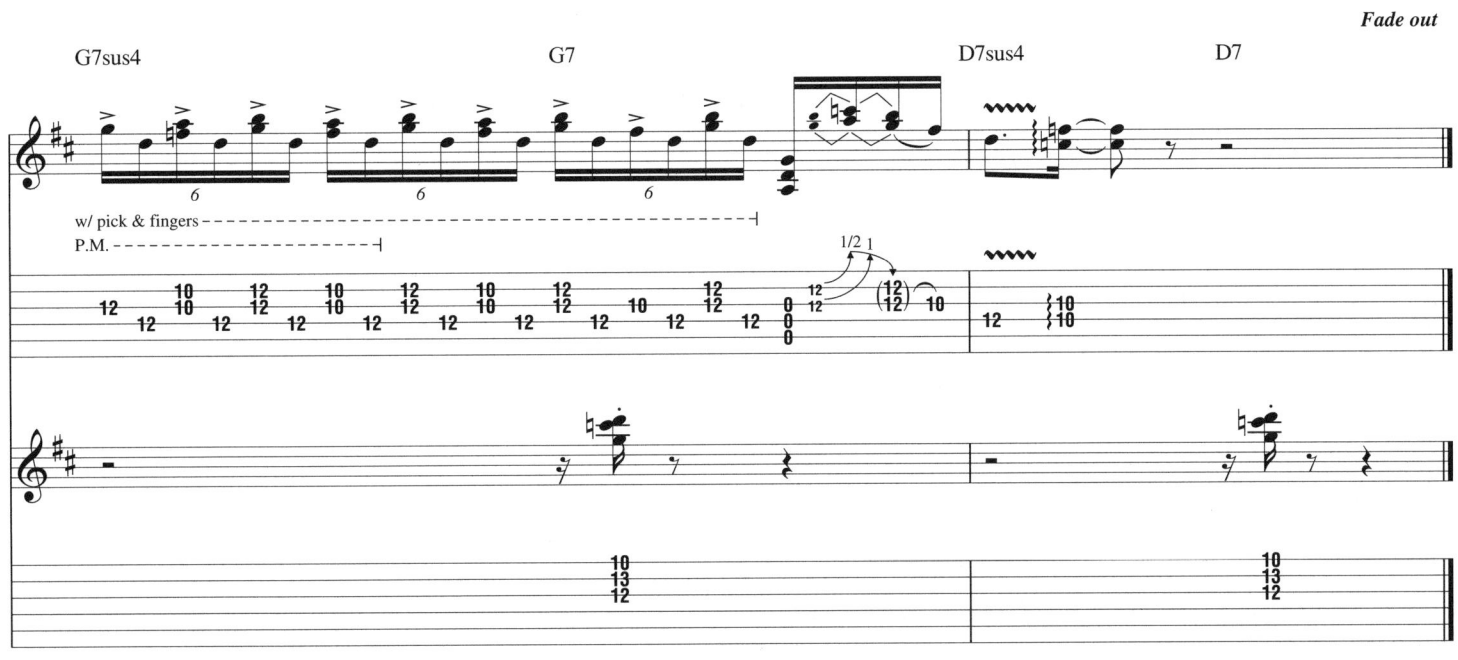

67

from *Dare to Be Different*
Guitar Boogie Shuffle
By Arthur Smith

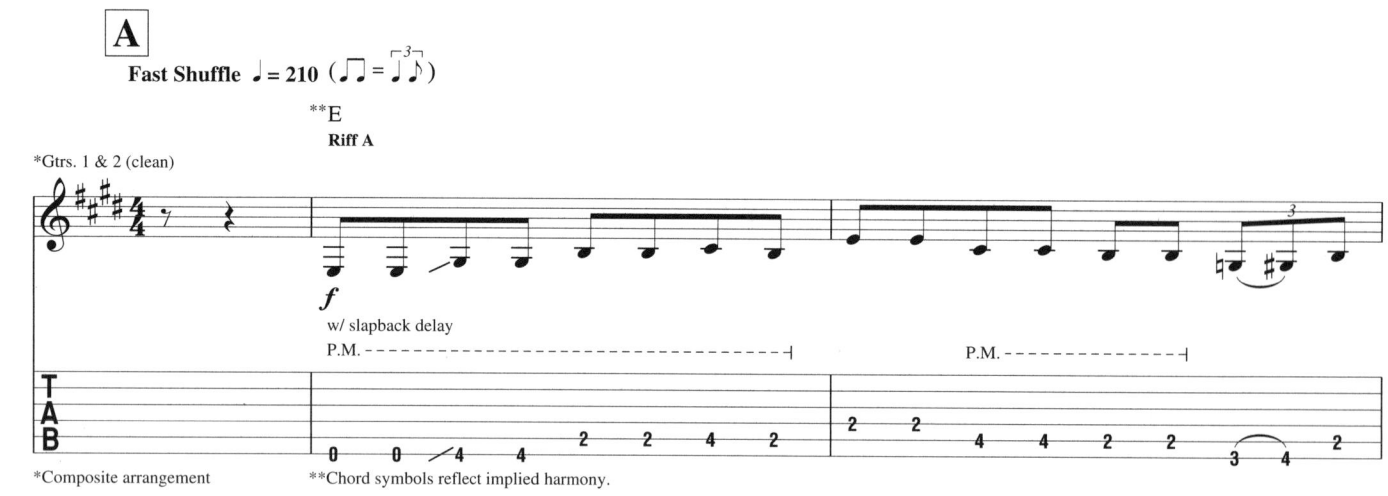

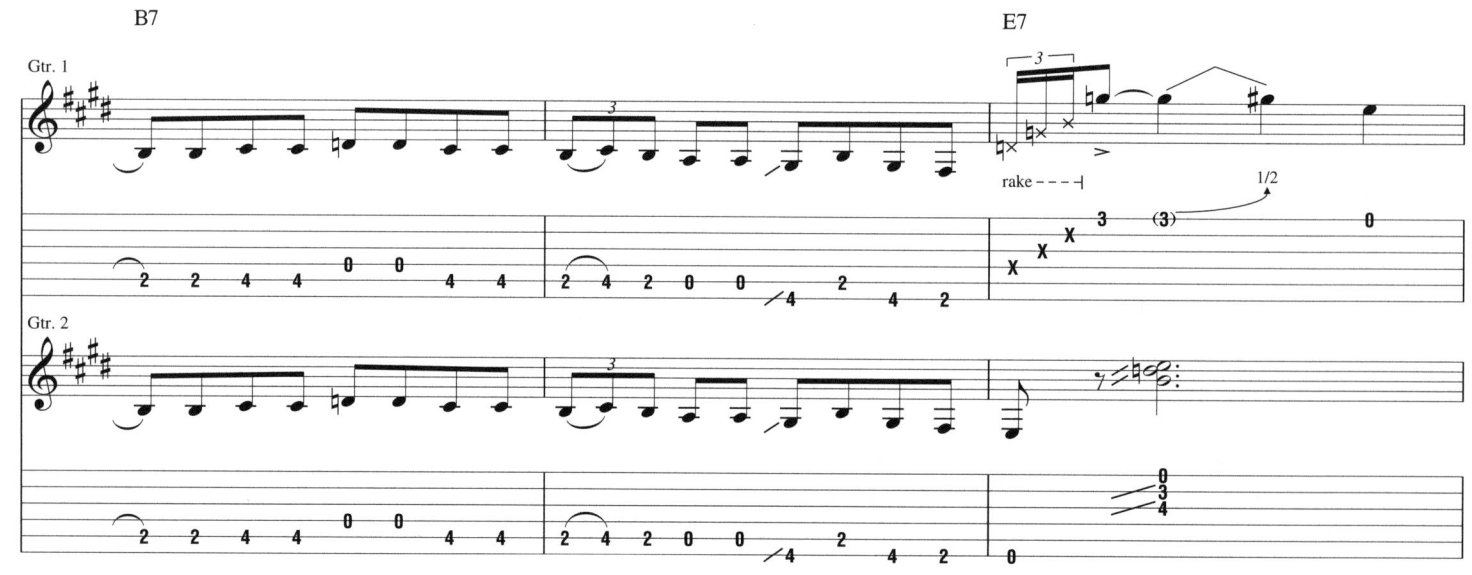

Copyright © 1946, 1959 Shapiro, Bernstein & Co., Inc., New York
Copyrights Renewed
International Copyright Secured   All Rights Reserved
Used by Permission

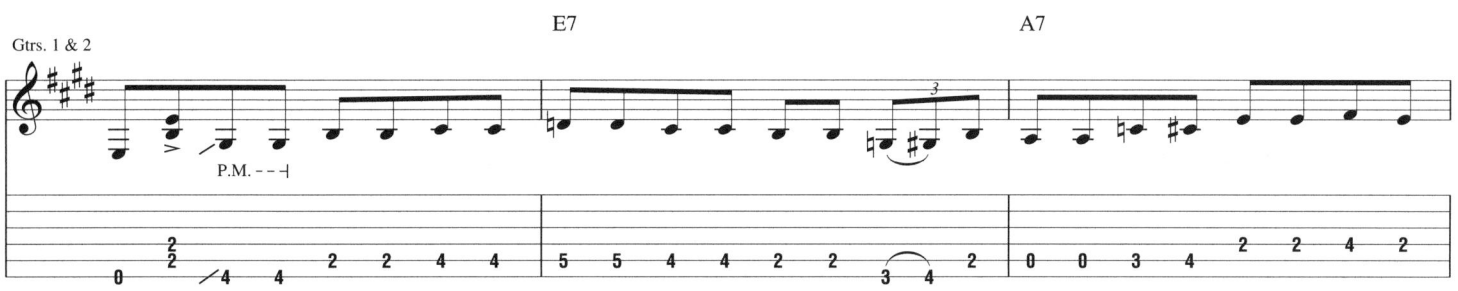

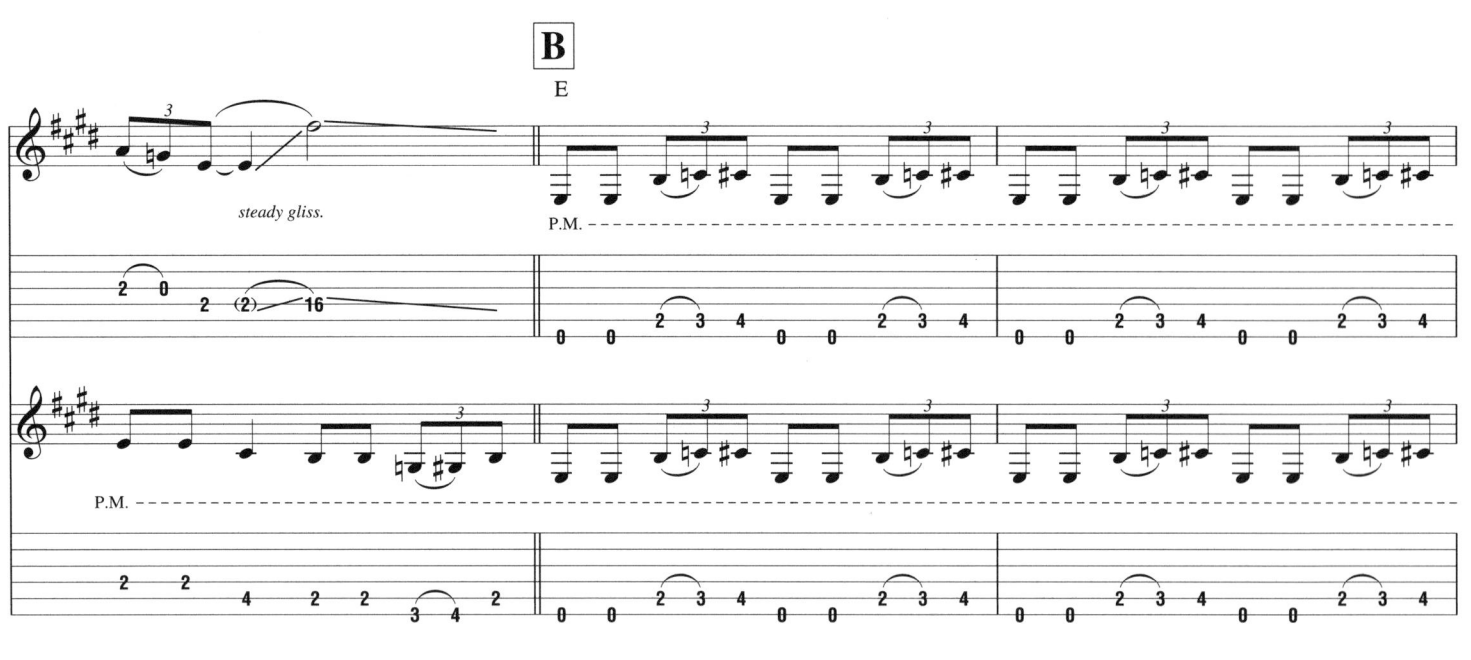
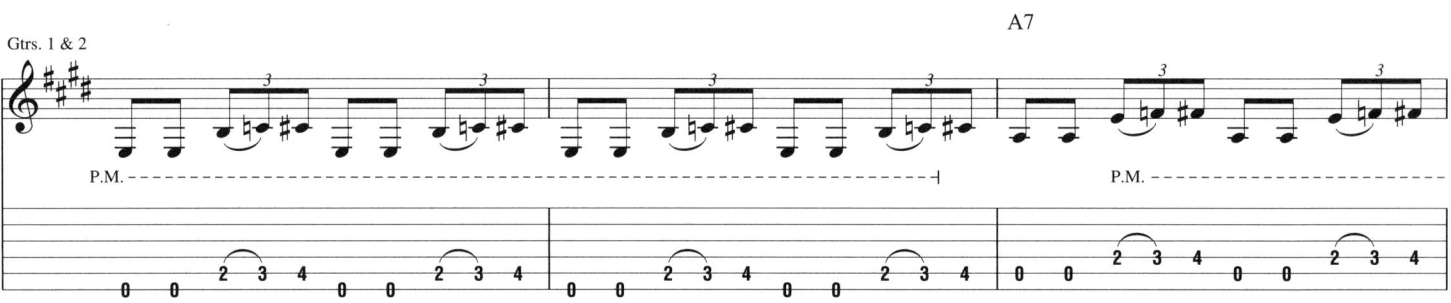
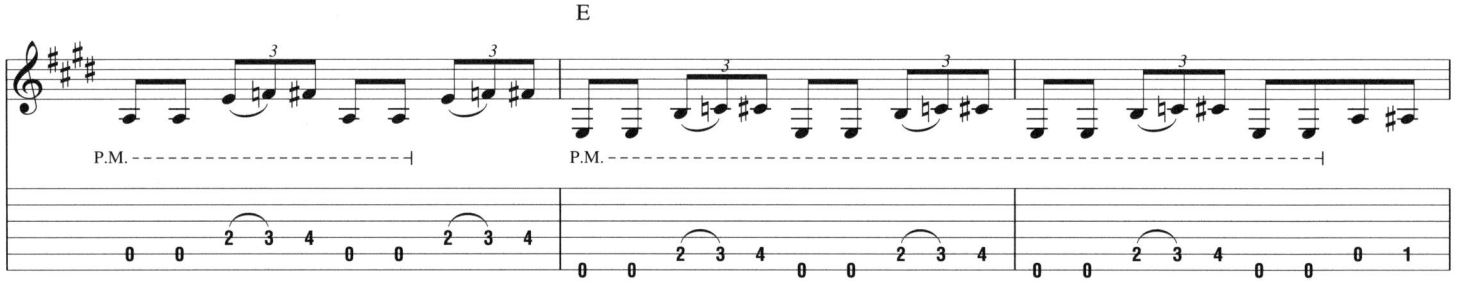

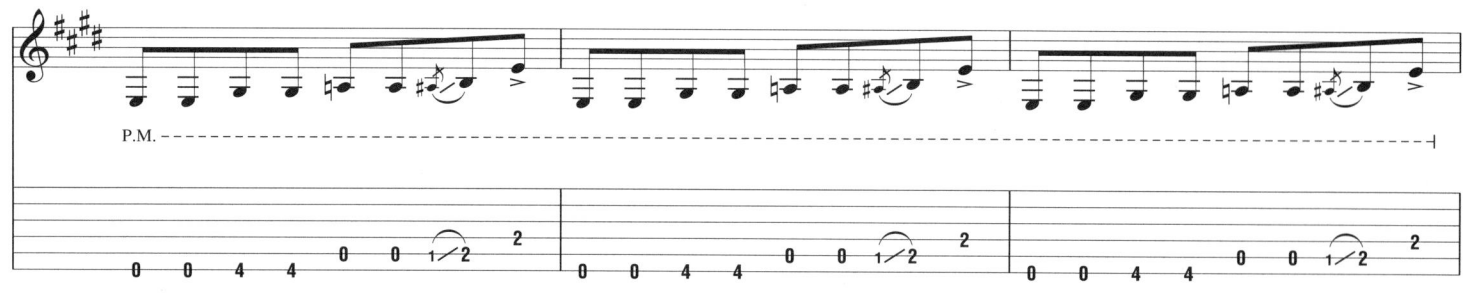

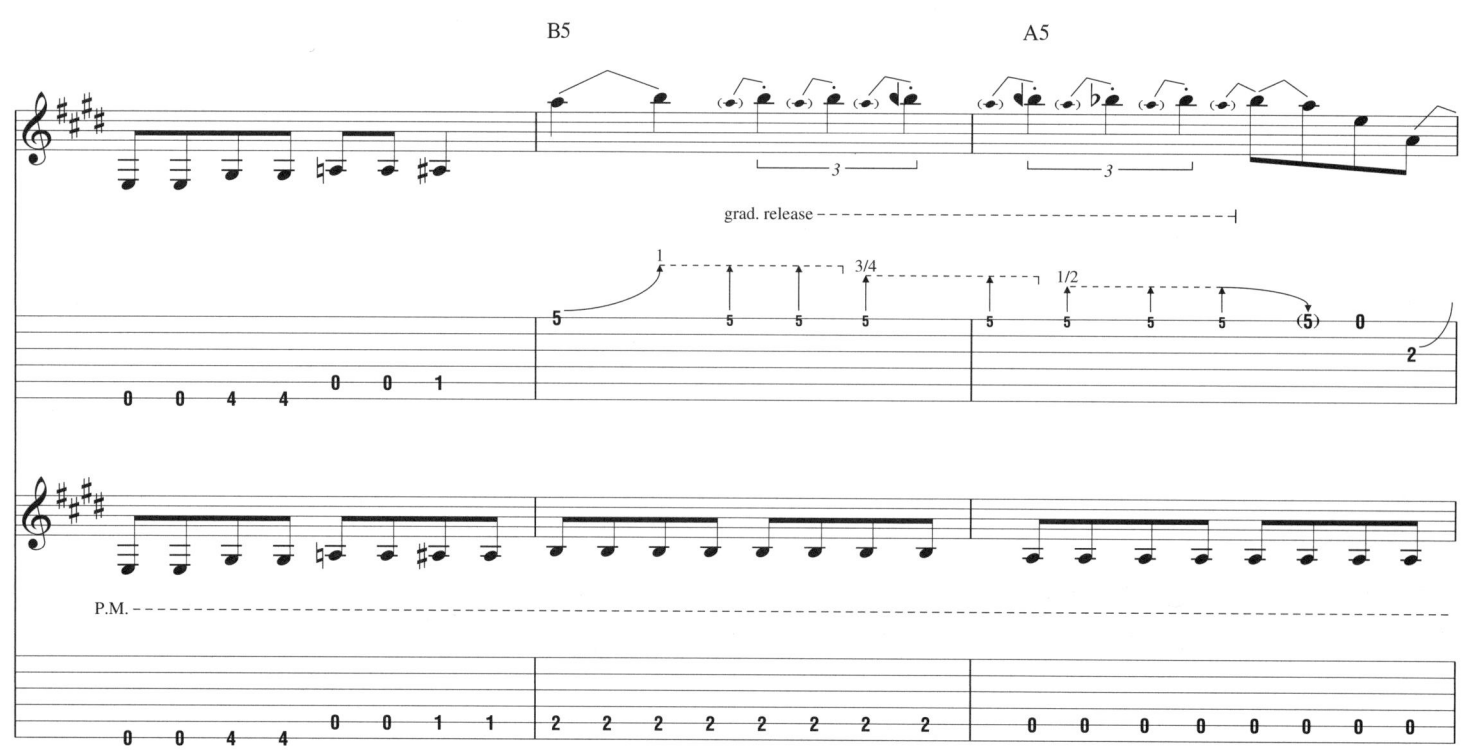

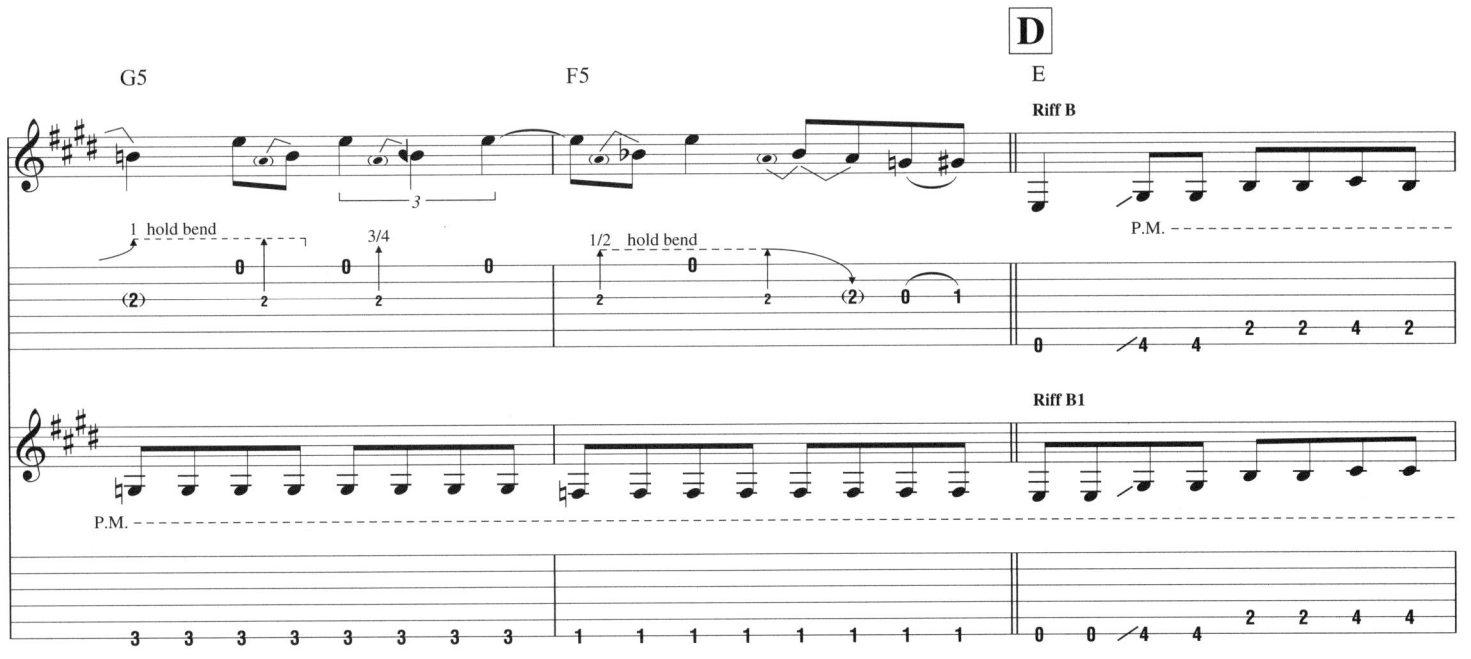

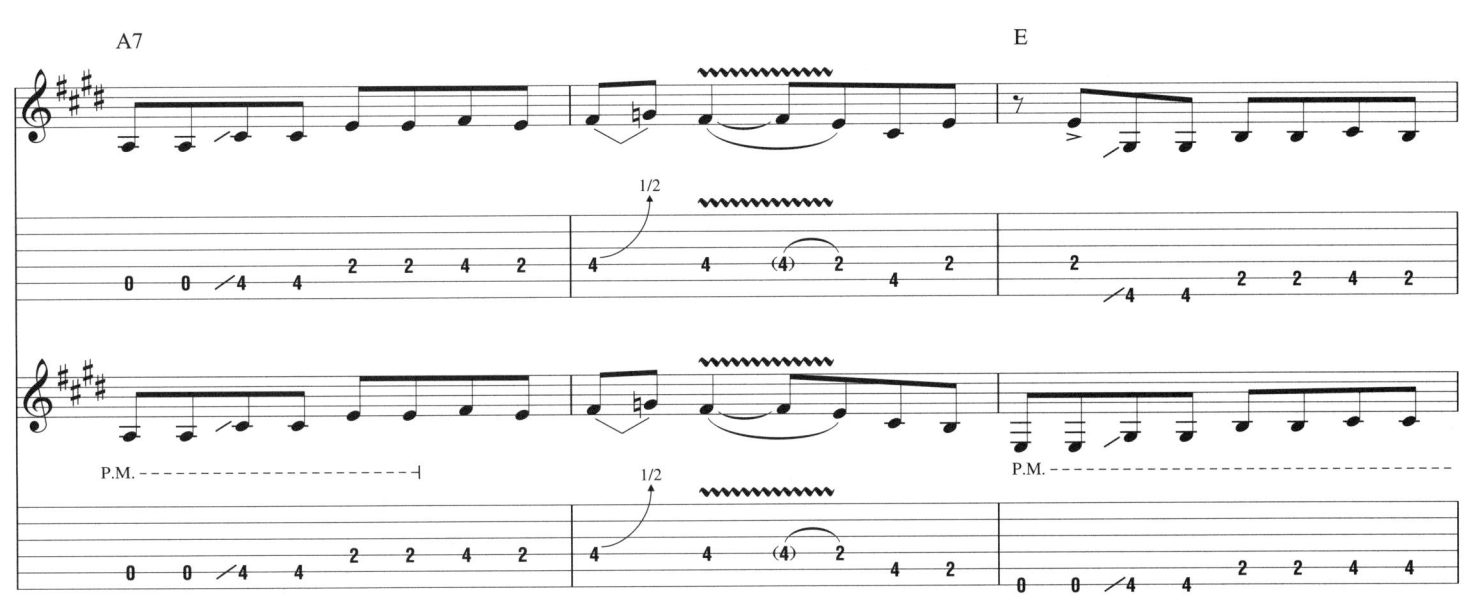

73

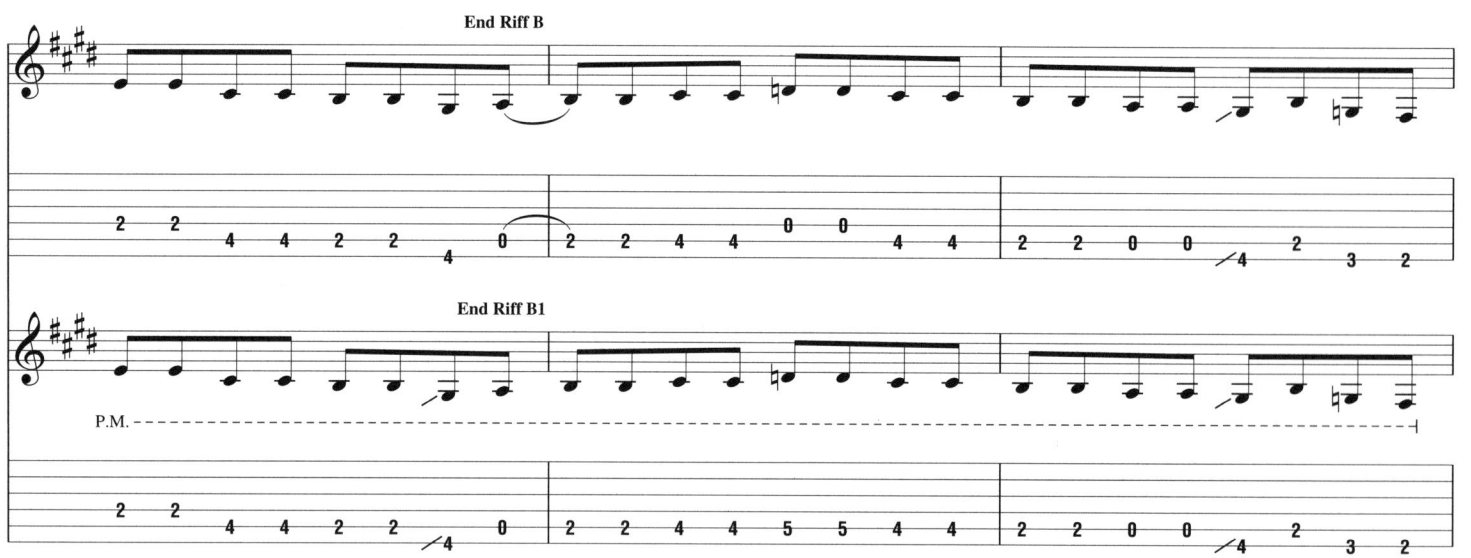
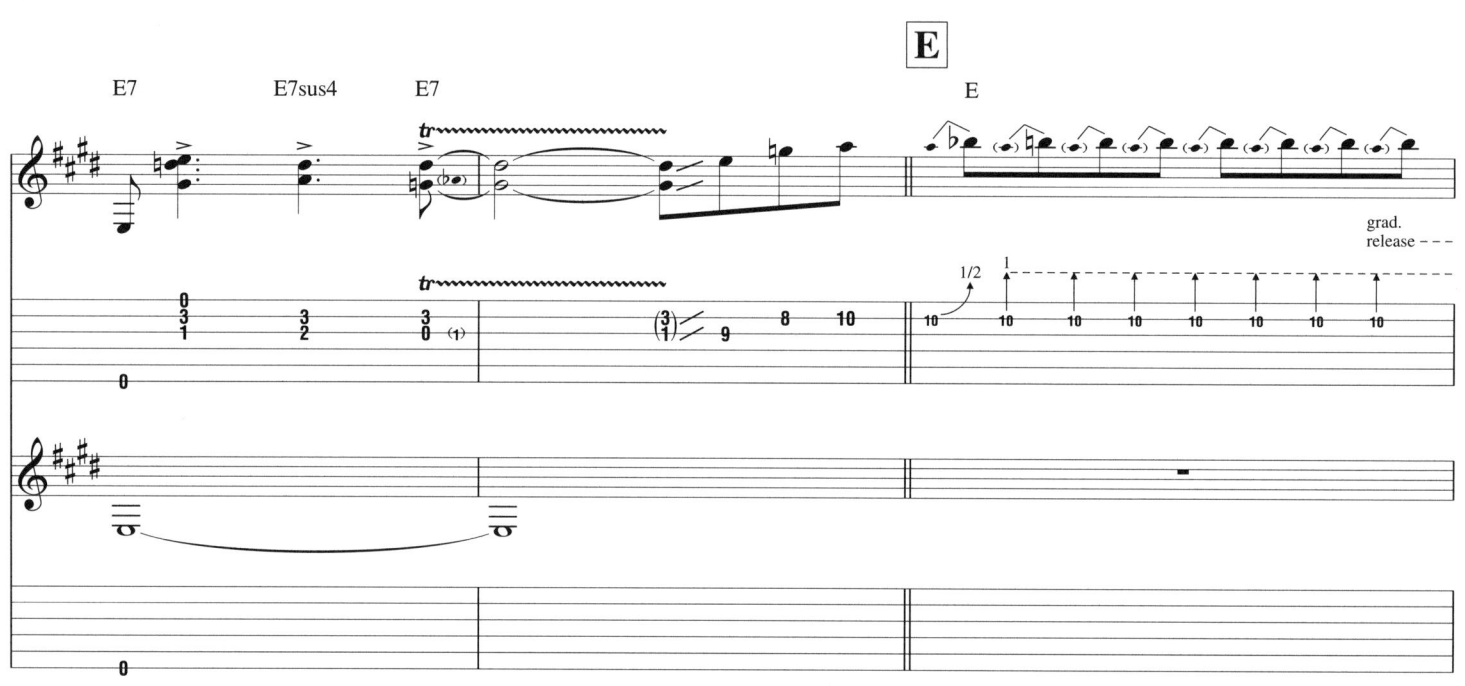
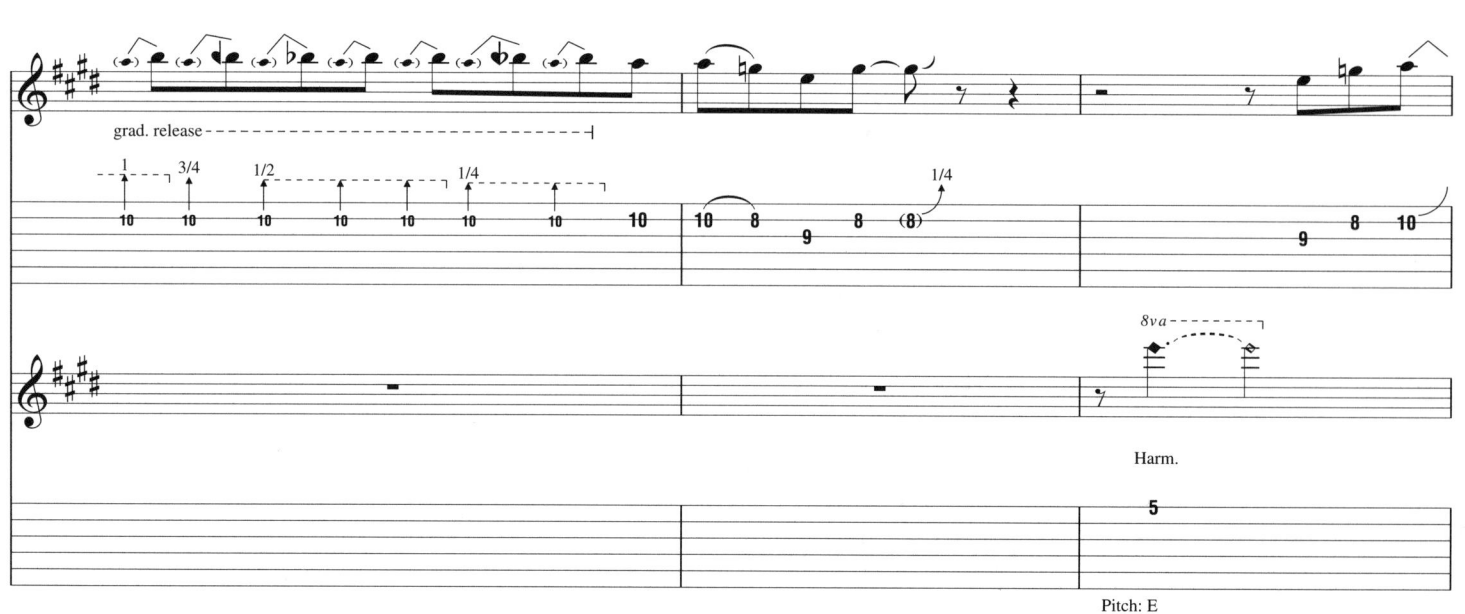

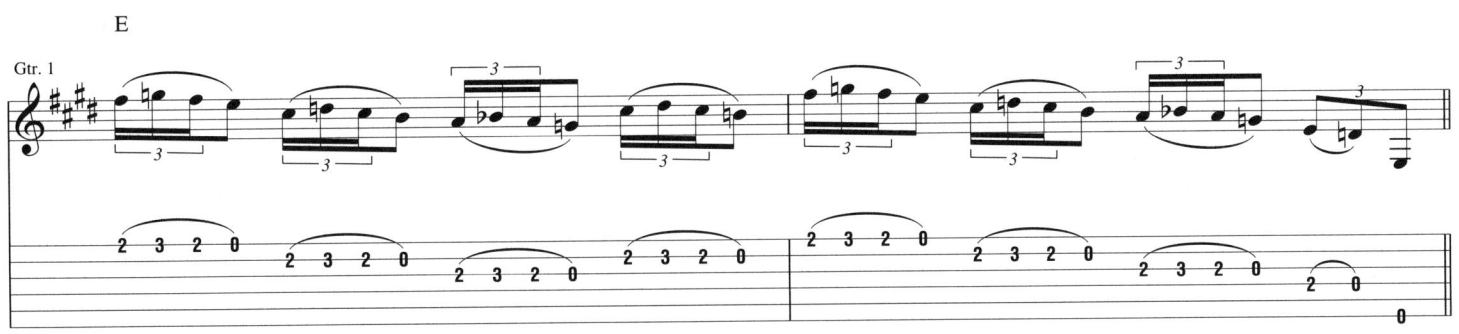

75

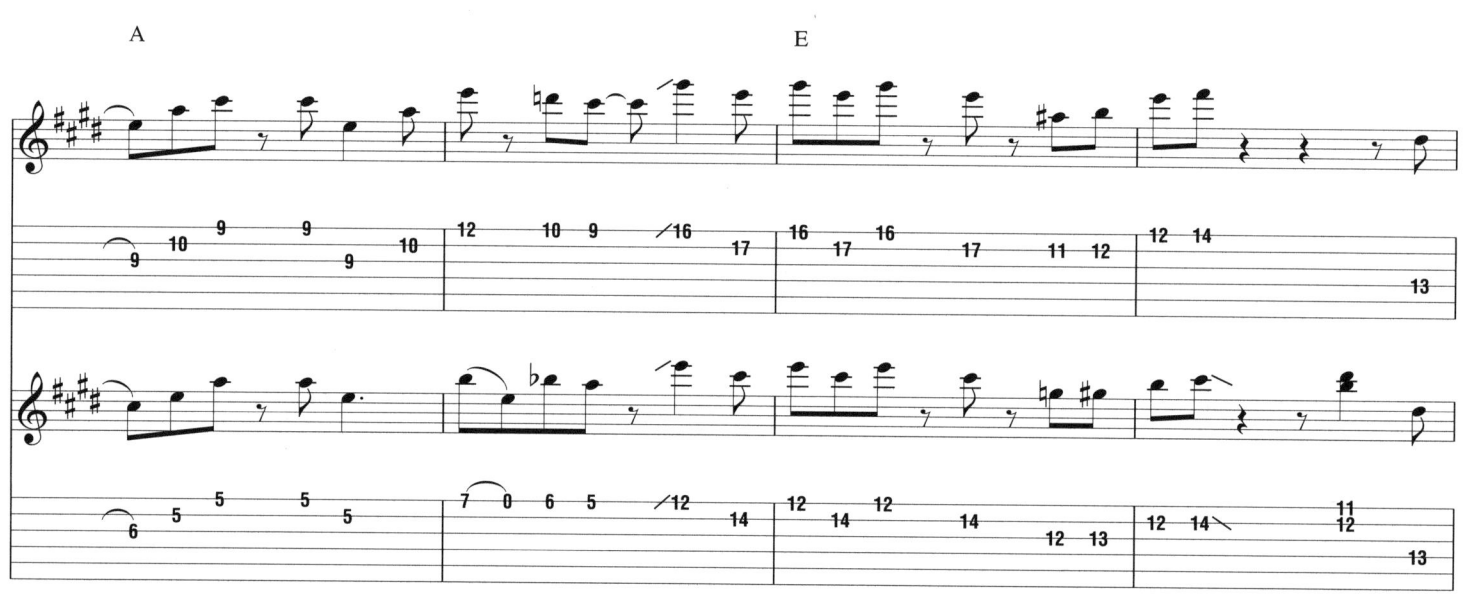
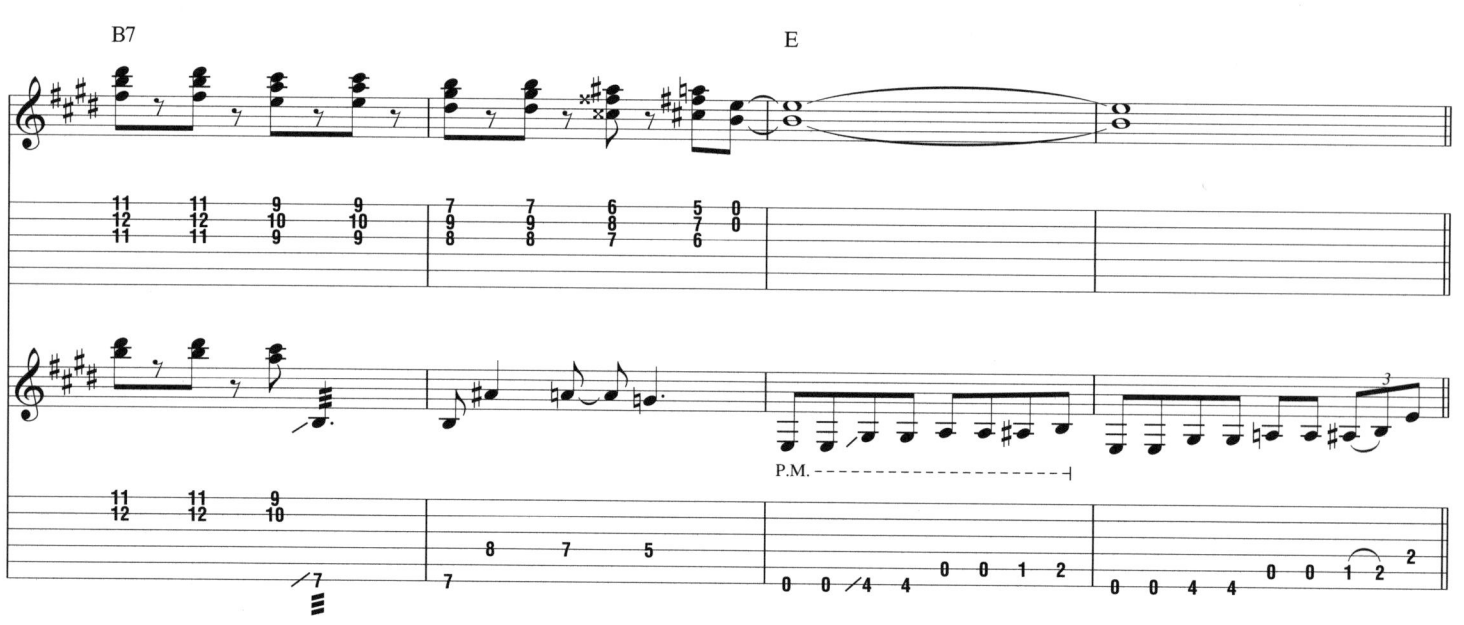

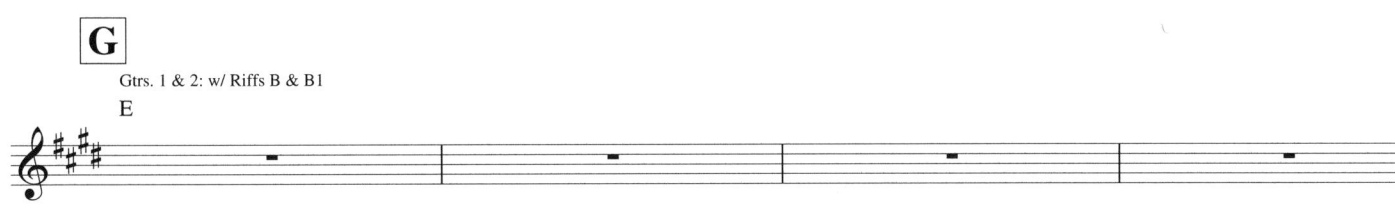
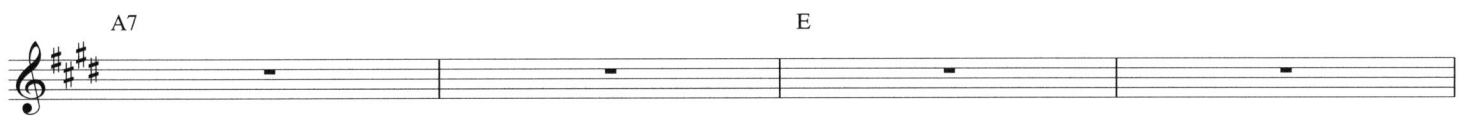
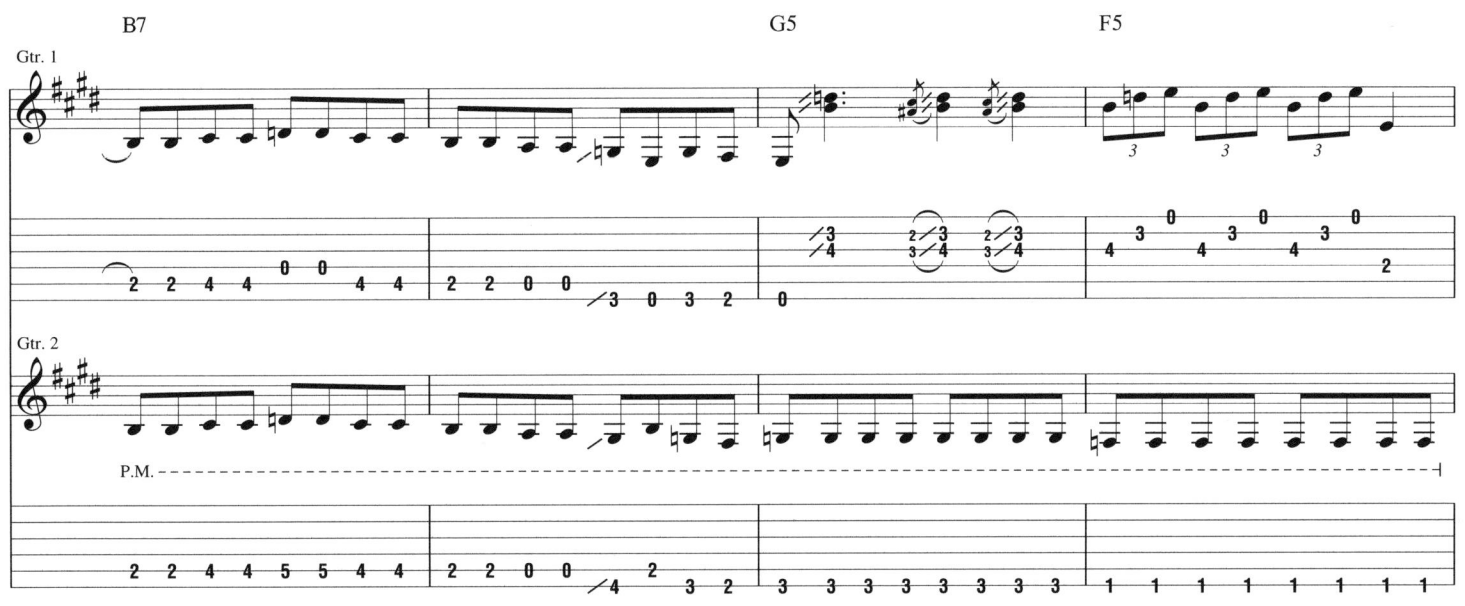
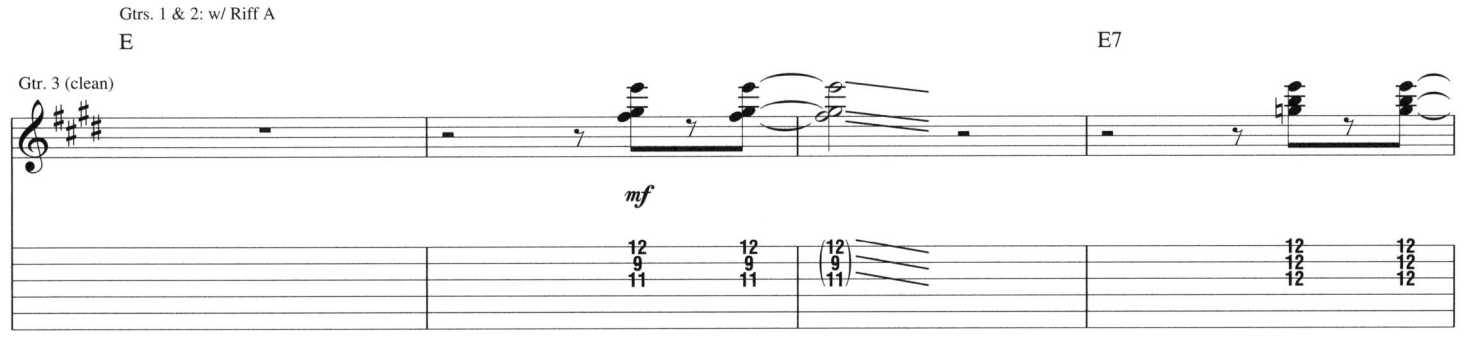
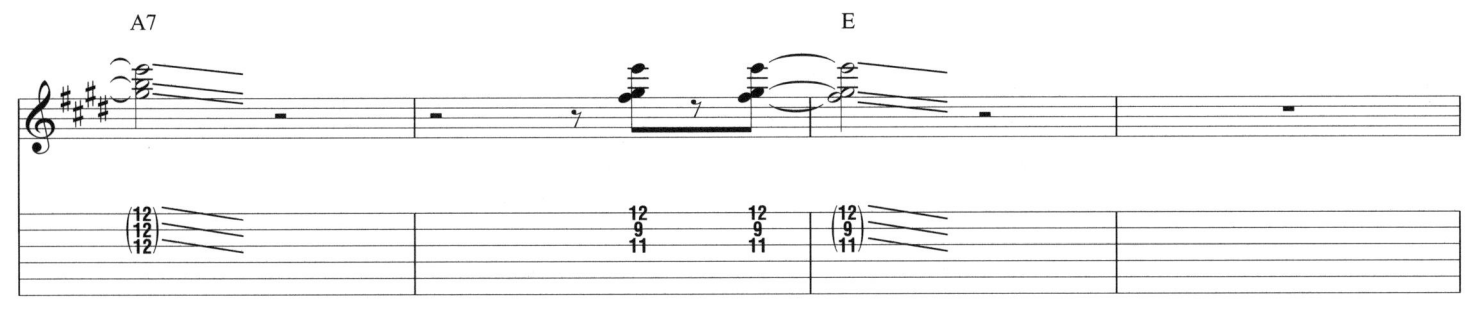

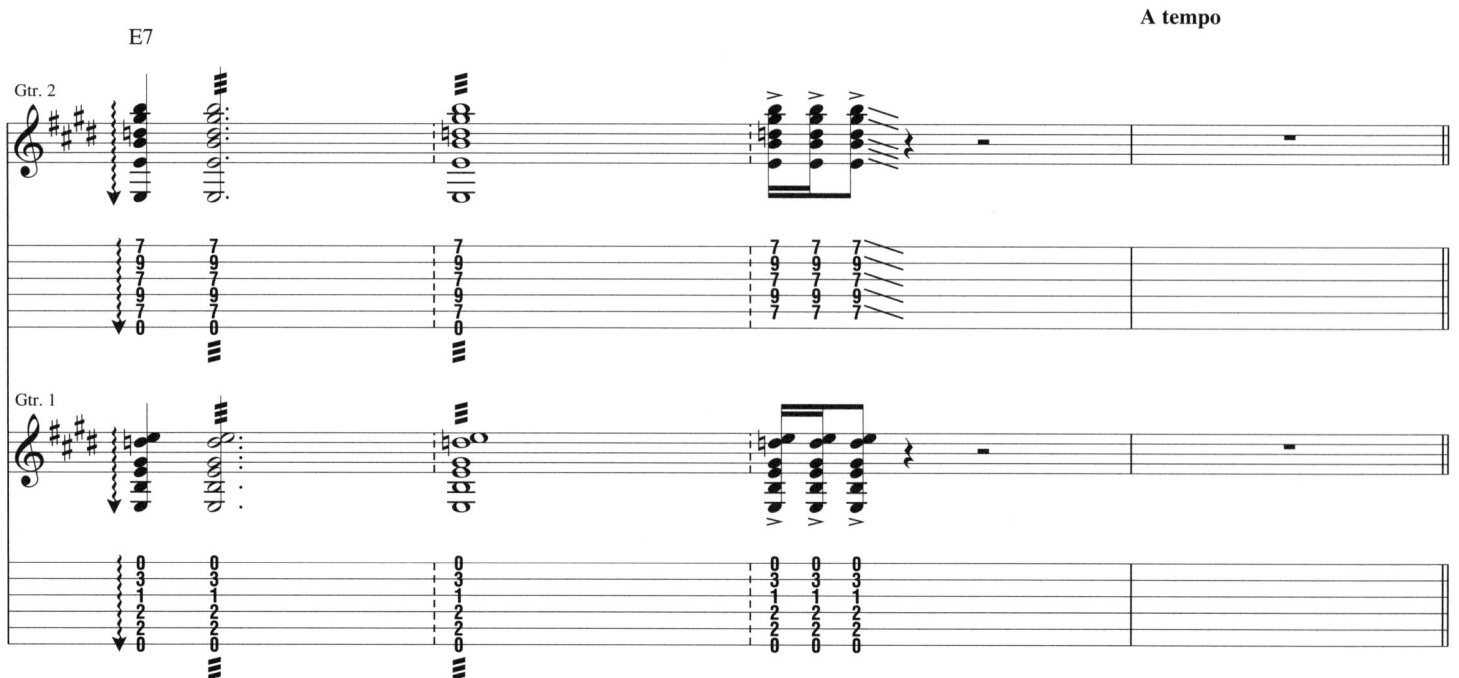

H
Gtrs. 1 & 2: w/ Riff B
E
Rhy. Fig. 1
Gtr. 3
A7
E
B7
A7
E
End Rhy. Fig. 1
*Tied to beat 1 on all recalls.
Gtr. 1
Gtr. 2
P.M.

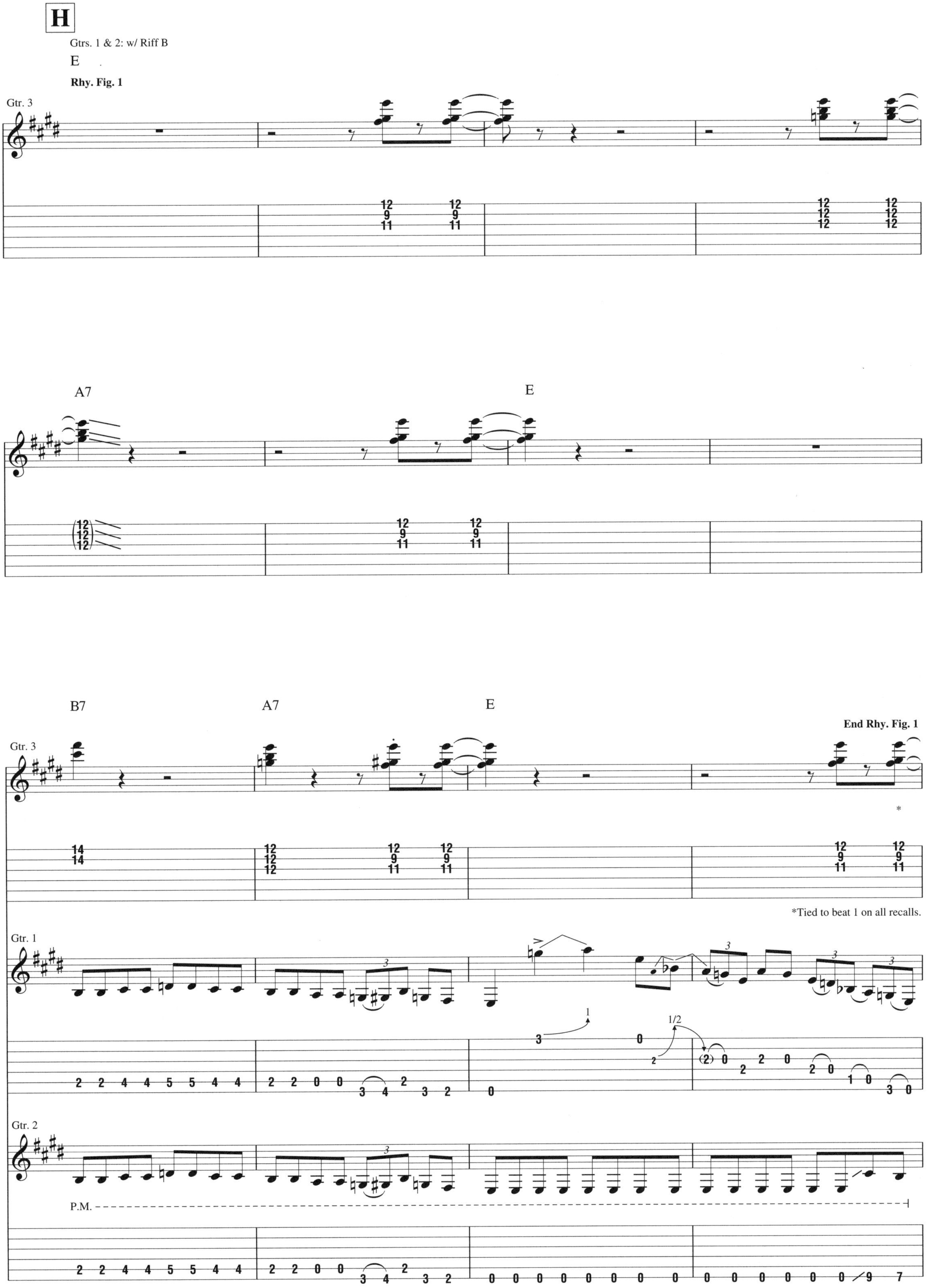

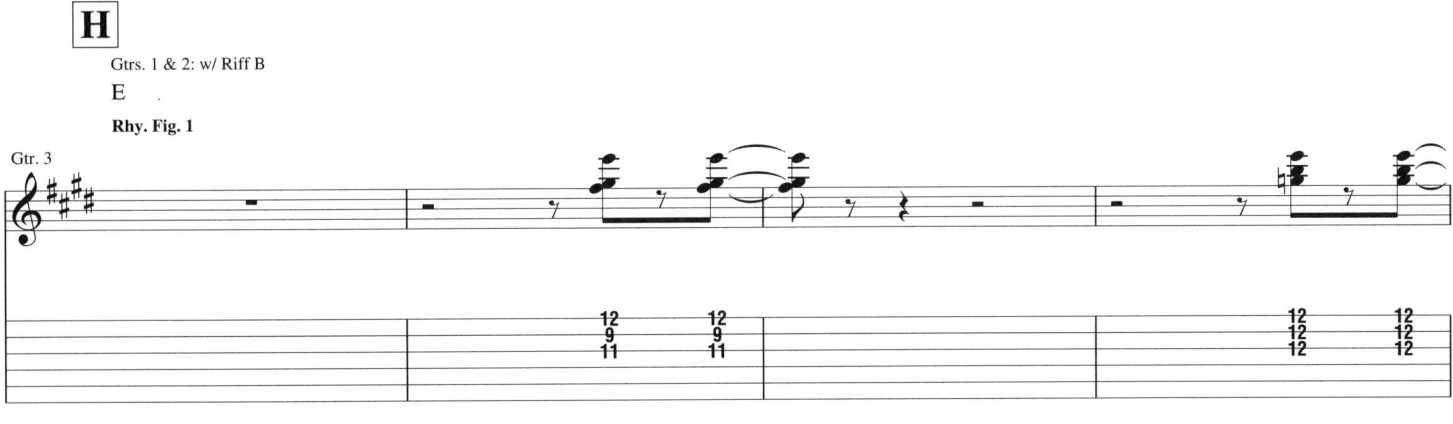

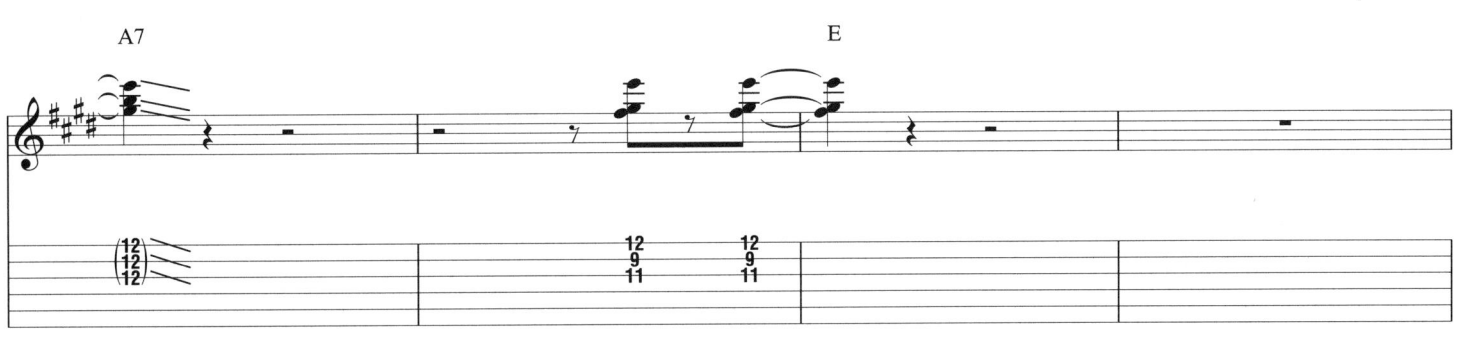

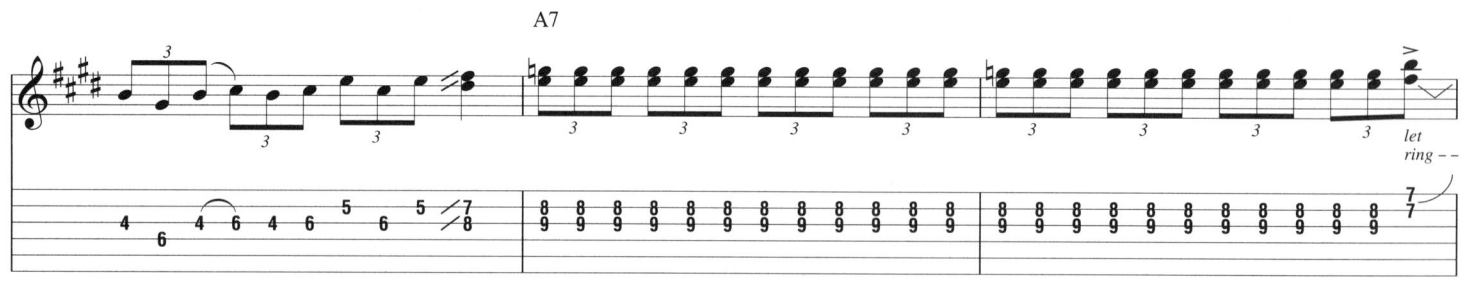
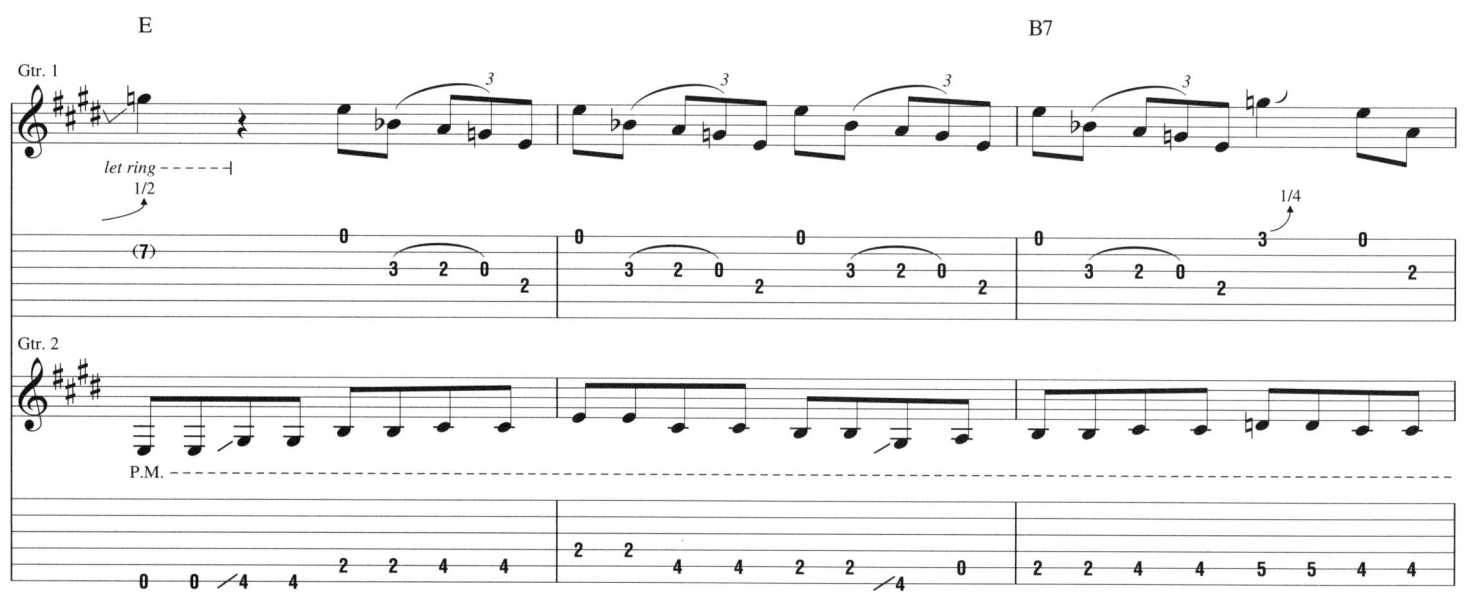
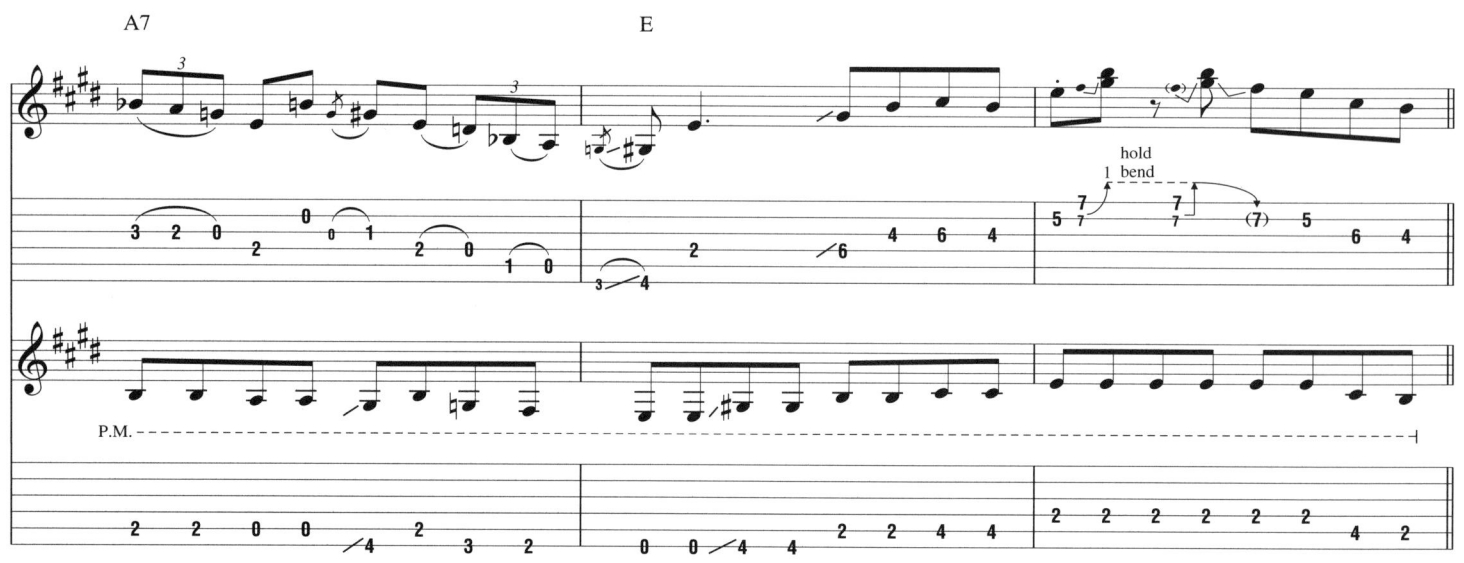

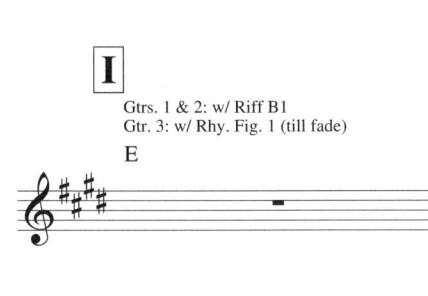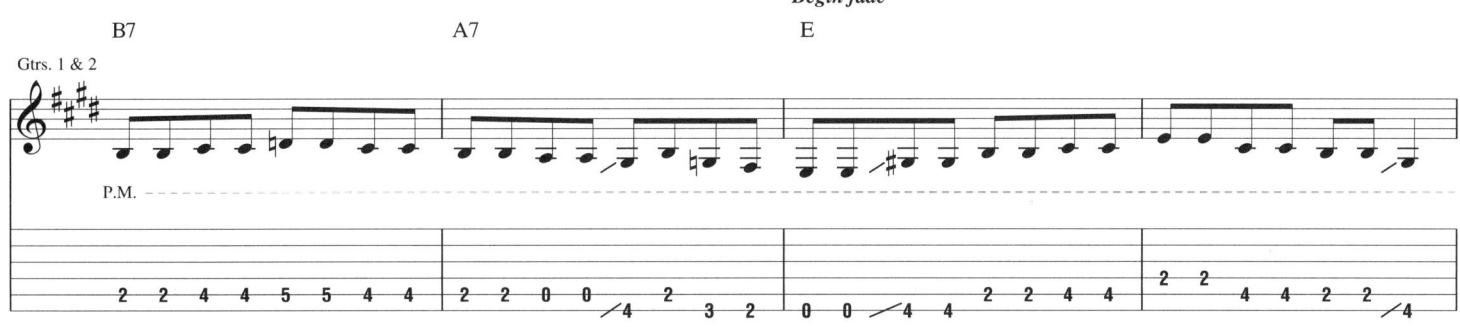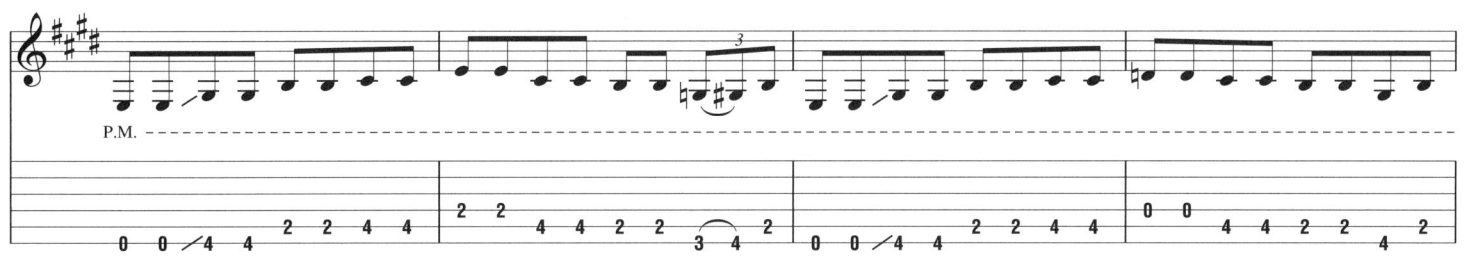

from *Dare to Be Different*
Hearts Grow Fonder
By Tommy Emmanuel

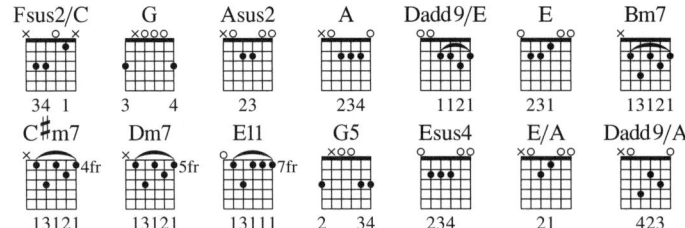

A

Moderately slow ♩ = 83

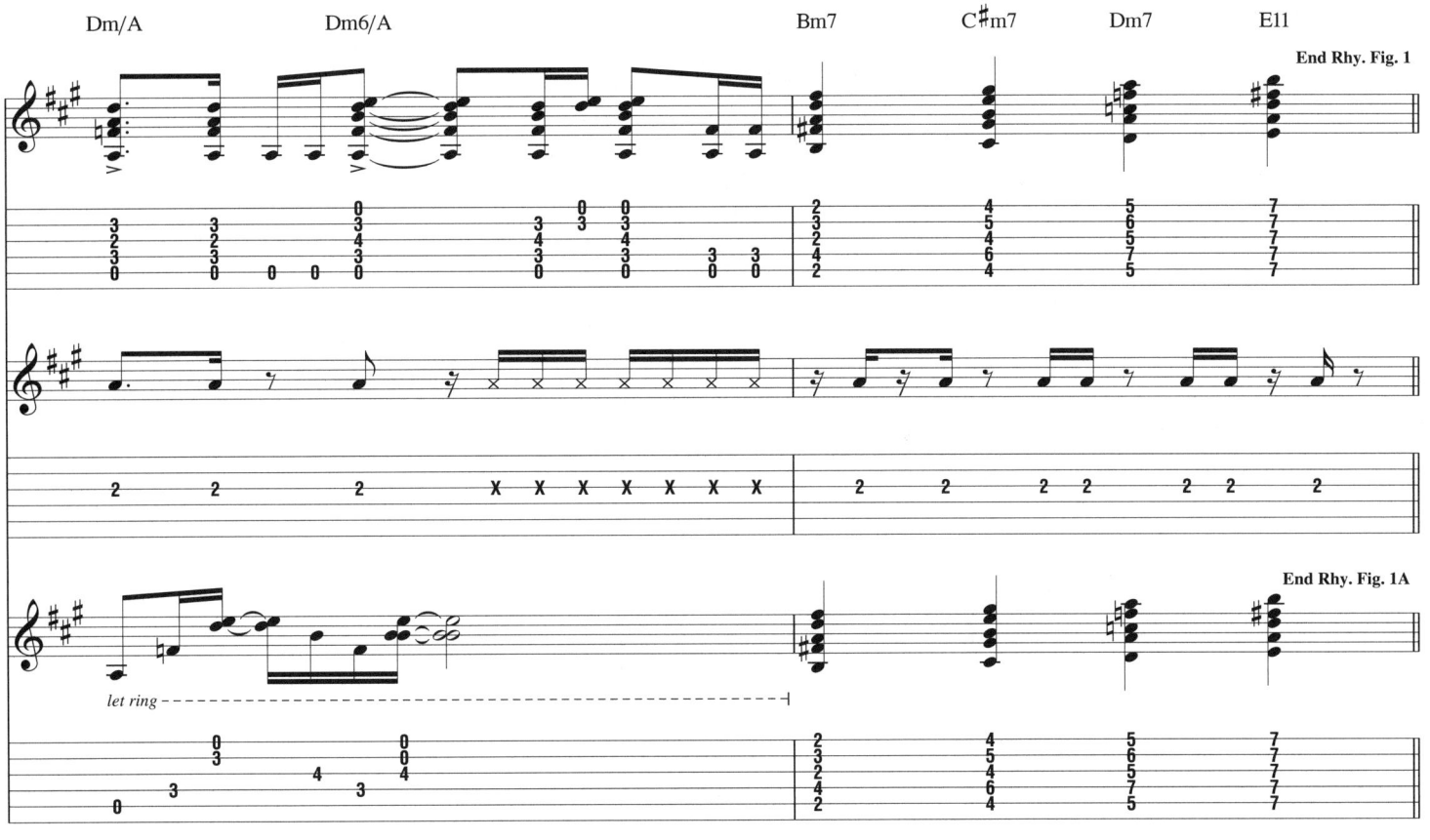
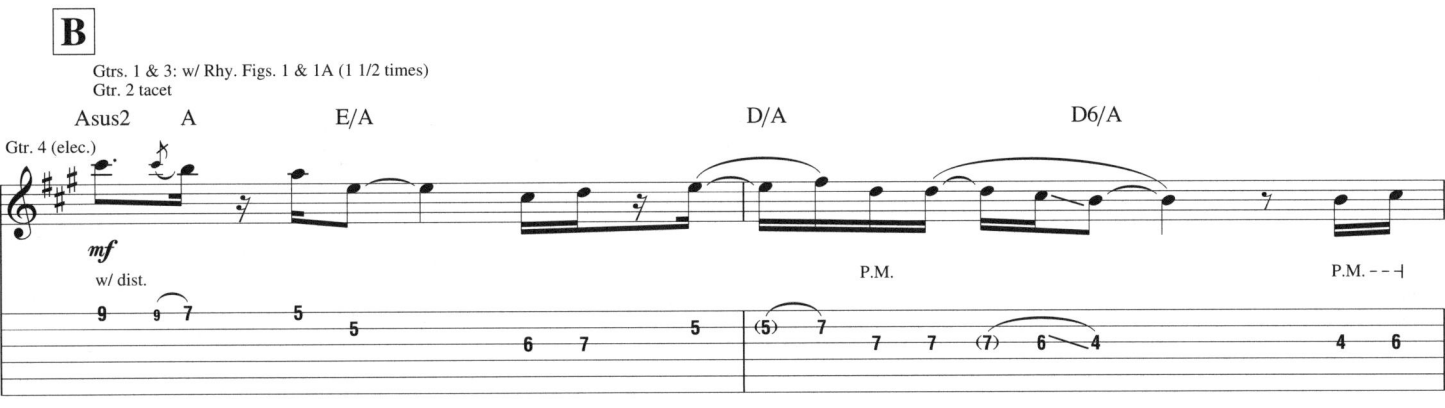
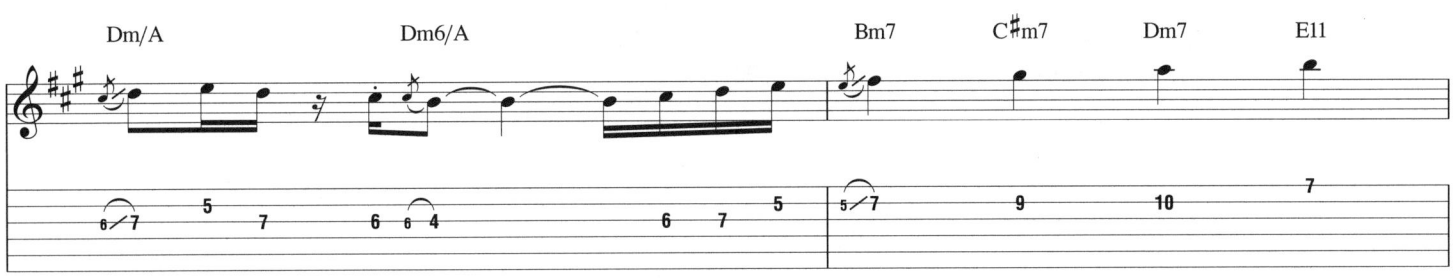
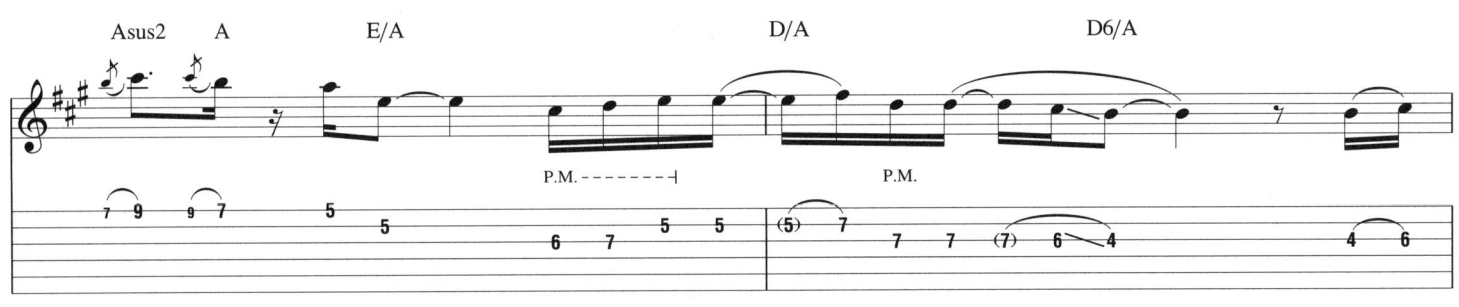

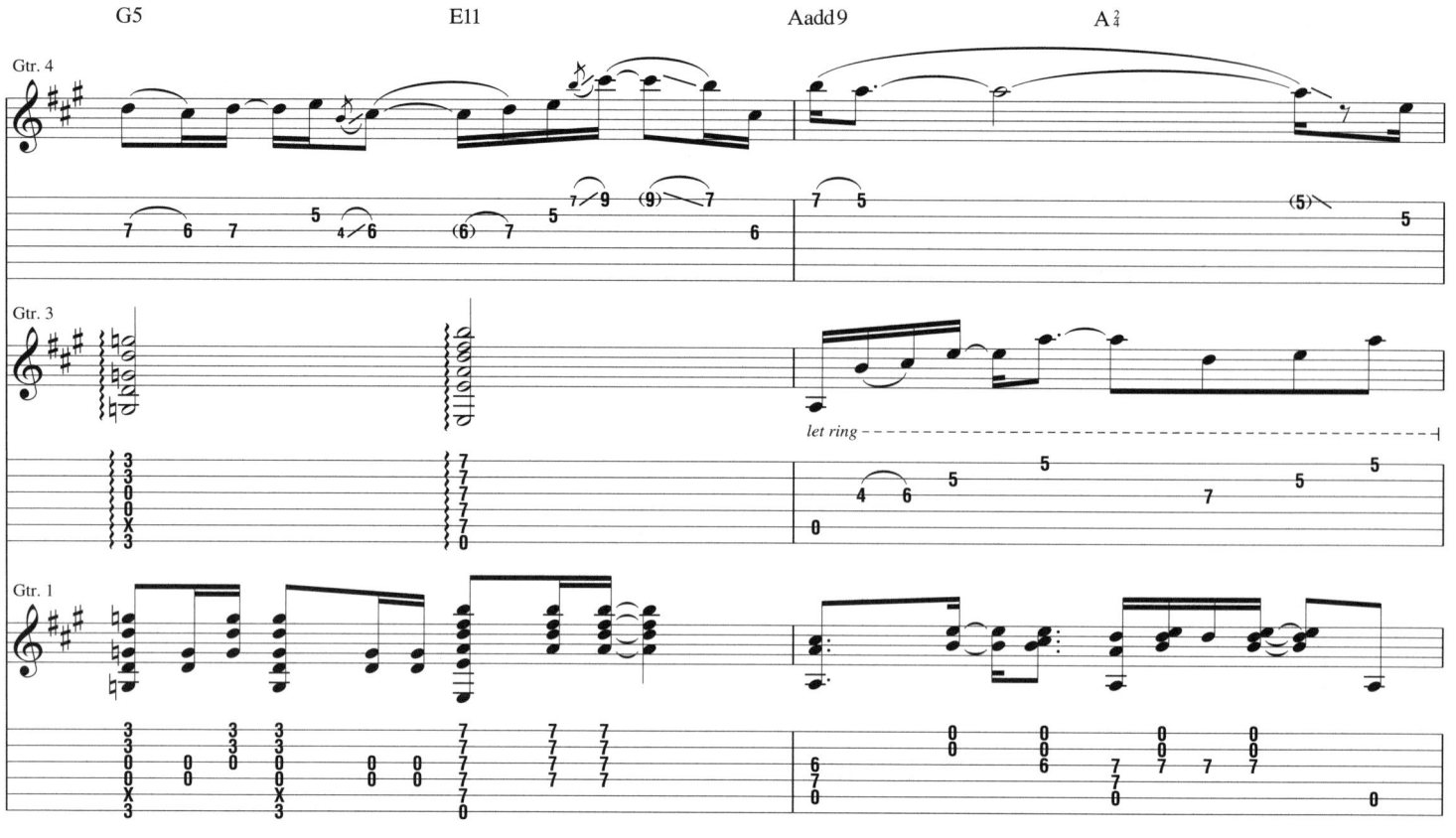
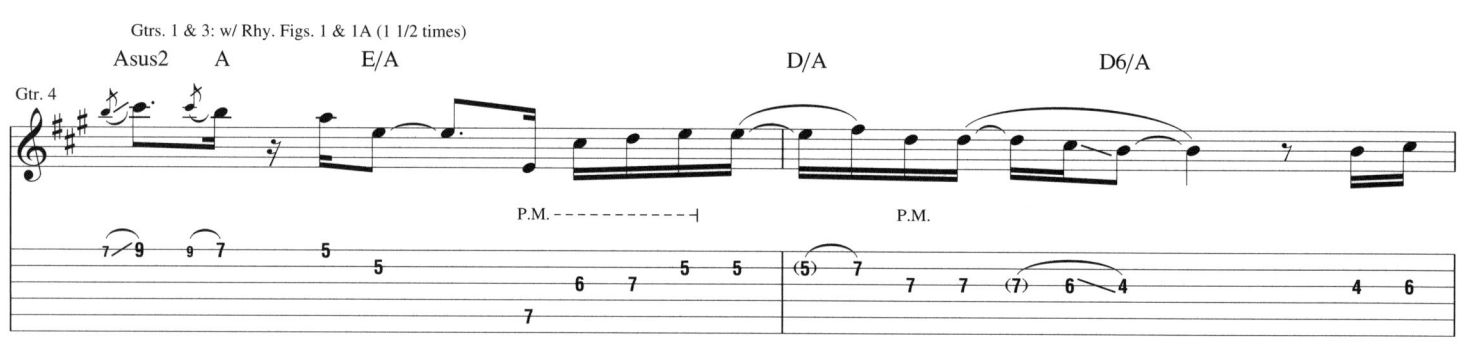
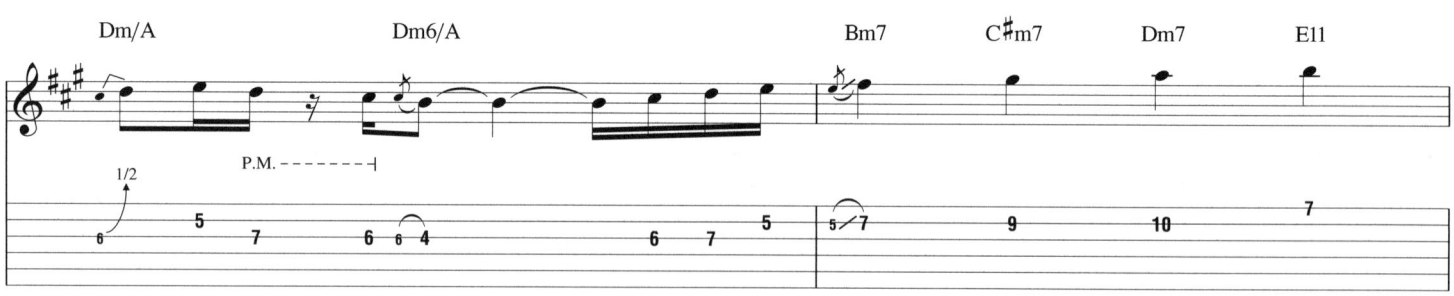
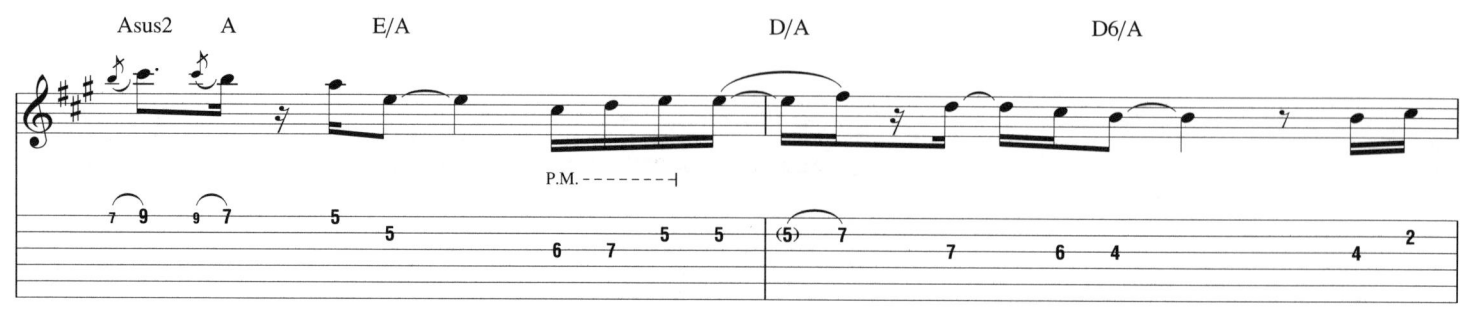

G5
E11
Aadd9
Gtr. 4
Gtr. 3
P.M.
Rhy. Fig. 2
End Rhy. Fig. 2
Gtr. 1
(cont. in slashes)
Gtr. 5 (elec.)
mf
w/ slight dist.
C
Gtr. 3 tacet
2nd time, Gtr. 6 tacet
Fsus2/C
G
Gtr. 1
Gtr. 4
simile on repeat
P.M.
Gtr. 5

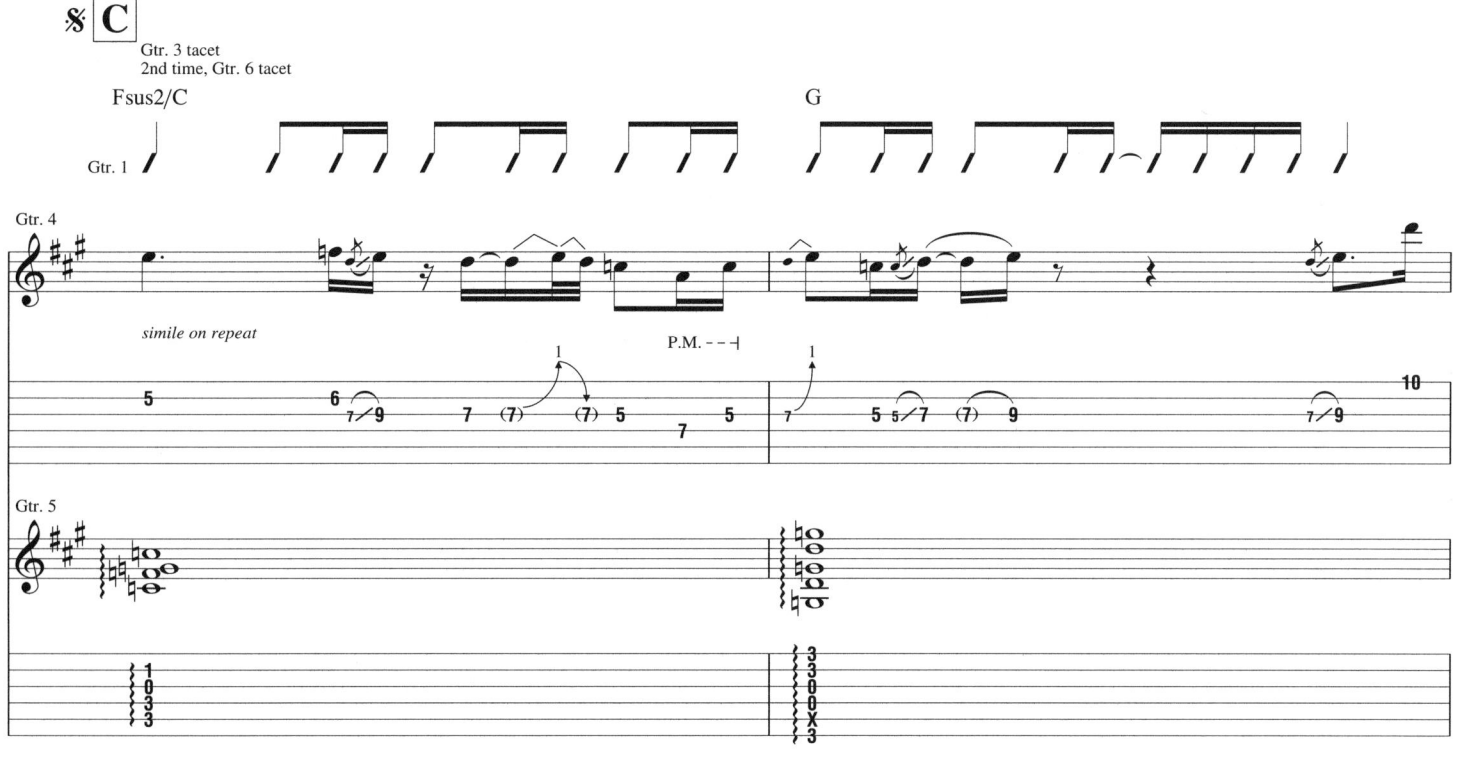

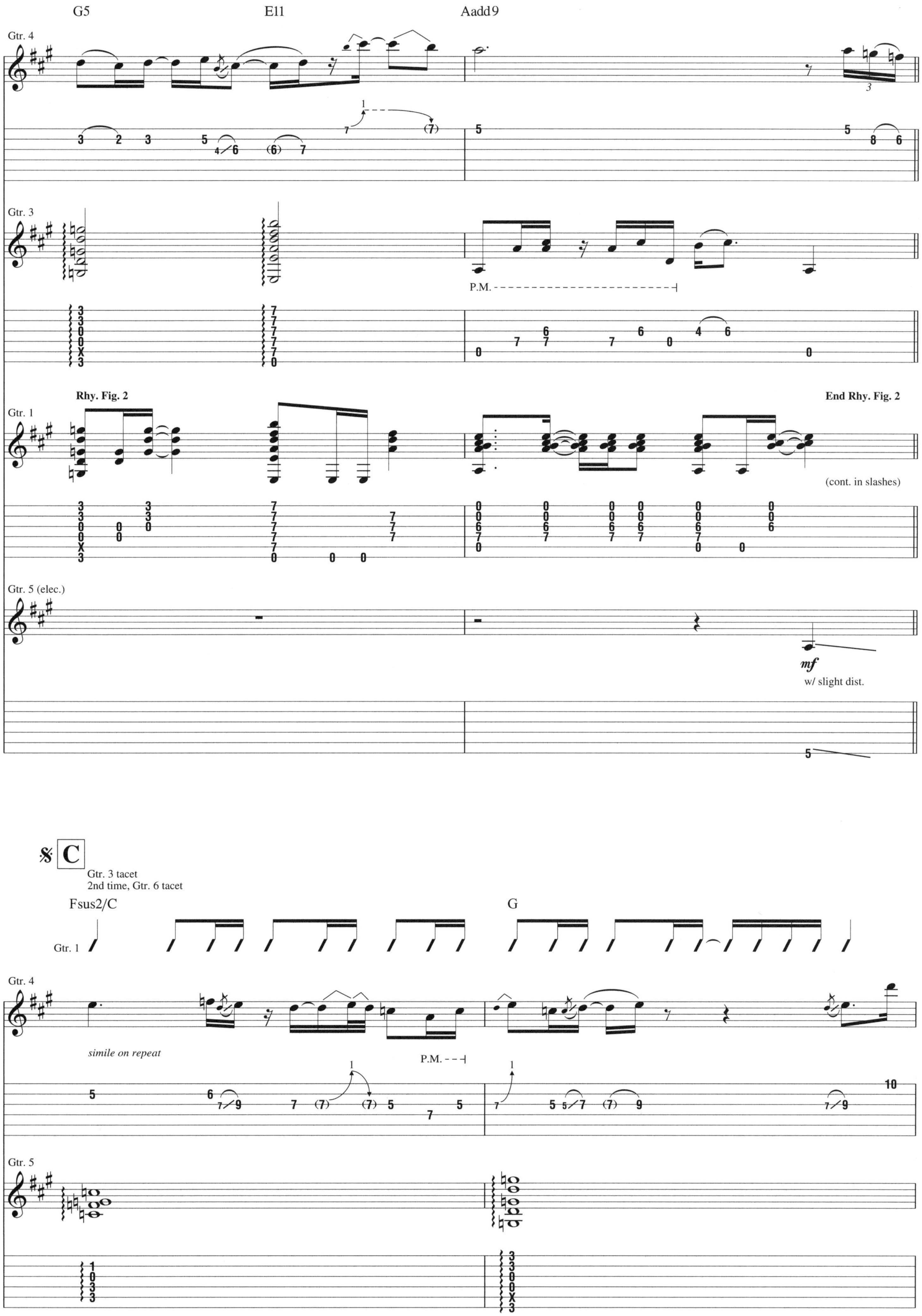

D

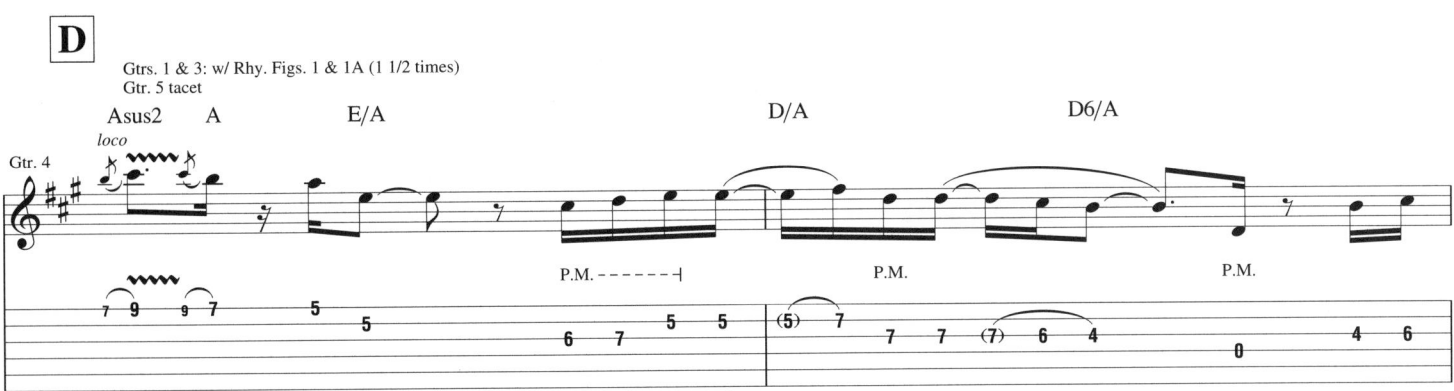

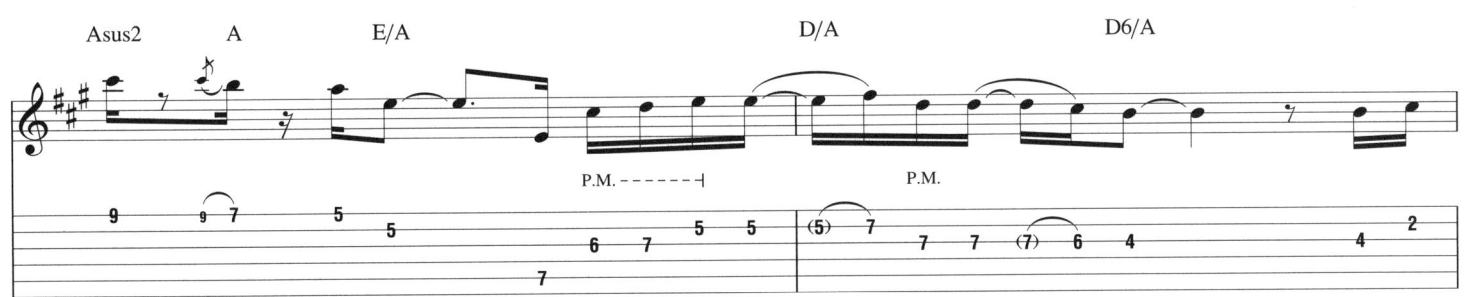
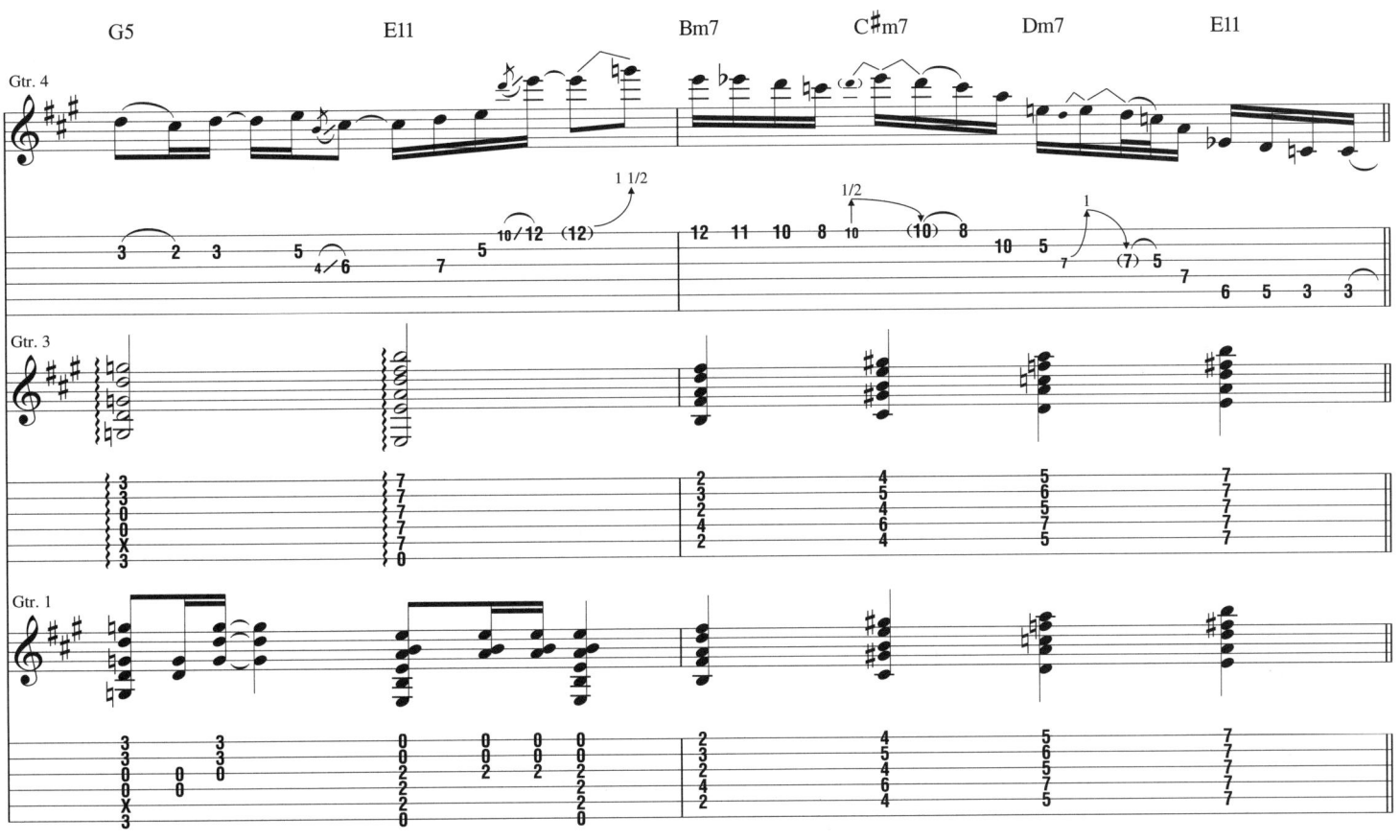

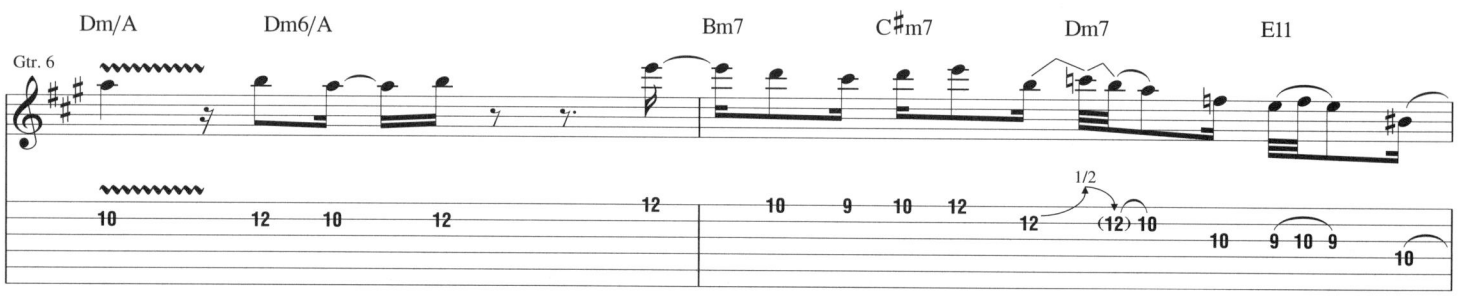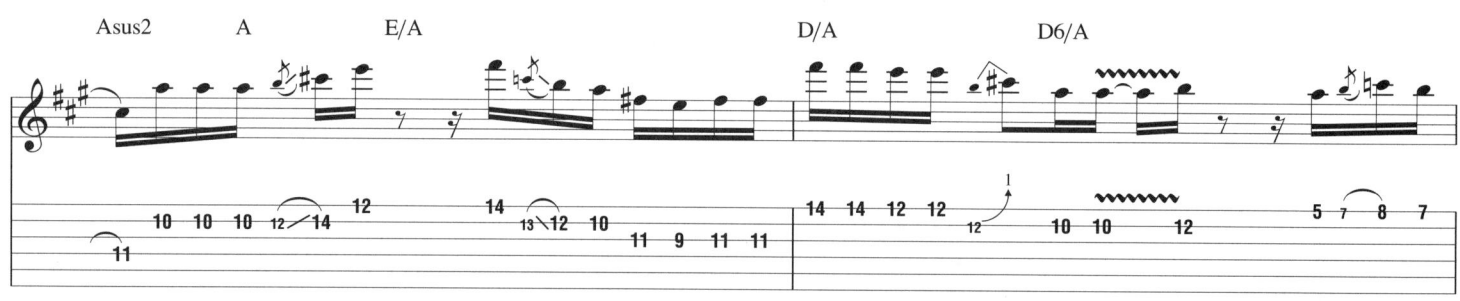

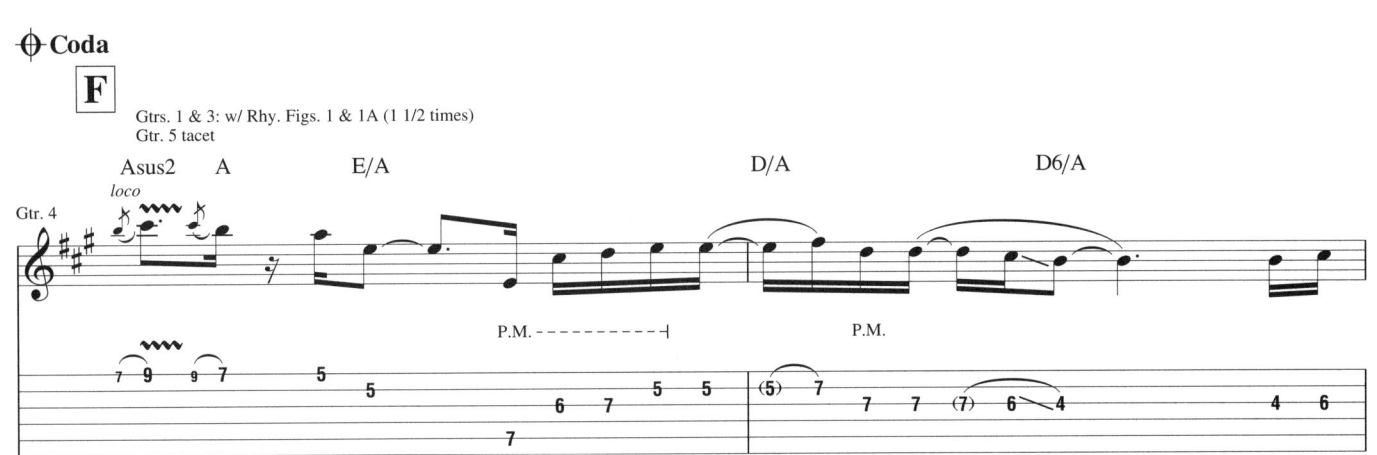
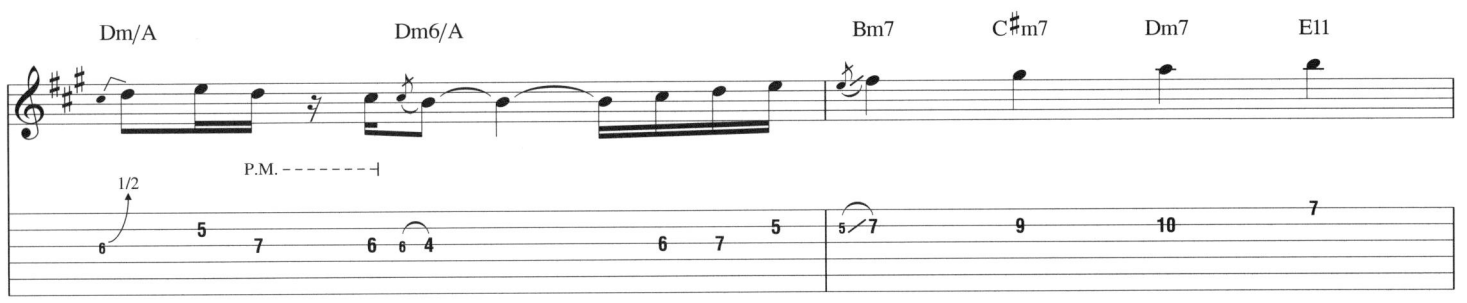
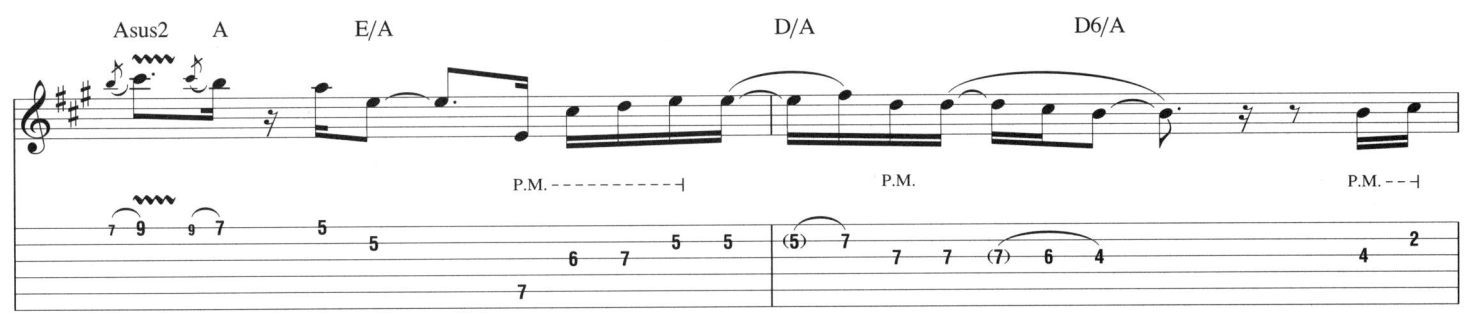
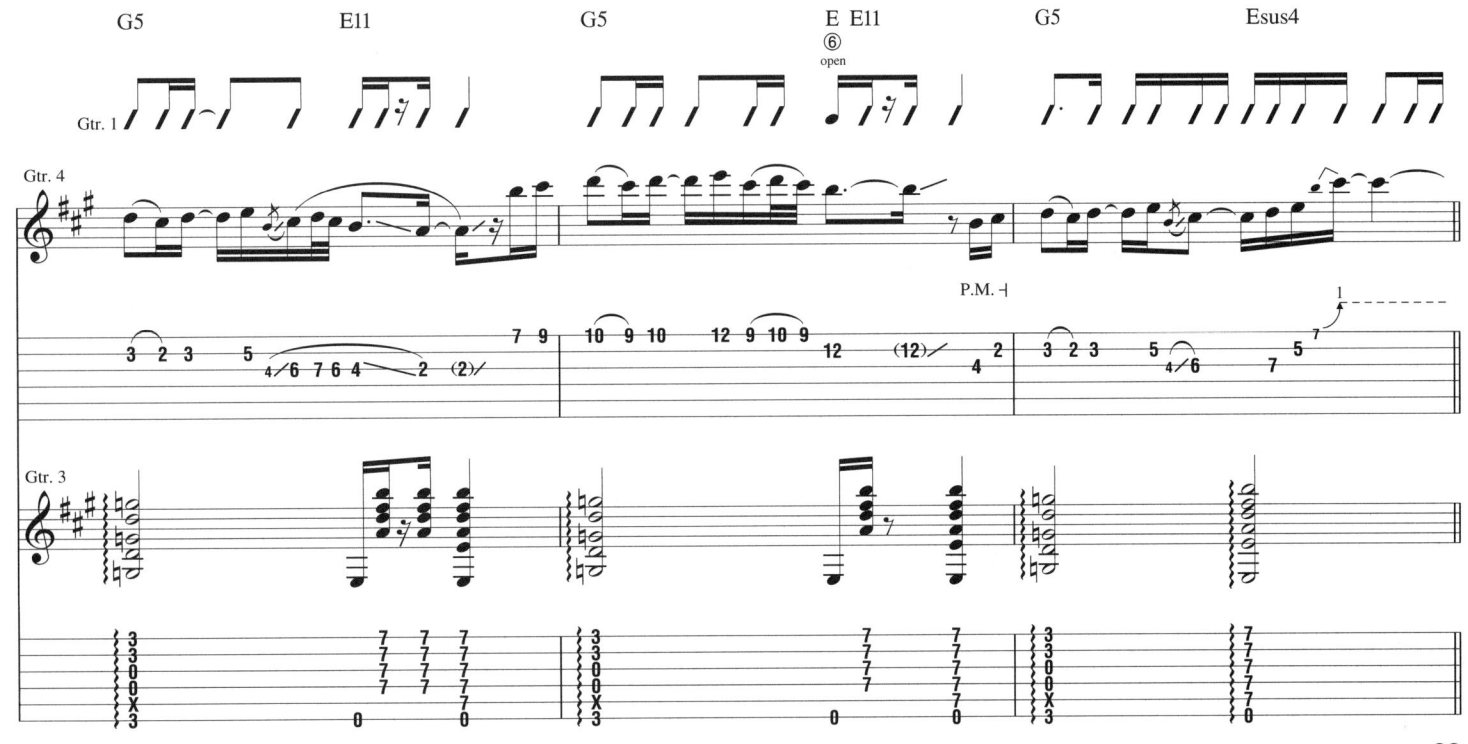

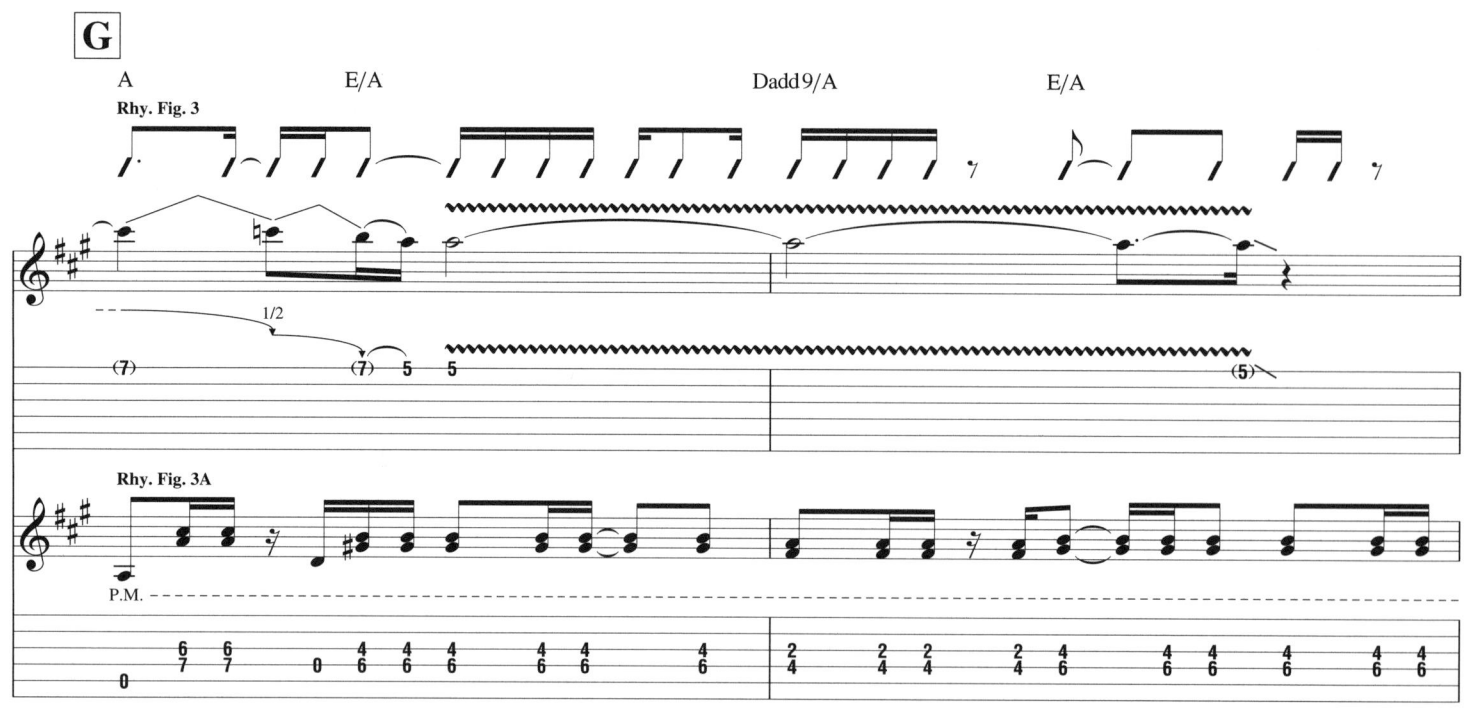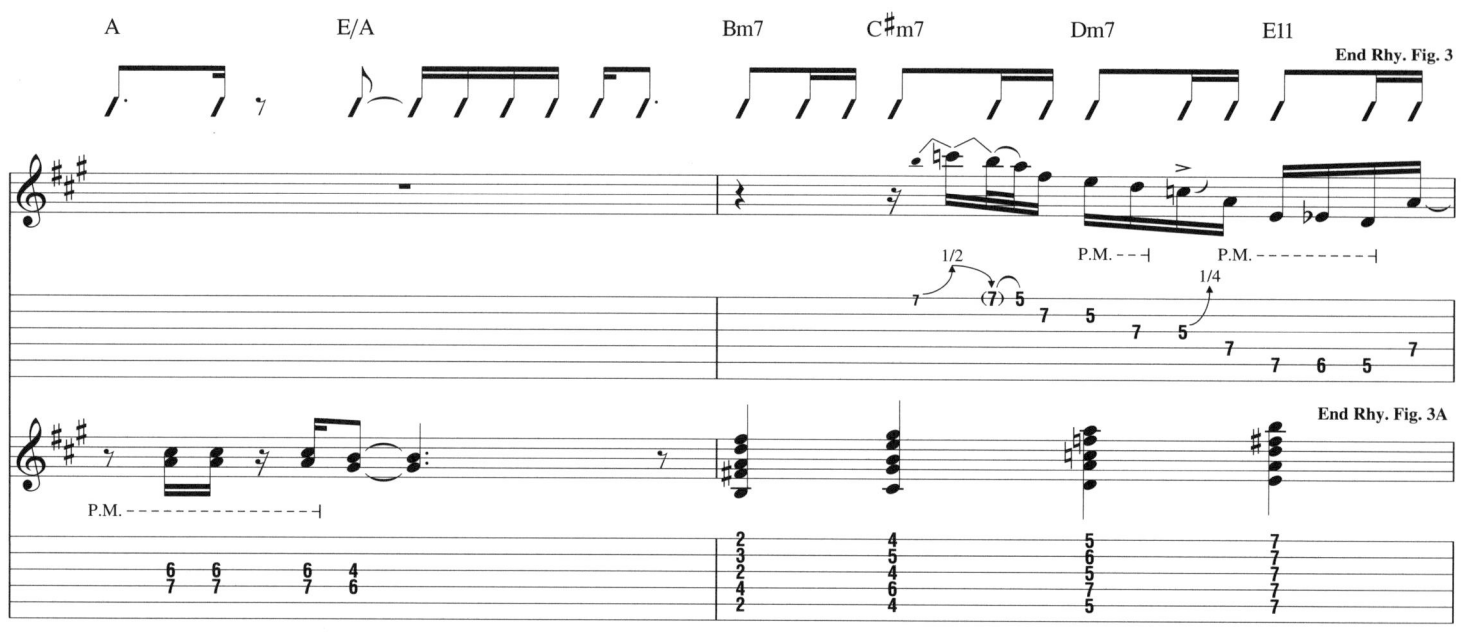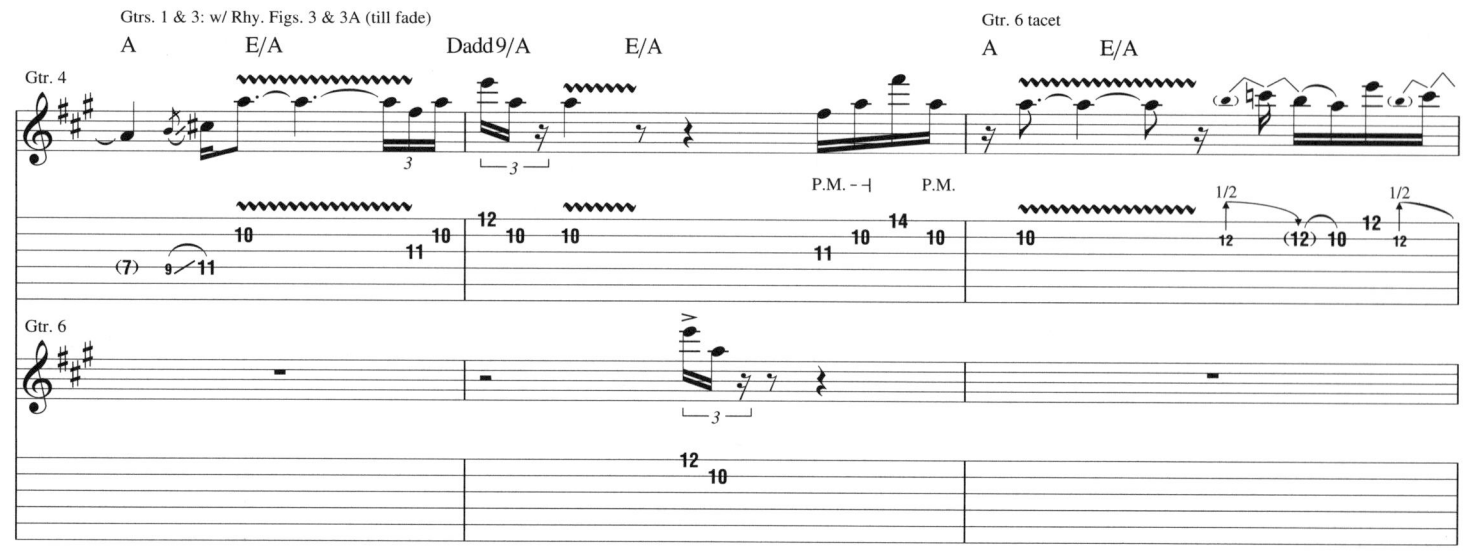

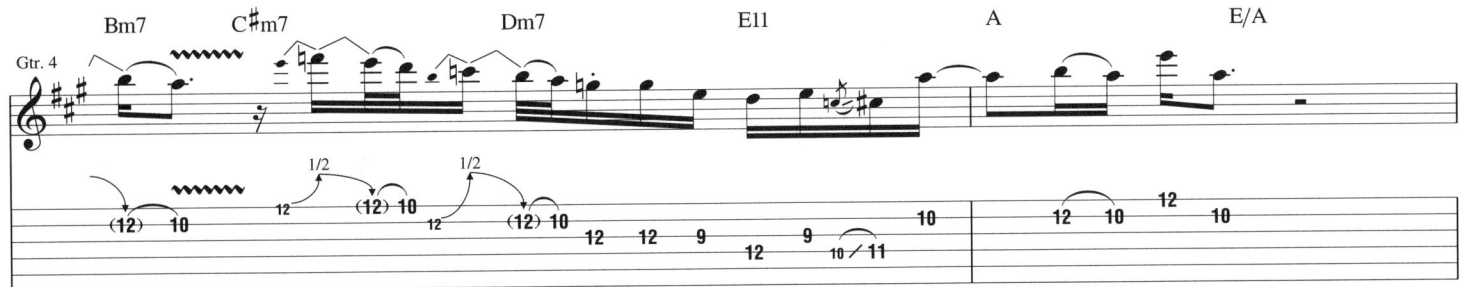

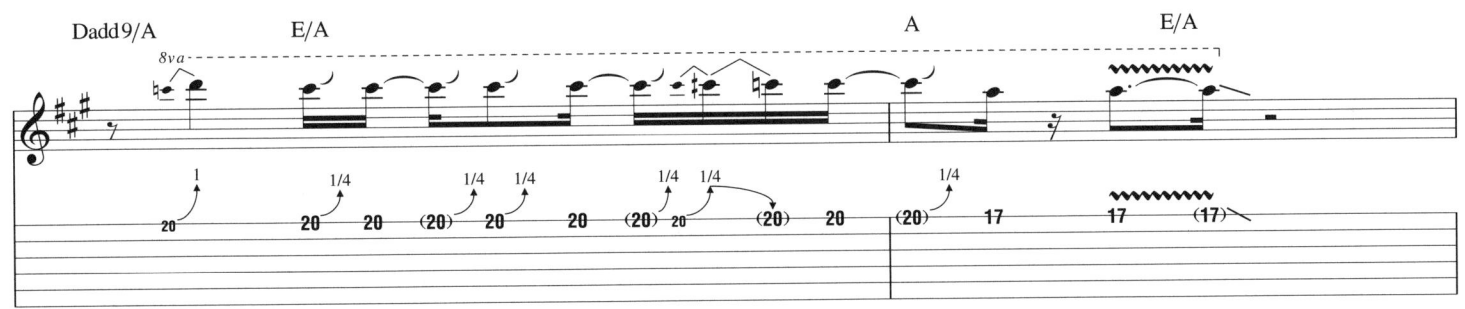
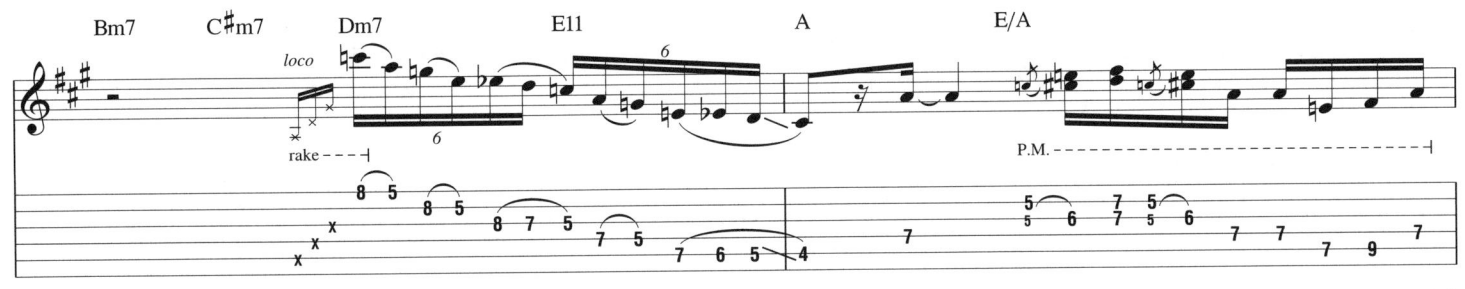

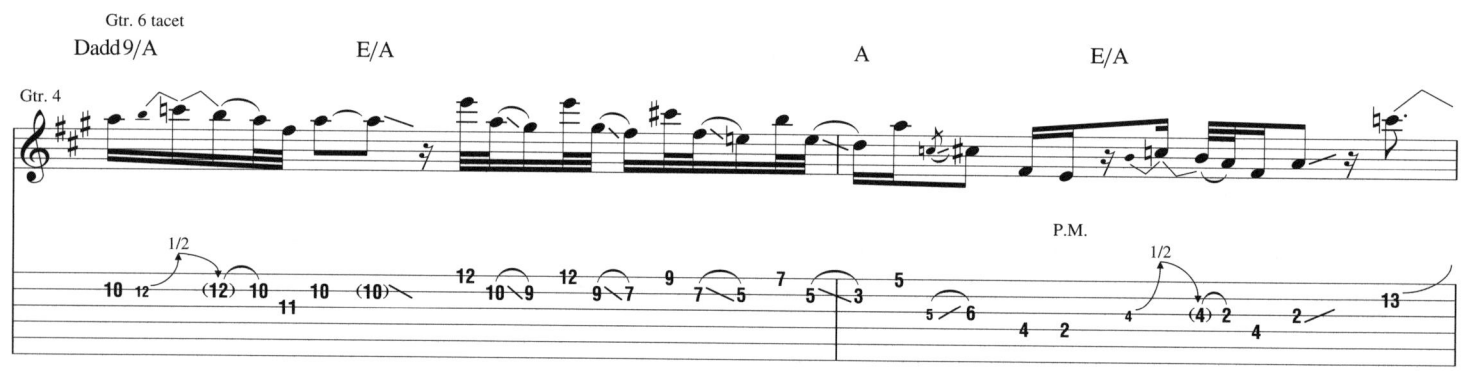
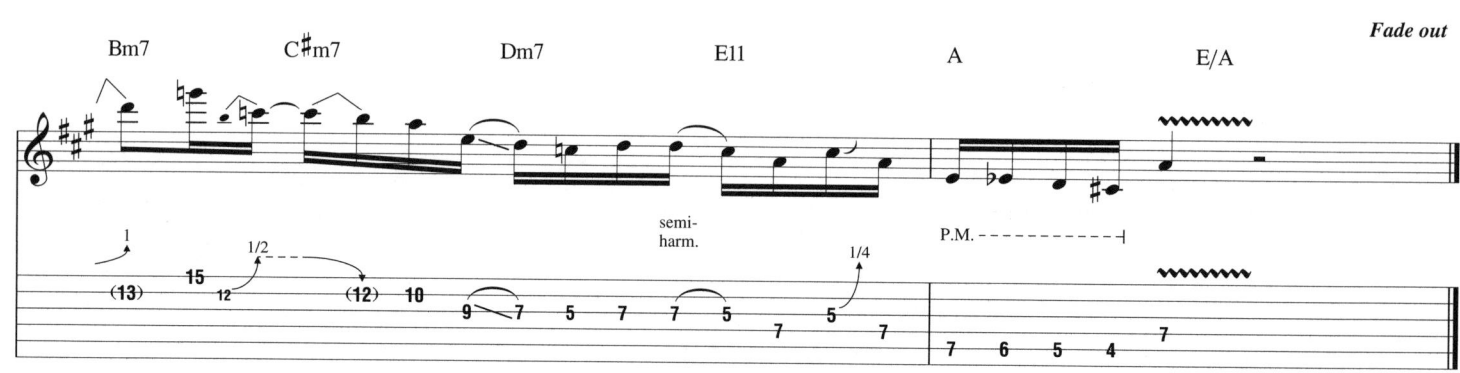

The Hunt
from *Classical Gas*
By Tommy Emmanuel

Gtr. 1: Drop D tuning:
(low to high) D-A-D-G-B-E

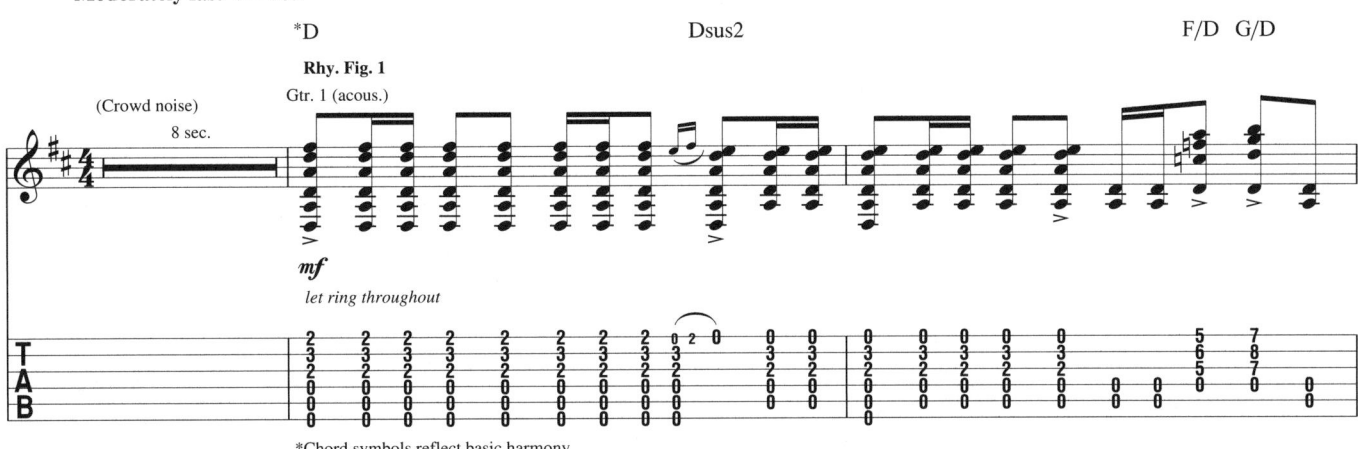

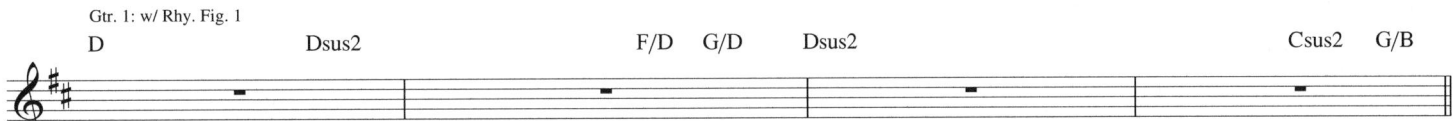

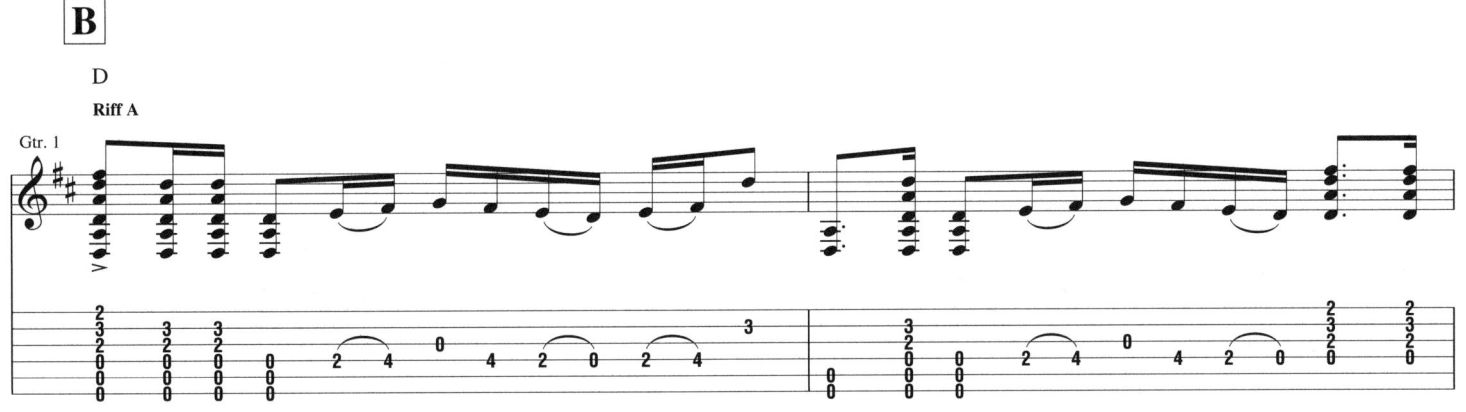

Copyright © 2002 UNIVERSAL MUSIC PUBLISHING PTY. LTD., Tommy Emmanuel Music and CHRIS GILBEY PTY. LTD.
All Rights in the United States and Canada Controlled and Administered by UNIVERSAL - POLYGRAM INTERNATIONAL PUBLISHING, INC.
All Rights Reserved   Used by Permission

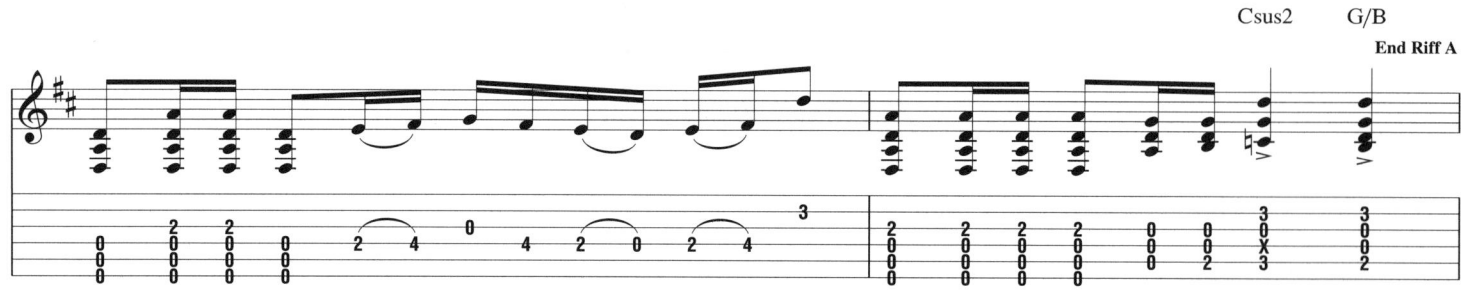
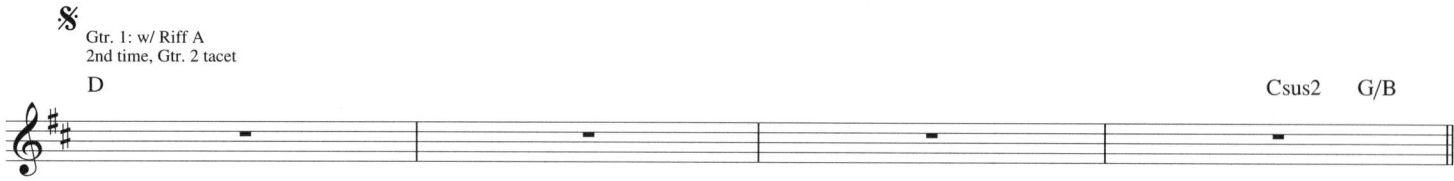
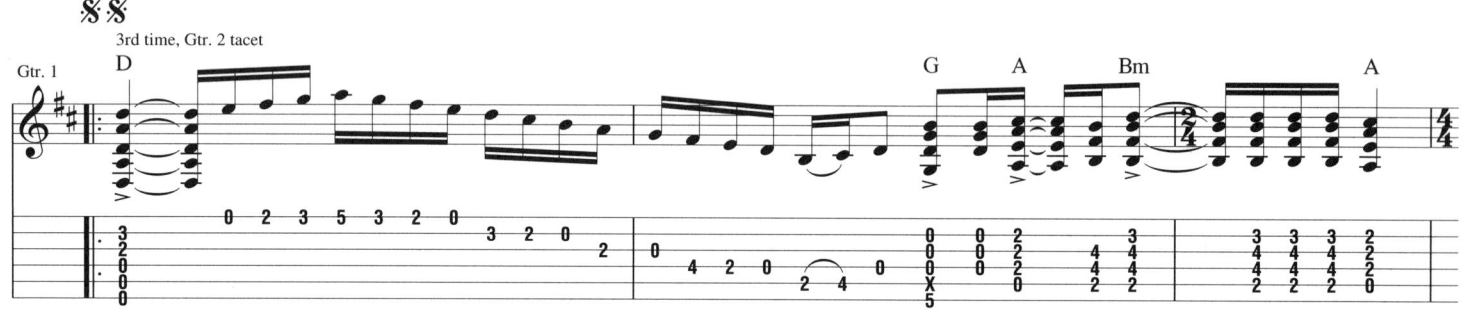

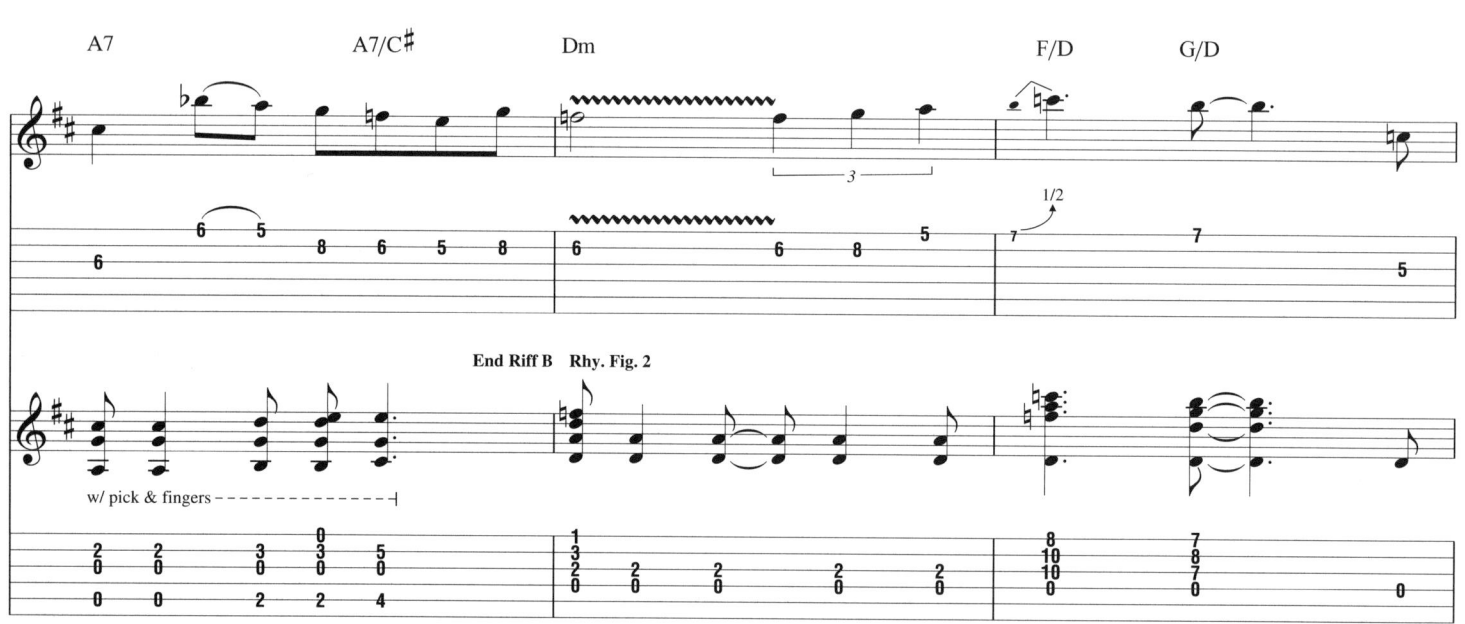
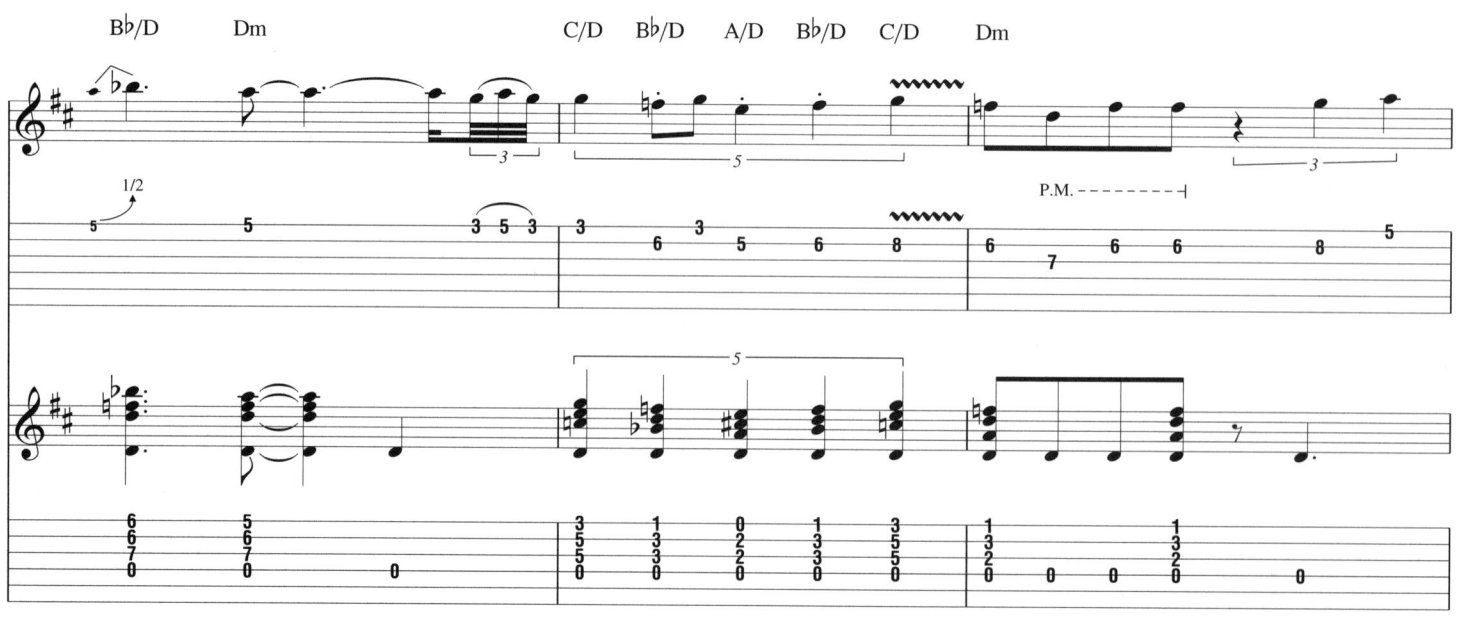

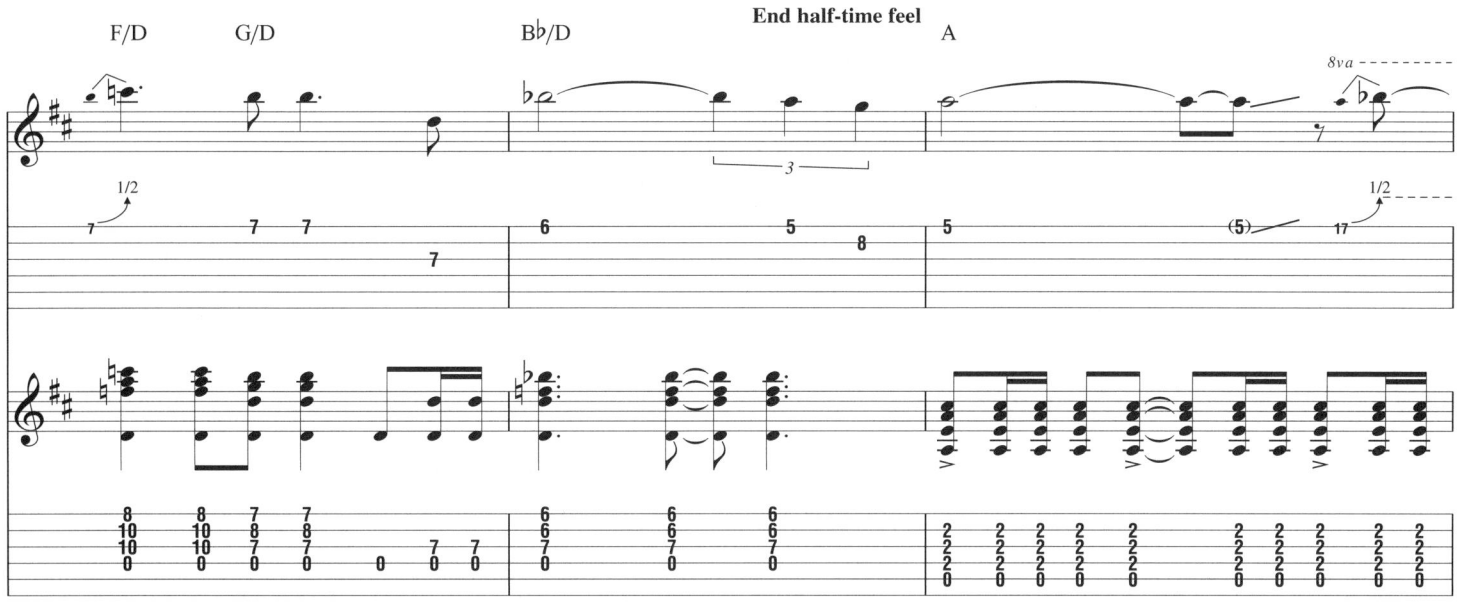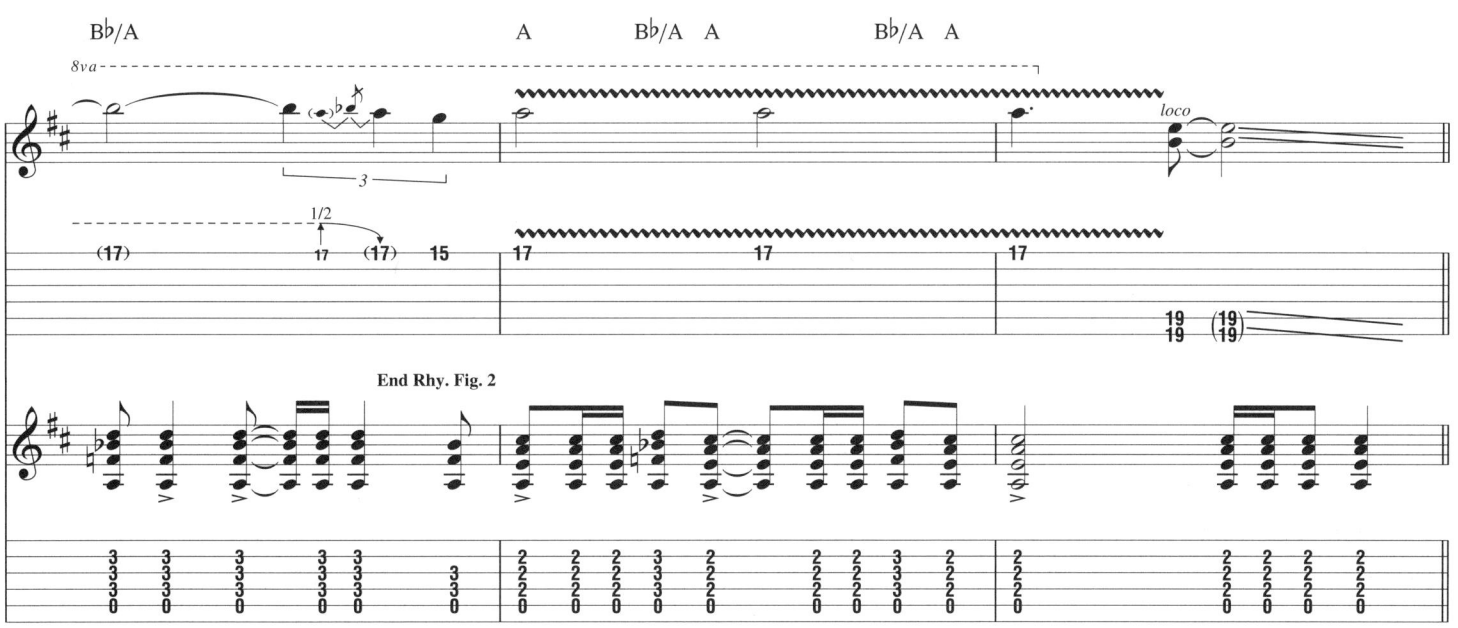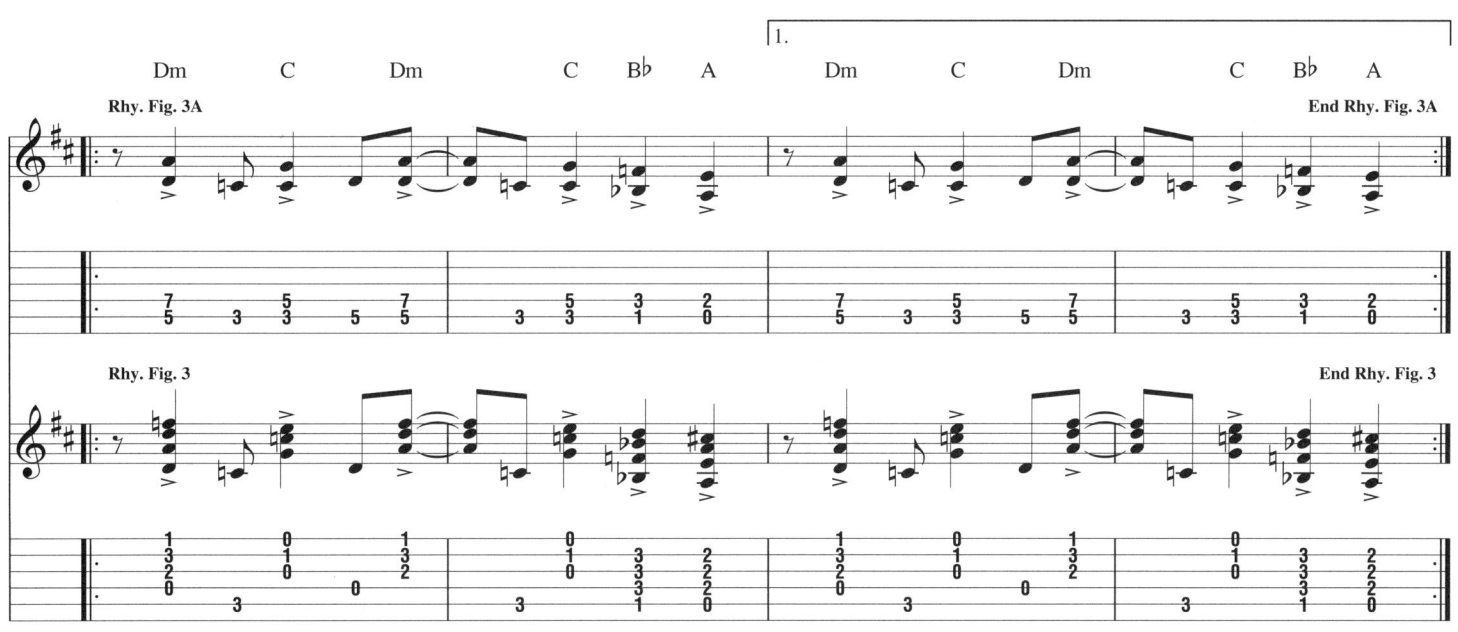

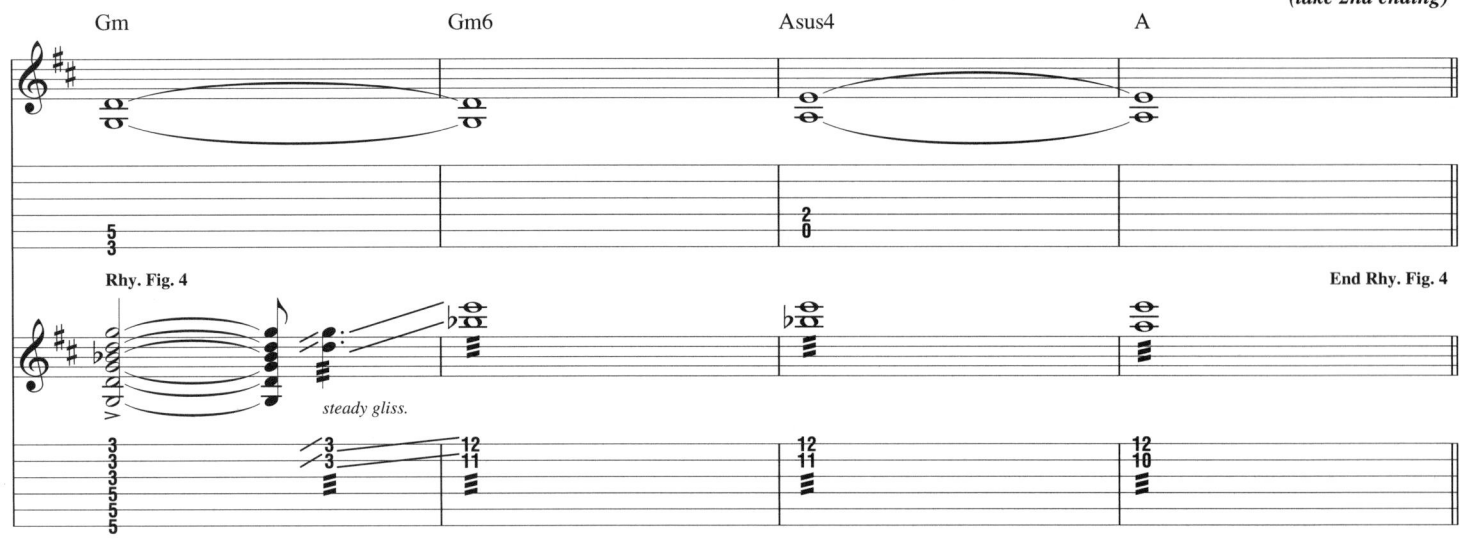

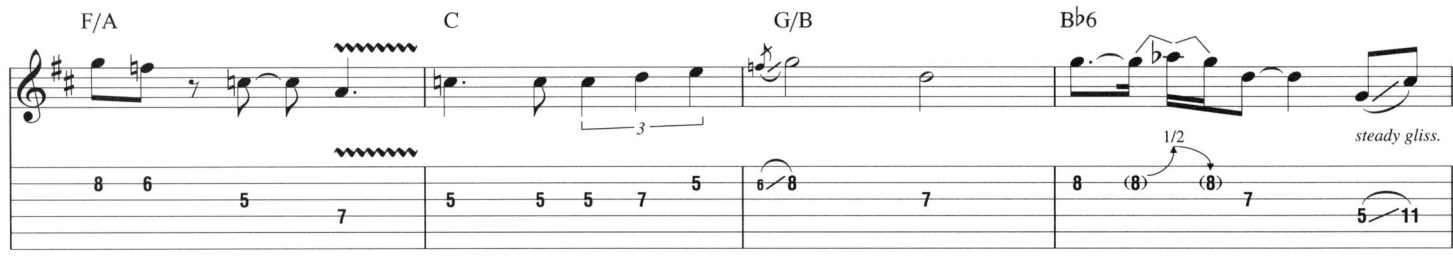
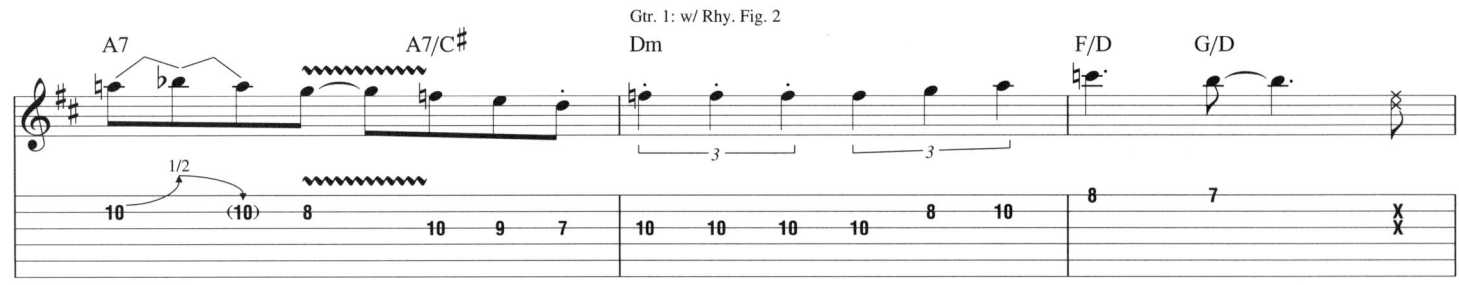
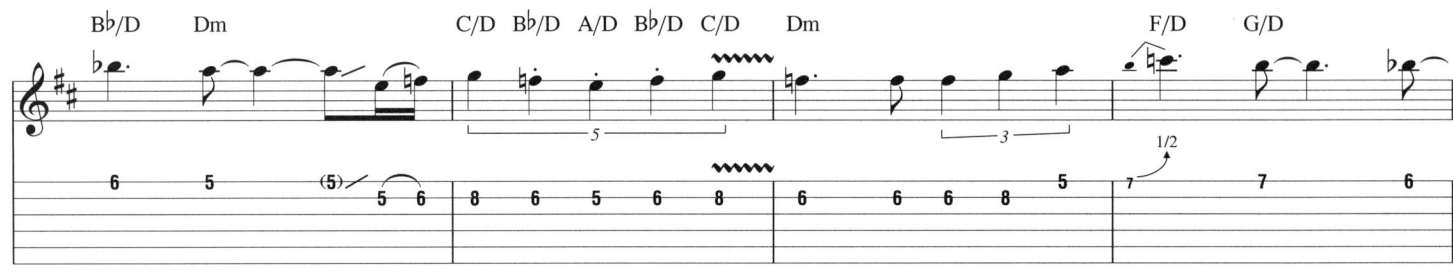

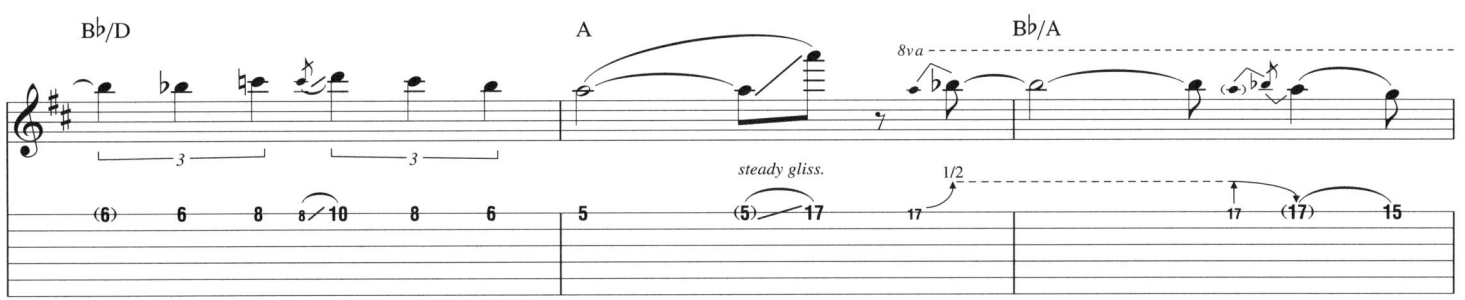
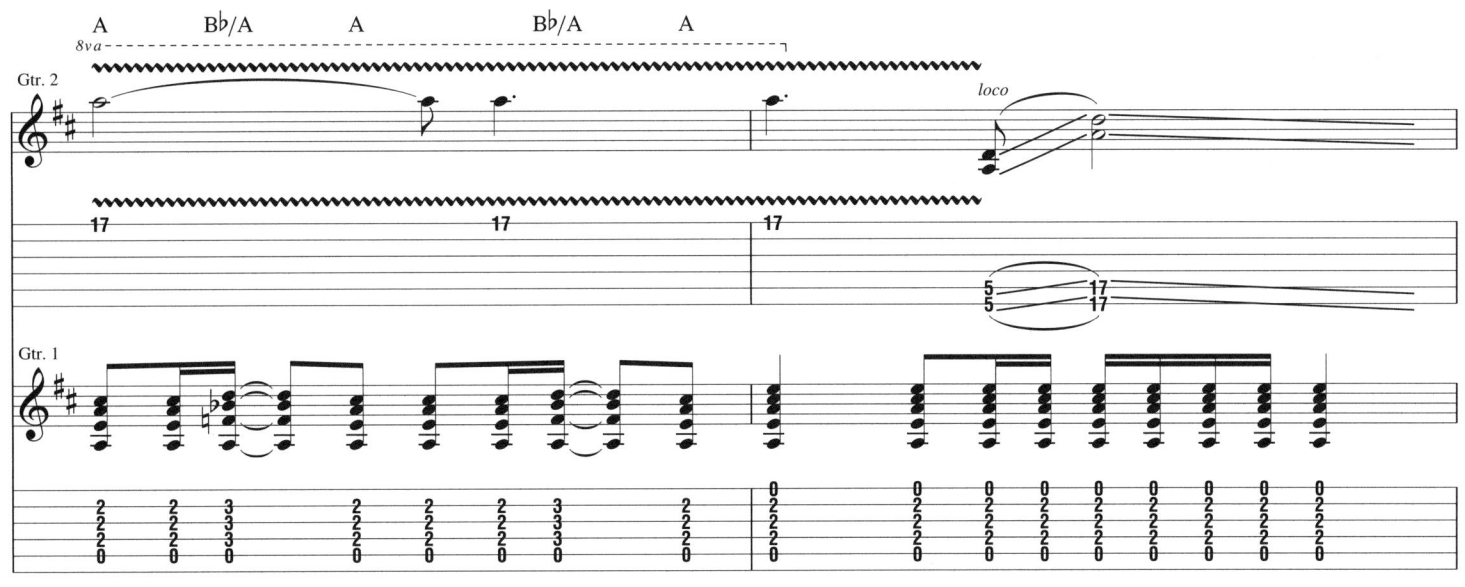
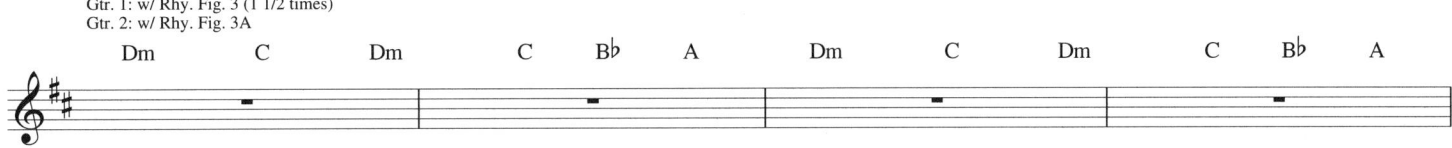

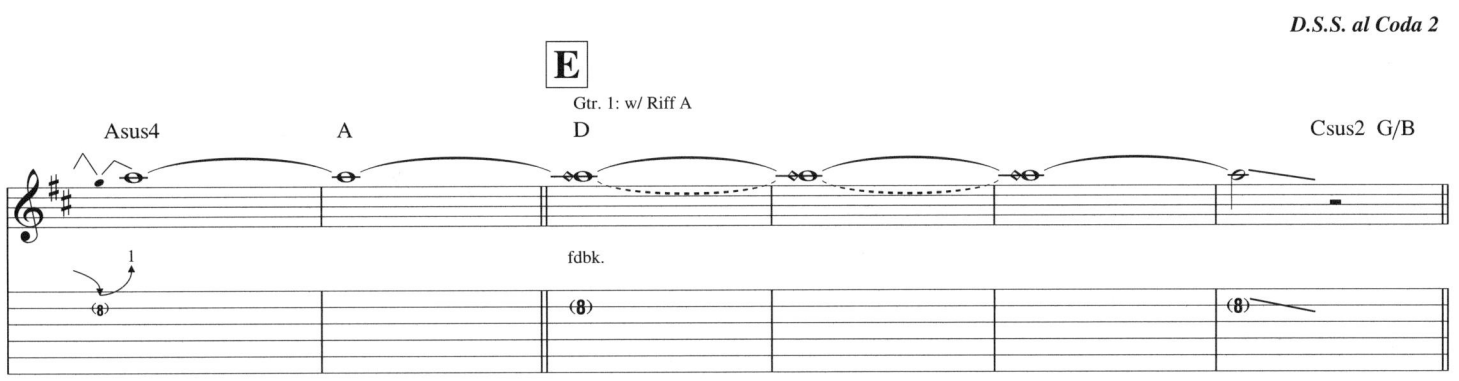

99

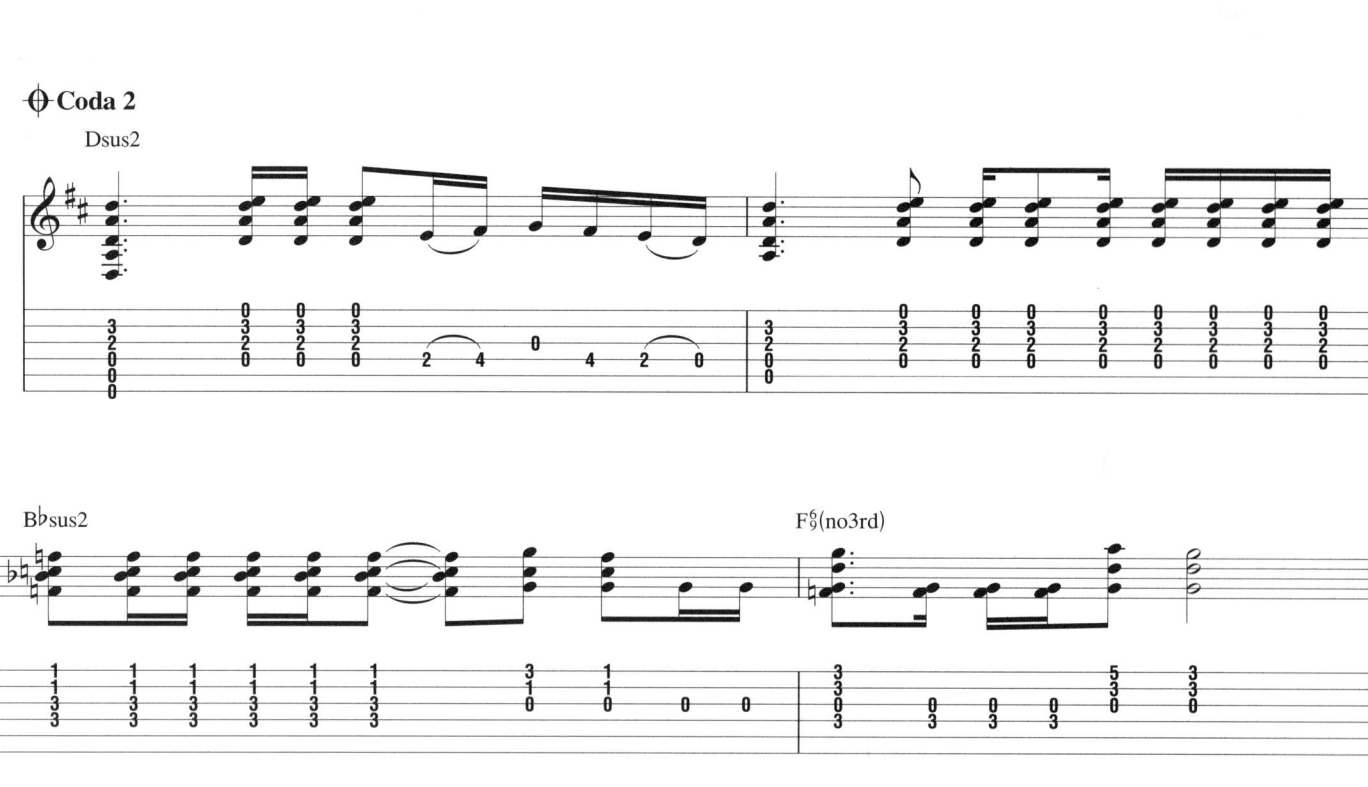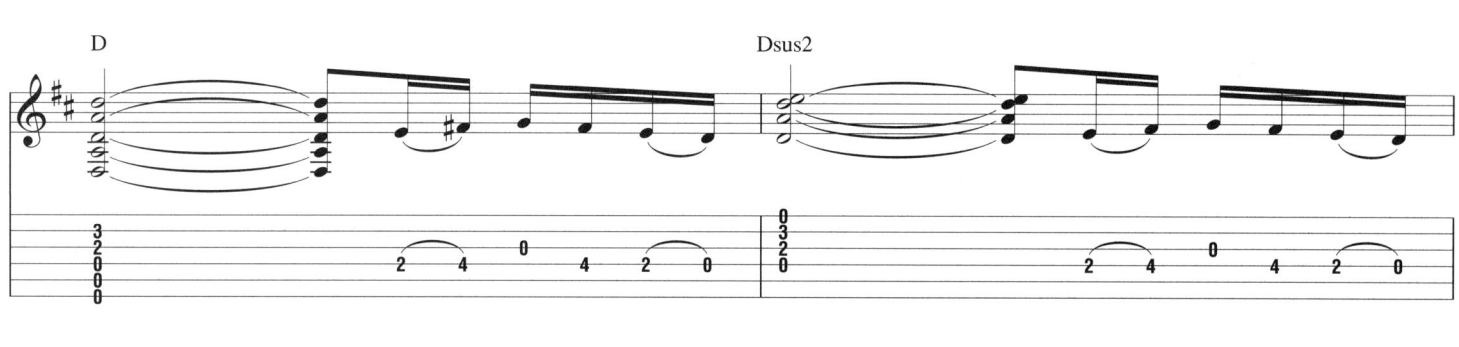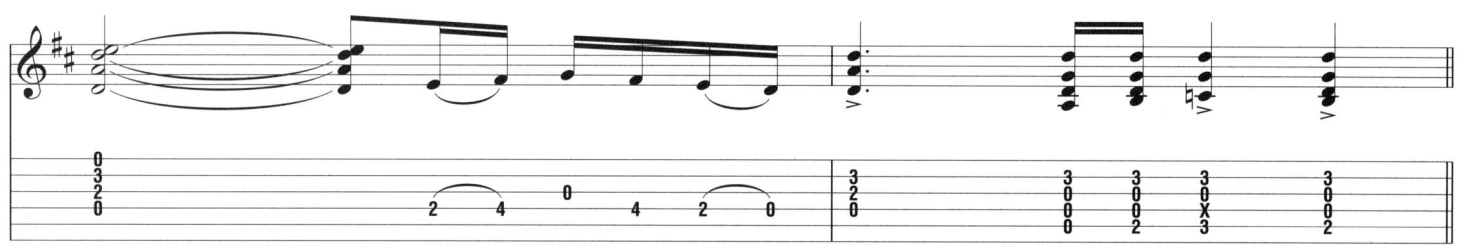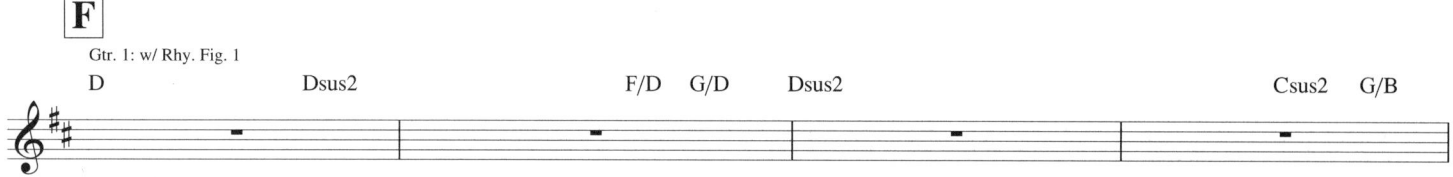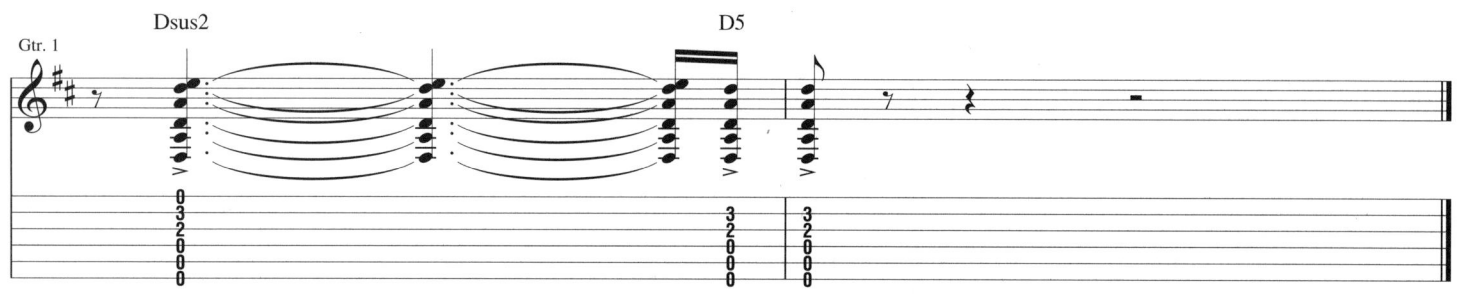

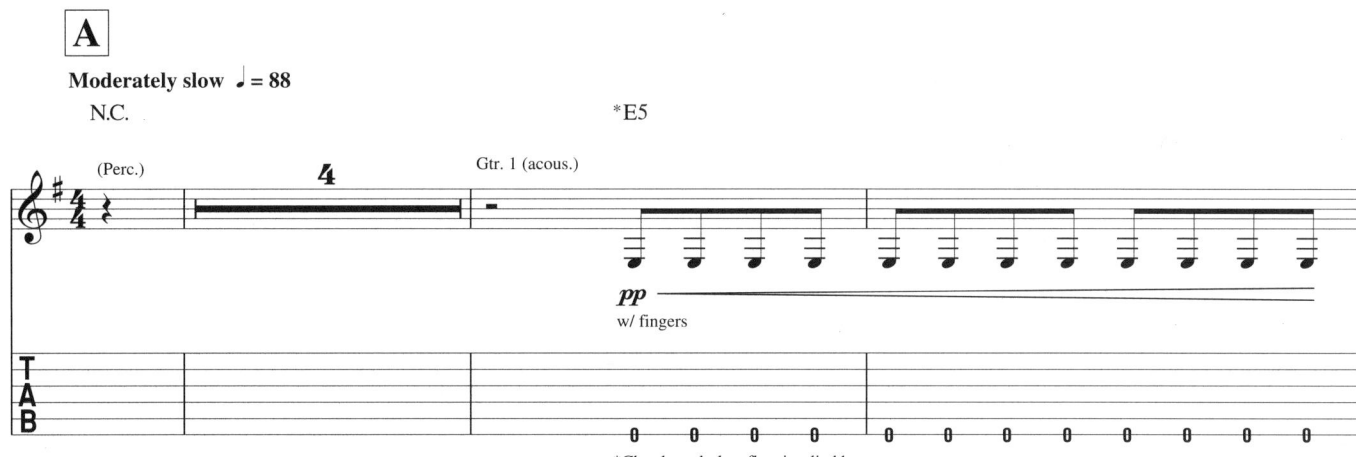
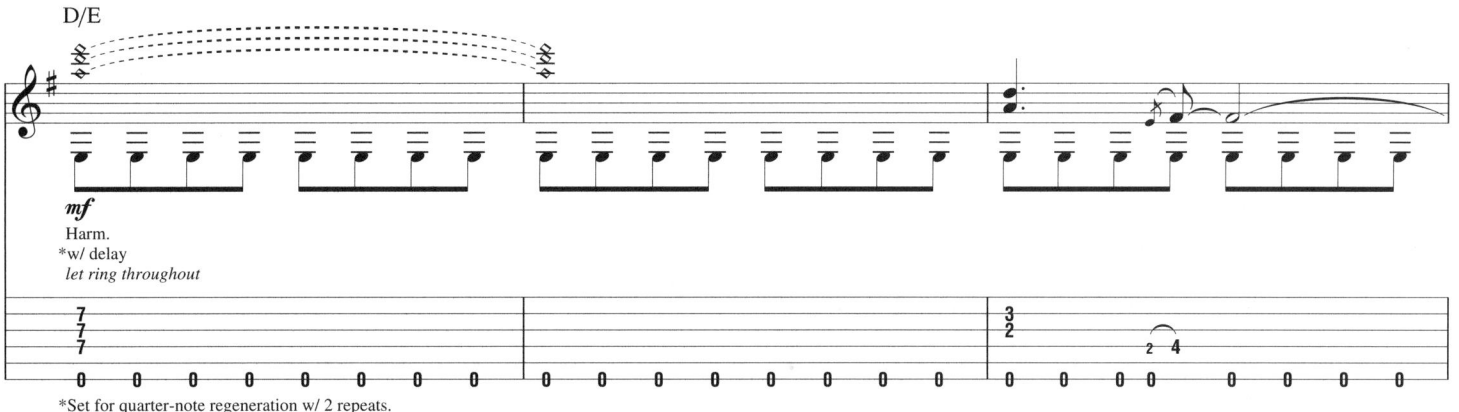
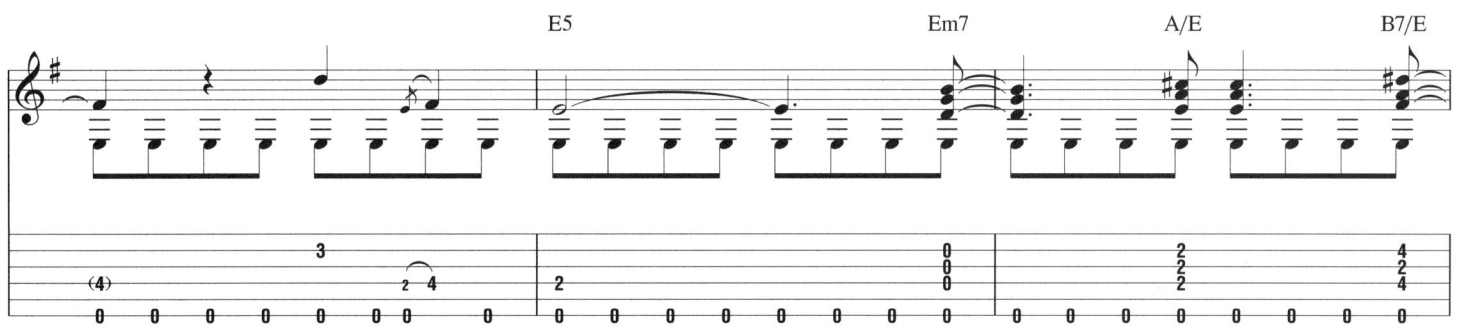
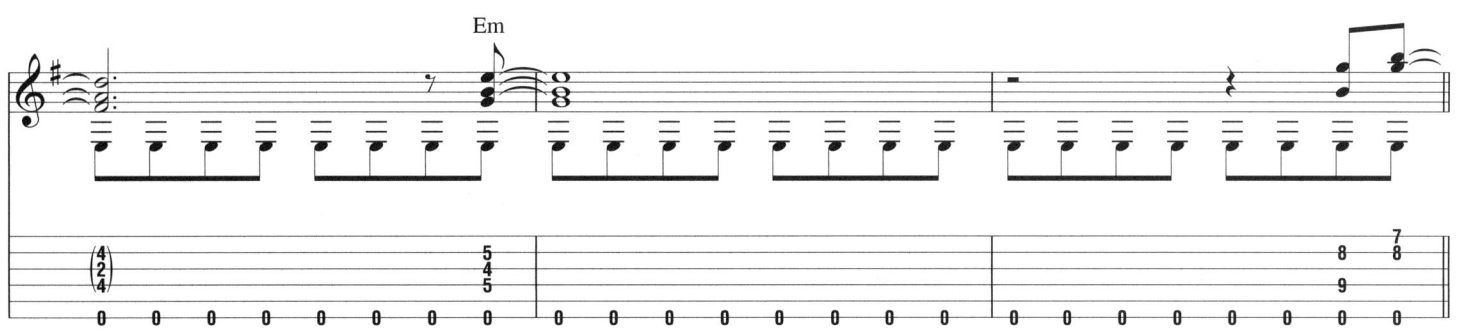

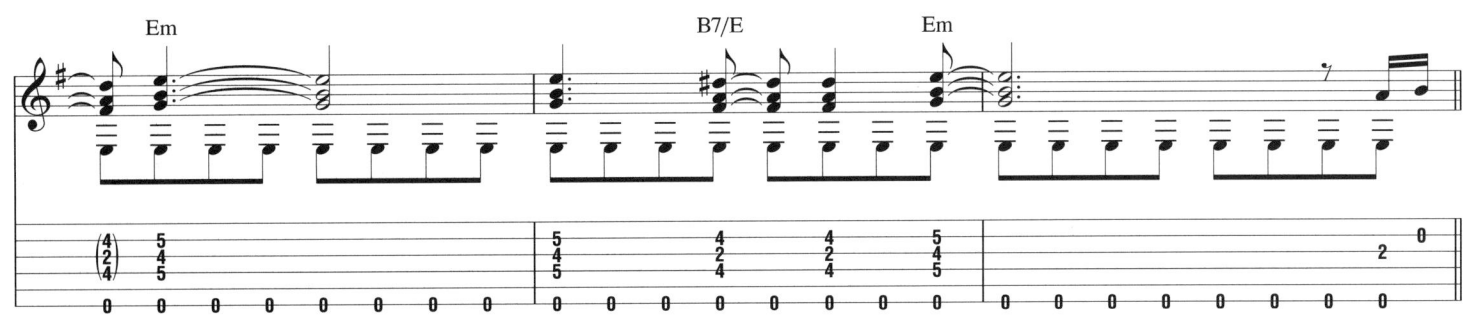
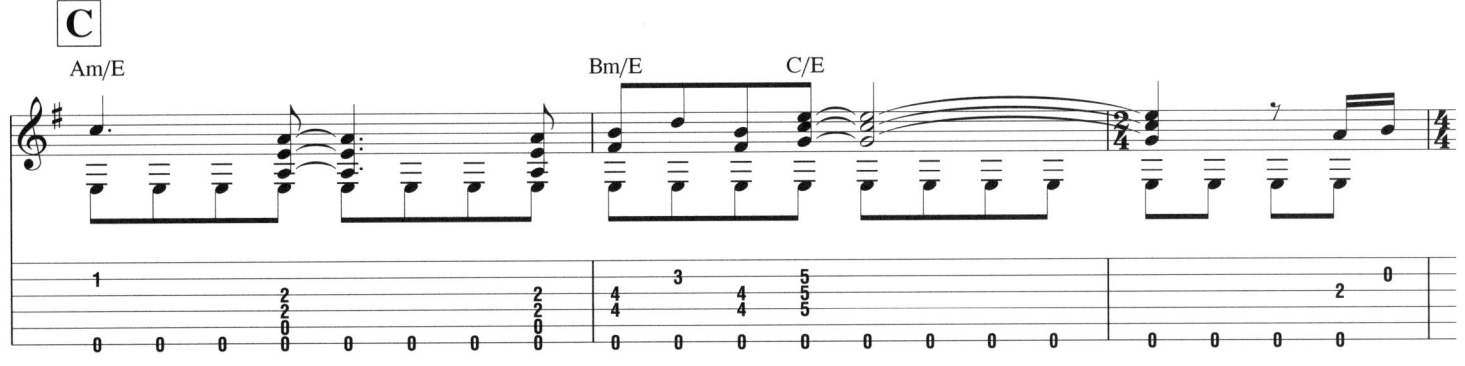
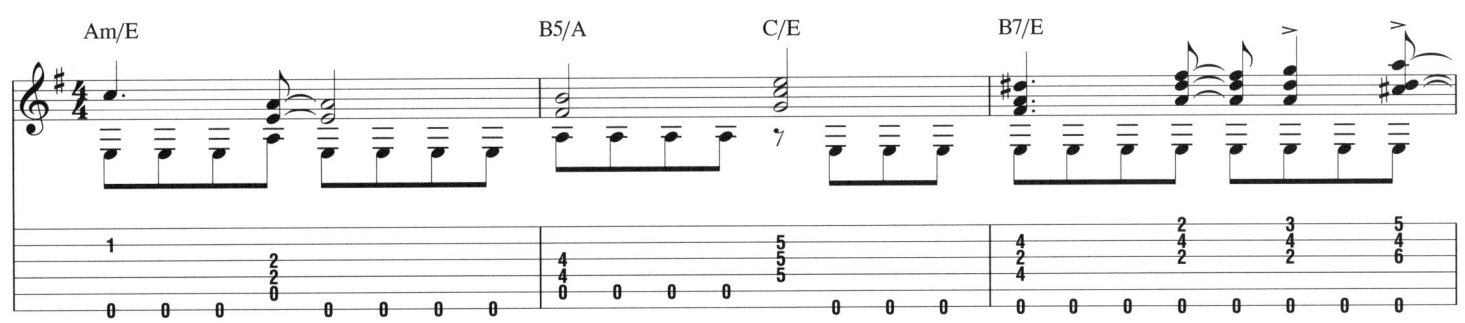
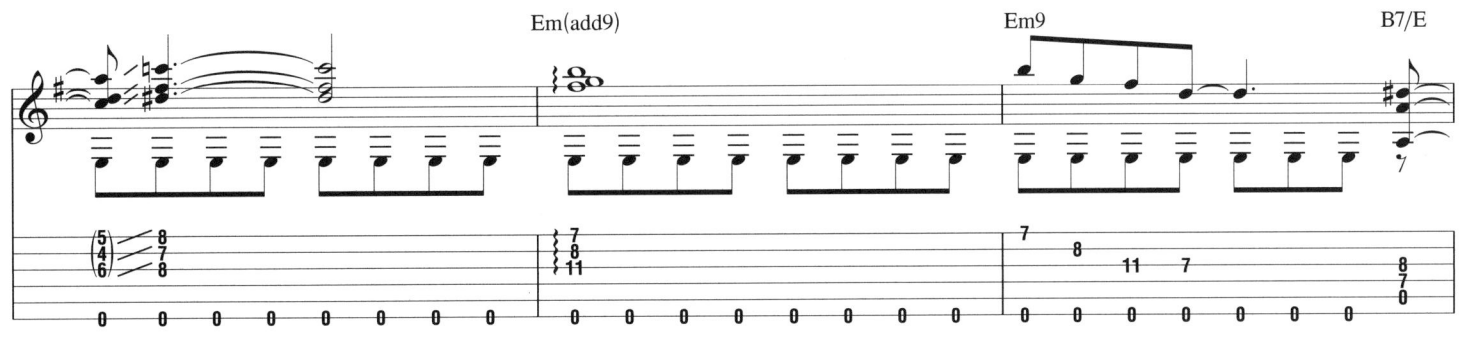
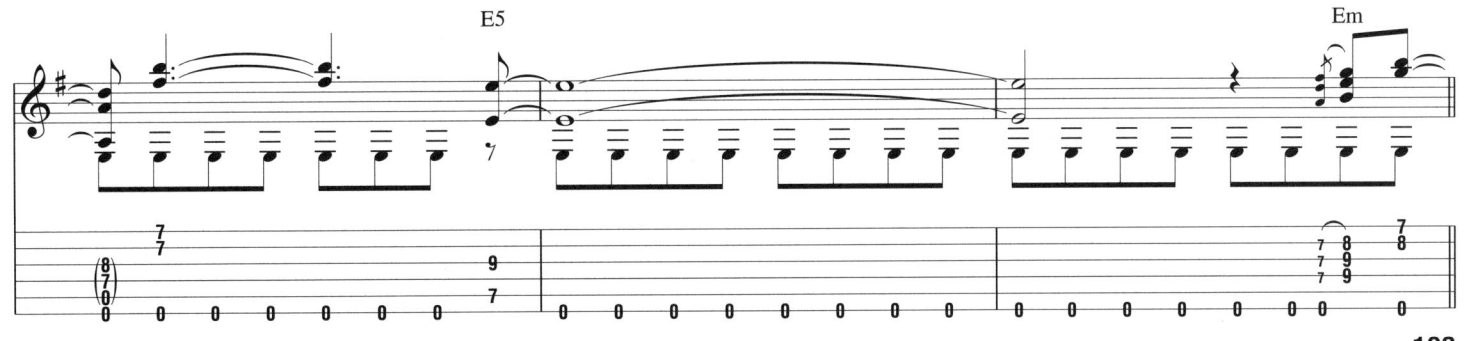

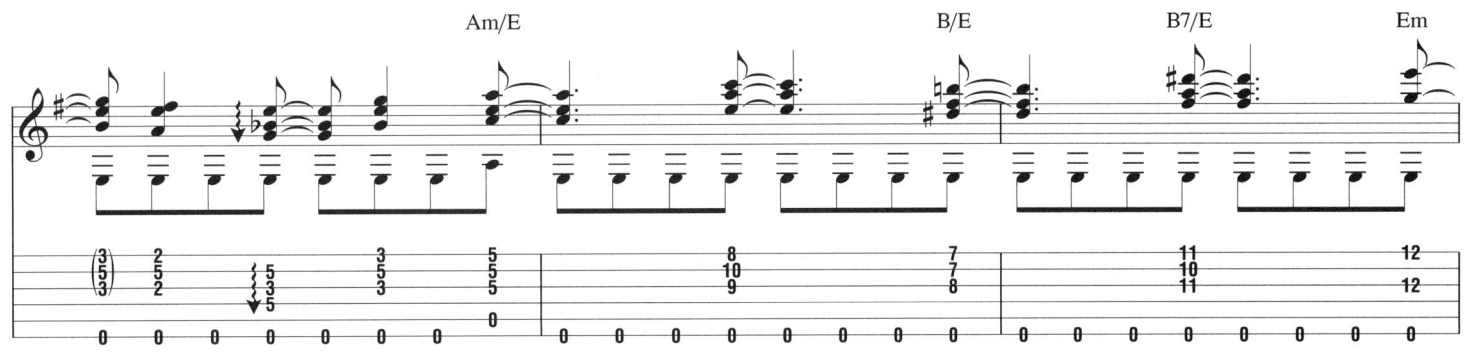
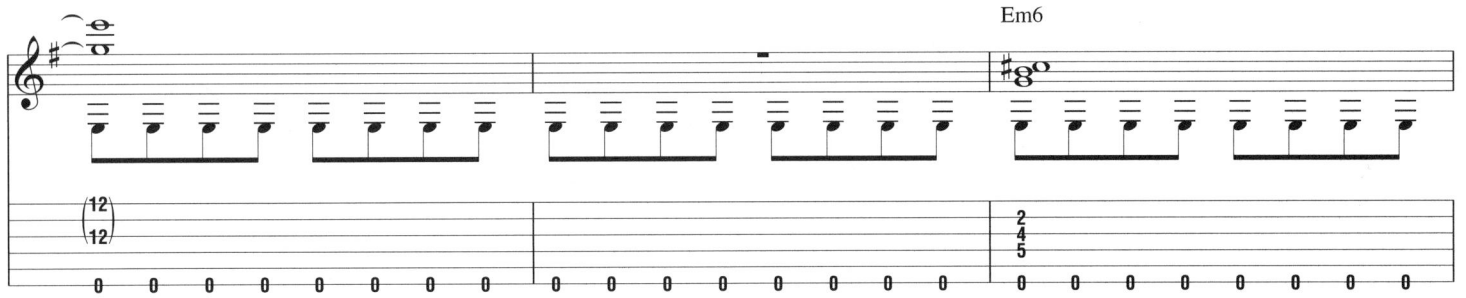
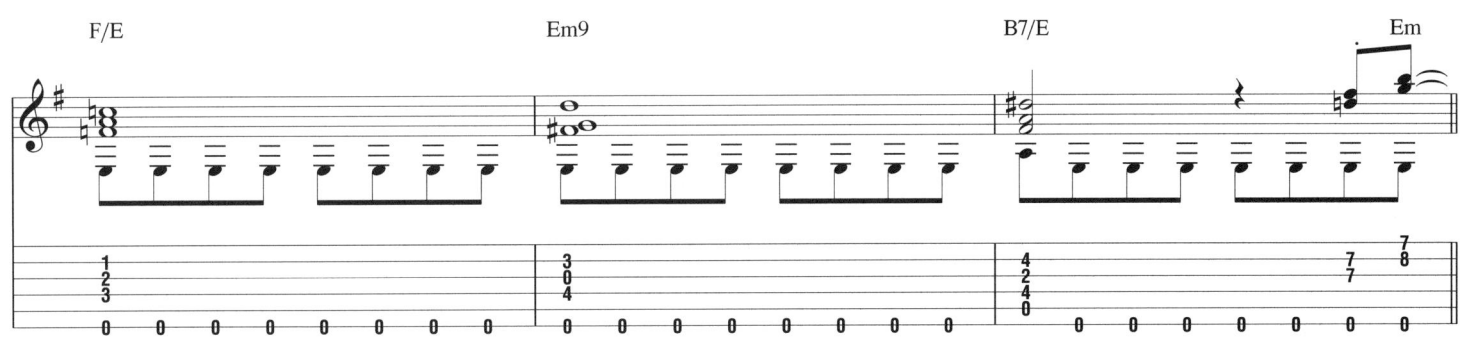
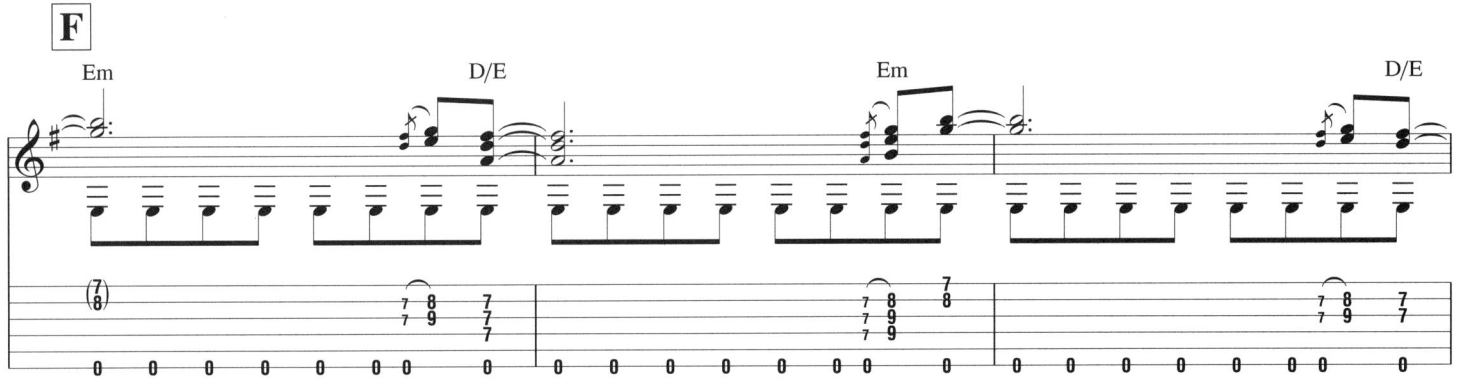
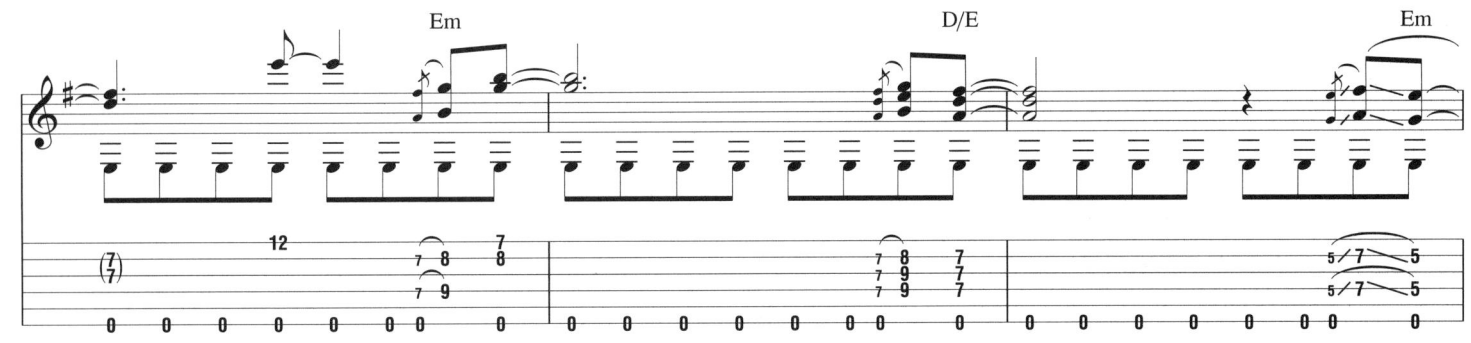

105

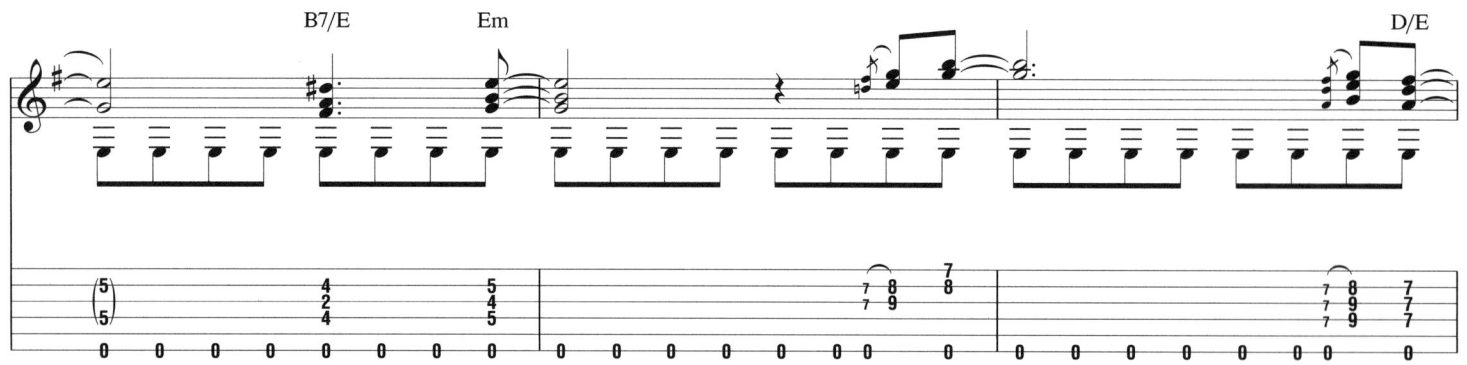
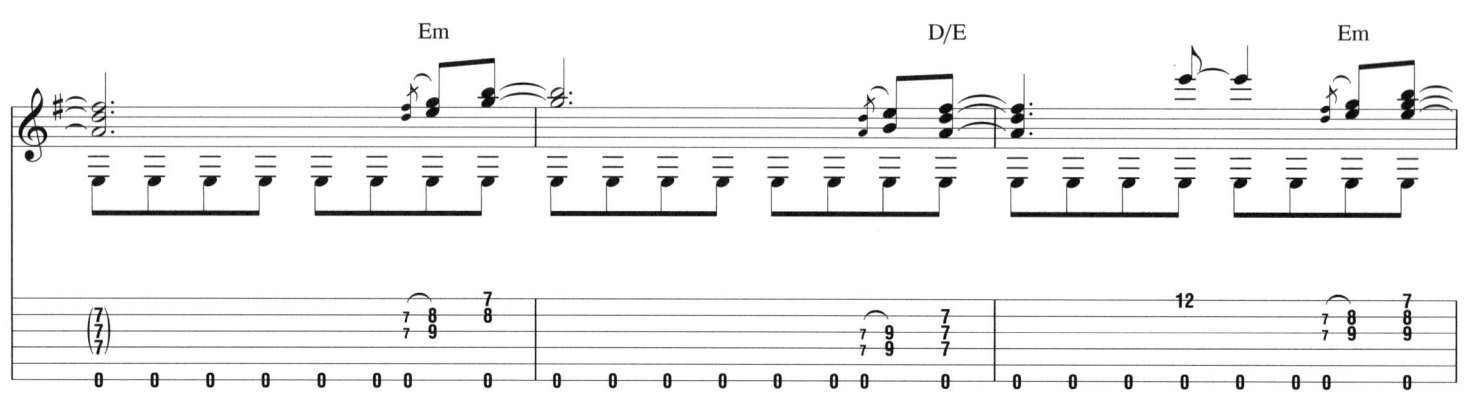
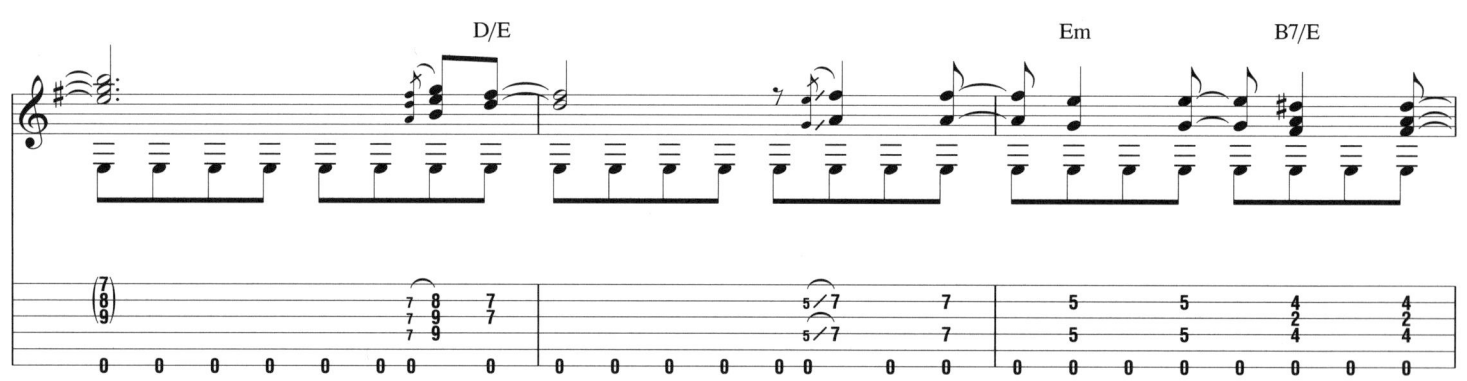

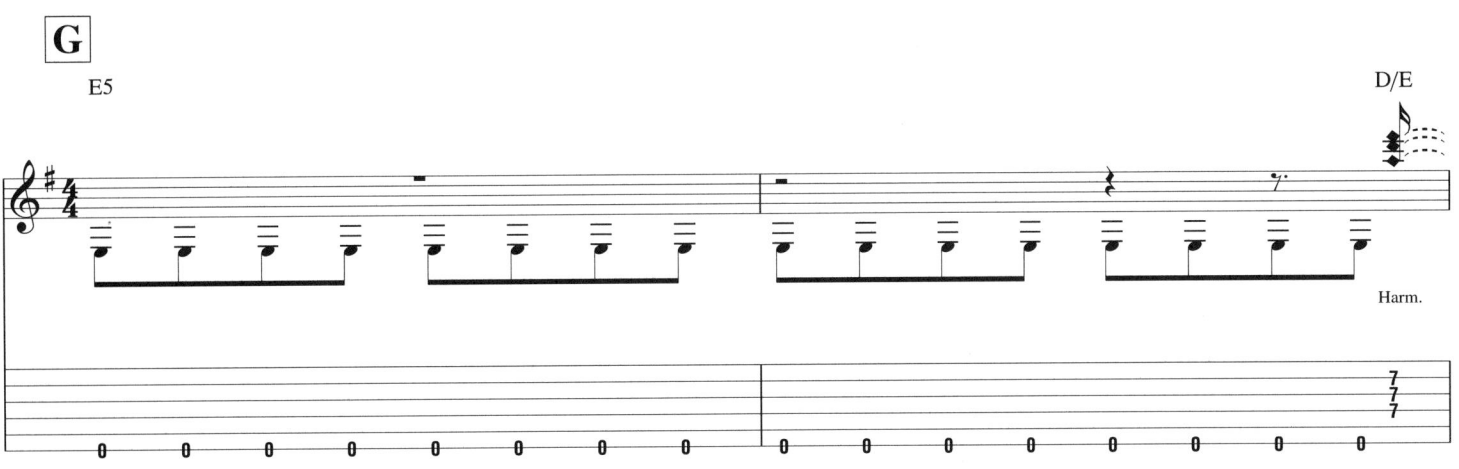
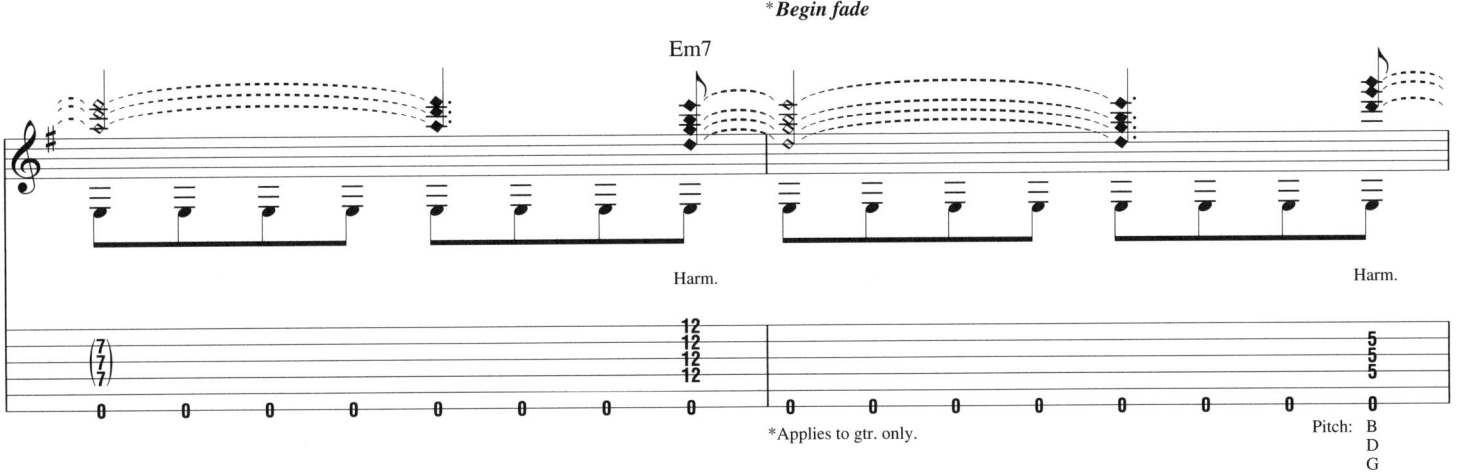

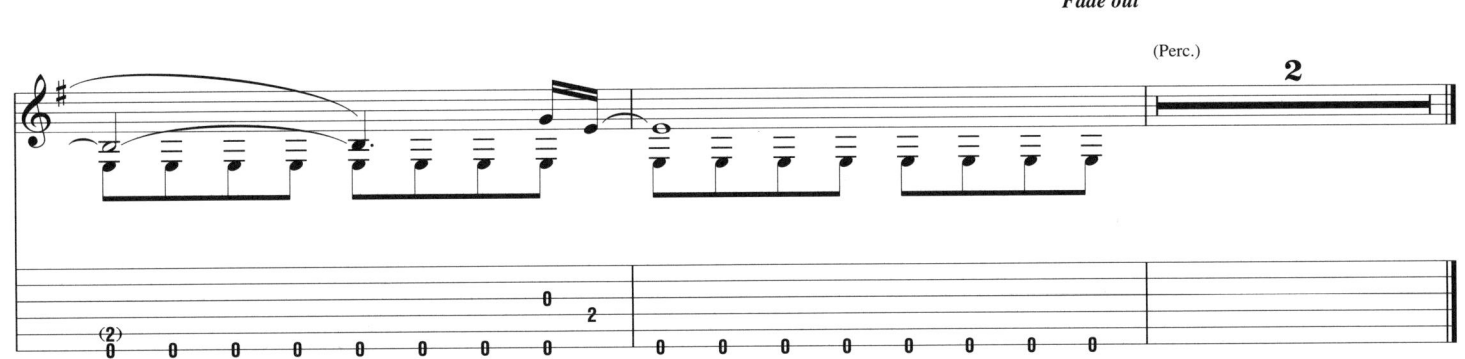

The Journey

from The Journey

By Tommy Emmanuel and David Hirschfelder

Drop D tuning:
(low to high) D-A-D-G-B-E

A

Moderately ♩ = 117

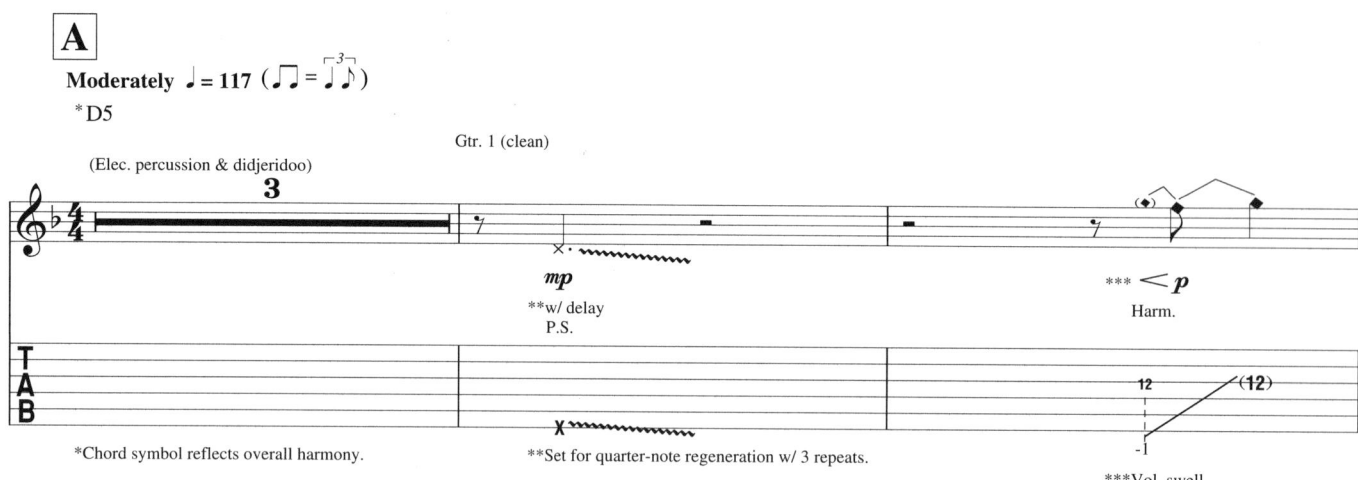

*Chord symbol reflects overall harmony.
**Set for quarter-note regeneration w/ 3 repeats.
***Vol. swell

B

†Dm7

†Chord symbols reflect implied harmony.

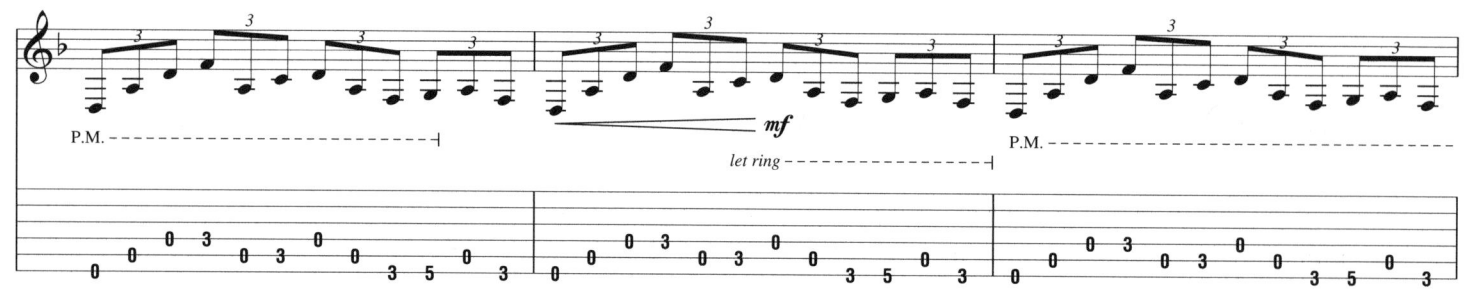

Copyright © 1993 UNIVERSAL MUSIC PUBLISHING PTY. LTD., TOMMY EMMANUEL MUSIC, CHRIS GILBEY PTY. LTD. and DEERFIELD PROD. PTY. LTD.
All Rights for UNIVERSAL MUSIC PUBLISHING PTY. LTD., TOMMY EMMANUEL MUSIC and CHRIS GILBEY PTY. LTD. in the
United States and Canada Controlled and Administered by UNIVERSAL - POLYGRAM INTERNATIONAL PUBLISHING, INC.
All Rights for DEERFIELD PROD. PTY. LTD. in the United States and Canada Controlled and Administered by
UNIVERSAL - SONGS OF POLYGRAM INTERNATIONAL, INC.
All Rights Reserved   Used by Permission

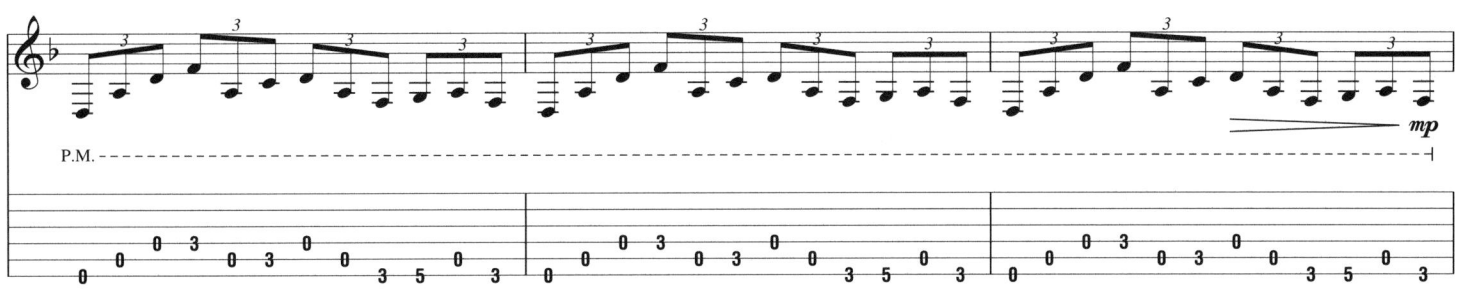
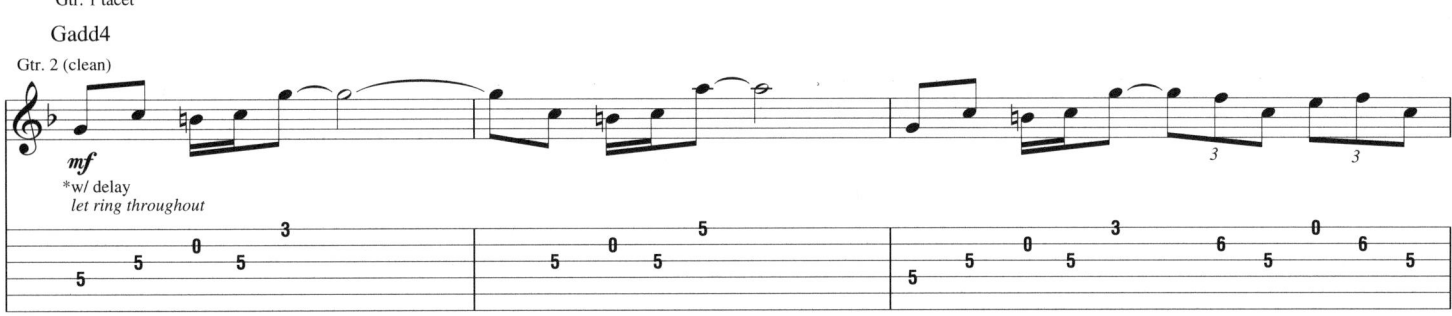
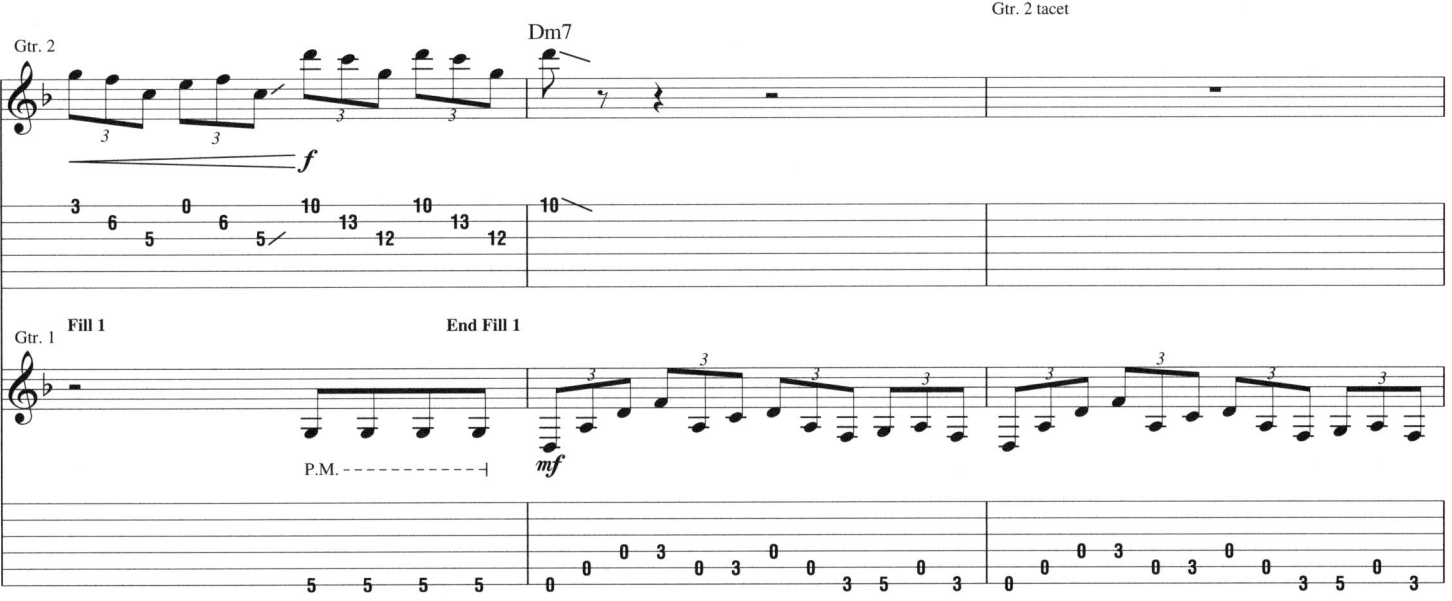
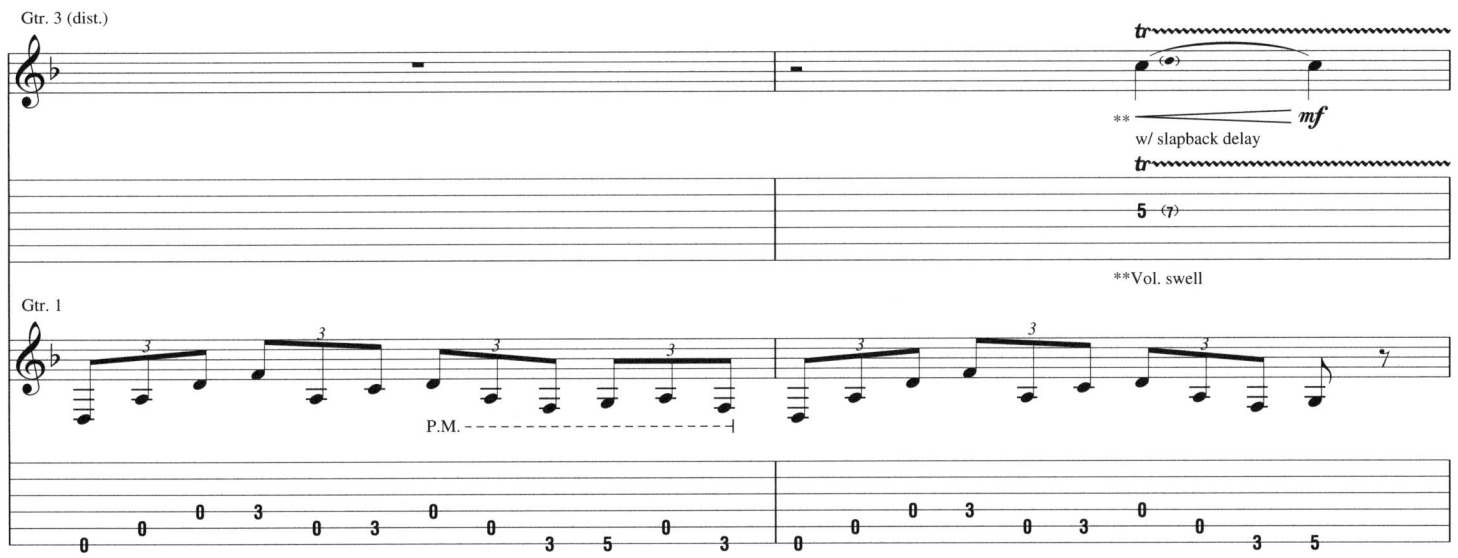

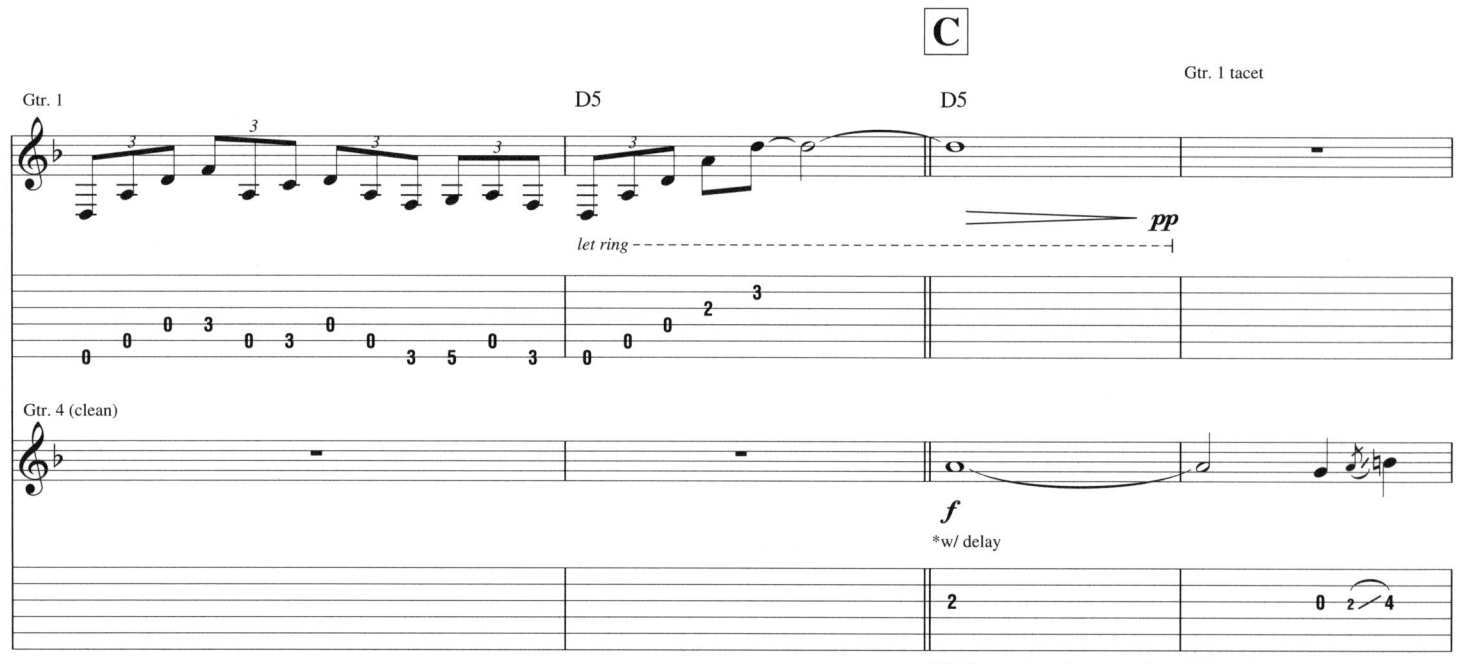

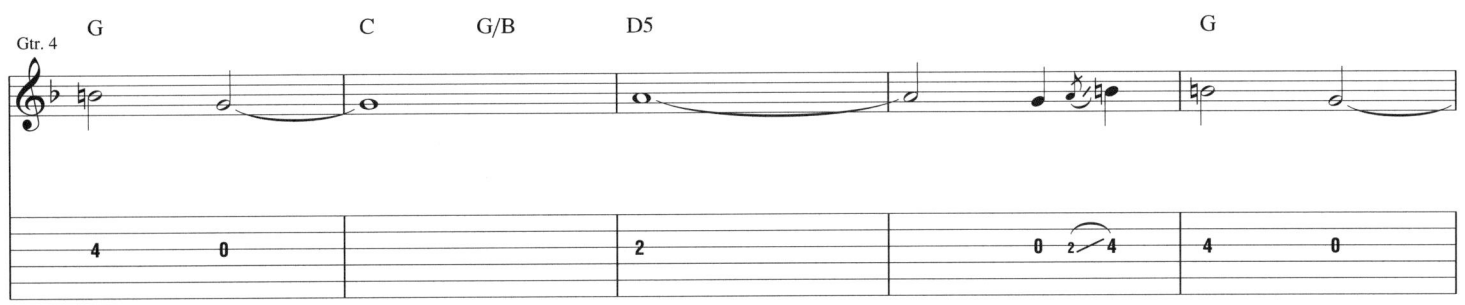

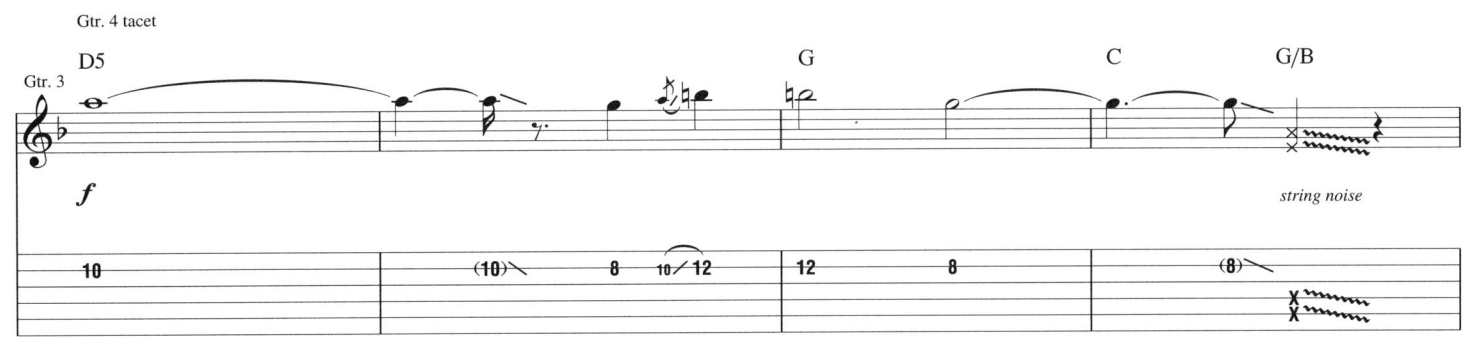
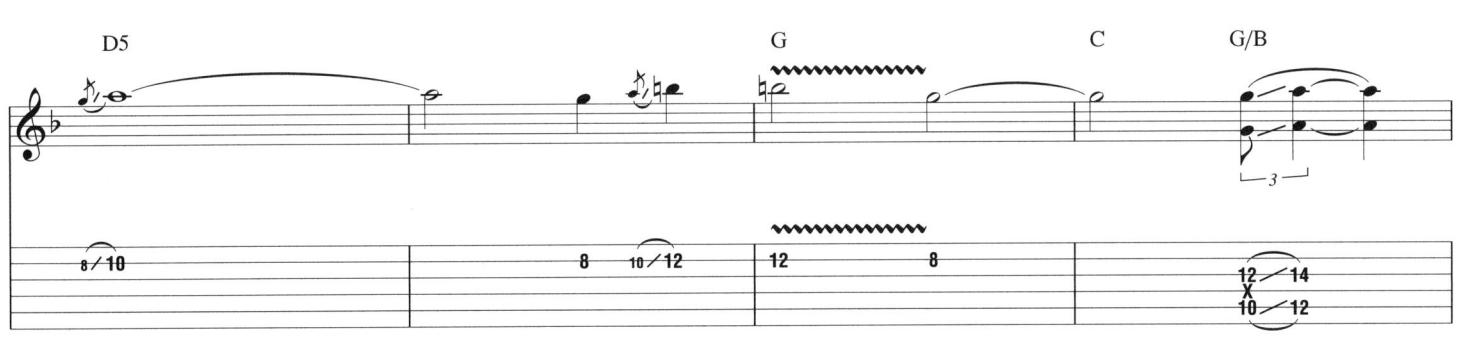
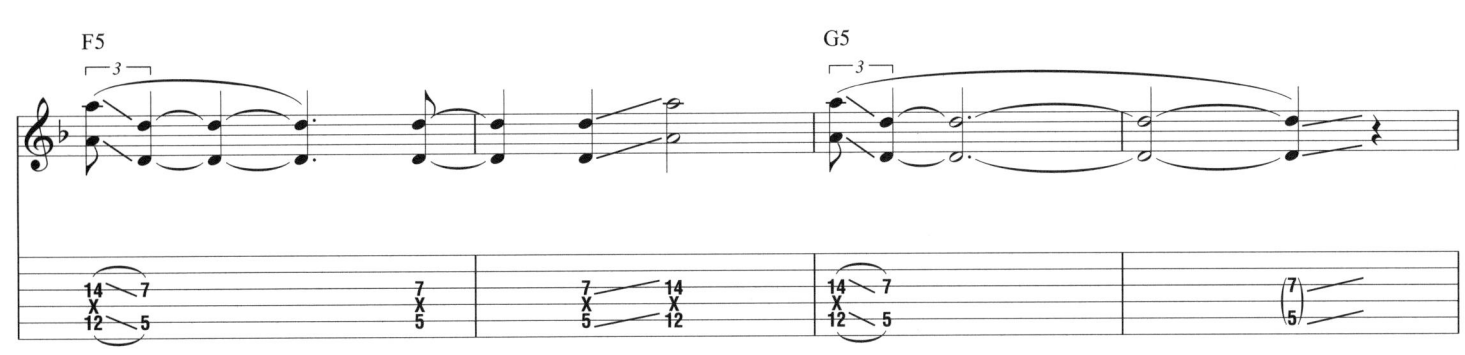

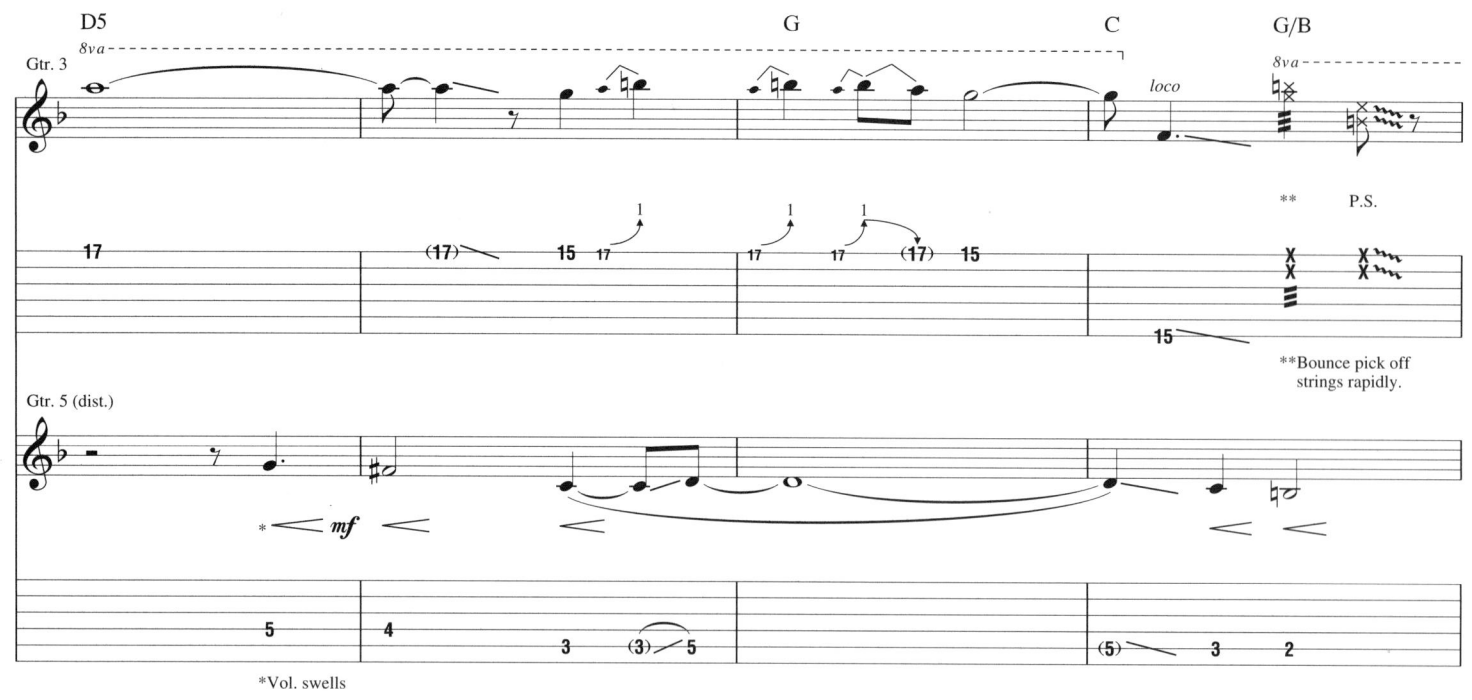
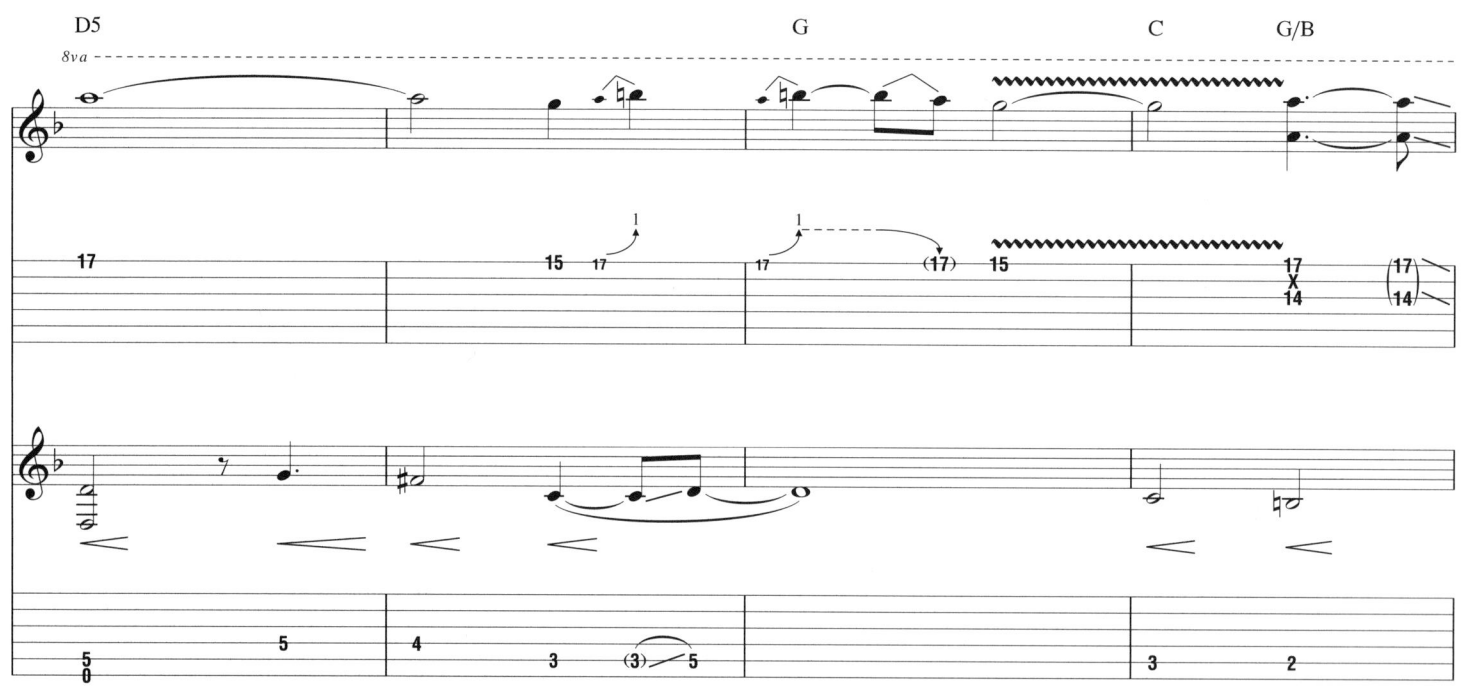

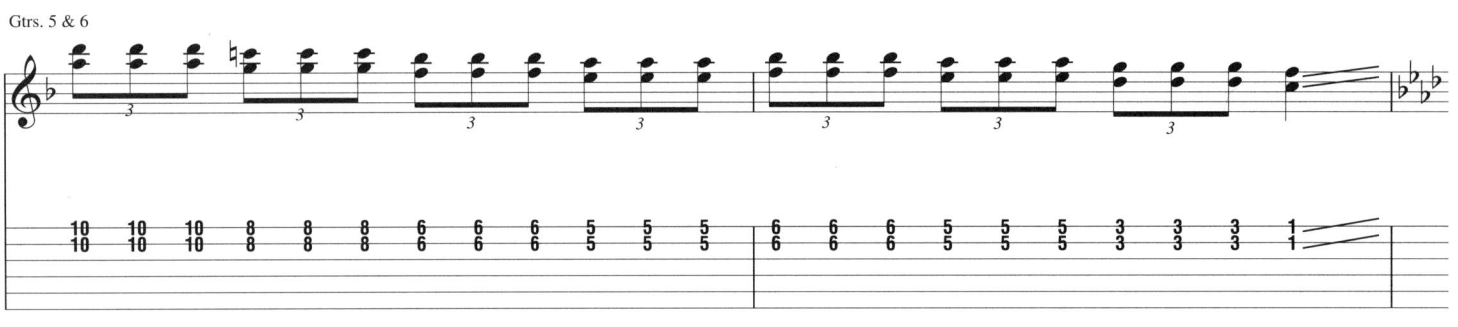

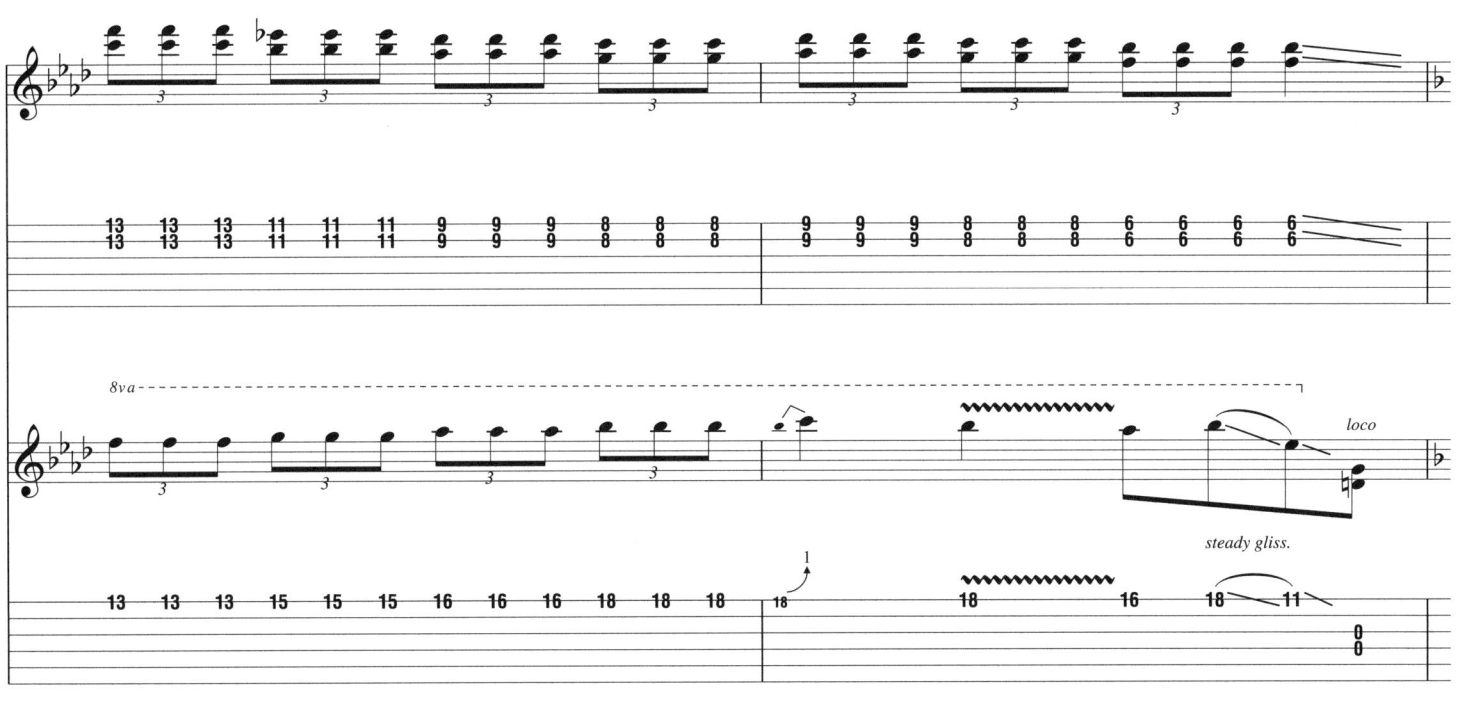
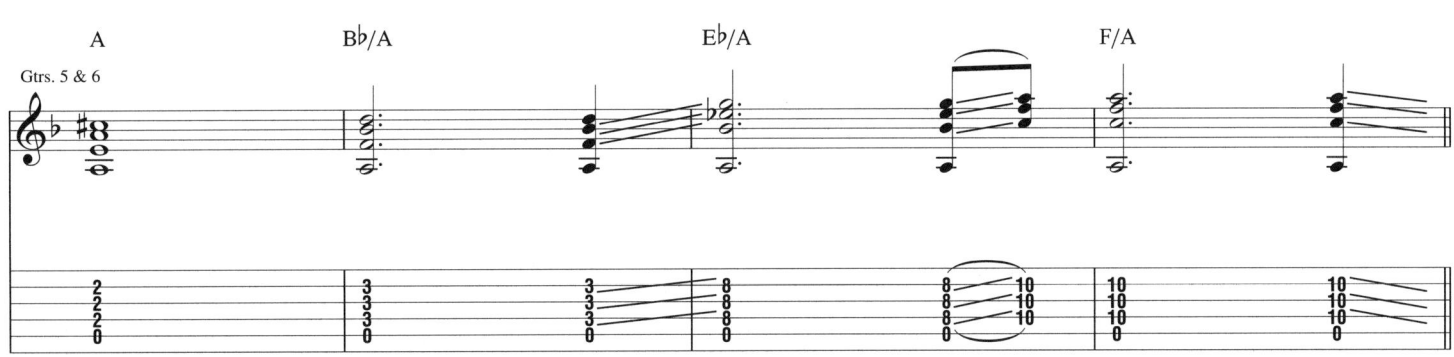

115

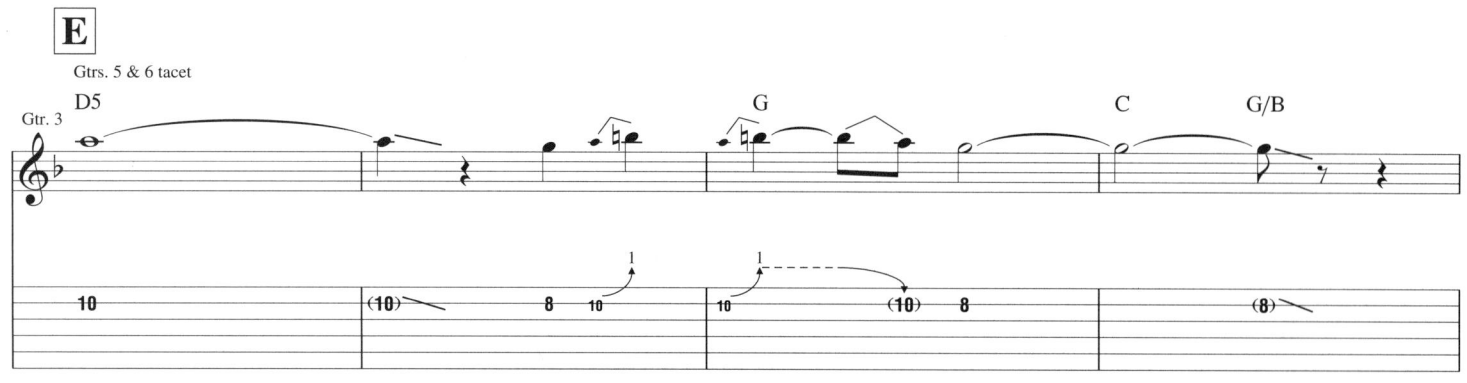

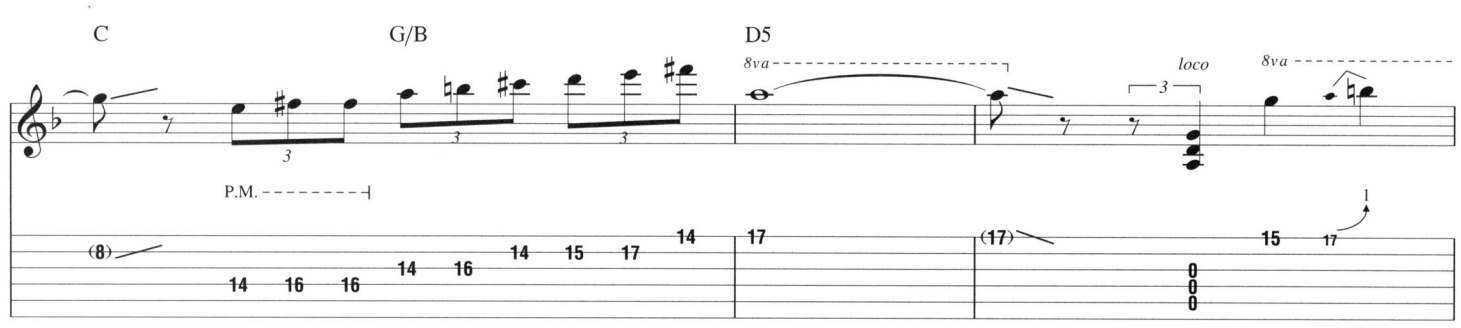
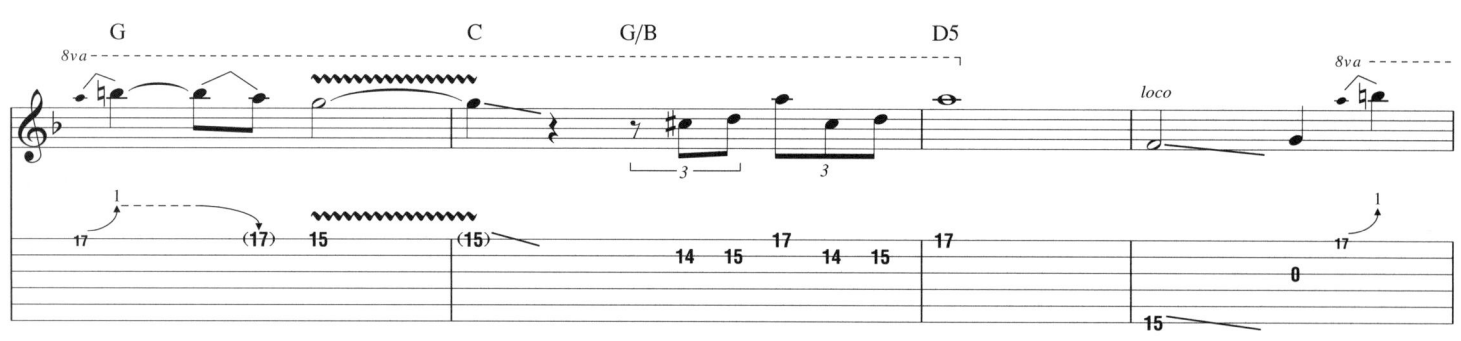
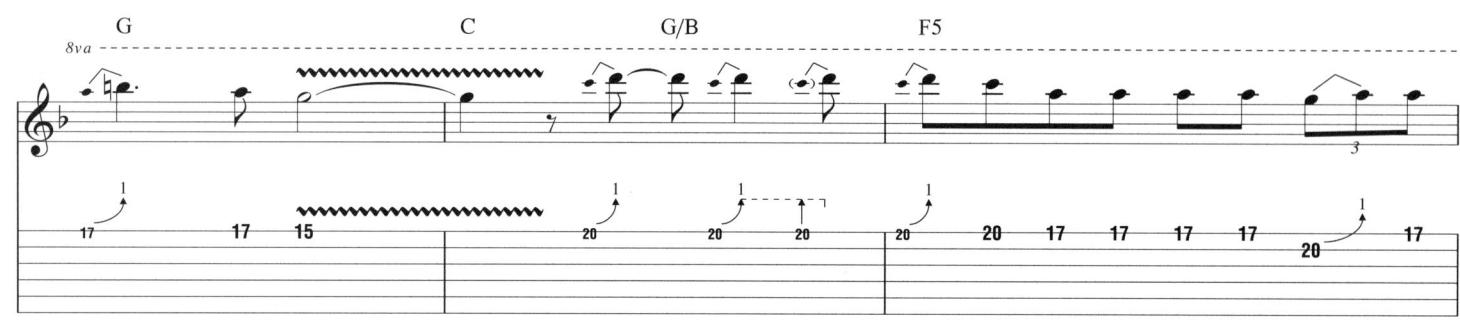

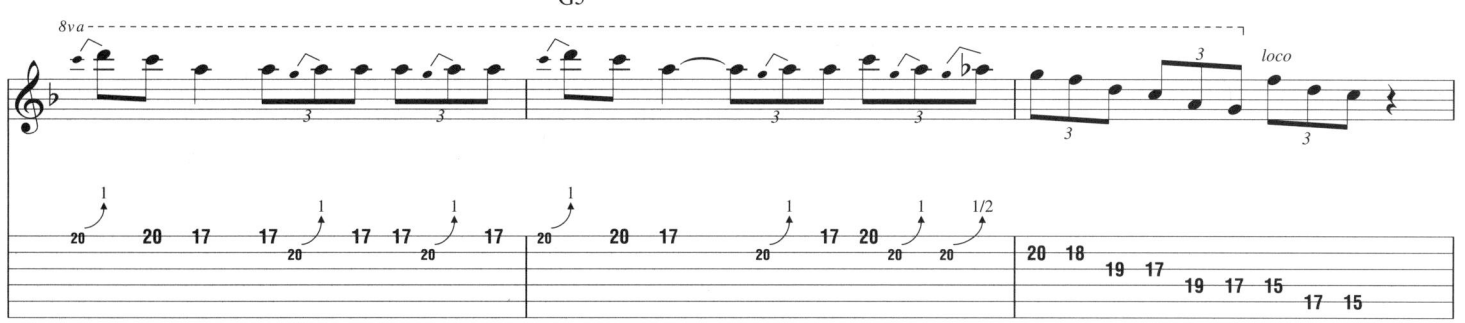
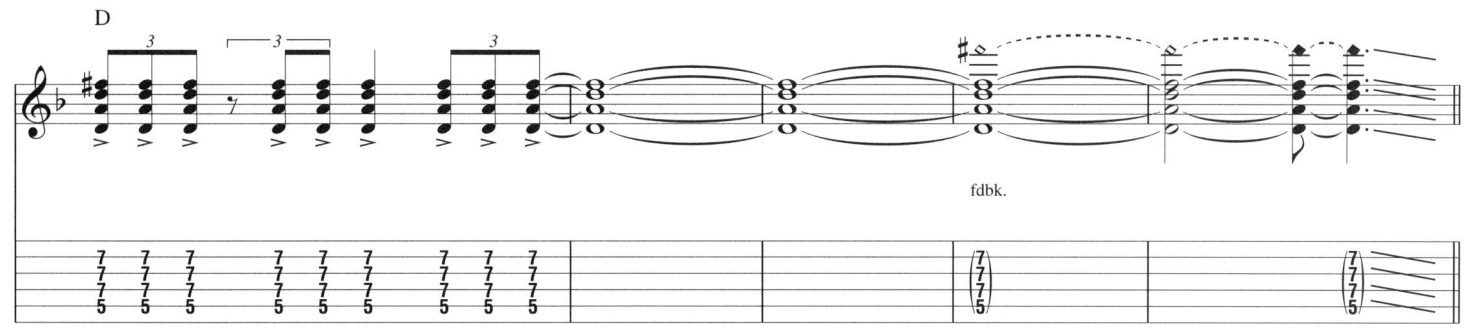

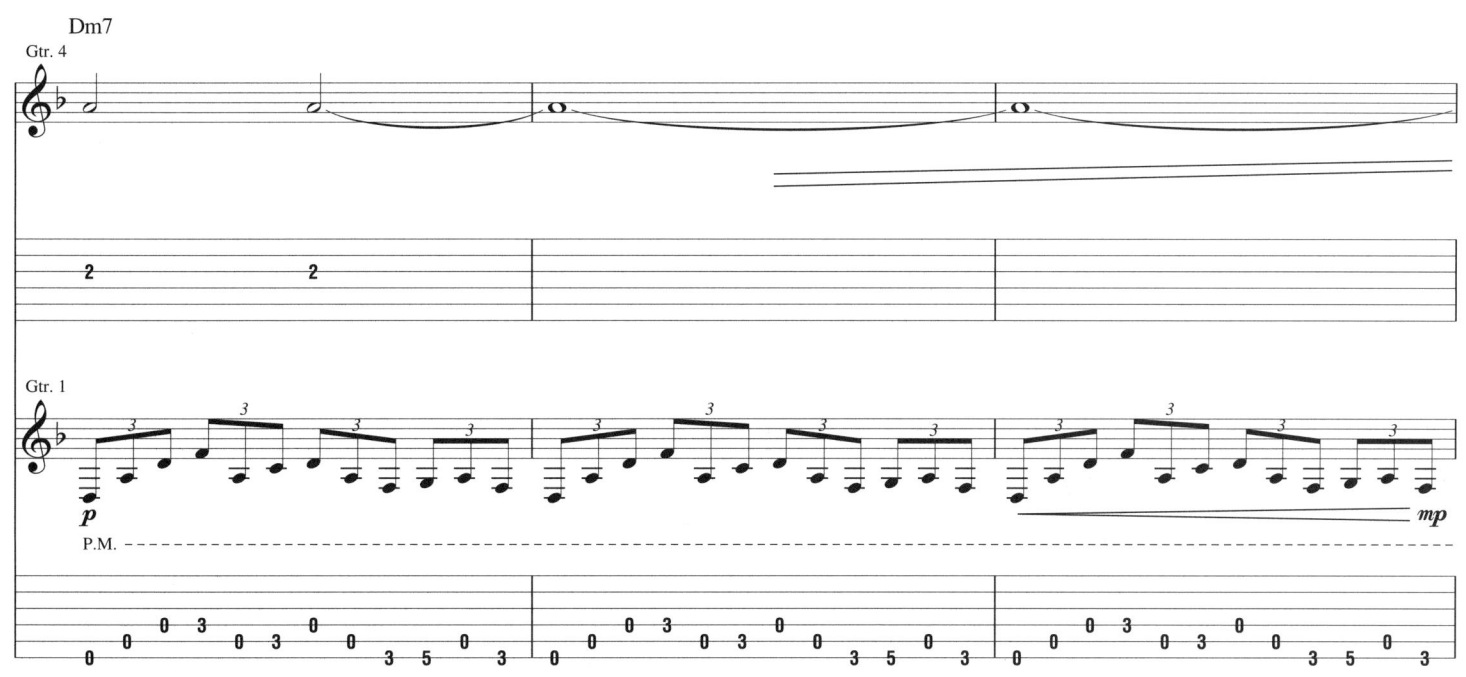

117

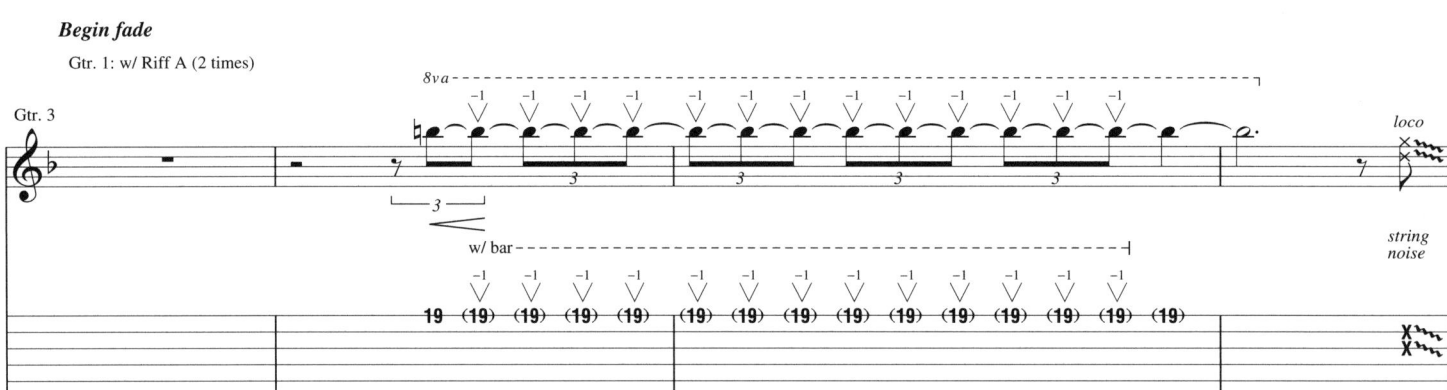
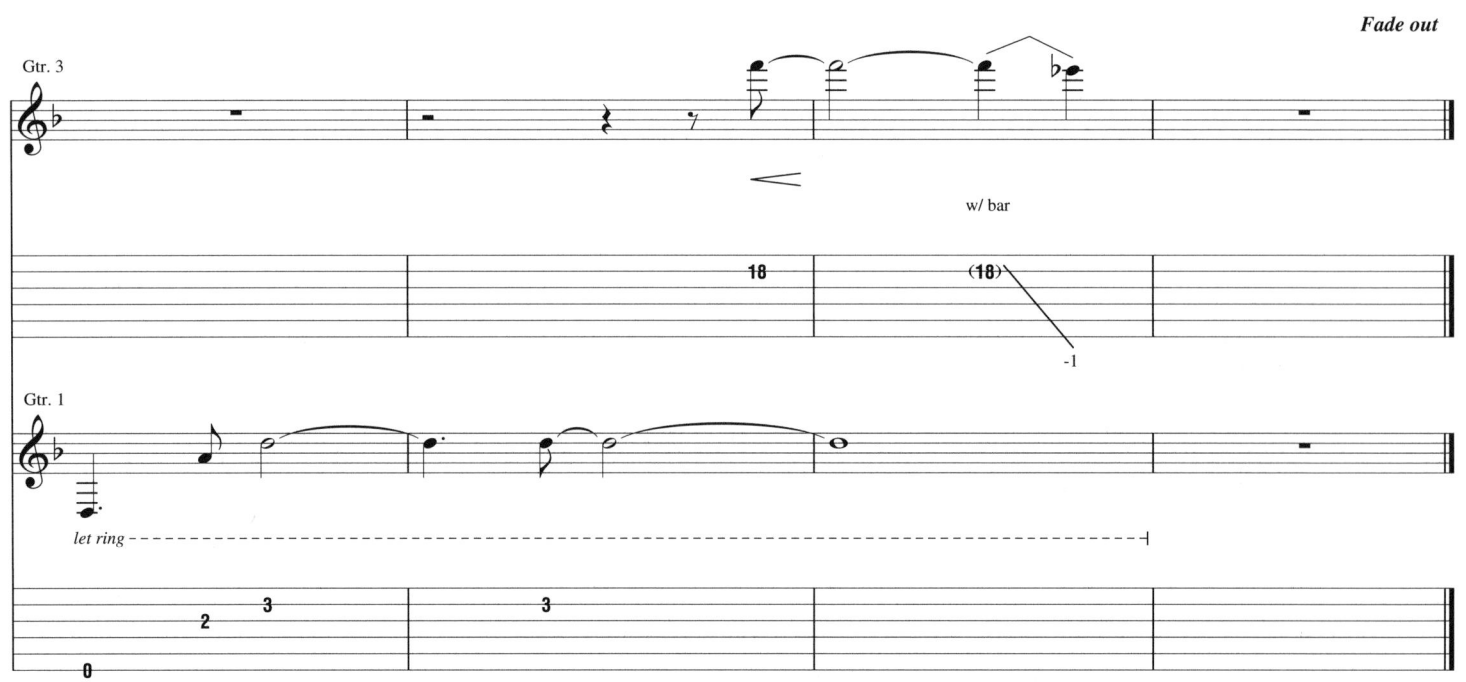

from *Determination*

Stevie's Blues

By Tommy Emmanuel

A

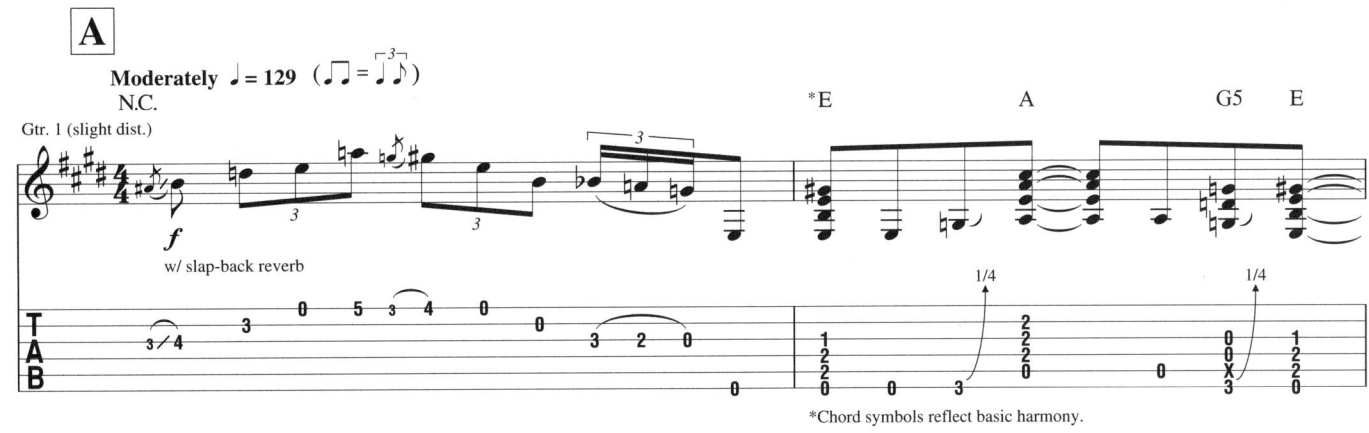

*Chord symbols reflect basic harmony.

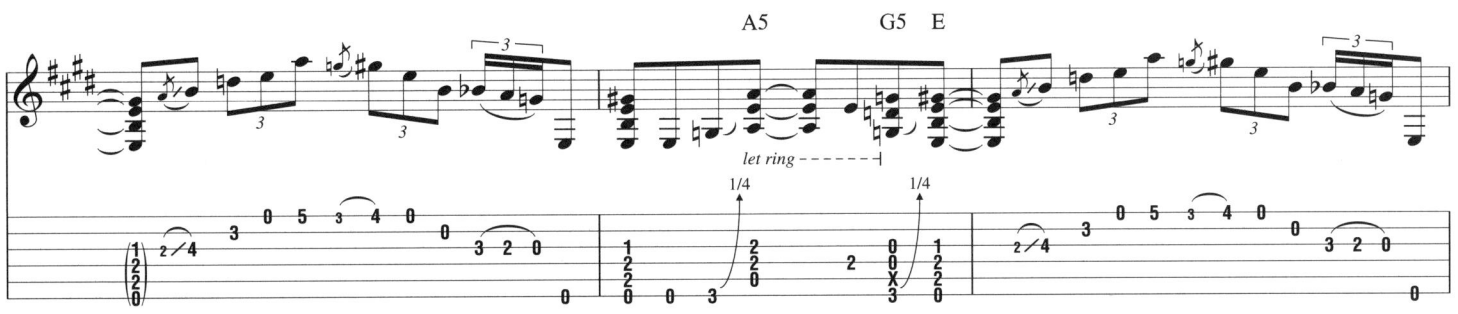

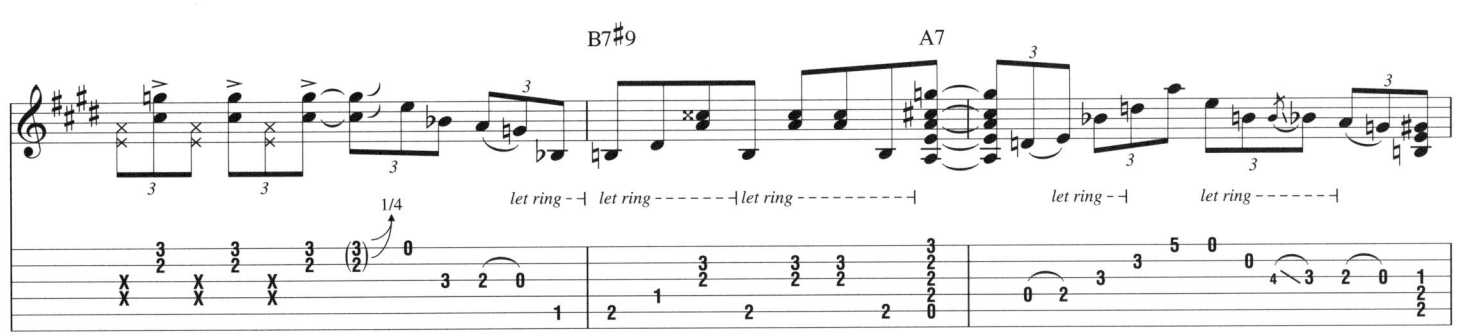

Copyright © 1993 UNIVERSAL MUSIC PUBLISHING PTY. LTD.
All Rights in the United States and Canada Controlled and Administered by UNIVERSAL - POLYGRAM INTERNATIONAL PUBLISHING, INC.
All Rights Reserved   Used by Permission

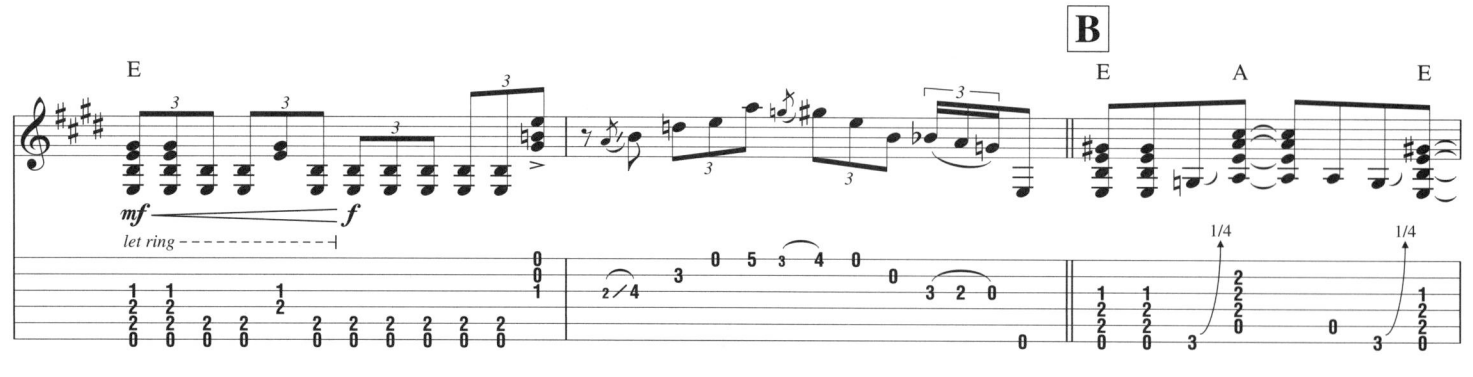
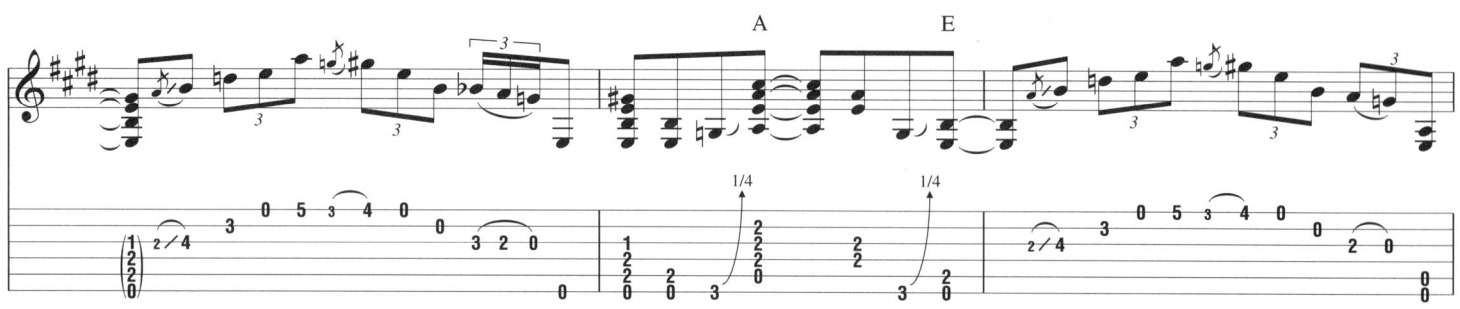
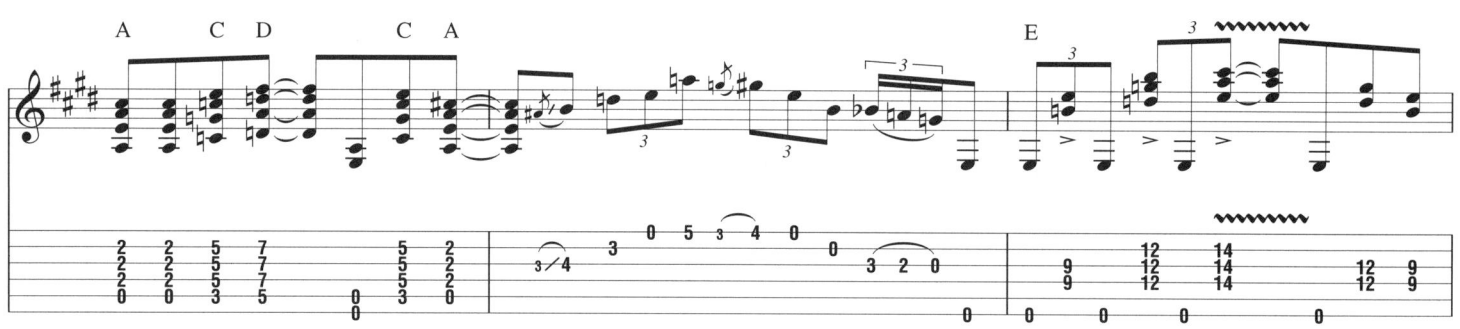

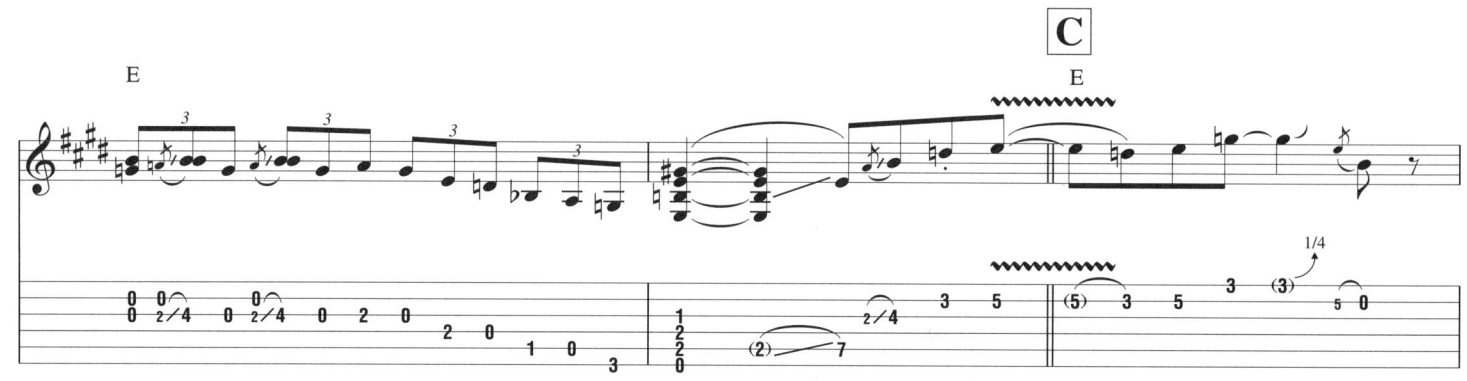

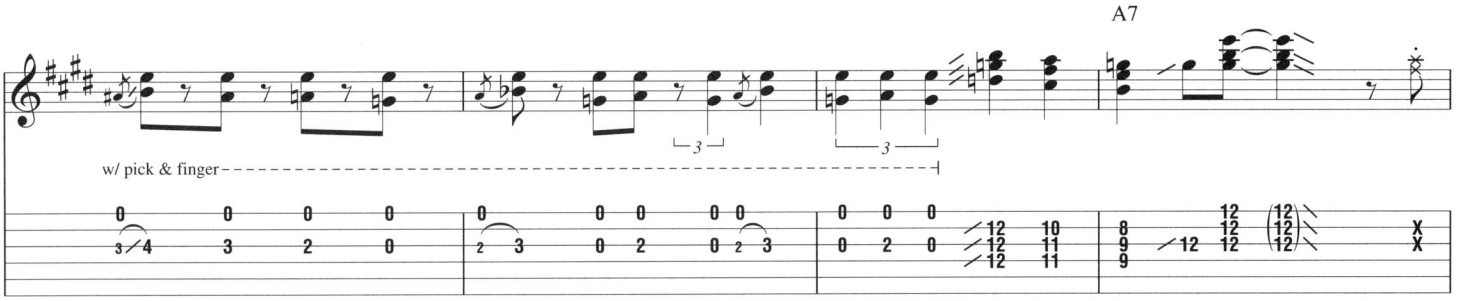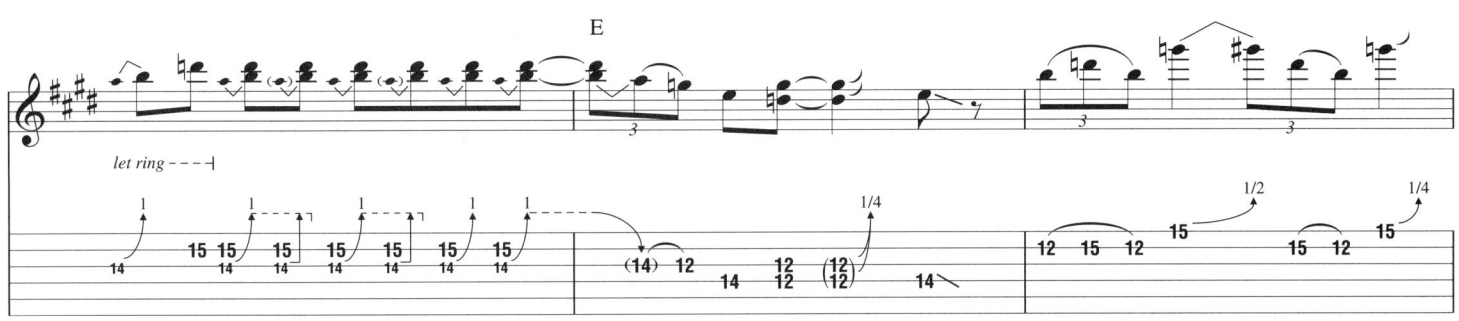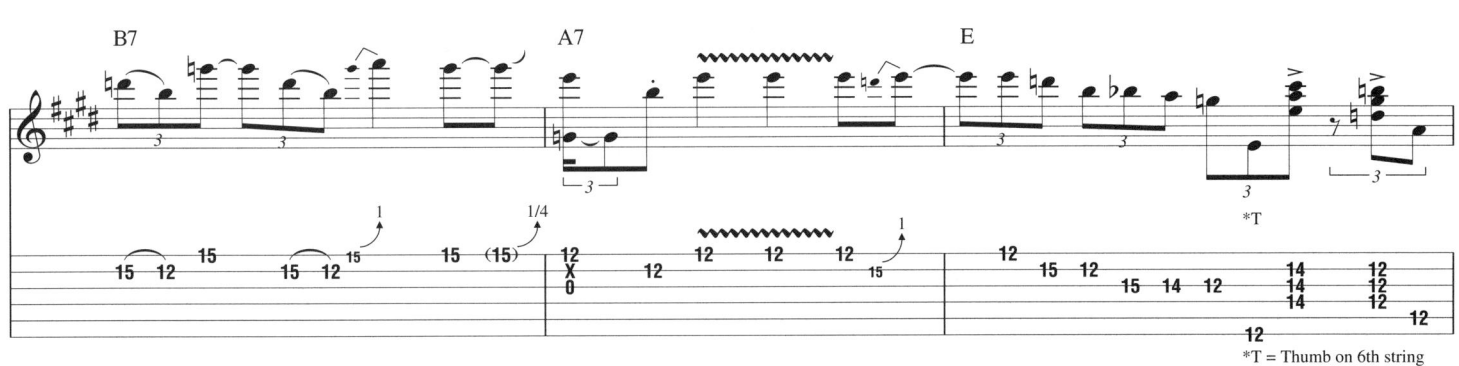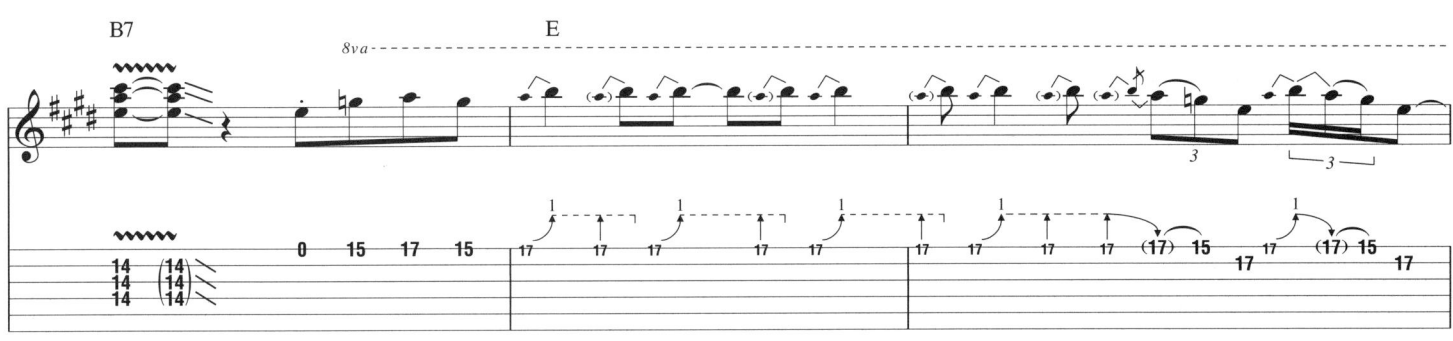

*T = Thumb on 6th string

**Played as even eighth notes.

121

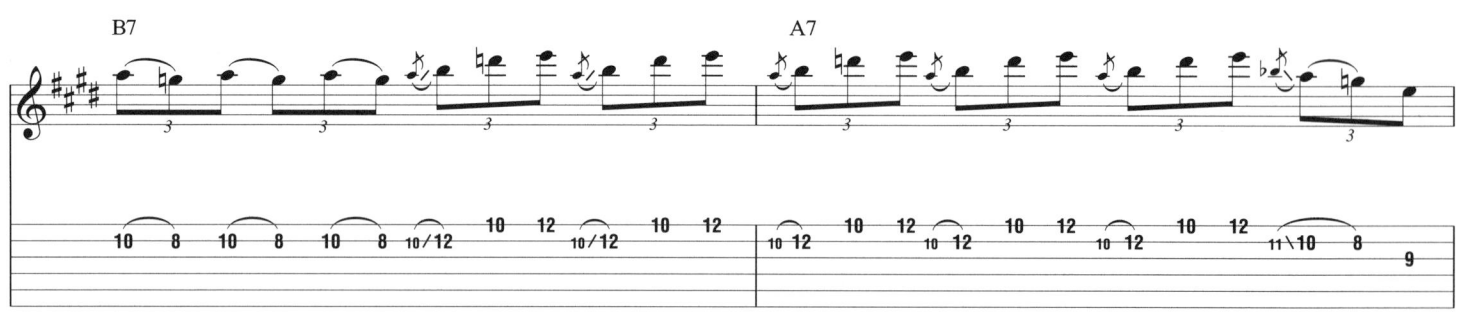

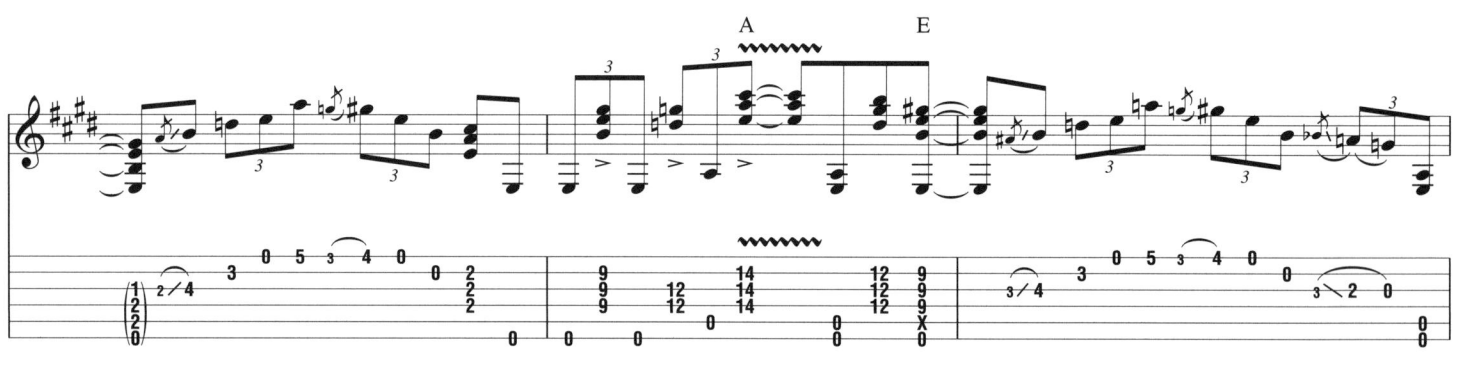
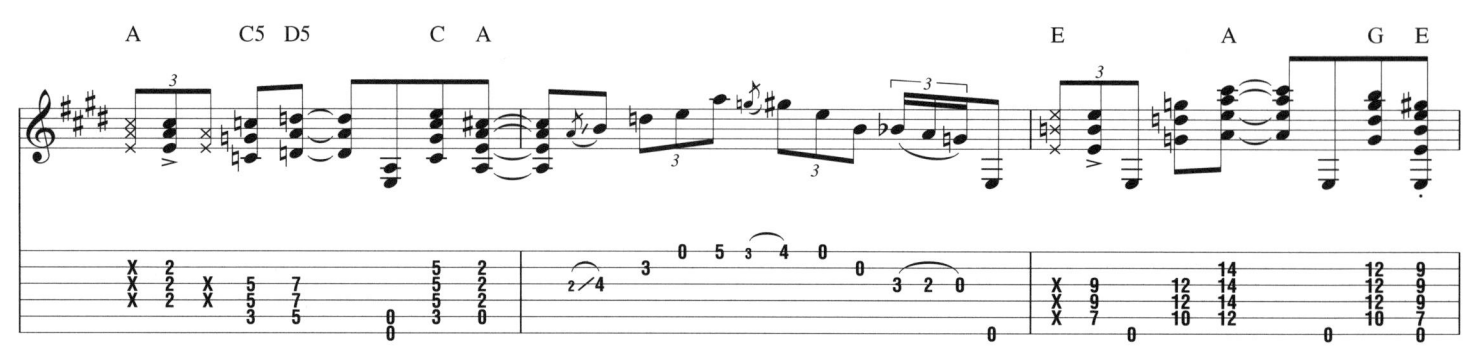

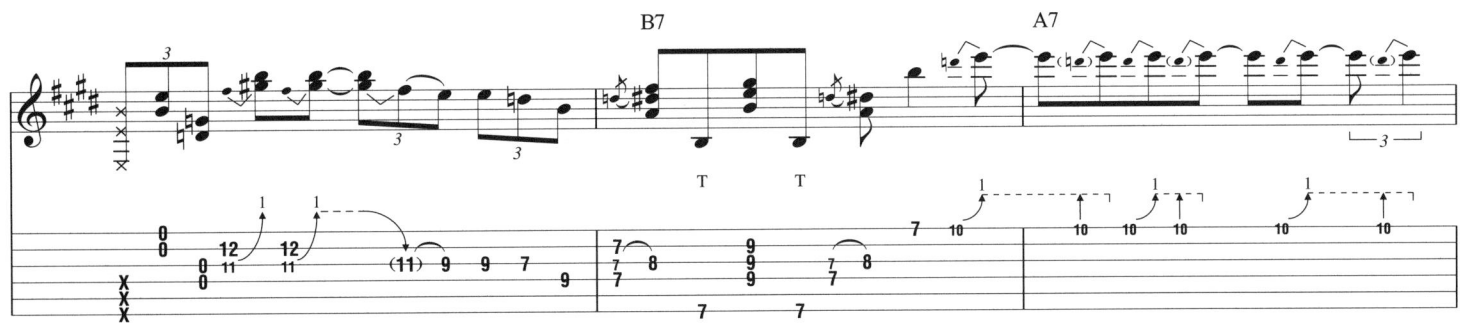
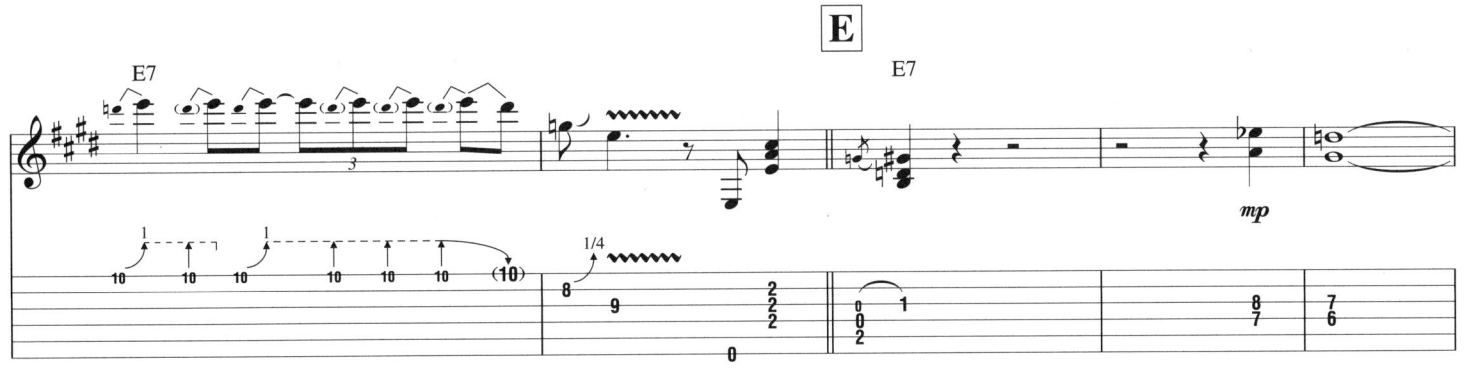
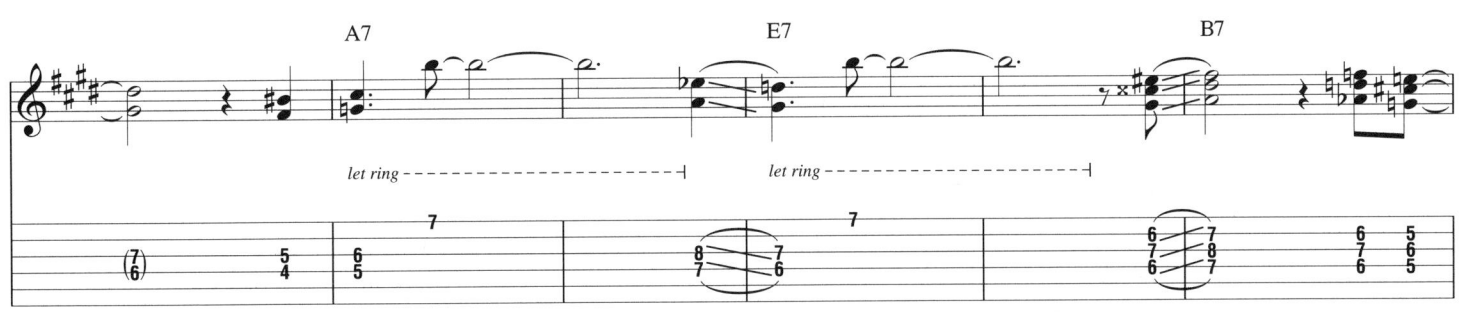
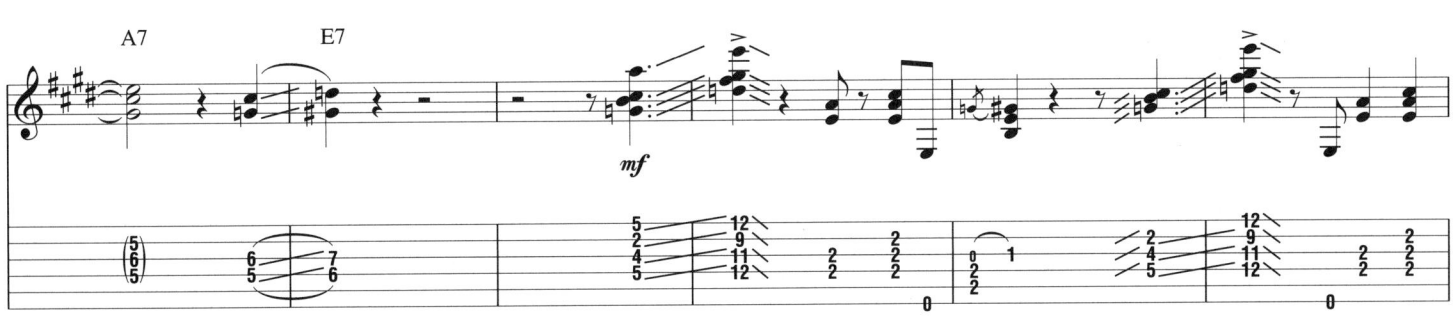
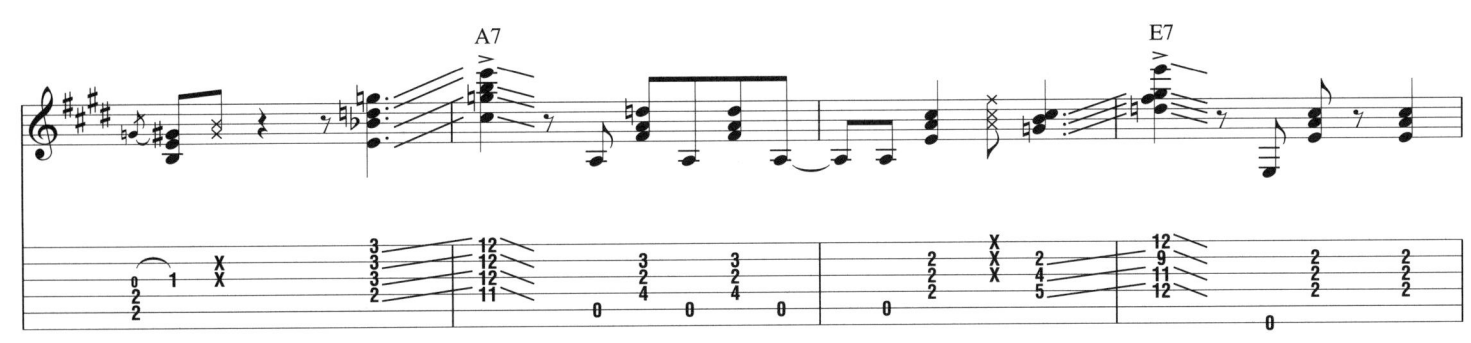

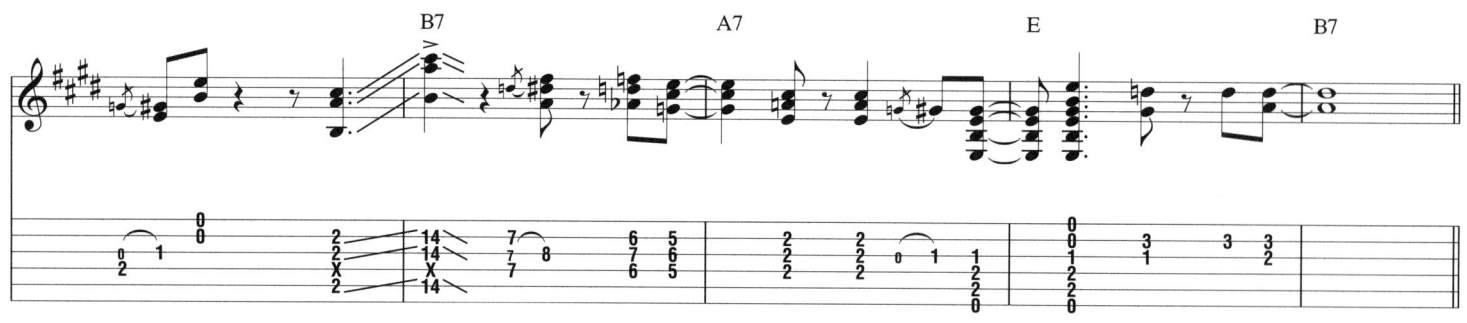
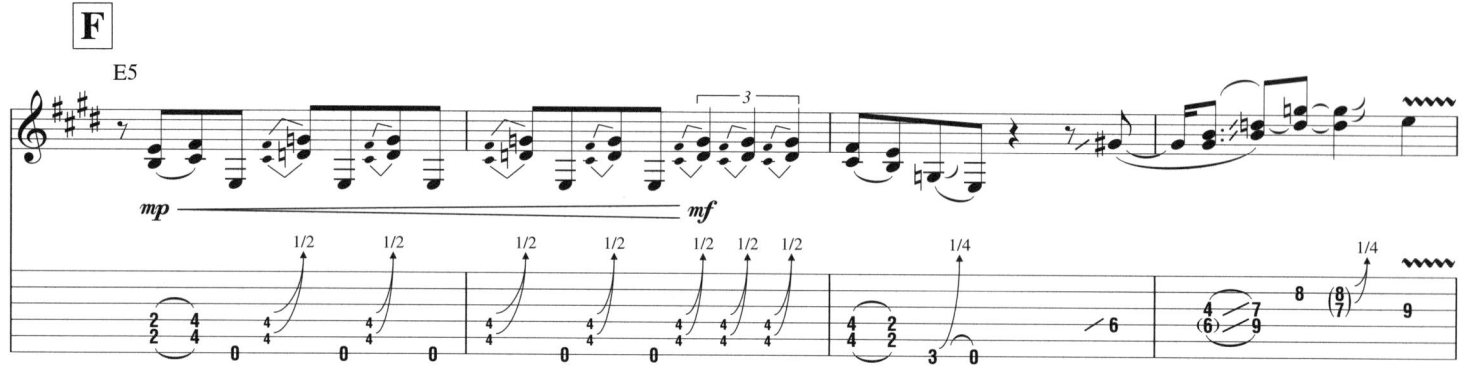
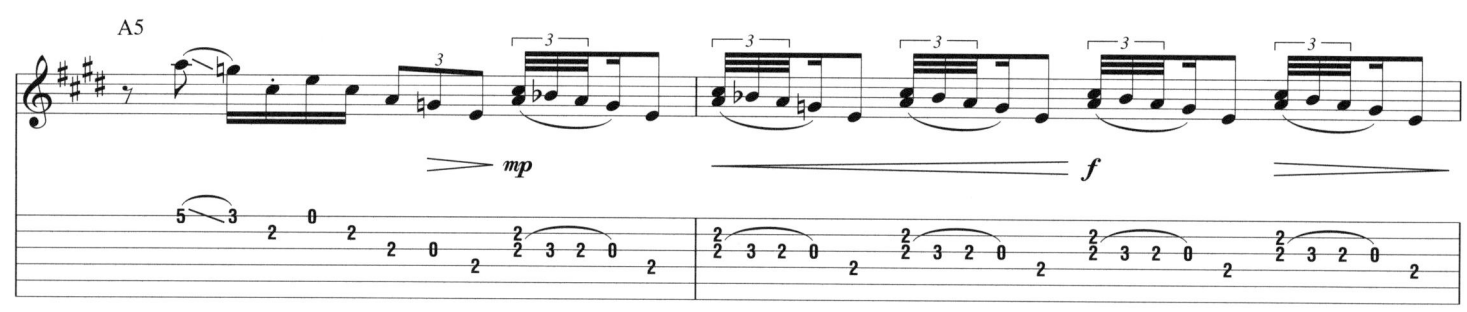

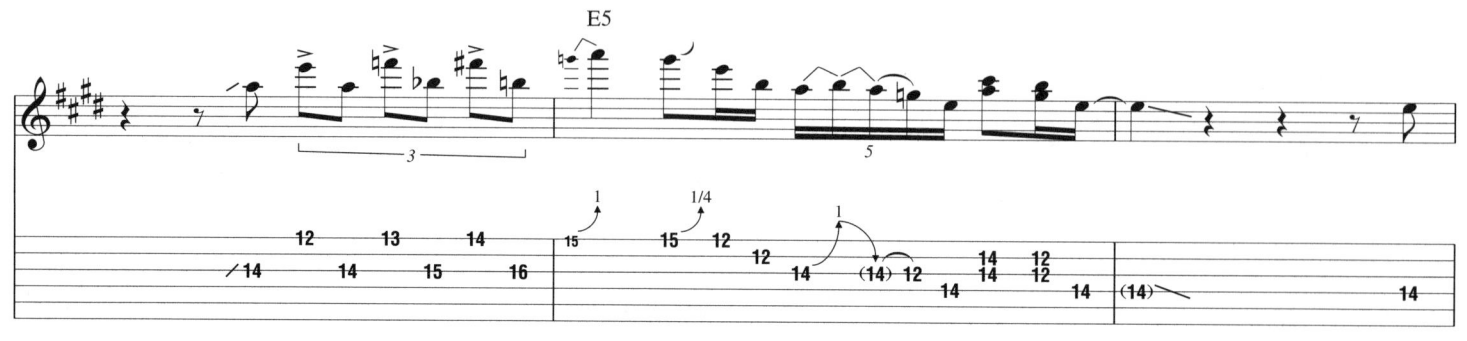

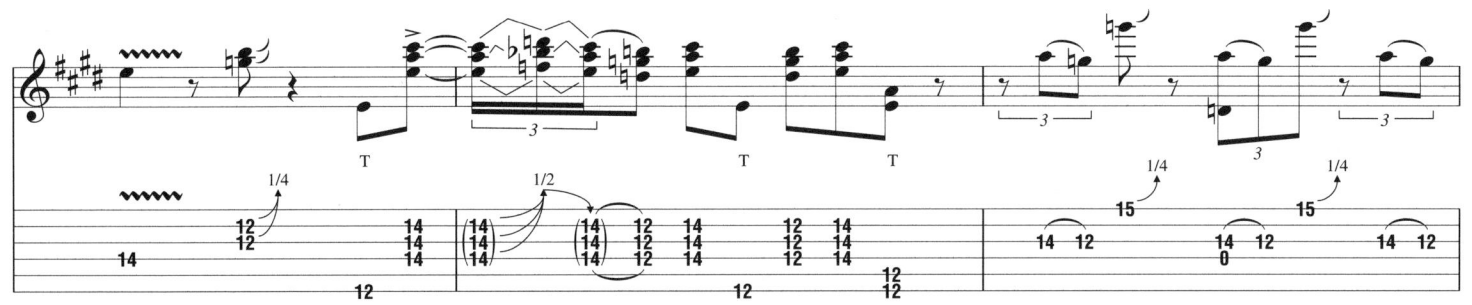
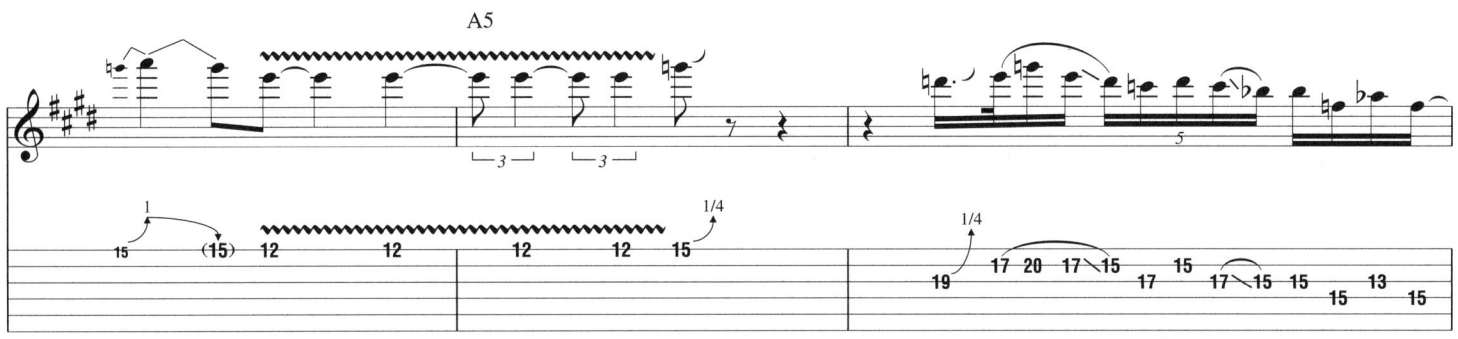
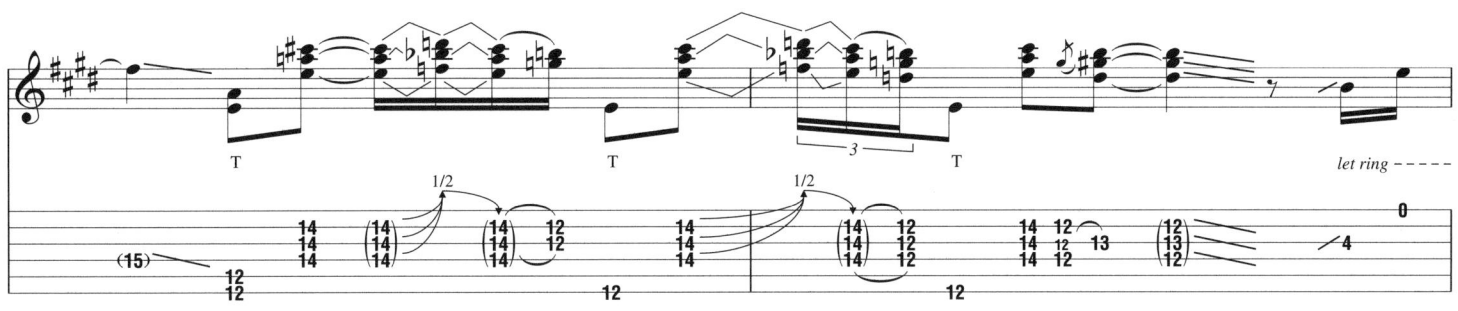

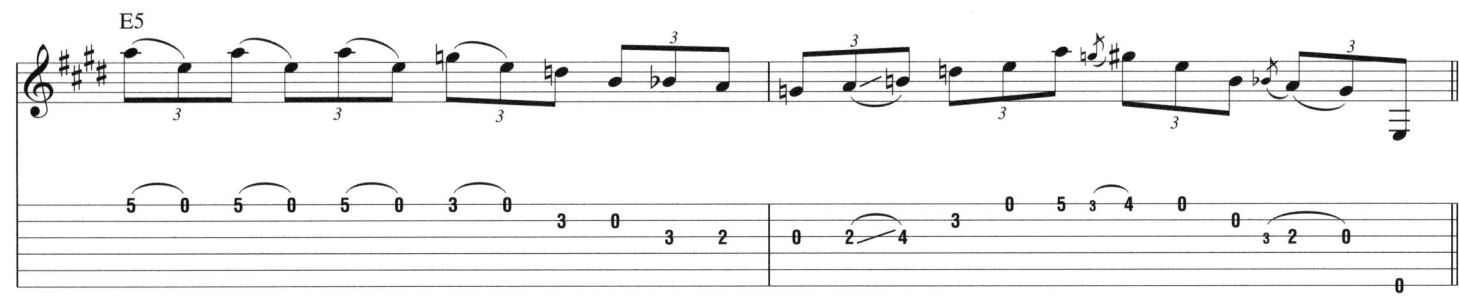

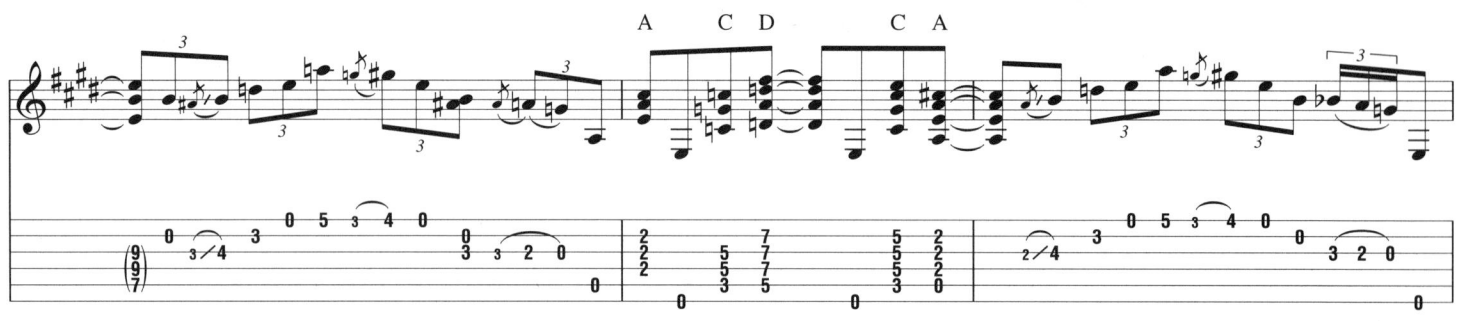
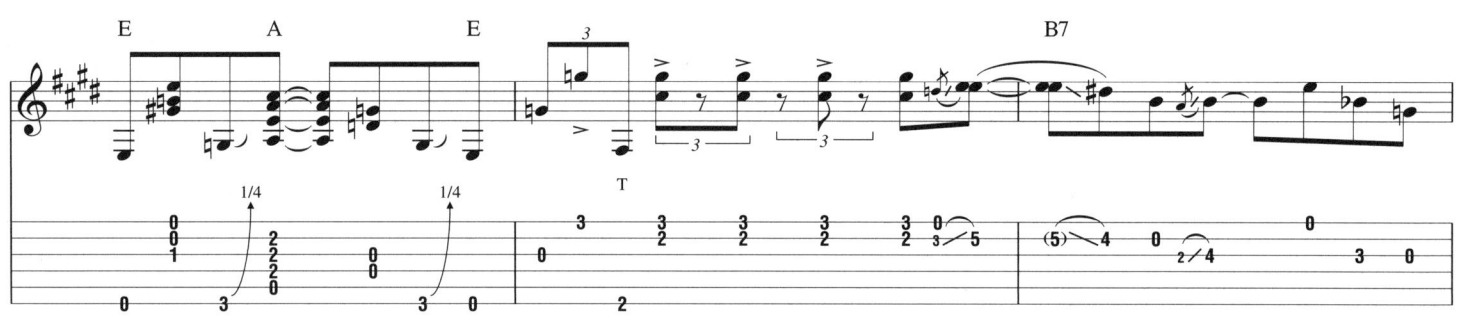
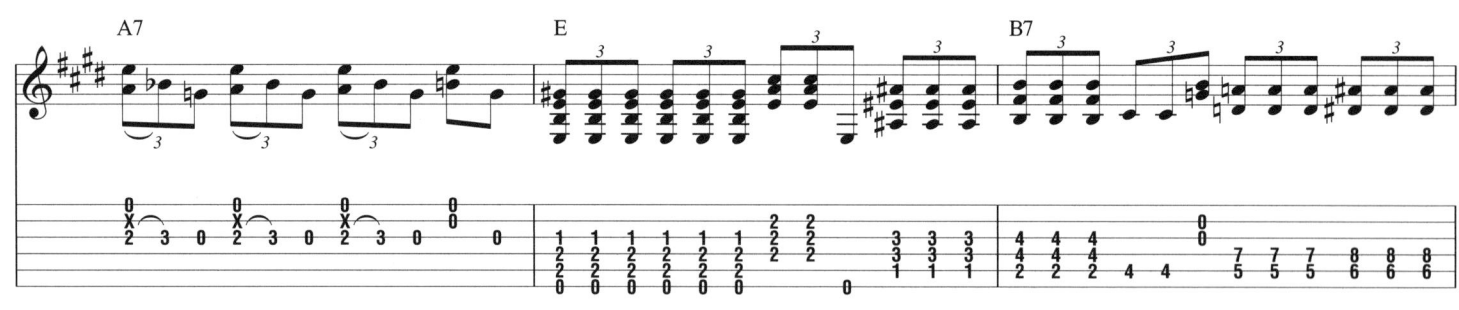
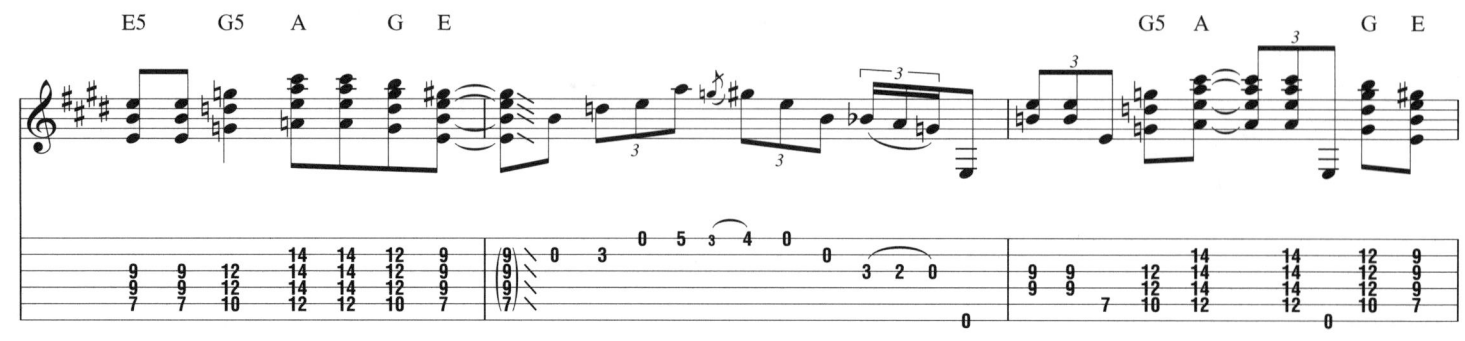

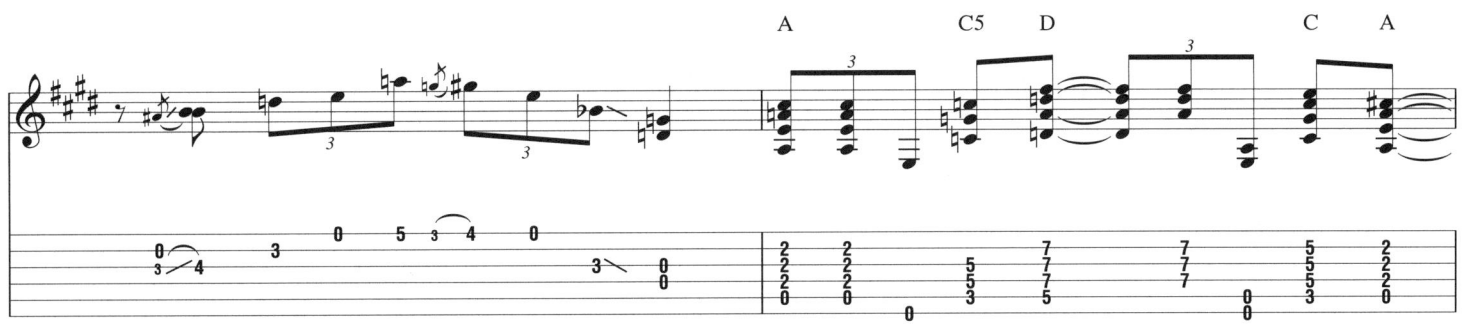
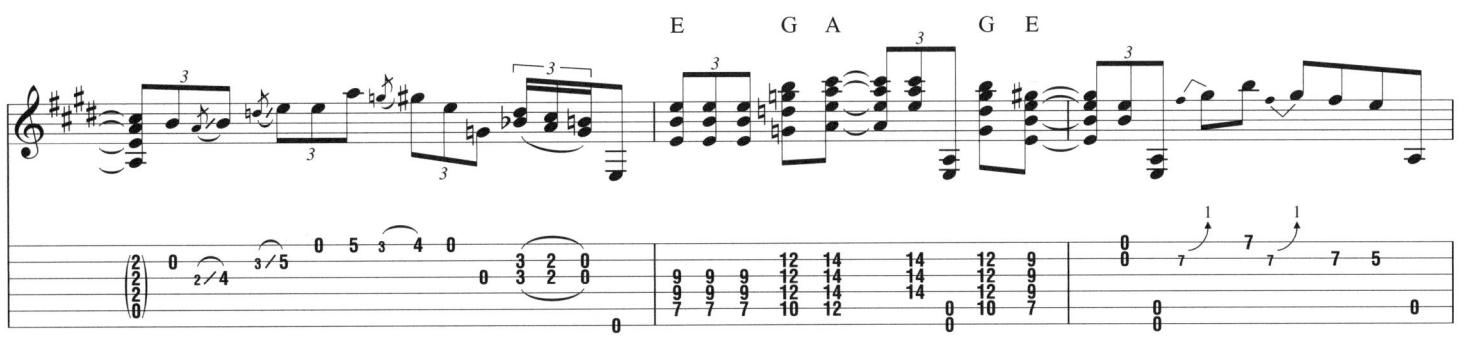

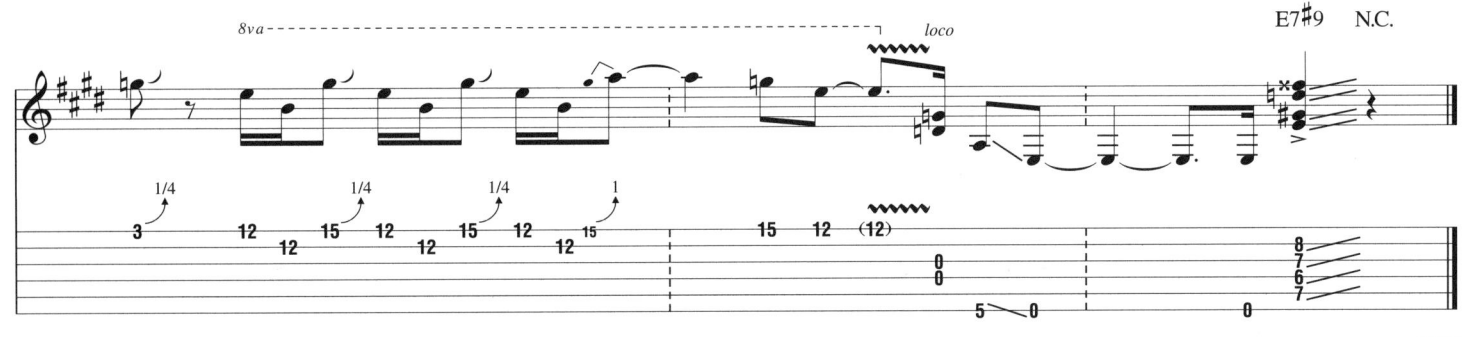

from *Up From Down Under*
Up From Down Under
By Tommy Emmanuel and Alan Mansfield

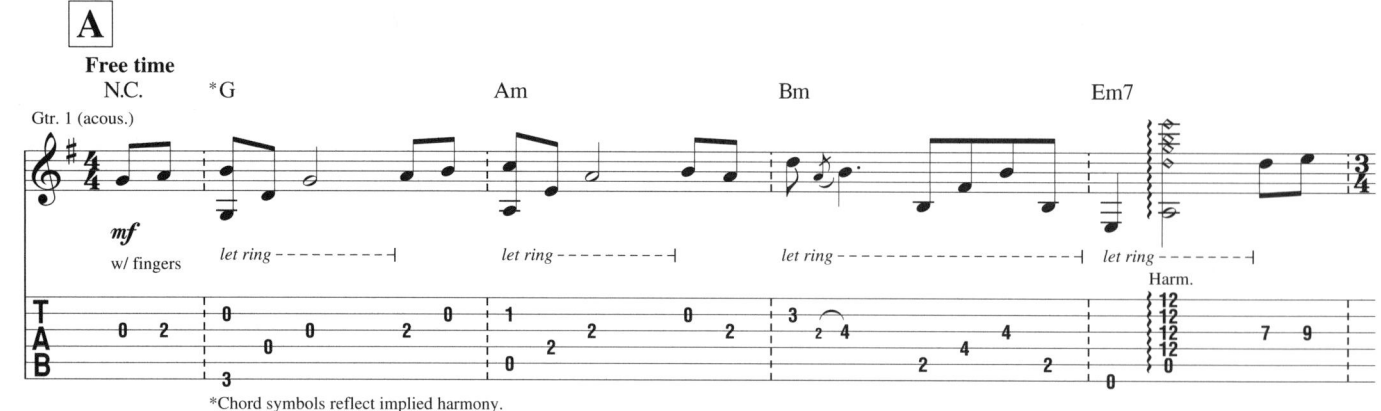

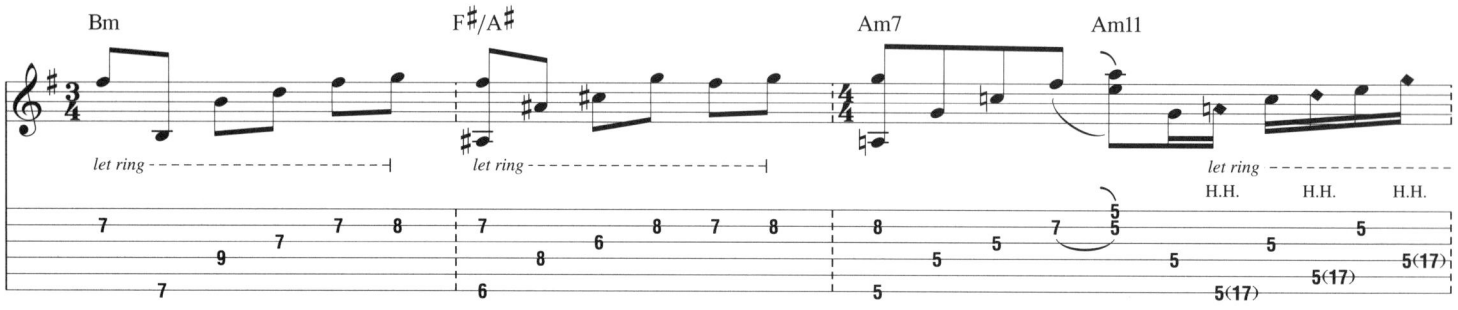

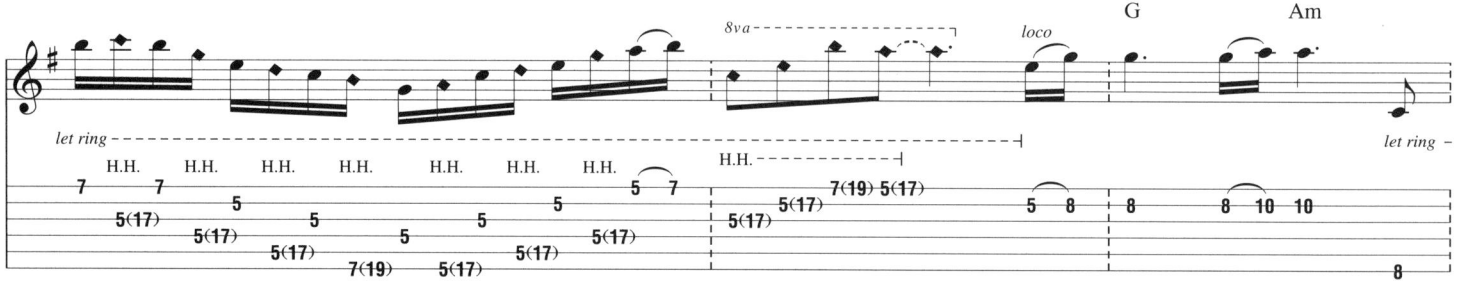

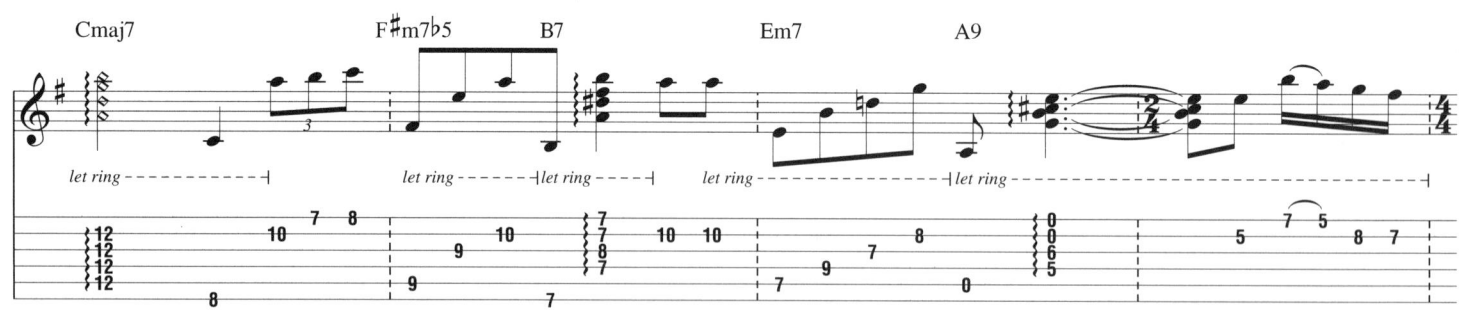

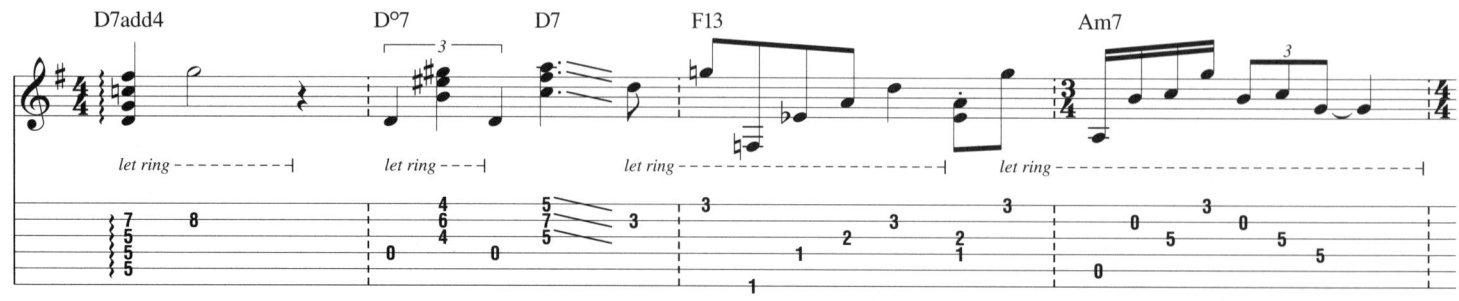

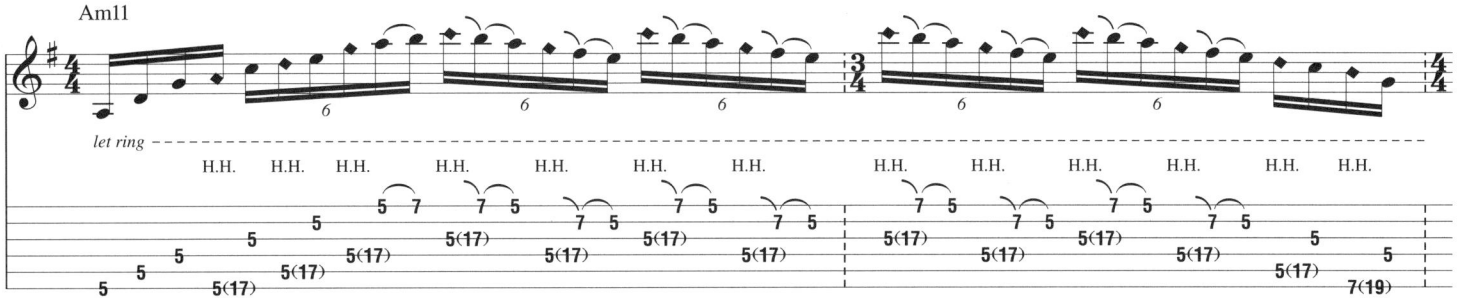
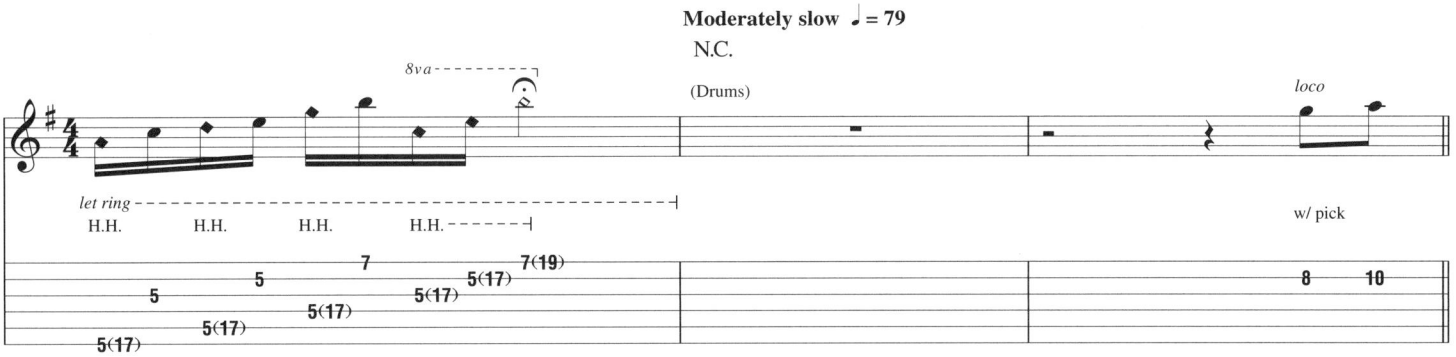
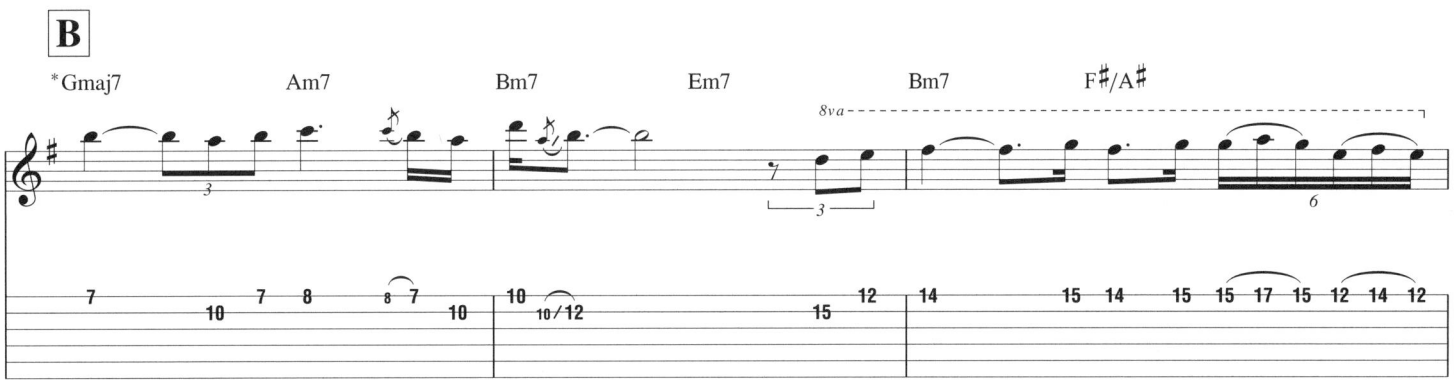

*Chord symbols reflect overall harmony.

129

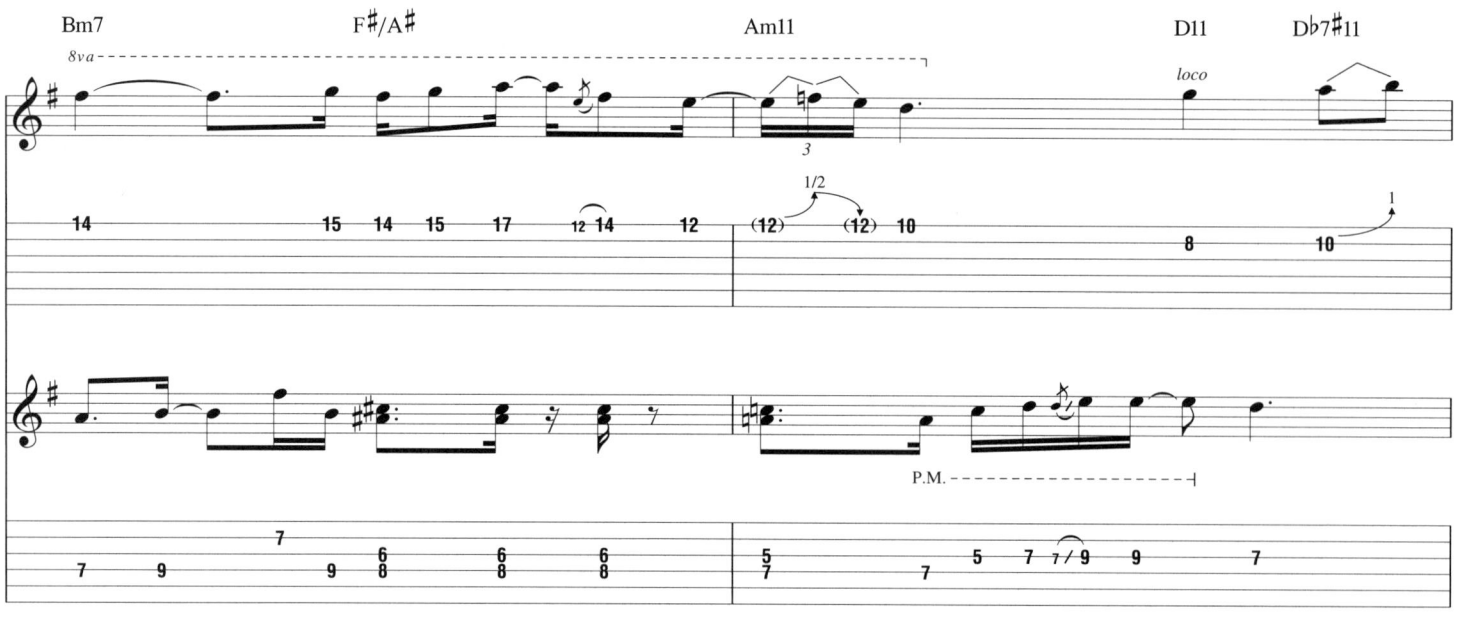
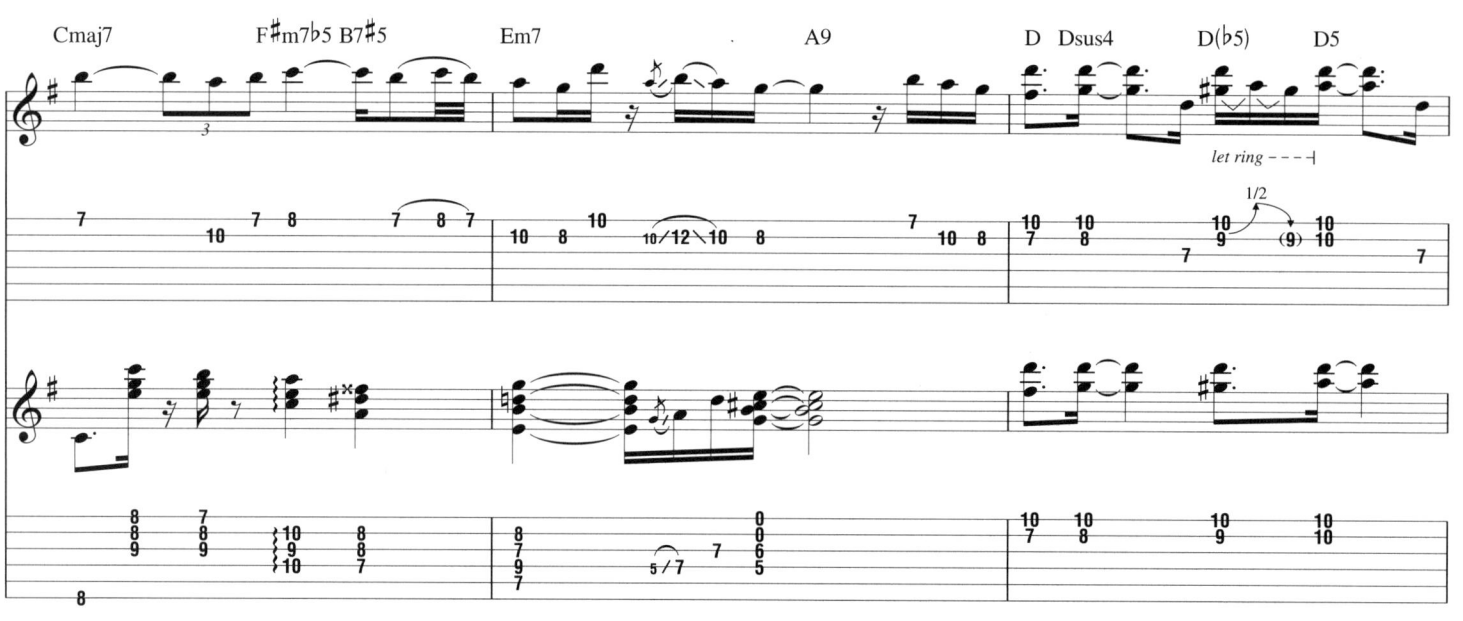
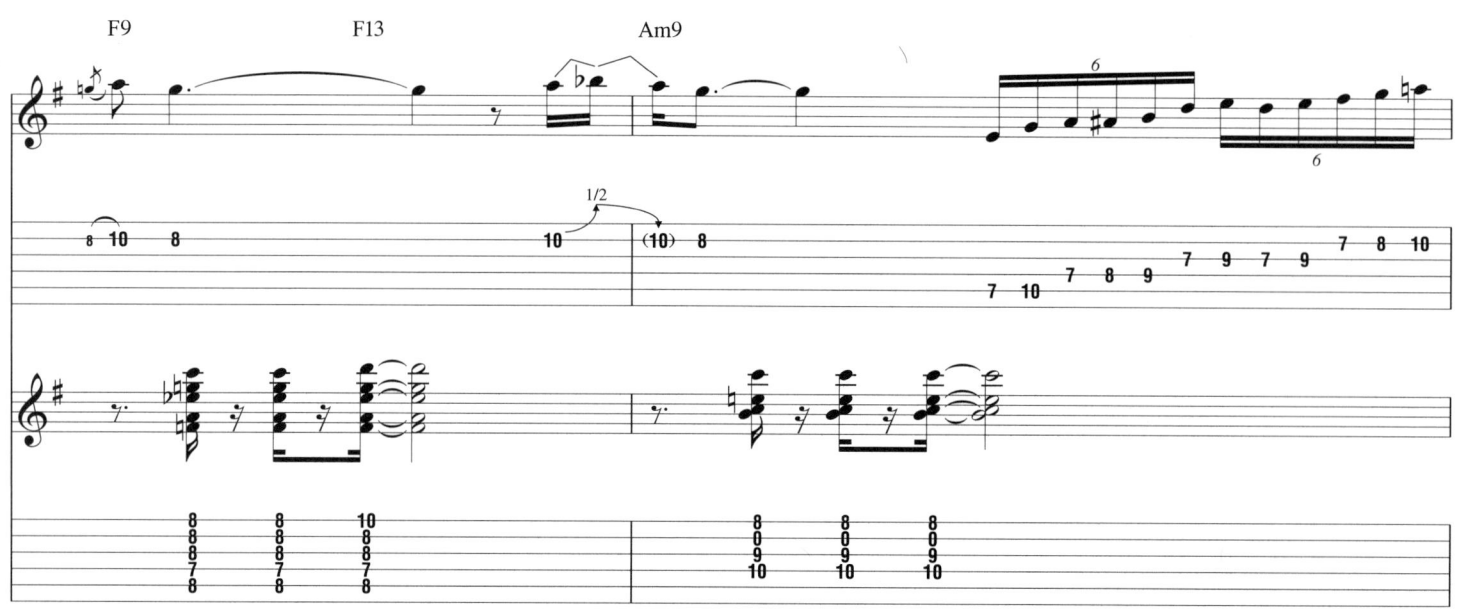

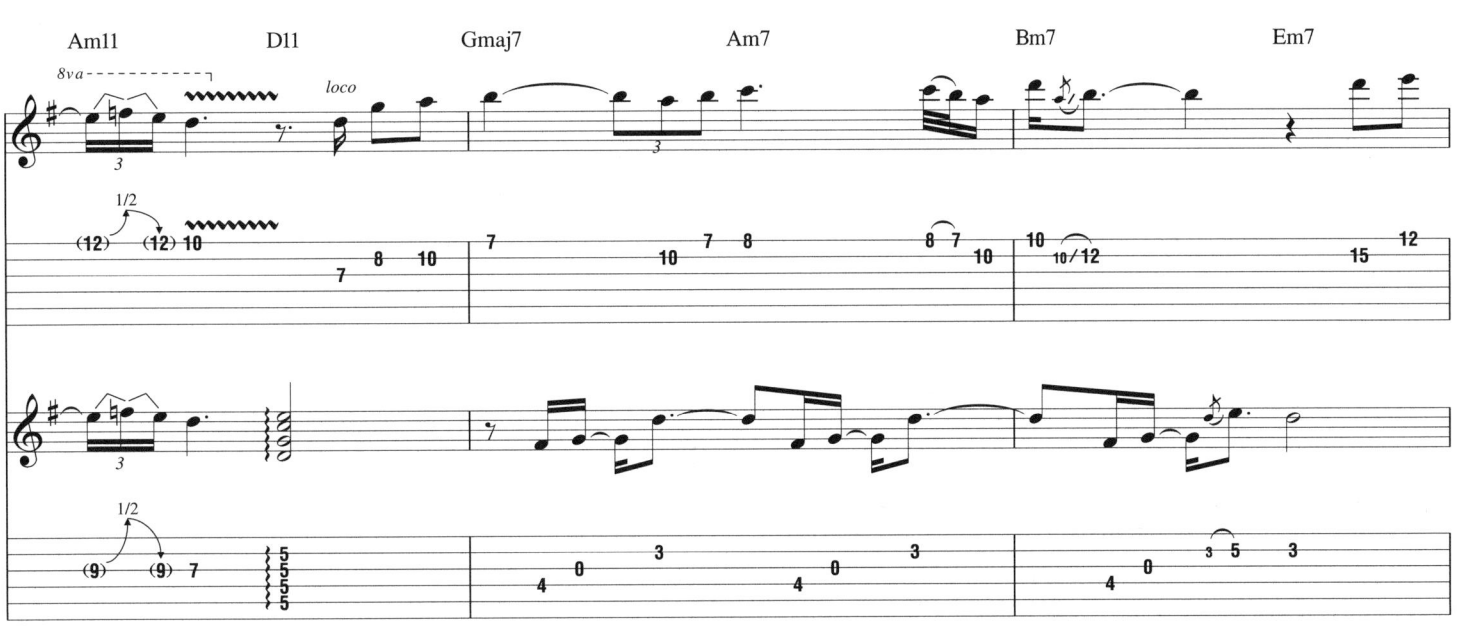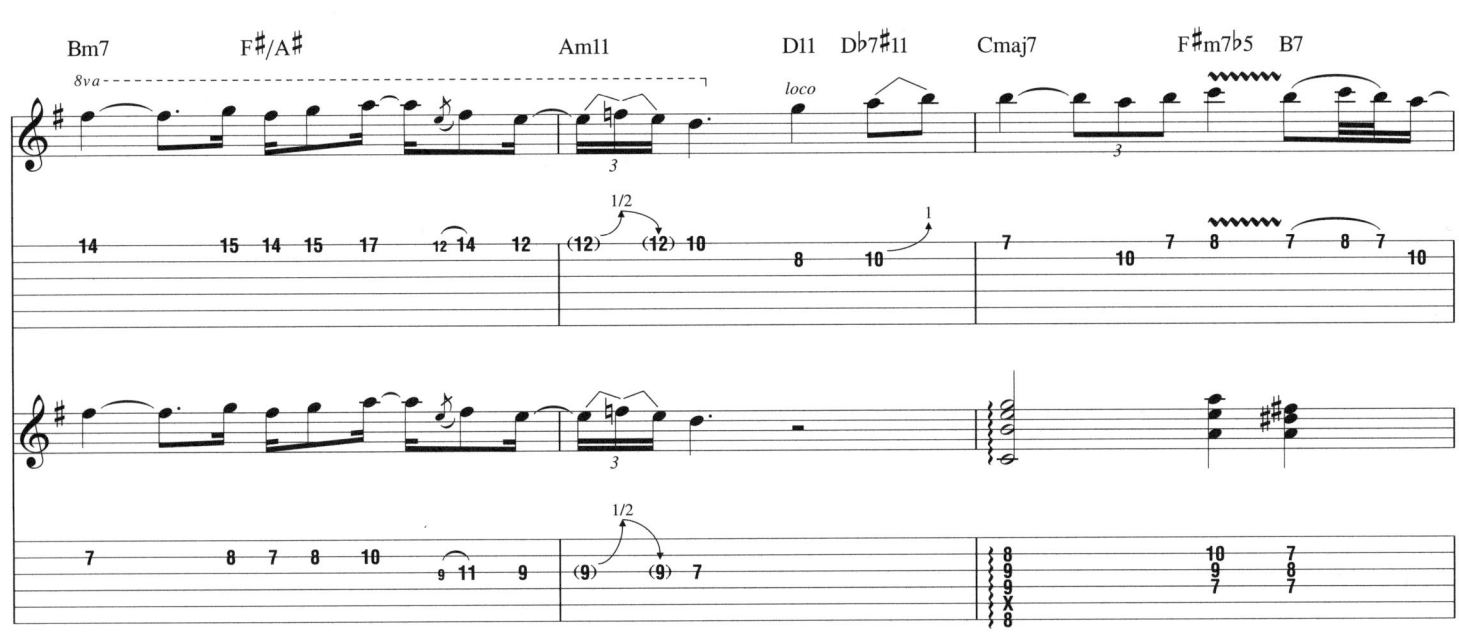

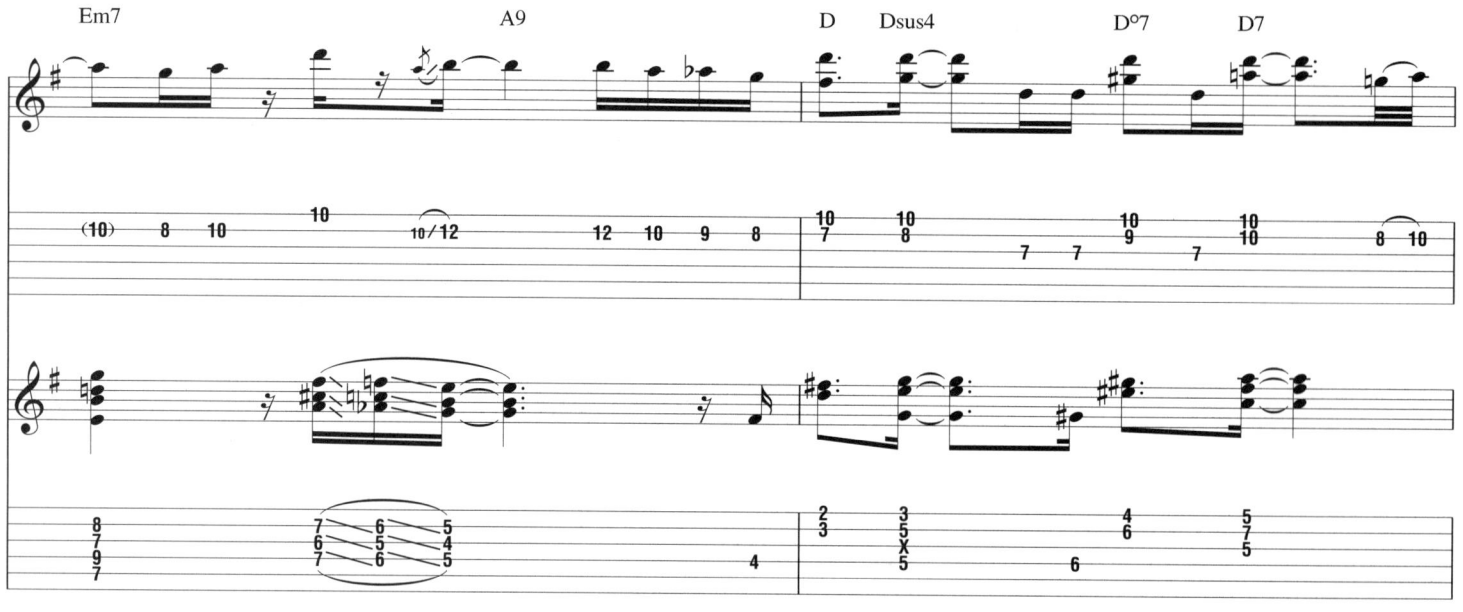

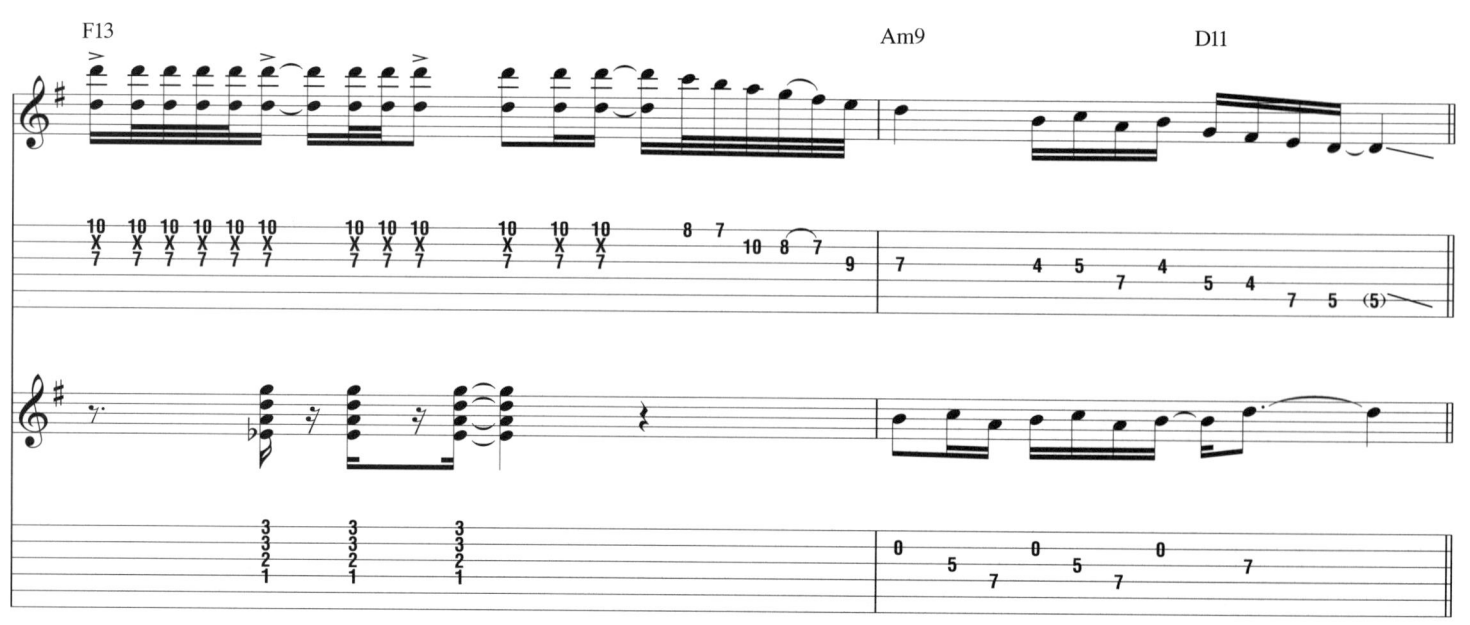

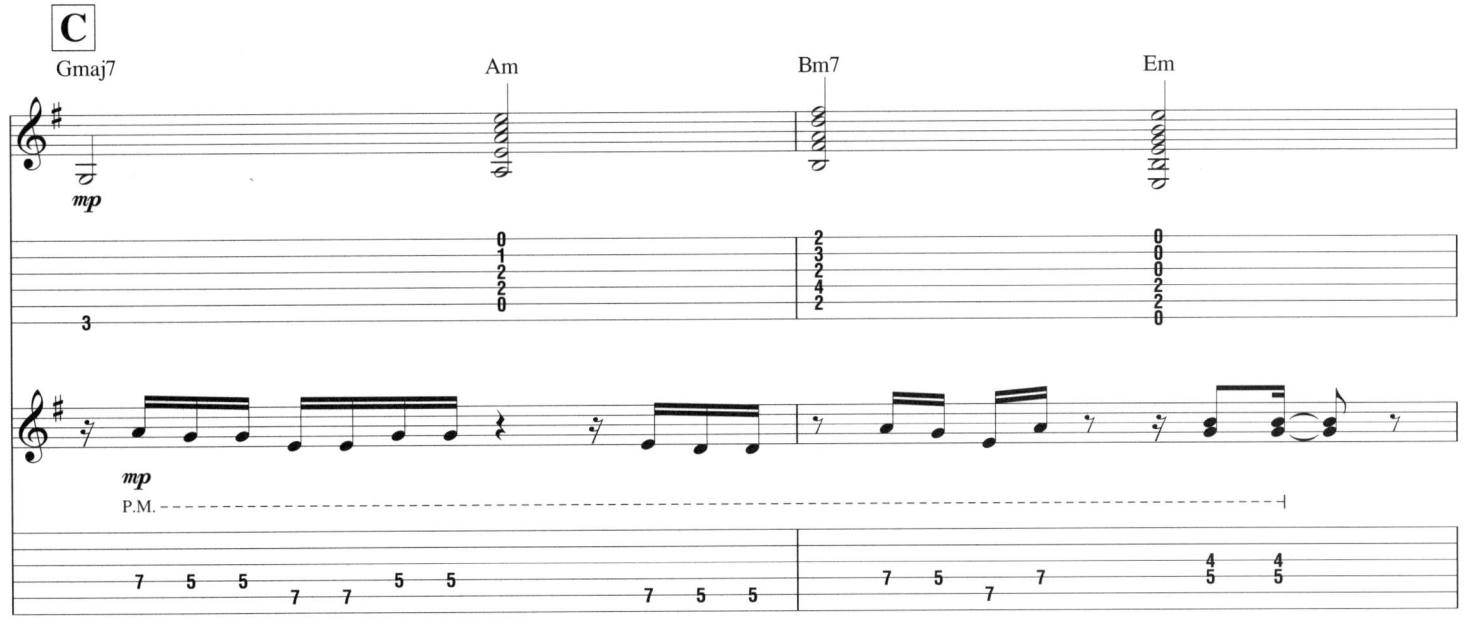

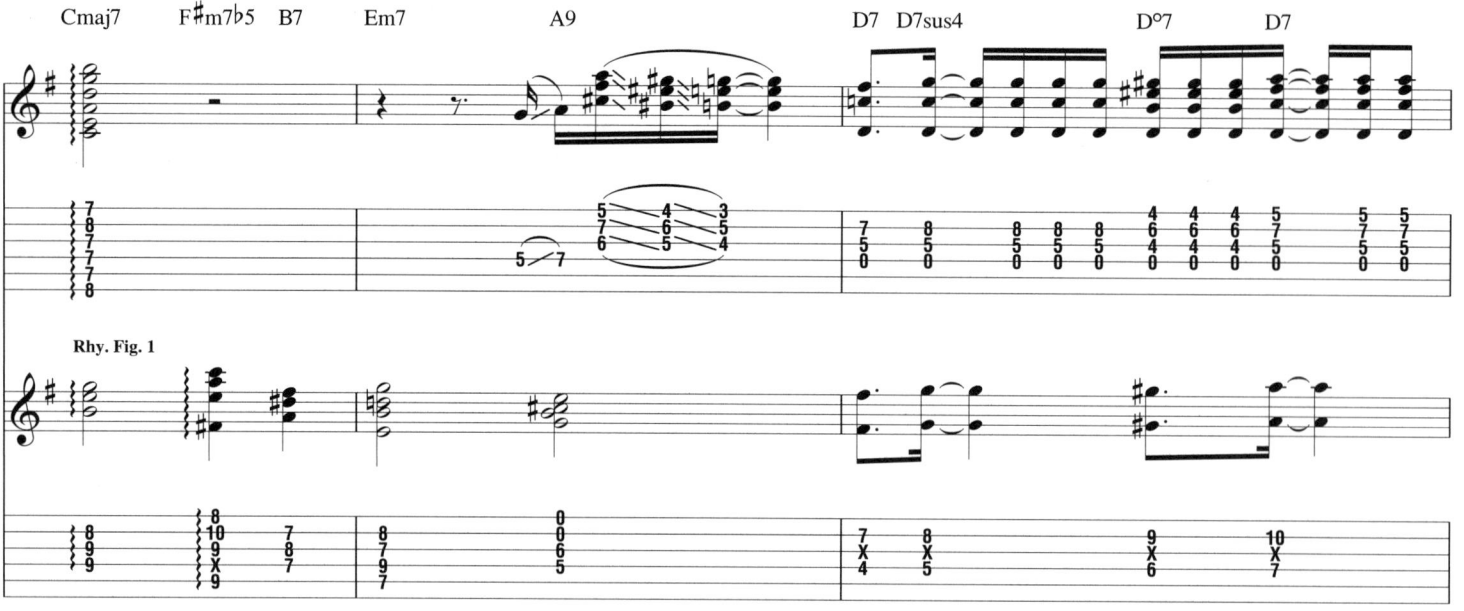
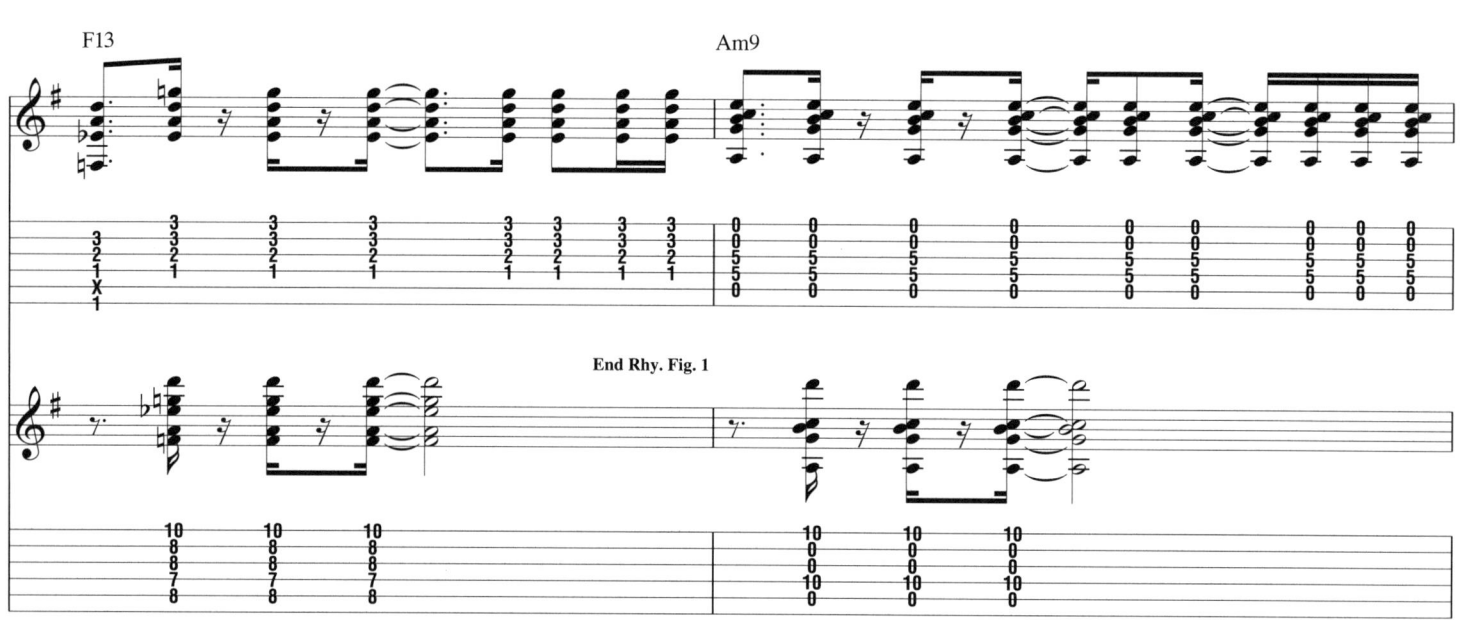
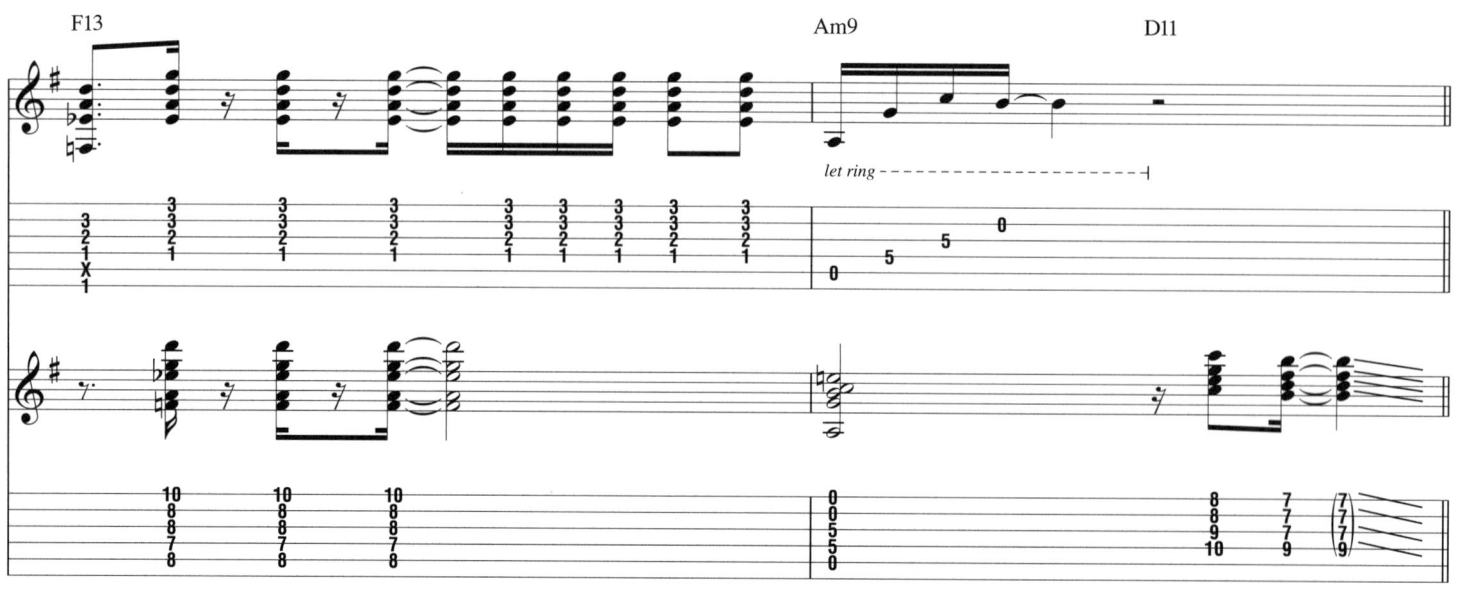

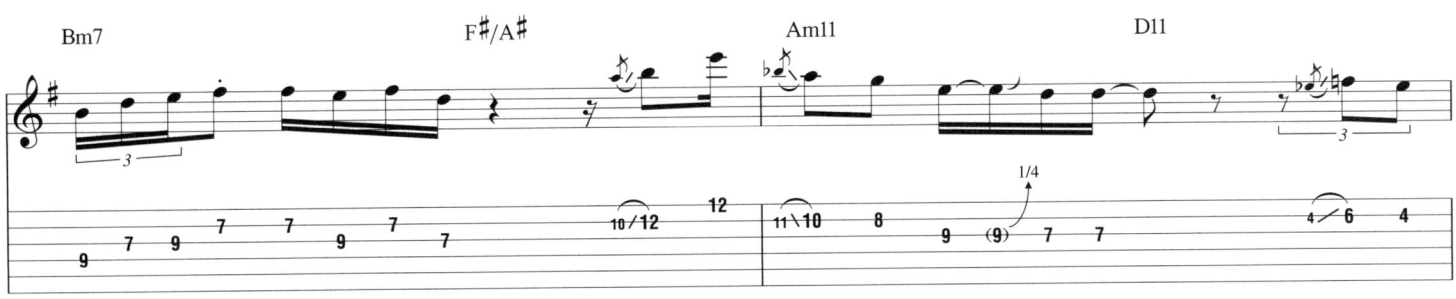
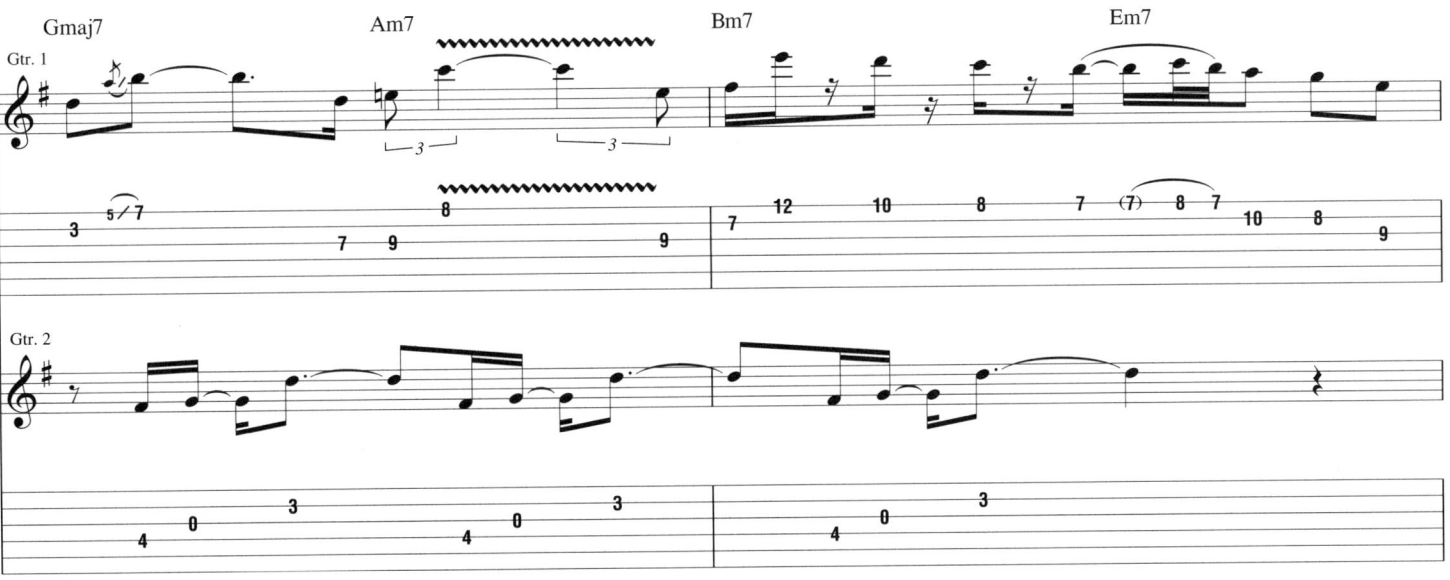
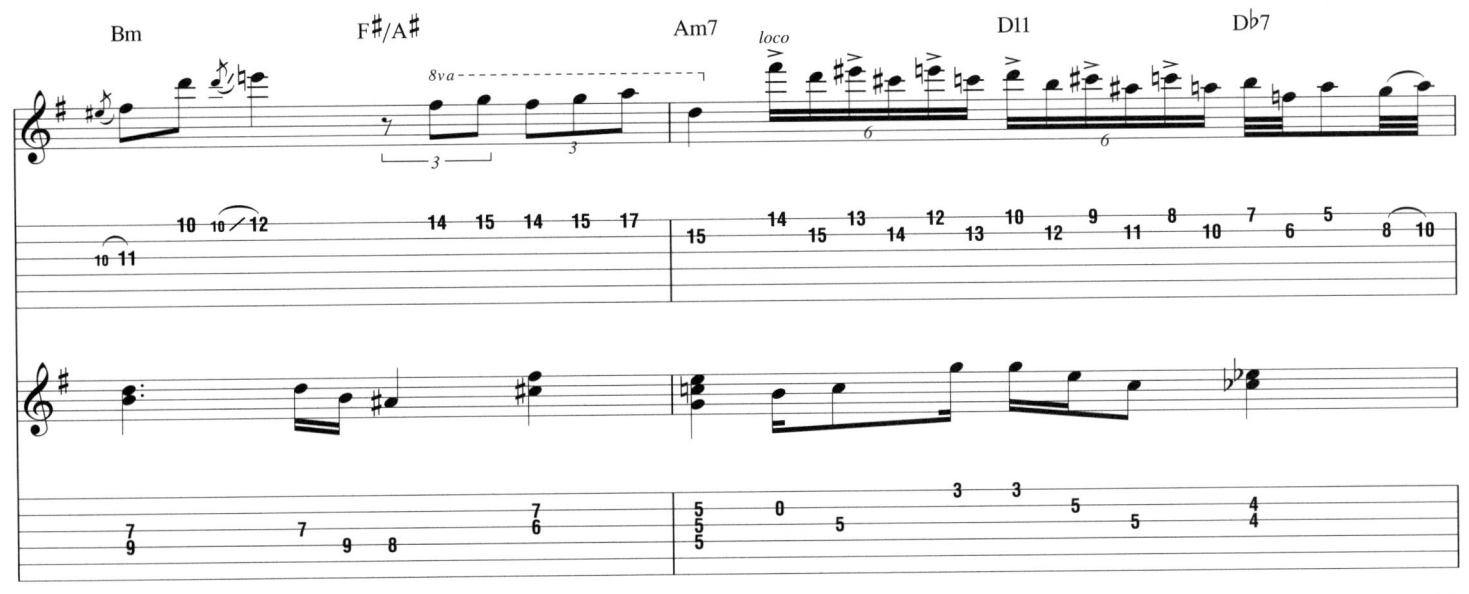

135

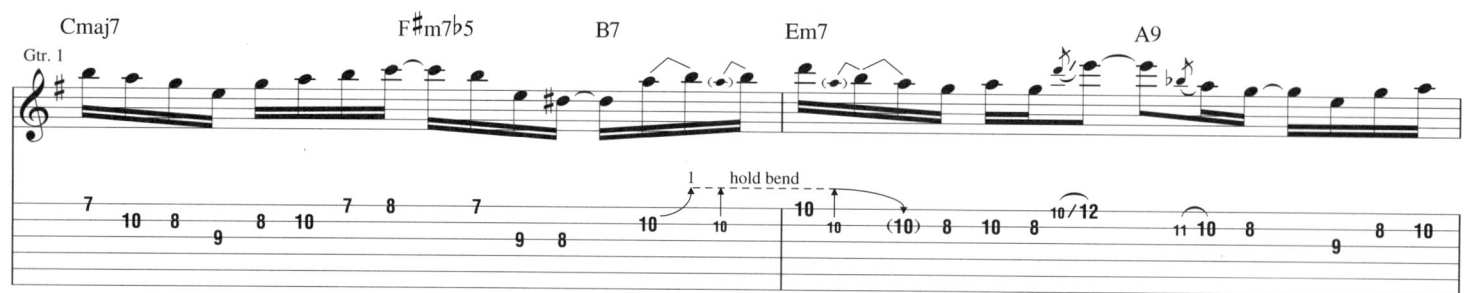
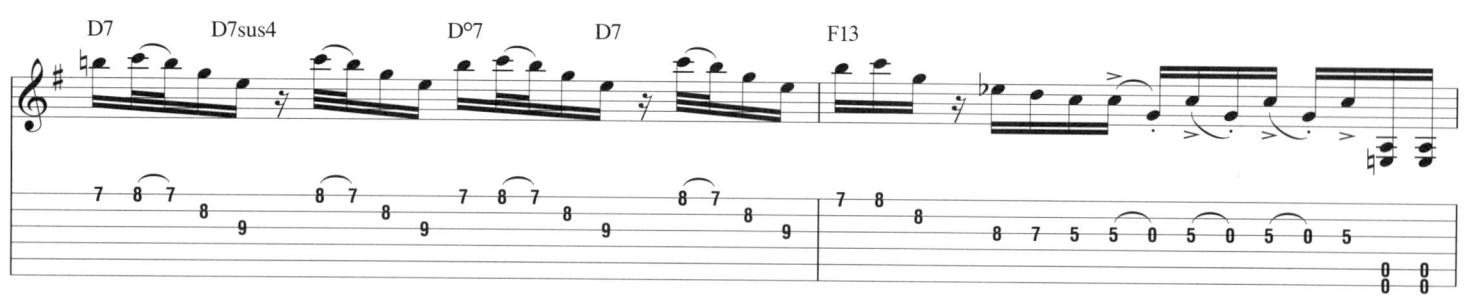
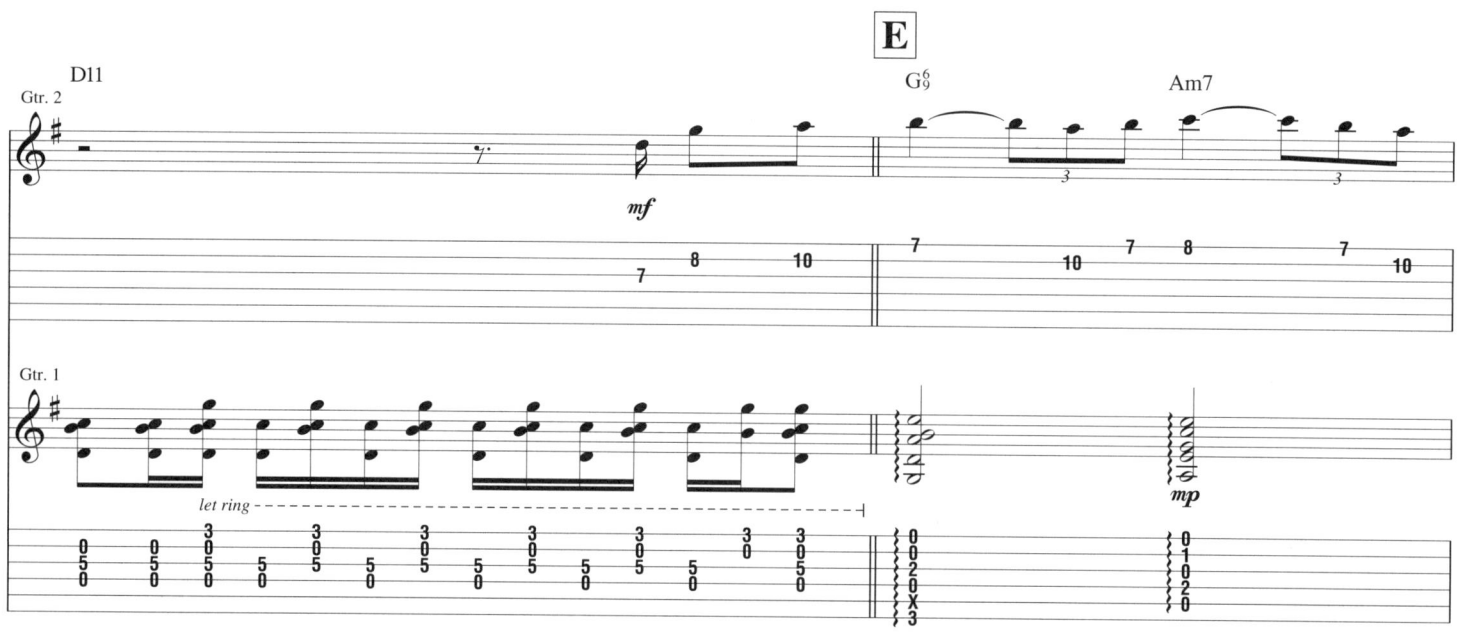

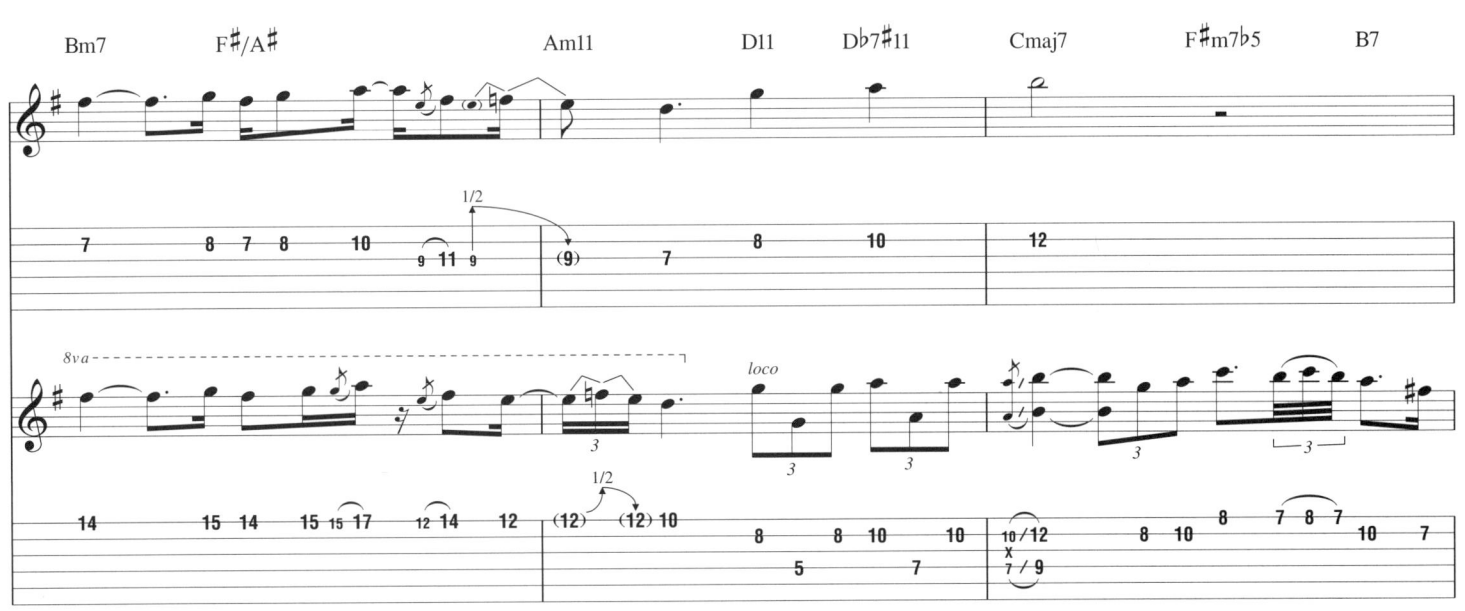

Am11
F13
1/2
let ring
F
Am9
Gtr. 2 tacet
Gtr. 1
Gtr. 3 (acous.)
mf
Gtr. 2
Gtr. 1 tacet
Gtr. 3
1/4

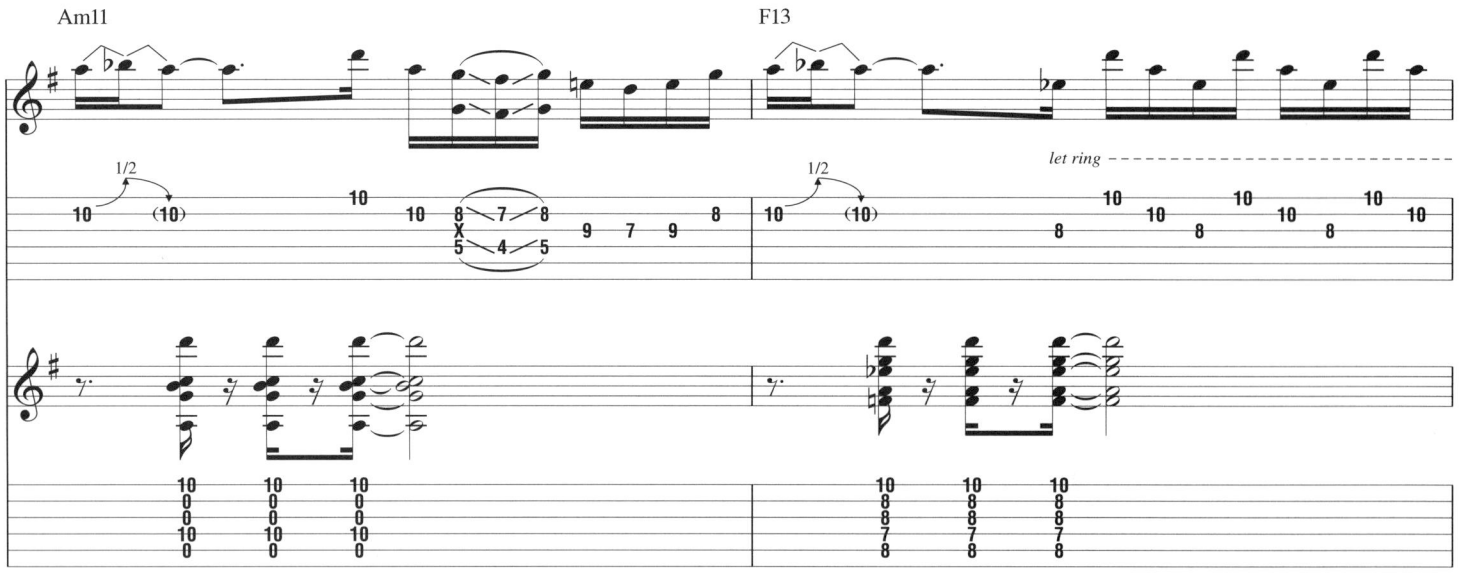

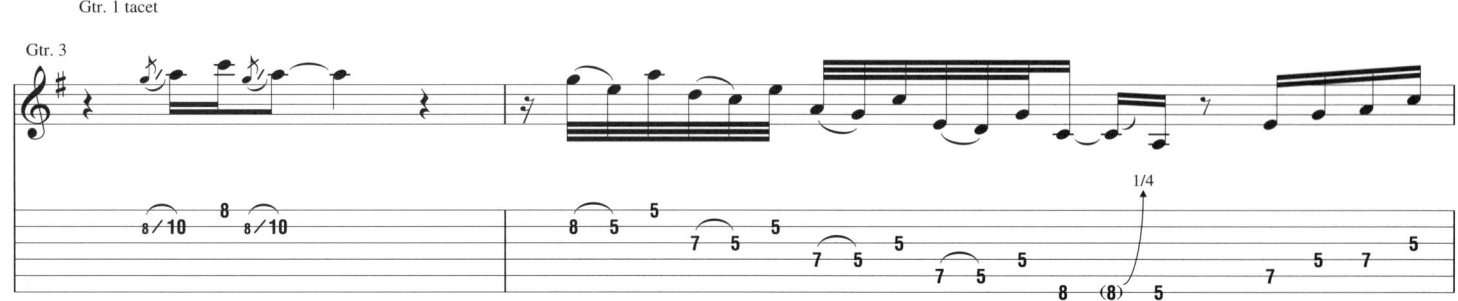

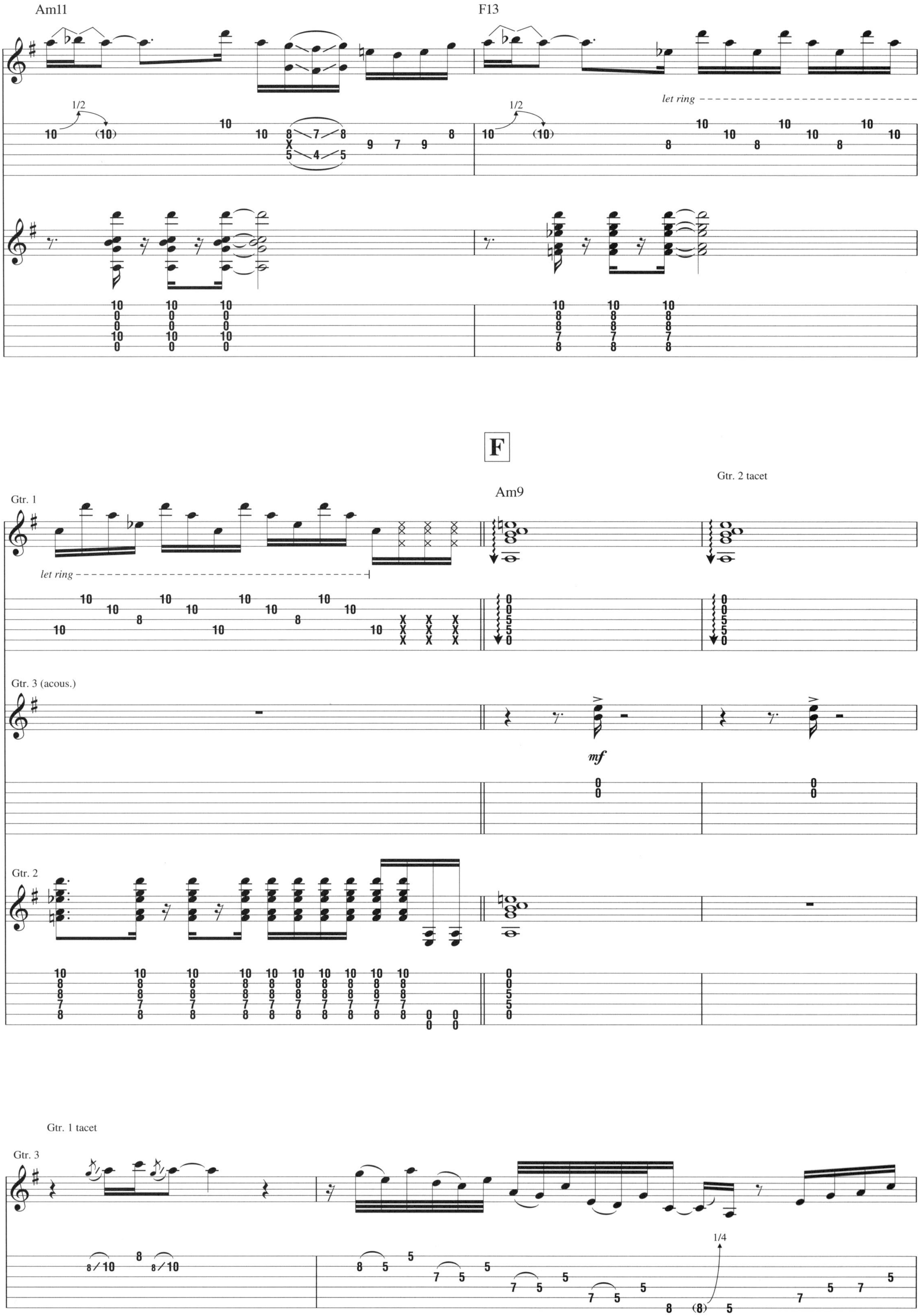

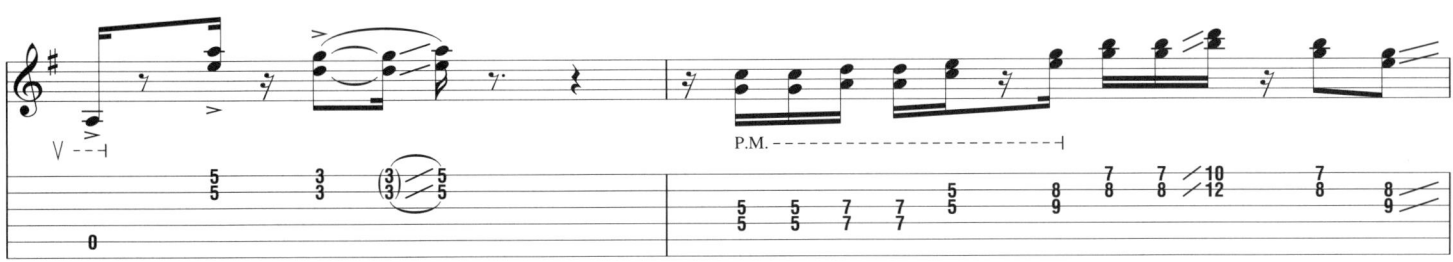
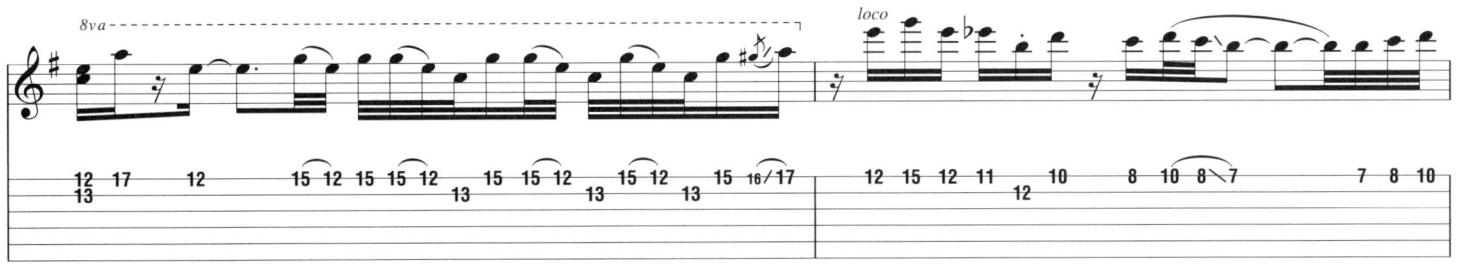

Begin fade

Fade out

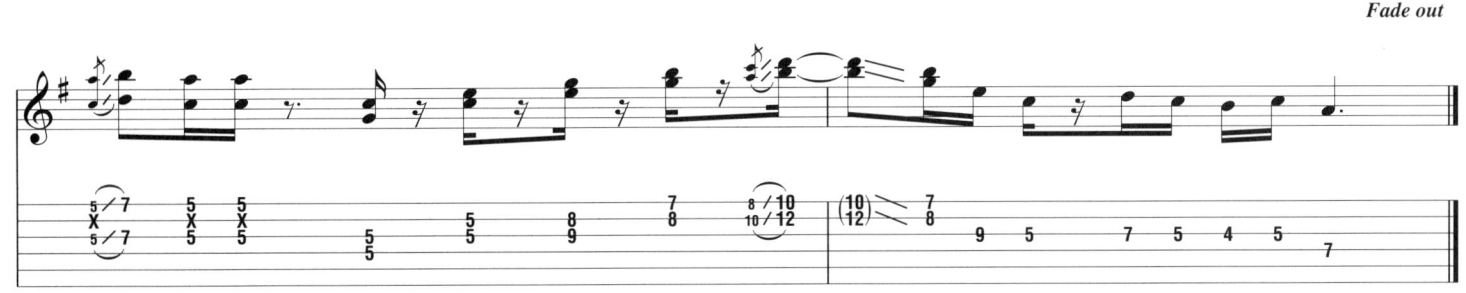

Guitar Notation Legend

Guitar music can be notated three different ways: on a *musical staff*, in *tablature*, and in *rhythm slashes*.

RHYTHM SLASHES are written above the staff. Strum chords in the rhythm indicated. Use the chord diagrams found at the top of the first page of the transcription for the appropriate chord voicings. Round noteheads indicate single notes.

THE MUSICAL STAFF shows pitches and rhythms and is divided by bar lines into measures. Pitches are named after the first seven letters of the alphabet.

TABLATURE graphically represents the guitar fingerboard. Each horizontal line represents a string, and each number represents a fret.

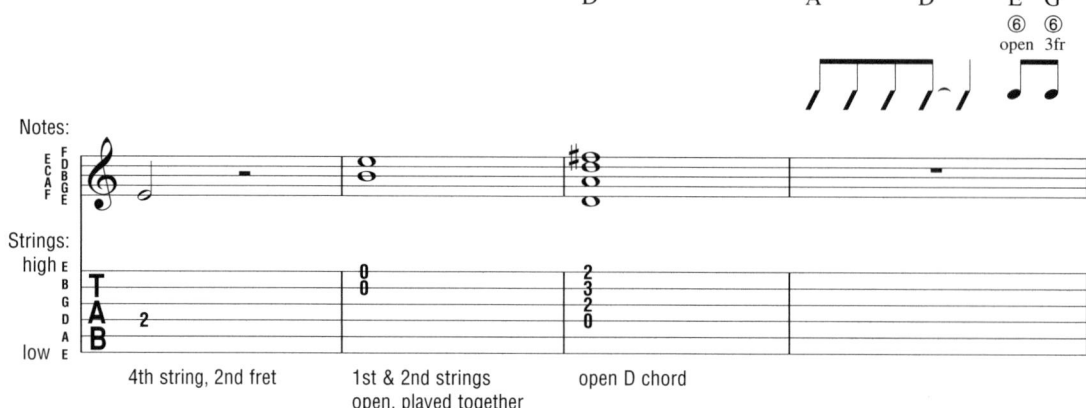

Definitions for Special Guitar Notation

HALF-STEP BEND: Strike the note and bend up 1/2 step.

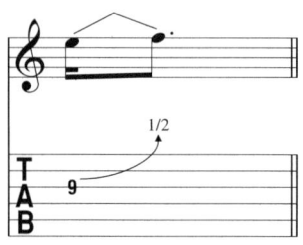

WHOLE-STEP BEND: Strike the note and bend up one step.

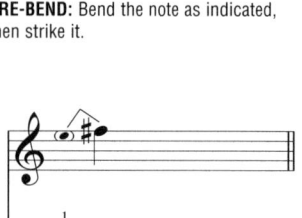

GRACE NOTE BEND: Strike the note and immediately bend up as indicated.

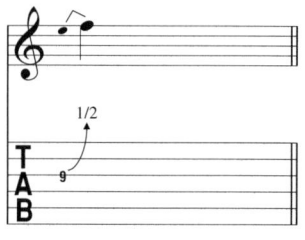

SLIGHT (MICROTONE) BEND: Strike the note and bend up 1/4 step.

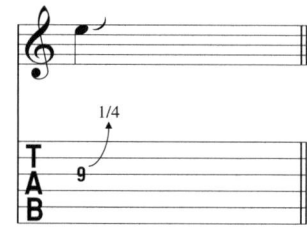

BEND AND RELEASE: Strike the note and bend up as indicated, then release back to the original note. Only the first note is struck.

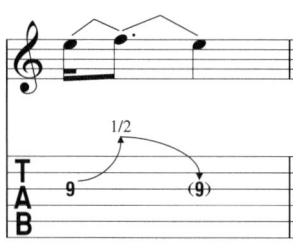

PRE-BEND: Bend the note as indicated, then strike it.

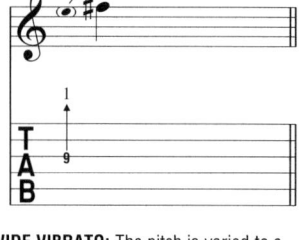

PRE-BEND AND RELEASE: Bend the note as indicated. Strike it and release the bend back to the original note.

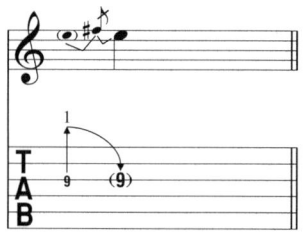

UNISON BEND: Strike the two notes simultaneously and bend the lower note up to the pitch of the higher.

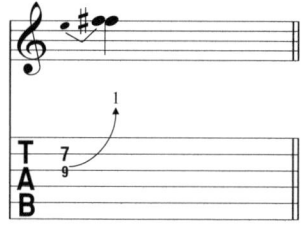

VIBRATO: The string is vibrated by rapidly bending and releasing the note with the fretting hand.

WIDE VIBRATO: The pitch is varied to a greater degree by vibrating with the fretting hand.

HAMMER-ON: Strike the first (lower) note with one finger, then sound the higher note (on the same string) with another finger by fretting it without picking.

PULL-OFF: Place both fingers on the notes to be sounded. Strike the first note and without picking, pull the finger off to sound the second (lower) note.

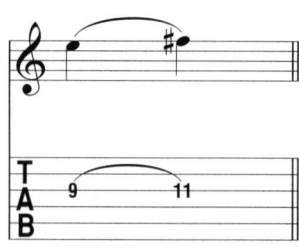
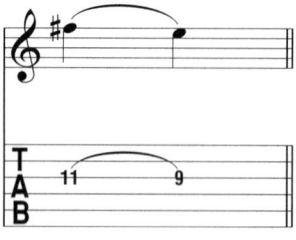
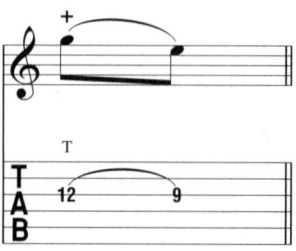

LEGATO SLIDE: Strike the first note and then slide the same fret-hand finger up or down to the second note. The second note is not struck.

SHIFT SLIDE: Same as legato slide, except the second note is struck.

TRILL: Very rapidly alternate between the notes indicated by continuously hammering on and pulling off.

TAPPING: Hammer ("tap") the fret indicated with the pick-hand index or middle finger and pull off to the note fretted by the fret hand.

NATURAL HARMONIC: Strike the note while the fret-hand lightly touches the string directly over the fret indicated.

PINCH HARMONIC: The note is fretted normally and a harmonic is produced by adding the edge of the thumb or the tip of the index finger of the pick hand to the normal pick attack.

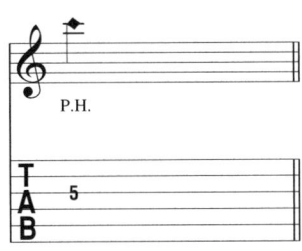

HARP HARMONIC: The note is fretted normally and a harmonic is produced by gently resting the pick hand's index finger directly above the indicated fret (in parentheses) while the pick hand's thumb or pick assists by plucking the appropriate string.

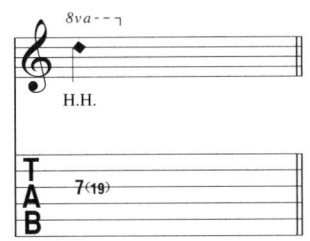

PICK SCRAPE: The edge of the pick is rubbed down (or up) the string, producing a scratchy sound.

MUFFLED STRINGS: A percussive sound is produced by laying the fret hand across the string(s) without depressing, and striking them with the pick hand.

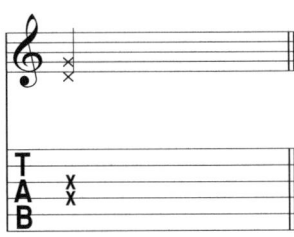

PALM MUTING: The note is partially muted by the pick hand lightly touching the string(s) just before the bridge.

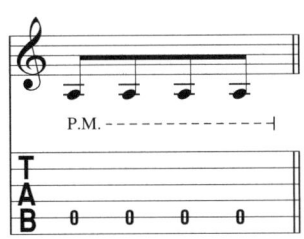

RAKE: Drag the pick across the strings indicated with a single motion.

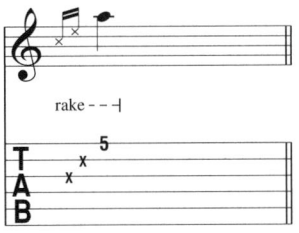

TREMOLO PICKING: The note is picked as rapidly and continuously as possible.

ARPEGGIATE: Play the notes of the chord indicated by quickly rolling them from bottom to top.

VIBRATO BAR DIVE AND RETURN: The pitch of the note or chord is dropped a specified number of steps (in rhythm), then returned to the original pitch.

VIBRATO BAR SCOOP: Depress the bar just before striking the note, then quickly release the bar.

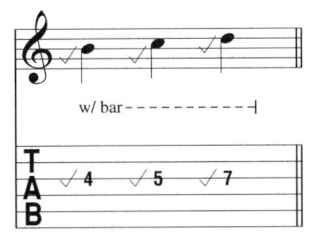

VIBRATO BAR DIP: Strike the note and then immediately drop a specified number of steps, then release back to the original pitch.

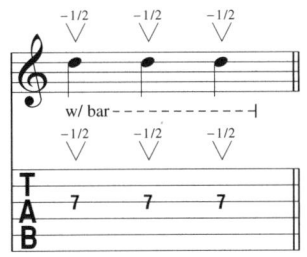

Additional Musical Definitions

 *(accent)* • Accentuate note (play it louder).

 *(accent)* • Accentuate note with great intensity.

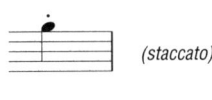 *(staccato)* • Play the note short.

 • Downstroke

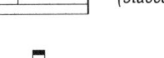 • Upstroke

D.S. al Coda • Go back to the sign (𝄋), then play until the measure marked "*To Coda*," then skip to the section labelled "**Coda**."

D.C. al Fine • Go back to the beginning of the song and play until the measure marked "*Fine*" (end).

Rhy. Fig. • Label used to recall a recurring accompaniment pattern (usually chordal).

Riff • Label used to recall composed, melodic lines (usually single notes) which recur.

Fill • Label used to identify a brief melodic figure which is to be inserted into the arrangement.

Rhy. Fill • A chordal version of a Fill.

tacet • Instrument is silent (drops out).

 • Repeat measures between signs.

 • When a repeated section has different endings, play the first ending only the first time and the second ending only the second time.

NOTE: Tablature numbers in parentheses mean:
1. The note is being sustained over a system (note in standard notation is tied), or
2. The note is sustained, but a new articulation (such as a hammer-on, pull-off, slide or vibrato) begins, or
3. The note is a barely audible "ghost" note (note in standard notation is also in parentheses).

FINGERPICKING GUITAR BOOKS

Hone your fingerpicking skills with these great songbooks featuring solo guitar arrangements in standard notation and tablature. The arrangements in these books are carefully written for intermediate-level guitarists. Each song combines melody and harmony in one superb guitar fingerpicking arrangement. Each book also includes an introduction to basic fingerstyle guitar.

FINGERPICKING ACOUSTIC
15 songs: Behind Blue Eyes • Best of My Love • Blowin' in the Wind • The Boxer • Dust in the Wind • Helplessly Hoping • Hey Jude • In My Life • Learning to Fly • Leaving on a Jet Plane • Tears in Heaven • Time in a Bottle • You've Got a Friend • and more.
00699614...$8.95

FINGERPICKING ACOUSTIC ROCK
15 songs: American Pie • Bridge over Troubled Water • Every Rose Has Its Thorn • Knockin' on Heaven's Door • Landslide • More Than Words • Norwegian Wood (This Bird Has Flown) • Suite: Judy Blue Eyes • Wanted Dead or Alive • and more.
00699764...$7.95

FINGERPICKING BACH
12 masterpieces from J.S. Bach: Air on the G String • Bourrée in E Minor • Jesu, Joy of Man's Desiring • Little Prelude No. 2 in C Major • Minuet in G • Prelude in C Major • Quia Respexit • Sheep May Safely Graze • and more.
00699793...$7.95

FINGERPICKING BALLADS
15 songs: Against All Odds • (Everything I Do) I Do It for You • Fields of Gold • Have I Told You Lately • It's All Coming Back to Me Now • Looks Like We Made It • Rainy Days and Mondays • Say You, Say Me • She's Got a Way • Your Song • and more.
00699717...$7.95

FINGERPICKING BEATLES
30 songs including: All You Need Is Love • And I Love Her • Can't Buy Me Love • Hey Jude • In My Life • Lady Madonna • Let It Be • Love Me Do • Michelle • Nowhere Man • Please Please Me • Something • Ticket to Ride • Yellow Submarine • Yesterday • and more.
00699049...$17.95

FINGERPICKING CHILDREN'S SONGS
15 songs: Any Dream Will Do • Do-Re-Mi • It's a Small World • Linus and Lucy • The Muppet Show Theme • Puff the Magic Dragon • The Rainbow Connection • Sesame Street Theme • Winnie the Pooh • Zip-A-Dee-Doo-Dah • and more.
00699712...$7.95

FINGERPICKING CHRISTMAS
20 classic carols: Away in a Manger • Deck the Hall • The First Noel • God Rest Ye, Merry Gentlemen • Hark! The Herald Angels Sing • It Came Upon the Midnight Clear • Jingle Bells • O Little Town of Bethlehem • Silent Night • What Child Is This • and more.
00699599...$7.95

FINGERPICKING CLASSICAL
15 songs: Ave Maria • Bourée in E Minor • Canon in D • Eine Kleine Nachtmusik • Für Elise • Habanera • Minuet in G Major (Bach) • Minuet in G Major (Beethoven) • New World Symphony • Pomp and Circumstance • and more.
00699620...$7.95

FINGERPICKING COUNTRY
17 classic favorites: Always on My Mind • By the Time I Get to Phoenix • Could I Have This Dance • Crazy • Green Green Grass of Home • He Stopped Loving Her Today • I Walk the Line • King of the Road • Tennessee Waltz • You Are My Sunshine • and more.
00699687...$7.95

FINGERPICKING DISNEY
15 songs: The Bare Necessities • Beauty and the Beast • Can You Feel the Love Tonight • Colors of the Wind • Go the Distance • If I Didn't Have You • Look Through My Eyes • Reflection • Under the Sea • A Whole New World • You'll Be in My Heart • and more.
00699711...$9.95

FINGERPICKING HYMNS
15 songs: Amazing Grace • Beneath the Cross of Jesus • Come, Thou Fount of Every Blessing • For the Beauty of the Earth • I've Got Peace like a River • Jacob's Ladder • A Mighty Fortress Is Our God • Rock of Ages • and more.
00699688...$8.95

FINGERPICKING MOZART
15 of Mozart's timeless compositions: Ave Verum • Eine Kleine Nachtmusik • Laudate Dominum • Minuet in G Major, K. 1 • Piano Concerto No. 21 in C Major • Piano Sonata in A • Piano Sonata in C • Rondo in C Major • and more.
00699794...$7.95

FINGERPICKING POP
Includes 15 songs: Can You Feel the Love Tonight • Don't Know Why • Endless Love • Imagine • Let It Be • My Cherie Amour • My Heart Will Go On • Piano Man • Stand by Me • We've Only Just Begun • Wonderful Tonight • and more.
00699615...$7.95

FINGERPICKING PRAISE
15 songs: Above All • Breathe • Draw Me Close • Great Is the Lord • He Is Exalted • Jesus, Name Above All Names • Oh Lord, You're Beautiful • Open the Eyes of My Heart • Shine, Jesus, Shine • Shout to the Lord • You Are My King • and more.
00699714...$7.95

FINGERPICKING ROCK
15 songs: Abracadabra • Brown Eyed Girl • Crocodile Rock • Free Bird • The House of the Rising Sun • I Want You to Want Me • Livin' on a Prayer • Maggie May • Rhiannon • Still the Same • When the Children Cry • and more.
00699716...$7.95

FINGERPICKING STANDARDS
17 fantastic songs: Can't Help Falling in Love • Fly Me to the Moon • Georgia on My Mind • I Just Called to Say I Love You • Just the Way You Are • Misty • Moon River • Unchained Melody • What a Wonderful World • When I Fall in Love • Yesterday • and more.
00699613...$7.95

FINGERPICKING WEDDING
15 tunes for the big day: Beautiful in My Eyes • Don't Know Much • Endless Love • Grow Old with Me • In My Life • The Lord's Prayer • This Is the Day (A Wedding Song) • We've Only Just Begun • Wedding Processional • You and I • and more.
00699637...$7.95

FINGERPICKING YULETIDE
16 holiday favorites: Blue Christmas • The Christmas Song • Frosty the Snow Man • A Holly Jolly Christmas • I'll Be Home for Christmas • Jingle-Bell Rock • Let It Snow! Let It Snow! Let It Snow! • Merry Christmas, Darling • Rudolph the Red-Nosed Reindeer • and more.
00699654...$7.95

For More Information, See Your Local Music Dealer, Or Write To:

HAL•LEONARD® CORPORATION
7777 W. BLUEMOUND RD. P.O. BOX 13819 MILWAUKEE, WI 53213

Prices, contents and availability subject to change without notice.

Visit Hal Leonard online at **www.halleonard.com**

PLAY THE CLASSICS
JAZZ FOLIOS FOR GUITARISTS

BEST OF JAZZ GUITAR
by Wolf Marshall • Signature Licks

In this book/CD pack, Wolf Marshall provides a hands-on analysis of 10 of the most frequently played tunes in the jazz genre, as played by the leading guitarists of all time. Features: All the Things You Are • How Insensitive • I'll Remember April • So What • Yesterdays • and more.
00695586 Book/CD Pack........................$24.95

GUITAR STANDARDS
Classic Jazz Masters Series

16 classic jazz guitar performances transcribed note for note with tablature: All of You (Kenny Burrell) • Easter Parade (Herb Ellis) • I'll Remember April (Grant Green) • Lover Man (Django Reinhardt) • Song for My Father (George Benson) • The Way You Look Tonight (Wes Montgomery) • and more. Includes a discography.
00699143 Guitar Transcriptions $14.95

JAZZ BALLADS FOR FINGERSTYLE GUITAR

21 standards, including: Cry Me a River • Easy to Love • In a Sentimental Mood • Isn't It Romantic? • Mood Indigo • My Funny Valentine • My Romance • Some Enchanted Evening • Stella by Starlight • The Way You Look Tonight • When I Fall in Love • and more.
00699028 Fingerstyle Guitar $12.95

JAZZ CLASSICS FOR SOLO GUITAR
arranged by Robert B. Yelin

This collection includes excellent chord melody arrangements in standard notation and tablature for 35 all-time jazz favorites: April in Paris • Cry Me a River • Day by Day • God Bless' the Child • It Might as Well Be Spring • Lover • My Romance • Nuages • Satin Doll • Tenderly • Unchained Melody • Wave • and more!
00699279 Solo Guitar $17.95

JAZZ FAVORITES FOR SOLO GUITAR
arranged by Robert B. Yelin

This fantastic 35-song collection includes lush chord melody arrangements in standard notation and tab: Autumn in New York • Call Me Irresponsible • How Deep Is the Ocean • I Could Write a Book • The Lady Is a Tramp • Mood Indigo • Polka Dots and Moonbeams • Solitude • Take the "A" Train • Where or When • more.
00699278 Solo Guitar $17.95

JAZZ FOR THE ROCK GUITARIST
by Michael Mueller

Take your playing beyond barre chords and the blues box! This book/CD pack will take you through the essentials of the jazz idiom with plenty of exercises and examples – all of which are demonstrated on the accompanying CD.
00695856 Book/CD Pack........................$14.95

JAZZ GEMS FOR SOLO GUITAR
arranged by Robert B. Yelin

35 great solo arrangements of jazz classics, including: After You've Gone • Alice in Wonderland • The Christmas Song • Four • Meditation • Stompin' at the Savoy • Sweet and Lovely • Waltz for Debby • Yardbird Suite • You'll Never Walk Alone • You've Changed • and more.
00699617 Solo Guitar $17.95

JAZZ GUITAR BIBLE

The one book that has all of the jazz guitar classics transcribed note-for-note, with standard notation and tablature. Includes over 30 songs: Body and Soul • Girl Talk • I'll Remember April • In a Sentimental Mood • My Funny Valentine • Nuages • Satin Doll • So What • Stardust • Take Five • Tangerine • Yardbird Suite • and more.
00690466 Guitar Recorded Versions $19.95

JAZZ GUITAR CHORD MELODIES
arranged & performed by Dan Towey

This book/CD pack includes complete solo performances of 12 standards, including: All the Things You Are • Body and Soul • My Romance • How Insensitive • My One and Only Love • and more. The arrangements are performance level and range in difficulty from intermediate to advanced.
00698988 Book/CD Pack $19.95

JAZZ GUITAR PLAY-ALONG
Guitar Play-Along Volume 16

With this book/CD pack, all you have to do is follow the tab, listen to the CD to hear how the guitar should sound, and then play along using the separate backing tracks. 8 songs: All Blues • Bluesette • Footprints • How Insensitive (Insensatez) • Misty • Satin Doll • Stella by Starlight • Tenor Madness.
00699584 Book/CD Pack $14.95

JAZZ STANDARDS FOR FINGERSTYLE GUITAR

20 songs, including: All the Things You Are • Autumn Leaves • Bluesette • Body and Soul • Fly Me to the Moon • The Girl from Ipanema • How Insensitive • I've Grown Accustomed to Her Face • My Funny Valentine • Satin Doll • Stompin' at the Savoy • and more.
00699029 Fingerstyle Guitar $10.95

JAZZ STANDARDS FOR SOLO GUITAR
arranged by Robert B. Yelin

35 chord melody guitar arrangements, including: Ain't Misbehavin' • Autumn Leaves • Bewitched • Cherokee • Darn That Dream • Girl Talk • I've Got You Under My Skin • Lullaby of Birdland • My Funny Valentine • A Nightingale Sang in Berkeley Square • Stella by Starlight • The Very Thought of You • and more.
00699277 Solo Guitar $17.95

101 MUST-KNOW JAZZ LICKS
by Wolf Marshall

Add a jazz feel and flavor to your playing! 101 definitive licks, plus a demonstration CD, from every major jazz guitar style, neatly organized into easy-to-use categories. They're all here: swing and pre-bop, bebop, post-bop modern jazz, hard bop and cool jazz, modal jazz, soul jazz and postmodern jazz.
00695433 Book/CD Pack........................$16.95

FOR MORE INFORMATION, SEE YOUR LOCAL MUSIC DEALER,
OR WRITE TO:

7777 W. BLUEMOUND RD. P.O. BOX 13819 MILWAUKEE, WI 53213

Visit Hal Leonard Online at **www.halleonard.com**

Prices, contents and availability subject to change without notice.

RECORDED VERSIONS®
The Best Note-For-Note Transcriptions Available

ALL BOOKS INCLUDE TABLATURE

00692015 Aerosmith – Greatest Hits..........$22.95	00692931 Jimi Hendrix – Axis: Bold As Love..........$22.95	00694975 Queen – Greatest Hits..........$24.95
00690603 Aerosmith – O Yeah! (Ultimate Hits)..........$24.95	00690608 Jimi Hendrix – Blue Wild Angel..........$24.95	00690670 Queensryche – Very Best of..........$19.95
00690178 Alice in Chains – Acoustic..........$19.95	00692932 Jimi Hendrix – Electric Ladyland..........$24.95	00690878 The Raconteurs – Broken Boy Soldiers..........$19.95
00694865 Alice in Chains – Dirt..........$19.95	00690017 Jimi Hendrix – Live at Woodstock..........$24.95	00694910 Rage Against the Machine..........$19.95
00690387 Alice in Chains – Nothing Safe: The Best of the Box..........$19.95	00690602 Jimi Hendrix – Smash Hits..........$19.95	00690055 Red Hot Chili Peppers – Blood Sugar Sex Magik..........$19.95
00690812 All American Rejects – Move Along..........$19.95	00690843 H.I.M. – Dark Light..........$19.95	00690584 Red Hot Chili Peppers – By the Way..........$19.95
00694932 Allman Brothers Band – Volume 1..........$24.95	00690869 Hinder – Extreme Behavior..........$19.95	00690379 Red Hot Chili Peppers – Californication..........$19.95
00694933 Allman Brothers Band – Volume 2..........$24.95	00690692 Billy Idol – Very Best of..........$19.95	00690673 Red Hot Chili Peppers – Greatest Hits..........$19.95
00694934 Allman Brothers Band – Volume 3..........$24.95	00690688 Incubus – A Crow Left of the Murder..........$19.95	00690852 Red Hot Chili Peppers – Stadium Arcadium..........$24.95
00690865 Atreyu – A Deathgrip on Yesterday..........$19.95	00690457 Incubus – Make Yourself..........$19.95	00690511 Django Reinhardt – Definitive Collection..........$19.95
00690609 Audioslave..........$19.95	00690544 Incubus – Morningview..........$19.95	00690779 Relient K – MMHMM..........$19.95
00690804 Audioslave – Out of Exile..........$19.95	00690790 Iron Maiden Anthology..........$24.95	00690643 Relient K – Two Lefts Don't Make a Right...But Three Do..........$19.95
00690884 Audioslave – Revelations..........$19.95	00690730 Alan Jackson – Guitar Collection..........$19.95	00690631 Rolling Stones – Guitar Anthology..........$24.95
00690820 Avenged Sevenfold – City of Evil..........$22.95	00690721 Jet – Get Born..........$19.95	00690685 David Lee Roth – Eat 'Em and Smile..........$19.95
00690366 Bad Company – Original Anthology, Book 1..........$19.95	00690684 Jethro Tull – Aqualung..........$19.95	00690694 David Lee Roth – Guitar Anthology..........$24.95
00690503 Beach Boys – Very Best of..........$19.95	00690647 Jewel – Best of..........$19.95	00690031 Santana's Greatest Hits..........$19.95
00690489 Beatles – 1..........$24.95	00690814 John5 – Songs for Sanity..........$19.95	00690796 Michael Schenker – Very Best of..........$19.95
00694929 Beatles – 1962-1966..........$24.95	00690751 John5 – Vertigo..........$19.95	00690566 Scorpions – Best of..........$19.95
00694930 Beatles – 1967-1970..........$24.95	00690845 Eric Johnson – Bloom..........$19.95	00690604 Bob Seger – Guitar Collection..........$19.95
00694832 Beatles – For Acoustic Guitar..........$22.95	00690846 Jack Johnson and Friends – Sing-A-Longs and Lullabies for the Film Curious George..........$19.95	00690803 Kenny Wayne Shepherd Band – Best of..........$19.95
00690110 Beatles – White Album (Book 1)..........$19.95	00690271 Robert Johnson – New Transcriptions..........$24.95	00690857 Shinedown – Us and Them..........$19.95
00692385 Chuck Berry..........$19.95	00699131 Janis Joplin – Best of..........$19.95	00690530 Slipknot – Iowa..........$19.95
00690835 Billy Talent..........$19.95	00690427 Judas Priest – Best of..........$19.95	00690733 Slipknot – Vol. 3 (The Subliminal Verses)..........$19.95
00692200 Black Sabbath – We Sold Our Soul for Rock 'N' Roll..........$19.95	00690742 The Killers – Hot Fuss..........$19.95	00120004 Steely Dan – Best of..........$24.95
00690674 blink-182..........$19.95	00694903 Kiss – Best of..........$24.95	00694921 Steppenwolf – Best of..........$22.95
00690831 blink-182 – Greatest Hits..........$19.95	00690780 Korn – Greatest Hits, Volume 1..........$22.95	00690655 Mike Stern – Best of..........$19.95
00690491 David Bowie – Best of..........$19.95	00690834 Lamb of God – Ashes of the Wake..........$19.95	00690877 Stone Sour – Come What(ever) May..........$19.95
00690873 Breaking Benjamin – Phobia..........$19.95	00690875 Lamb of God – Sacrament..........$19.95	00690520 Styx Guitar Collection..........$19.95
00690764 Breaking Benjamin – We Are Not Alone..........$19.95	00690823 Ray LaMontagne – Trouble..........$19.95	00120081 Sublime..........$19.95
00690451 Jeff Buckley – Collection..........$24.95	00690676 John Lennon – Guitar Collection..........$19.95	00690771 SUM 41 – Chuck..........$19.95
00690590 Eric Clapton – Anthology..........$29.95	00690781 Linkin Park – Hybrid Theory..........$22.95	00690767 Switchfoot – The Beautiful Letdown..........$19.95
00690415 Clapton Chronicles – Best of Eric Clapton..........$18.95	00690782 Linkin Park – Meteora..........$22.95	00690830 System of a Down – Hypnotize..........$19.95
00690074 Eric Clapton – The Cream of Clapton..........$24.95	00690783 Live – Best of..........$19.95	00690799 System of a Down – Mezmerize..........$19.95
00690716 Eric Clapton – Me and Mr. Johnson..........$19.95	00690743 Los Lonely Boys..........$19.95	00690531 System of a Down – Toxicity..........$19.95
00694869 Eric Clapton – Unplugged..........$22.95	00690876 Los Lonely Boys – Sacred..........$19.95	00694824 James Taylor – Best of..........$16.95
00690162 The Clash – Best of..........$19.95	00690720 Lostprophets – Start Something..........$19.95	00690871 Three Days Grace – One-X..........$19.95
00690828 Coheed & Cambria – Good Apollo I'm Burning Star, IV, Vol. 1: From Fear Through the Eyes of Madness..........$19.95	00694954 Lynyrd Skynyrd – New Best of..........$19.95	00690737 3 Doors Down – The Better Life..........$22.95
00690593 Coldplay – A Rush of Blood to the Head..........$19.95	00690752 Lynyrd Skynyrd – Street Survivors..........$19.95	00690683 Robin Trower – Bridge of Sighs..........$19.95
00690838 Cream – Royal Albert Hall: London May 2-3-5-6 2005..........$22.95	00690577 Yngwie Malmsteen – Anthology..........$24.95	00690740 Shania Twain – Guitar Collection..........$19.95
00690856 Creed – Greatest Hits..........$22.95	00690754 Marilyn Manson – Lest We Forget..........$19.95	00699191 U2 – Best of: 1980-1990..........$19.95
00690401 Creed – Human Clay..........$19.95	00694956 Bob Marley – Legend..........$19.95	00690732 U2 – Best of: 1990-2000..........$19.95
00690819 Creedence Clearwater Revival – Best of..........$19.95	00694945 Bob Marley – Songs of Freedom..........$24.95	00690775 U2 – How to Dismantle an Atomic Bomb..........$22.95
00690572 Steve Cropper – Soul Man..........$19.95	00690657 Maroon5 – Songs About Jane..........$19.95	00690575 Steve Vai – Alive in an Ultra World..........$22.95
00690613 Crosby, Stills & Nash – Best of..........$19.95	00120080 Don McLean – Songbook..........$19.95	00660137 Steve Vai – Passion & Warfare..........$24.95
00690289 Deep Purple – Best of..........$17.95	00694951 Megadeth – Rust in Peace..........$22.95	00690116 Stevie Ray Vaughan – Guitar Collection..........$24.95
00690784 Def Leppard – Best of..........$19.95	00690768 Megadeth – The System Has Failed..........$19.95	00660058 Stevie Ray Vaughan – Lightnin' Blues 1983-1987..........$24.95
00690347 The Doors – Anthology..........$22.95	00690505 John Mellencamp – Guitar Collection..........$19.95	00694835 Stevie Ray Vaughan – The Sky Is Crying..........$22.95
00690348 The Doors – Essential Guitar Collection..........$16.95	00690646 Pat Metheny – One Quiet Night..........$19.95	00690015 Stevie Ray Vaughan – Texas Flood..........$19.95
00690810 Fall Out Boy – From Under the Cork Tree..........$19.95	00690558 Pat Metheny – Trio: 99>00..........$19.95	00690772 Velvet Revolver – Contraband..........$22.95
00690664 Fleetwood Mac – Best of..........$19.95	00690040 Steve Miller Band – Young Hearts..........$19.95	00690071 Weezer (The Blue Album)..........$19.95
00690870 Flyleaf..........$19.95	00690794 Mudvayne – Lost and Found..........$19.95	00690447 The Who – Best of..........$24.95
00690808 Foo Fighters – In Your Honor..........$19.95	00690611 Nirvana..........$22.95	00690589 ZZ Top Guitar Anthology..........$22.95
00690805 Robben Ford – Best of..........$19.95	00694883 Nirvana – Nevermind..........$19.95	
00694920 Free – Best of..........$19.95	00690026 Nirvana – Unplugged in New York..........$19.95	
00690848 Godsmack – IV..........$19.95	00690807 The Offspring – Greatest Hits..........$19.95	
00690601 Good Charlotte – The Young and the Hopeless..........$19.95	00694847 Ozzy Osbourne – Best of..........$22.95	
00690697 Jim Hall – Best of..........$19.95	00690399 Ozzy Osbourne – Ozzman Cometh..........$19.95	
00690840 Ben Harper – Both Sides of the Gun..........$19.95	00690866 Panic! At the Disco – A Fever You Can't Sweat Out..........$19.95	
00694798 George Harrison – Anthology..........$19.95	00694855 Pearl Jam – Ten..........$19.95	
00692930 Jimi Hendrix – Are You Experienced?..........$24.95	00690439 A Perfect Circle – Mer De Noms..........$19.95	
	00690661 A Perfect Circle – Thirteenth Step..........$19.95	
	00690499 Tom Petty – Definitive Guitar Collection..........$19.95	
	00690428 Pink Floyd – Dark Side of the Moon..........$19.95	
	00690789 Poison – Best of..........$19.95	
	00693864 The Police – Best of..........$19.95	

Prices and availability subject to change without notice. Some products may not be available outside the U.S.A.

FOR A COMPLETE LIST OF GUITAR RECORDED VERSIONS TITLES, SEE YOUR LOCAL MUSIC DEALER, OR WRITE TO:

Visit Hal Leonard online at www.halleonard.com   0607